Childhood Bilingualism

Childhood Bilingualism:
Aspects of Linguistic Cognitive, and Social Development

Edited by

Peter Homel
Michael Palij
Doris Aaronson
New York University

LAWRENCE ERLBAUM ASSOCIATES, PUBLISHERS
1987   Hillsdale, New Jersey   London

Lawrence Erlbaum Associates, Inc., Publishers
365 Broadway
Hillsdale, New Jersey 07642

Library of Congress Cataloging-in-Publication Data
Childhood bilingualism.

   Contains revised papers presented at a Conference on
Childhood Bilingualism, held at New York University,
June 25–26, 1982.
   Includes bibliographies and index.
   1. Bilingualism in children.   2. Language acquisition.
3. Child development.   I. Homel, Peter. II. Palij,
Michael.   III. Aaronson, Doris.   IV. Conference on
Childhood Bilingualism (1982 : New York University)

P115.2.C48 1987   404'.2   86-8955
ISBN 0-89859-806-0

Printed in the United States of America
10 9 8 7 6 5 4 3 2 1

Contents

Preface

This volume is based primarily on a conference on childhood bilingualism held at New York University on June 25 and 26, 1982. The idea for the conference grew out of a series of discussions between two of the editors, Peter Homel and Michael Palij, who had substantial interests in exploring the nature of bilingual cognition and the effect of bilingualism on psychological development. We, the editors, were struck by the wealth of research but were appalled by the lack of communication between researchers in ''mainstream'' developmental psychology—those looking at language development in monolingual children—and researchers looking at similar developmental processes in bilingual children. We thought it would be of great interest and practical value to bring together researchers from both areas in an attempt to stimulate dialogue and interaction between the two groups.

The first step toward holding the conference was taken when Paul Dores, of SUNY, Stony Brook, gave us a copy of a request for proposals for the Society for Research in Child Development's (SRCD) series of study groups and summer institutes. Our initial proposal to SRCD for funding for a summer study group focused on four areas of child development and how bilingualism might affect each one: language acquisition, cognitive functioning, social cognition and communication, and personality and emotional development. SRCD approved the proposal, adding the issue of bidialectism and its relationship to bilingualism as another area of focus.

The volume contains most of the presentations made at the conference and follows, with minor changes, the general organization of the conference. During each session, two ''bilingual'' researchers (i.e., doing research in the bilingualism) presented a general review of the issues within a topic area and gave examples of their own research within this context. A "monolingual" researcher (i.e., one oriented toward research in monolingual development) then presented a discussion of the issues raised by the two bilingual researchers, indicating the points of contact and departure between bilingual and monolingual research.

ACKNOWLEDGMENTS

We thank SRCD for recognizing the importance of the study of childhood bilingualism and for providing funding for the conference. In particular, we thank Dorothy H. Eichorn of the University of California—Berkeley, who was the Executive Officer of SRCD at the time of the conference, and Viola Moulton Buck, her assistant; Gray Garwood of Tulane University, who was the chairperson in charge of SRCD's study group program; and largaret Spencer of Emory University, who was SRCD's observer at the conference.

Many people were very helpful at various stages, in both making the conference a reality and helping to complete this book. We thank Dick Koppenaal, Chairman of the Psychology Department of New York University, for his support of the conference. We also acknowledge the following people and departments at New York University for their help in setting up the conference: Peter Chepus of the Office for Funded Accounts, Michael Robbins of the Budget and Fund Accounting Department, and Sherry Daulet of the Psychology Department, who helped in handling the expenses for the conference; Jacqueline Downing of the Physics Department, and Grace Sun of the Housing Office, who helped make the arrangements for conference space and housing for the conference participants; the Catering Service of New York University for providing refreshments and meals during the conference; and Felix Scherer of the Psychology Department, for his technical assistance in setting up the equipment for the conference. We are also deeply thankful to Sally Thomason and Laura Brighenti for both their moral support and material help before, during, and after the conference.

Above all, we are indebted to Larry Erlbaum and Carol Lachman of Lawrence Erlbaum Associates. Many difficulties are attendant with publishing a book that tries to span an area as large as childhood bilingualism. We sincerely feel that without their help and seemingly inexhaustible patience, the preparation of this volume would not have been possible.

Childhood Bilingualism

I

INTRODUCTION

Childhood Bilingualism: Introduction and Overview

Peter Homel
Michael Palij
Doris Aaronson
New York University

In 1962, Peal and Lambert published the results of a study comparing bilingual and monolingual children on various measures of intelligence and achievement. Their findings were surprising, at least in light of certain assumptions that had been prevalent in child psychology up to that time. They found no evidence to indicate any sort of intellectual deficiency in bilingual children. The performance of bilinguals on all measures was either equivalent or superior to that of their monolingual comparison group. These results were in clear contradiction to a belief that had come to be accepted as truism by psychologists and laymen alike, especially in North America: The acquisition of two languages in childhood impairs intellectual development—it leads to mental confusion or difficulties in coordinating language and thought in children. The results obtained by Peal and Lambert suggested that there are no detrimental effects of bilingualism, and there may even be some cognitive advantages.

Peal and Lambert's study had a major impact on at least two aspects of childhood bilingualism. First, it sparked a renewed interest in the study of childhood bilingualism among psychologists and educators. Second (and perhaps even more important), it provided one of the major justifications for the establishment of bilingual education programs during the late 1960s and early 1970s, especially in Canada and the United States.

The number of studies dealing with childhood bilingualism increased dramatically throughout the rest of the 1960s and 1970s. Most of this research concentrated on cognitive development, basically replicating the results of Peal and Lambert either with different measures of cognitive performance or with different samples of bilingual children. A few studies looked at the social and personal aspects of growing up with two languages. Yet another set of studies considered the social phenomena closely related to bilingualism—biculturalism and bidialectism—and the role they play in the development of the child.

By 1982, research into childhood bilingualism had proliferated to such an extent that a major effort was necessary to bring together the available data on childhood bilingualism and provide some theoretical framework within which to understand them. On June 21–22, 1982, a study group was held at New York University entitled "Childhood Bilingualism: Aspects of Cognitive, Social, and Emotional Development." Sponsored under the auspices of the Society for Research in Child Development and organized by Peter Homel and Michael Palij with the help of Doris Aaronson, the aims of this study group were (a) to summarize the current work on bilingualism and make it accessible to mainstream developmental psychologists; and (b) to provide researchers in both the bilingual and the monolingual research areas an opportunity to develop an integrated model of the developmental processes operating in the bilingual child.

The structure of the study group was specifically designed to achieve these ends. Researchers in bilingualism from a number of disciplines, including psychology, education, and linguistics, were invited to deliver papers reviewing specific aspects of childhood bilingualism. The papers were organized into sections covering the following areas of interest: language acquisition, cognitive development, social and emotional development, and the relationship of biculturalism and bidialectism to bilingualism. Each section also included a "monolingual" discussant—a researcher in the particular area (e.g., language acquisition) whose own work had been done primarily with monolingual children. This structure encouraged discussion and dialogue not only among scientists from various areas of bilingual research, but also between bilingual and monolingual researchers looking at similar aspects of child development.

It was not the purpose of the conference to evaluate existing governmental policies about bilingual education nor to make recommendations for changing such policies. Rather, the conference was intended to provide an impartial summary and synthesis of the research in childhood bilingualism and bilingualism's effect on development. Ultimately, however, it was hoped that providing such a compilation of information about childhood bilingualism would prove to be of benefit to those involved making policy decisions concerning bilingualism and bilingual education.

The present volume is the end result of the SRCD study group on childhood bilingualism. It is intended as something more than a record of the proceedings of papers and presentations given during the two days during which the study group met. In preparing their manuscripts for this book, the original participants in the study group were encouraged to revise their original presentations in light of comments or discussions that arose during the course of the study group, as well as to address points of convergence or divergence they saw between their own presentations and those of the others. The result is a far greater degree of integration among the various papers than would have been possible in a proceedings-type volume.

The book is divided into several topic areas: (a) language acquisition and processing; (b) cognitive functioning, style, and development; (c) social and emotional development; and (d) bidialectism and bilingualism. Following the structure of the conference (at which most of these papers were originally presented), each topic area has two or three chapters written by researchers in bilingualism and a discussion chapter by a researcher whose main work has been in a monolingual context. The following is a brief overview of these chapters.

INTRODUCTION

The accompanying chapter in the Introductory section is by Peter Homel and Michael Palij and it provides a social and historical description of bilingualism and language policy in four countries: Canada, the Soviet Union, the United States and the People's Republic of China. In their concluding section, Homel and Palij discuss the future of bilingualism and linguistic diversity in each country, as well as some of the possible psychological relationships between childhood bilingualism and the social context in which it occurs.

LANGUAGE ACQUISITION AND PROCESSING

The first chapter in this section by Kenji Hakuta focuses on the processes involved in the acquisition of a second language and how these processes contrast with those involved in first language acquisition. Hakuta examines these processes and how they are affected by such factors as cognitive maturity, similarity in linguistic structure of the first and second language, transfer from the first language to the second, and age effects. He concludes by arguing that the best way to guide future research in first and second language acquisition is to adopt a conceptual framework that identifies language universals and typologies (i.e., categorical membership features that identify how one language systematically differs from another). Within this framework, research on second language acquisition is seen to be complementary to research on first language acquisition instead of being separate from or tangential to it.

Next, James Cummins examines the interrelationships among bilingualism, linguistic proficiency, and metalinguistic awareness. According to Cummins, it is easy to misperceive these factors as being categorical (saying, for example, that a child is either bilingual or not), thereby glossing over the fact that these factors constitute continua—that the performance of individual children may vary considerably along any one of these factors. Cummins provides a two-dimensional scheme for understanding the interrelationship among these three factors: one dimension reflects the degree to which there is "contextual" support for understanding a communication (by context Cummins means the sociocultural setting in which the communication is being made); the second dimension reflects the degree of cognitive involvement for the task to be performed.

The first dimension ranges from one extreme, which can be referred to as context-embedded—where a communication is embedded in an appropriate situation, a context in which to understand the communication—to the other extreme of being context-reduced, where there are very few contextual aids in interpreting the communication. The dimension of cognitive involvement ranges from those tasks that require little cognitive processing to those that are very demanding in processing demands. This model allows Cummins to characterize a number of different studies on bilingual proficiency and metalinguistic awareness.

The chapter by Aaronson and Ferres examines some of the differences they have found in English language processing by native English speakers and Chinese-English bilinguals. Striking differences between the two groups seem to be directly attributable to differences in the structures of the English and Chinese languages. One of the most intriguing conclusions drawn from these results is that traditional grammatical categories found in English may not have exact counterparts in Chinese. Differences in linguistic performance appear to be related to the bilingual's knowledge and experience with the differences in both languages, especially when the languages derive from different language families.

Martin Braine provides a discussion of these three chapters focusing on the implications of each for theory building and future research by monolingual researchers in language acquisition and processing.

BILINGUALISM AND COGNITIVE DEVELOPMENT

Palij and Homel examine the question of how bilingualism affects cognitive development in Chapter 7. This chapter is divided into three subsections: (a) a historical review of studies relating cognitive development and processing to bilingualism, (b) theoretical issues involved in directing research in this area, and (c) methodoligical problems with past and present studies and the use of contemporary statistical techniques in constructing more comprehensive and valid models.

The next chapter by Edward DeAvila examines how intelligence and cognitive style, interest and motivation, and educational opportunity and access all interact to influence school behaviors. DeAvila argues that the poor academic performance seen in many school situations is not directly related to students being bilingual, or even directly related to other factors that are related to being bilingual. Instead, it is the interaction of the three previously stated factors that gives rise to the poor academic performance. For school performance to improve, these factors must be faced and effectively dealt with. DeAvila reviews a study that clearly identifies these factors and suggests one means of improving students' school performance.

Joseph Glick concludes this section with a discussion of the chapters by Palij and Homel, and DeAvila. He raises issues regarding the role of traditional goals in education and how the methods for implementing them often overlook the specific needs of students. This becomes particularly important in the consideration of classroom goals and performance of students from different sociocultural backgrounds and ethnolinguistic groups.

BILINGUALISM AND SOCIAL DEVELOPMENT

In this section, Chapter 10 by Donald Taylor focuses on social psychological factors that promote or inhibit the acquisition of a second language. Taylor stresses the importance of intergroup relations, the sociocultural goals of each group, and how these factors influence the acquisition of second language by children from different groups. He describes a possible model for depicting such intergroup situations: a 2 × 2 classification scheme where one dimension reflects either positive or negative relations among groups, and the other dimension reflects whether a group desires to maintain its own culture and language. Taylor details the social and psychological consequences that follow from each of these possible conditions within this scheme and provides examples from contemporary society.

Wallace Lambert's chapter is concerned with how experiences in bilingual and bicultural settings affect the attitudes and perspectives of the developing child. He goes on to show how these attitudes and perspectives then influence language learning and the development of bilingualism. Lambert presents examples of some of the historical forces that have affected both social attitudes and research in Canada. He also reviews the findings of the Canadian language-immersion programs and how attitudes and language learning were affected within them.

E. Tory Higgins provides the discussion for this section. He ties together the threads common to the several chapters and indicates how new research on the role of social cognition may provide additional insights into the relationship between social reality and cognitive functioning.

BIDIALECTISM

Although the distinction between what constitutes linguistic variation and what constitutes dialectal variation may be contestable, bilingualism itself may be described as language variation at the interlanguage level and bidialectism as the study of language variation at the intralanguage level. Dialects represent systematic and coherent linguistic systems that operate within a larger monolingual framework. For example, Black English has specific features that identify it as a bona fide language system that also uses many Standard English grammatical forms and words.

William Hall and William Nagy examine how differences in communication patterns between black and white children can be attributed to differences in the children's cultural background. Hall and Nagy report that black children use *state* words like "think," "know," "happen," "see," and "want" much less often in their classrooms than they do at home, where the level of usage of such words is comparable to the home-usage level by white children. Apparently black children experience some sort of discontinuity between their home and school environments that results in reduced usage of state words in school. This finding contradicts the notion that black children come from linguistically deprived backgrounds and indicates that the problems that black children encounter in school may be due to factors that are far more subtle than has been previous considered.

Next, John Roy, in his chapter, reviews the development of Black English and contrasts its development with that of bilingualism by immigrant groups who had not forcibly been brought to American shores. He begins with the development of Black Creole and discusses how various social processes caused it to give rise to the more familiar Black English of contemporary times. He points out that this pattern of development apparently differs from that of other dialects, particularly regional dialects. Black English represents a convergence toward Standard English from Black Creole, whereas other dialects usually represent a divergence from Standard English to their present form. Roy concludes by examining the factors that make it important for teachers of English to be sensitive to the dialectal background of their students.

William Stewart provides the discussion chapter for this last section and describes some of the linguistic and psychological implications of cross-dialectal communication.

CONCLUDING REMARKS

This volume is intended to serve a dual function. On one hand, for those unfamiliar with bilingual research, it provides a comprehensive summary of past work in this area. We feel that there are many aspects of bilingual research that can cast light on research done in other areas of developmental psychology, and vice versa. For those familiar with bilingual research, this book should serve a heuristic function, providing a source of ideas for future investigation. Many of the chapters presented here highlight the need to take into account the mediating role of social and cultural factors; others describe possible research designs and statistical procedures that might be used to handle such multivariate situations.

We hope that this book will stimulate further research into the complex relationship between bilingualism and psychological development and provide a more comprehensive view of the linguistic, cognitive, social, and emotional processes involved in the development of the bilingual child.

REFERENCES

Peal, E., & Lambert, W. E. (1962). The relation of bilingualism to intelligence. *Psychological Monographs, 76*, 1–23 (No. 546).

Bilingualism and Language Policy: Four Case Studies

Peter Homel
Michael Palij
New York University

In this chapter, we examine the language policies of four countries: Canada, the Soviet Union, the United States, and the People's Republic of China. In particular, we try to indicate the different perspective that each of these countries has taken with regard to linguistic diversity and bilingualism and how this is reflected in the manner in which each country approaches bilingual education.

We first present a general overview of each country, including a description of the general linguistic and ethnic composition of the country, as well as some of the past and present trends in policy of the particular country toward minority languages and bilingualism. We then discuss some of the implications certain social policies may have for the psychological development of bilingual children.

CANADA

Canada is officially a bilingual country, with English and French enjoying equal status as the languages of government. Of a total population of approximately 24 million in 1976, 67% of all Canadians reported English as their first language and 26% reported French (Beaujot & McQuillian, 1982). The French speakers are concentrated primarily in the provinces of Quebec (87% of the population of the province) and New Brunswick (34%). In addition to English and French, programs for the maintenance of languages spoken by Native Indian groups and the Inuktitut (Eskimo), as well as those spoken by major immigrant groups (German, Italian, Hungarian, and Ukrainian), are also supported by the Canadian government.

The total rate of bilingualism in Canada is 13%. The breakdown is 33% for

French Canadians; 8% for English Canadians. One cause of such different rates of bilingualism among French and English speakers appears to be the geographical distribution of bilingualism. Approximately 57% of all bilinguals in Canada live in Quebec province. In fact, 35% of all bilinguals in Canada live in the Montreal area (Beaujot & McQuillian, 1982).

The English and French each established colonies in Canada in the 17th century. By the mid-18th century, the number of English settlers had increased enormously as compared with the French. In 1763, after defeat by England in the Seven Years' War, France was forced to cede all of her territories in Canada to the British.

Over the years, a number of official concessions were made to French-speaking Canadians. The Quebec Act of 1774 recognized Quebec as a French-speaking area and allowed the French there to maintain their own religious and public institutions. In particular, the Catholic Church remained in control of the educational system in Quebec. These concessions were maintained under the Confederation Act of 1867, which also gave all Canadians the right to political participation at both the national and provincial levels.[1]

Unfortunately, the official rights accorded the French failed to offset widespread social and economic discrimination that they experienced from the English-speaking majority (Whitaker, 1984). One of the major means of control over the French was the use of English in almost all aspects of government, commerce, and higher education. Added to this was the generally conservative role of the Catholic Church in French Canadian society, encouraging the passive acceptance of the status quo among the French.

Even in Quebec, with its majority of French speakers, the English-speaking community still succeeded in maintaining political control at both the local and the provincial levels by means of their economic power. They owned most of the businesses and factories and tended to show favor either to other native English speakers or to those French who were fairly well assimilated into the English-speaking culture.

By the 1960s, however, there was a growing movement in the major French-speaking areas calling for the Canadian government to show a greater recognition of the linguistic and political rights of French speakers. It was in response to this that a Royal Commission on Bilingualism and Biculturalism was convened between 1965 and 1968 to look into these problems. On the basis of the suggestions of the commission, the Official Languages Act was adopted in 1969, declaring that English and French were to be the official languages of Canada and that they possess equal status in terms of their use in all aspects of government.

The primary purpose of the act was to encourage bilingualism at an institu-

---

[1]Kaalt (1977) has also suggested that, in deference to the French Canadians who would have seen such an attempt as the first step in its own assimilation, attempts to assimilate other non-English speaking groups who came as immigrants were not as strong in Canada as they were in the U.S.

tional level in an effort to provide equal social and governmental services for both English and French speakers. Coupled with this, however, were official efforts in support of educational opportunities for minority students, as well as the establishment of programs of bilingual education and second language instruction for both French and English speakers.

According to Grosjean (1982), the results of the Official Languages Act appear to be encouraging. For example, census results indicate that a growing number of Native English speakers especially in Quebec are learning and using French. On the other hand, however, about a third of the French children outside of Quebec province apparently still do not receive instruction in their native language.

One of the fears expressed among French Canadians is that because they constitute a minority group within Canada, the general encouragement of bilingualism might result in an increased tendency toward assimilation of French Canadian speakers into the dominant English-speaking community. This would compound the loss of French speakers that is already taking place in Quebec as a result of the low birth rate among the French, the migration of French speakers to other, non-French speaking areas of Canada, the preference of new immigrants settling in Quebec to learn English rather than French, among other factors (Beaujot & McQuillian, 1982).

The late 1960s and early 1970s witnessed the growth of a separatist movement among the French in Quebec. The *Parti Quebecois* came into power in Quebec province with a platform calling for the preservation of a French speaking Quebec and a greater degree of autonomy of the province from the rest of English-speaking Canada. In 1977, under the administration of the Parti Quebecois, an act was passed making French the only official language of the province. Businesses were required to adopt French as the language of everyday affairs, children of immigrants were compelled to learn French in schools, and children of English-speaking parents were allowed to be taught in English only if their parents could prove that they themselves had been taught in English in the province.

The federal government of Canada generally maintained a policy that sought to counter the separatist movement among the French in Quebec while at the same time continuing to encourage a bilingual Canada. In 1982, a new Canadian constitution was proclaimed that essentially contained all the provisions of the original Act of Confederation of 1867, as well as all of the amendments that had been made to it over the years. In addition, it contained certain proposals that had been worked out with the leaders of the various provinces.

Among these was a Charter of Rights and Freedoms that contained a provision giving parents the right to choose either English or French as the language of instruction for their children in any province where the numbers warranted it. This charter served as the basis for the Canadian Supreme Court's decision in 1984 to strike down the provision of the Quebec Act that restricted English instruction to children of parents who had been educated in English in Quebec.

On the other hand, the Canadian government's actions with regard to the province of Manitoba seemed to underscore the government's dedication to the cause of bilingualism. Although Manitoba had entered the Canadian Confederation as a bilingual province in 1870, the provincial government subsequently rescinded the language rights of its French-speaking minority. In 1979, the Canadian Supreme Court ordered that these rights be restored. After 4 years of delay by Manitoba, a bill was passed in the Canadian Parliament in support of the original court decision to restore bilingualism in Manitoba.

In summary, Canada appears to have established a long-term commitment to encouraging and maintaining bilingualism at both the national and the provincial levels. Practically, this may be viewed as an effort to ensure that both French- and English-speaking Canadians enjoy equal access to social services, business, and education. More important, however, this may be viewed as a solution to the general problem of reconciling the demands of national unity with the needs of its multilingual–multicultural society.

One indication of the success of this policy may be the fact that ethnic polarization has become less of an issue in recent years. This notion has some support in the apparent decline of the Parti Quebecois during the early 1980s, which culminated in the defeat of the party in the provincial elections of 1985. On the other hand, Whitaker (1984) has suggested that the decline of the Parti Quebecois may have been the unintentional result of its own efforts. Because of its language programs, it may have succeeded in strengthening the French identity of Quebec, thus relieving the very anxiety that had originally compelled French speakers to support the Parti Quebecois. In any case, bilingualism in Canada appears to be a key element in its national policy, and there are no indications at this time of any movement away from that position.

THE SOVIET UNION

The Soviet Union (the Union of Soviet Socialist Republics), with a population of approximately 262 million people, is a constitutional federation consisting of 15 member republics. The largest is the Russian Socialist Federalist Soviet Republic (RSFSR), which serves as the center of the Soviet government. The remaining republics are referred to as "national" republics. They correspond more or less to the traditional homelands of the major non-Russian national or ethnic groups that make up at least half the population of the Soviet Union.[2]

---

[2]The popular practice of using the term "Russia" to refer to the Soviet Union (which even Soviets are prone to do) thus represents a failure to appreciate the extent of ethnic and linguistic diversity in that nation. It parallels the use of the term "America" in referring to the United States something that has often been criticized by the other peoples of both North and South America.

There are some 130 distinct languages spoken within the borders of the Soviet Union (Comrie, 1981; Isayev, 1977). Some idea of the extent of linguistic diversity in the Soviet Union can be gotten from the following list of major language families spoken in the Soviet Union, as well as some prominent examples of each family:

1. *Indo-European,* including the Slavic languages (Russian, Ukrainian, and Byelorussian), Baltic languages (Lithuanian, Latvian), Iranian languages (e.g., Tadjik and Kurd), Moldavian (a romance language similar to Romanian), Yiddish, and Armenian.
2. *Altaic,* including the Turkic languages (e.g., Uzbek, Kazakh, Azerbaijani), Mongolic languages (Buryat and Kalmyk), and the Tungus-Manchu languages.
3. *Uralic,* including the Finno-Ugaric languages (e.g., Estonian, Karelian, and Mordovian) and the Samodic group.
4. *Iberian-Caucasic,* including the Kartvelian languages (e.g., Georgian), along with the Abkhaz-Adyghe, the Nakh, and the Daghestani languages.
5. *Paleo-Asiatic,* including the Chukchi-Kachatdal and Eskimo languages.

In the Soviet census, a distinction is made between national or ethnic identity and native language (Narodnoe Khozjajstvo SSSR 1922-1982, 1982). For example, Russian is the declared language of 58.6% of the total population of the Soviet Union. This group can be further divided into ethnic Russians who live within the borders of the RSFSR (approximately 114 million according to the 1979 census); ethnic Russians who live in the other republics of the Soviet Union (24 million); and nonethnic Russians who declare Russian as their native language (13 million, or 5% of the total population).

Other major languages (presented in order of percentage of speakers) spoken in the Soviet Union include: Ukrainian (14%), Uzbek (4%), Byelorussian (3%), Kazakh (2.2%), Tatar (2.2%), Azerbaijani (1.8%), Armenian (1.3%), Georgian (1.3%), Lithuanian (1.1%), Moldavian (0.91%), Tadjik (0.86%), Chuvash (0.61%), Latvian (0.58%), Kirghiz (0.58%), and Estonian (0.37%), Bilinguals make up 21.5% of the total population of the Soviet Union (Comrie, 1981). Among non-Russians the rate is 42.6%; among Russians, it is 3.1%. Even among those Russians living in non-Russian areas, the rate of bilingualism still tends to be far lower than that for the non-Russians in the particular area.

The linguistic and ethnic diversity of the Soviet Union is a direct result of its prerevolutionary past. The Russian empire was formed as the result of a series of military conquests between the 16th and 19th centuries. During the course of this period, what had begun as the relatively small principality of Moscow-Suzdal expanded west as far as Poland and the Carpathian mountains, south as far as the Black Sea and the Caucasus Mountains, north as far as Finland and the Arctic, and east as far as China and the Pacific Ocean.

The language policies which the tsarist government adopted toward individual non-Russian minorities in these conquered areas were based primarily on political considerations specific to each group. A relatively liberal approach to language policy was adopted for Estonia and Finland. At the time of their annexation by the Russian empire, these areas already had high levels of culture and industry comparable to those in western European countries. Moreover, both regions were already under the political and economic domination of nonindigenous minority ethnic groups—ethnic Swedes composed the ruling elite in Finland, with Germans holding power in Estonia. These minorities maintained their dominant status by serving as overseers and government officials for the Russians. The Russian government accorded these minority groups a limited degree of political and linguistic freedom in return for their loyalty.

The case of the Ukrainians represents a more extreme policy. To discourage Ukrainian separatism, an imperial decree was issued in 1876 banning the public use of Ukrainian (Savchenko, 1970). It prohibited, among other things, the teaching of Ukrainian in schools, the publication of original works and translations in Ukrainian, and the public performance of plays and songs in Ukrainian. The general ban against the use of Ukrainian remained in effect until the Revolution of 1905.

For the rest of the non-Russian languages within the Russian empire, discouragement was carried on through a policy of social neglect rather than of restrictions. In those regions, no schooling was allowed in the native language aside from that connected with religious training or missionary work. More able non-Russian students were encouraged to learn Russian and to assimilate into Russian culture in order to succeed in government or business.

Despite the efforts of the tsarist government, nationalistic movements steadily developed within several ethnic groups during the 19th century. As a result, a number of these groups attempted to form their own independent (and, in some cases, socialist) governments during the period of the Bolshevik Revolution. However, faced with the potential loss of raw materials and food from many of these areas, the Bolsheviks took immediate military action against these nationalist groups. At the same time, the Bolsheviks adopted policies designed to gain favor among the non-Russian minorities.

Thus, one of the aims of the new Soviet state, as outlined by Lenin in 1917, became the full and equal development of all ethnic and linguistic minorities in the Soviet Union (Comrie, 1981; Kreindler, 1982). There was to be no official language for the new Soviet state. All Soviet citizens were to have complete freedom to use their native languages in private and in public. Public usage included the right to use one's native language for addressing public meetings, corresponding with the government, and giving testimony in court. Moreover, all Soviet citizens were guaranteed the right to receive an education in and to have access to literature and cultural materials in their native languages.

In addition, the establishment of a system of national republics gave the major ethnic groups at least some degree of autonomy and self-government, although primary power always lay with the central government in Moscow. Each national republic was allowed to use its native language as the official language of government. Each national republic was given control over local aspects of educational policy and over the development of the national culture.

The 1920s witnessed an active campaign aimed at encouraging the development of non-Russian languages and ethnic cultures. For languages with an already existing written language and literary tradition, programs were created for setting up schools, publishing newspapers and books, and so on. For those languages without a writing system or for which the already existing systems of writing were cumbersome and unsuited to easy acquisition, linguists were sent to study the languages and develop writing systems for them.

Under Stalin's leadership in the 1930s, however, a general retrenchment occurred in Soviet policy with increasingly greater emphasis being placed on the need to unify the nation and develop centralized control of the state. This led to a growing encouragement of the use of Russian as a common language for communication among members of different ethnic groups.

Many of the non-Russian writers, intellectuals, and scientists who came into prominence during the previous decade either perished during the purges of the 1930s or were forced to conform to more ideologically acceptable (and less nationalistic) topics of writing or research (Luckyj, 1975; Simirenko, 1969). Yet another example of retrenchment was the discontinuance of the publication of materials in some languages (e.g., Lapp, Karelian) on the excuse that they had very few speakers, most of whom were bilingual in other, more prevalent languages.

As a result of the emphasis on national unity during the Second World War, the 1940s saw increases in the greater prominence given to Russian than to the non-Russian languages. This trend was exemplified by Stalin's victory toast of 1945, wherein he publicly referred to Russia as the nation that served as the "leading force of the Soviet Union" (Bilinsky, 1964). Russian was proclaimed as the language of high culture, as well as the language of socialism. As a result, linguistic reforms were effected in various non-Russian languages to bring them closer in appearance to Russian. These reforms consisted primarily of changes in grammar and orthography based on Russian patterns, and the introduction of many Russian loan words or calques, which often replaced words that had already been well established in the particular language.

After Stalin's death in 1953, there was a period of relaxation in the Soviet Union that lasted until the resignation of Khruschev in 1964. An official acknowledgment was made of the contribution of the non-Russian nationalities to the life and culture of the Soviet Union: The development of an international culture was not to result in the leveling and disappearance of national traditions.

Non-Russian minorities were granted greater concessions in educational policy and in literary and intellectual freedom of expression.

Since the late 1960s, however, the Soviet government appears to have returned to a tacit policy encouraging the status of Russian as the official language of the Soviet Union. It is considered to be the only language with the status of a *lingua franca* within the Soviet Union and is the only language that can be used in communication with individuals from other nations.

There has also been a general acceptance of the eventual consolidation of smaller ethnic groups and languages into larger ones, with the eventual goal of developing a unified Soviet People with a common Soviet language—Russian. Bilingualism appears to be encouraged as part of this gradual incorporation of smaller language groups into larger ones. According to Isayev (1977): "...bilingualism should be viewed as a transitional stage to monolingualism which will be reached by the smaller ethnic groups when their assimilation into the corresponding nations is complete" (pp. 199–200).

Evidence indicates an active policy of promoting both the assimilation of non-Russian minorities and the increased use of Russian vis-à-vis the non-Russian national languages. The non-Russian republics in the European portion of the Soviet Union have shown steady decreases in the percentages of their native ethnic populations with a corresponding increase in the percentages of persons declaring themselves as being ethnically Russian.

Similarly, there has been a steady decline in the number of copies and number of titles of books and publications in non-Russian languages, with a corresponding increase in the number of imprints in Russian (Lewis, 1972). Scientific and technical journals that were formerly published in non-Russian languages are now published in Russian, presumably to make them more accessible to readers both within and outside the Soviet Union.

Yet another trend is indicated by the fact that non-Russian parents have increasingly begun to send their children to Russian-language schools rather than to native-language schools in order to increase their children's chances of success in entering institutions of higher education (Comrie, 1981; Kreindler, 1982). Even in the national language schools, Russian is a compulsory subject in the early grades, and efforts have been underway to introduce it as early as kindergarten and preschool classes.

In short, it appears that bilingualism is currently being viewed as a transitory phenomenon in the Soviet Union—a necessary part of the process of assimilating non-Russian minorities into a Russian-speaking Soviet nation. Part of the justification for this may be demographic. Brunner (1981) reports that birth rates among ethnic Russians, as well as among the non-Russian nationalities in the European portions of the Soviet Union (Ukrainians, Byelorussians, Estonians, etc.), have been declining considerably over the past 2 decades. Over the same period, birth rates among the Muslim-Turkic nationalities (Uzbeks, Kazakhs, Azerbaijanis, etc.) have increased.

On the basis of his demographic data, Brunner (1981) has estimated that, at present, ethnic Russians probably constitute only 49% of the total of all draft-age males and that by 1995 they will constitute only 46%. Considering the Slavic groups as a whole, he estimates that they now are 67% of all draft age males and that by 1995 that figure will decline to 62%. If these figures are reflective of general trends in the Soviet population, ethnic Russians may soon come to constitute a minority group within the Soviet Union. Current efforts to inculcate among the non-Russian minorities a sense of identity with a Russian-speaking Soviet culture may be an attempt to offset such future demographic changes in the ethnic Russian population.

In her review of language policy in the Soviet Union, Kreindler (1982) commented that it is paradoxical that the country which was one of the first to champion the rights of minority populations to develop and maintain their own languages should now be moving away from that original policy. She points to the further irony that the Soviet Union appears to be doing so at the same time that other nations seem to have awakened to the linguistic and educational needs of their own minority groups.

THE UNITED STATES

The United States is often thought of as a linguistically and ethnically homogenous nation. Although there is no legal basis for it, English has come to assume the role of the official language of the United States. The vast numbers of non-English speaking immigrants who came to the U.S. over the past 200 plus years presumably were all assimilated into the English-speaking mainstream, leaving behind their original languages and ethnic ties. A single "American" culture thus developed from the amalgamation of many immigrant groups into one national "melting pot." This culture perhaps shows influences from the many diverse groups that went into its formation, but it still constitutes a monolithic entity of language and culture.

This notion of the homogeneity of language and culture in the U.S. came under critical scrutiny and reappraisal during the 1960s and 1970s (Glazer & Moynihan, 1970; Greer, 1974; Novak, 1977). As a result, the commonly accepted "melting pot" image of the United States was found to be only partially correct. Although the U.S. is a nation that primarily uses English as a language of communication, and there appears to be a distinct U.S. culture, the U.S. is neither linguistically nor culturally homogenous.

The Harvard Encyclopedia of American Ethnic Groups (Thernstrom, Orlov, & Handlin, 1980) estimates that there are at least 106 distinct ethnic groups in the U.S. and cautions that this is a conservative estimate because related groups were occasionally collapsed into a single category (e.g., the entry for American Indians actually comprises some 170 different groups).

More evidence comes from the 1980 census data (U.S. Department of Commerce 1980 Census, 1983) which reports that of a total of 210 million people in the U.S., 25 million reported speaking a language other than English at home. About 7 million of these non-English speakers were under the age of 17. The major non-English languages appear to be: Spanish (11.1 million speakers); Italian (1.6 million); German (1.59 million); French (1.55 million); and Polish (820 thousand).[3]

The Bilingual Education Act of 1968 provided federal support for the establishment and funding of bilingual education programs in those areas where non-English speaking children from low income families comprised a large portion of the school population. The original intention of the act was that bilingual education should remedy situations wherein non-English speaking children were, as a result of their inability to speak English, deprived of the opportunity for an adequate education. It was expected that English would be introduced with the child's home language and its use expanded until the child could function adequately in English. Then the child would be transferred to a regular, English-speaking classroom.

However, because bilingual programs were administered at the state and local levels, interpretation of policy was often subject to the needs and desires of the local community. Actual implementation of bilingual education often varied from its original intent, so that it is difficult to describe bilingual education in the U.S. as a unitary program or phenomenon. Some school systems only offered English-as-a-Second Language (ESL) programs, which were essentially remedial programs in which the primary language of instruction was English. Other systems offered instruction in both English and the children's native language but made the use of the native language only transitional, building up the children's competence sufficiently for them to attend regular, English-speaking classes. Other systems developed programs aimed at maintaining the child's native language and at teaching English. Children in such programs received instruction in both their native language and English, and often received, instruction about the history and culture of their particular national or ethnic group as well.

Efforts to consolidate federal policy toward bilingual education were stimulated by two events that occurred in 1974. In the case of *Lau v. Nichols,* (1974), the Supreme Court affirmed that the failure to provide educational assistance programs to non-English speaking children was in violation of Title VI of the Civil Rights Act, which forbade discrimination on the basis of race, color, or national origin in the operation of any federally assisted programs. In response to

---

[3]WHile the figure of 25 million as the total number of people speaking a language other than English in the U.S. is quite impressive, even that may be an underestimate. Fishman (1980b) has pointed out a number of problems involved in collecting census data and has suggested that the number of non-English speakers in the U.S. may be as high as 40 million.

this, the Department of Health, Education, and Welfare issued guidelines for local school systems recommending bilingual education as a specific solution to rectifying this situation.

The Bilingual Education Act was amended by Congress in 1974 to make it more explicit in intent and design. Bilingual education was defined as "instruction given in, and study of, English and to the extent necessary to allow a child to progress effectively through the education system, the native language of the children of limited English speaking ability" (pp. 186-187). The act stipulated that bilingual education should include instruction in the children's own language in addition to English and should offer instruction dealing with aspects of the native cultural heritage of the children as well. Finally, it allowed for bilingual instruction for children other than those from low income families. Congress renewed this act in 1984; it remained essentially unchanged except for a provision allowing for 4% of the funds allocated to local educational systems for bilingual education to be used for "alternative instructional methods" of their own choosing—methods placing more stress on English as the primary language of instruction.

The concept of bilingual education as a means of maintaining the linguistic and cultural identities of minority children has met with considerable opposition from various individuals and groups who still support the idea of a linguistically and culturally homogenous U.S. A reflection of this opinion is seen in recent attempts by the Department of Education to rescind many of the regulations for the conduct of bilingual education programs, in particular, the regulations specifying bilingual education as the only approach to providing adequate education for the minority language child (Fiske, 1985; U.S. Department of Education, 1984). Some of the alternatives suggested include a return to more traditional ESL programs (Keefe, 1985).

Such attempts by the Department of Education are intended to give greater autonomy to local school systems to use whatever method of instruction is best to teach minority language students—either bilingual instruction or some means of remedial instruction conducted in English. Critics, however, have charged that such a policy is merely a ploy to weaken and eventually do away with bilingual education (Garcia, 1985; Howe, 1985).

Although questions about the relative usefulness of different approaches to educating children of non-English speaking background appear to be under consideration in the U.S. government, the need for such programs appears to be more crucial than ever. Demographic projections of changes in the number of non-English speaking background individuals in the U.S. indicate that this population may increase to 34.7 million in 1990 and 39.5 million by the year 2000. The number of persons in this category under the age of 14 will increase to 5.4 million by 1990 and to 7.7 million by the year 2000. The future disposition and development of the latter group will be heavily dependent on the decisions concerning bilingual education now being made by the U.S. government.

THE PEOPLE'S REPUBLIC OF CHINA

The People's Republic of China (PRC), with over one billion people, is the most populous nation in the world. The official language policy of the PRC is similar to that of the Soviet Union, a not surprising situation, considering the close relationship the Chinese communists enjoyed with the Soviet Union at least in their early years. The rights of minority nationalities are guaranteed by the constitution of the PRC adopted in 1954 (Lehmann, 1975). Discrimination against national minorities and their languages is prohibited, and all national minorities are granted full rights to use and develop their written languages.

The languages of the PRC are predominately Sino-Tibetan. *Han,* the official designation for the Chinese language, is spoken by 95% of the population. Han itself is divided into nine major sublanguage groupings: *Mandarin* [4](spoken in Beijing and in the provinces of Ganshu, Shaanxi, Sichuan, Hubei, and Yunan), with about 665 million speakers; Xiang (spoken in Hunan province), with 50 million; *Gan* (spoken largely in Jiangxi province), with about 25 million; *Huizhou* (spoken in southern Anhui province), with 4 million; *Wu* (spoken in Shanghai and Zhejiang province), with 85 million; *Minnan* (spoken in southern Fujian province), with 10 million; *Minbei* (spoken in northern Fujian province), with 12 million; *Hakka* (spoken throughout southern China), with 40 million; and *Yue* (or Cantonese), with 55 million (Moser, 1985).

The use of the term *dialect* to refer to different sublanguages of Han is somewhat misleading; the differences between these groupings may be as great as those between, for example, Spanish and French. Moreover, Mandarin itself can be further subdivided into at least five different dialect groups, each with its own subdialects.

The dialect spoken in Beijing was designated the official language of the Republic of China in 1911 and was retained in that function by the communist regime when it came into power in 1949. It is usually referred to as *Putonghua,* or the common language. Moreover, the pronunciation of Chinese characters that is taught in schools has been standardized, based upon the pronunciation that these characters have in the Beijing dialect area. In addition to Putonghua, *Pinyin,* a system for transcribing Chinese characters that is based on the Latin alphabet, has also been introduced as a device for facilitating the learning of standard Chinese characters. Children are first taught to read in Pinyin and then gradually introduced to the Chinese characters themselves.

Aside from the dialect groups of Han, there are some 58 other minority nationalities making up some 6% of the population of the PRC (about 56 million people). The major minority languages are: *Chuang,* with 7.8 million speakers;

---

[4]The term "Mandarin" is no longer used in the PRC as its use is associated with the prerevolutionary era. Often it is referred to as "the common language" or *putonghua* (see the discussion in the text following).

Hui, with 3.9 million; *Uighur,* with 3.9 million; *Miao,* with 2.6 million; *Yi,* with 3.3 million; *Tibetan,* with 2.8 million; *Manchu-Tungus,* with 2.4 million; *Mongol,* with 1.6 million; *Puyi,* with 1.3 million; and *Korean,* with 1.2 million (Dreyer, 1976).

Autonomous national districts exist in areas with large concentrations of national minorities. Such districts have the same degree of autonomy and power as the national republics in the Soviet Union. However, all governmental institutions in those districts (e.g., judicial courts) are required to use the local minority language, and public documents are written in both Putonghua and the local language. Instruction is in the local language at both the elementary and middle school levels, and Chinese from the Han-speaking areas who work or live in minority language areas are required to learn the local language (Mei, 1984).

Like the Soviet Union, the PRC has had to contend throughout its history with the problem of reconciling ethnic and linguistic plurality with the social and economic goals of a centralized communist state. Also as in the Soviet Union, periods of relative accommodation to the interests of minority groups (as indicated for example, by support for the system of autonomous national districts) have alternated with more radical attempts to eliminate special consideration for minority groups and to assimilate them into the Han-speaking mainstream. The latter tendency was especially evident during the Cultural Revolution of the 1960s. With the widespread disruption of Chinese society during this period, many of the government-sponsored agencies and services for supporting non-Han minority groups were effectively destroyed and had to be painstakingly rebuilt during the 1970s.

Since the Cultural Revolution, the PRC appears to have returned to a more balanced policy toward its minorities, supporting the maintenance of non-Han languages and cultures while at the same time encouraging the learning of Putonghua by all citizens of the PRC. The present view is typified by the following statement issued by the Commission on Language Reform in 1984: "Because of the variety of languages in China, everyone is required to speak the common language. The policy is not to replace one's own dialect but to become bilingual in one's own language and the common language [Putonghua]" (Mei, 1984, p. 78). The use of Putonghua is being encouraged in all aspects of public life: government and legislature, the military, mass media, school instruction, and the work place. In addition, schools are beginning to create incentives for learning Putonghua, for example, holding contests and competitions within and between schools, through the use of peer monitoring, and so on.

Any conclusions about the role of bilingualism in the language policy of the PRC must be guarded because of the paucity of information. Moreover, the information that is available has come principally from groups that, having toured China by official invitation (e.g., Lehman, 1975; Mathias & Kennedy, 1980; Mei, 1984), have based much of their reports on information provided by government sources. From this information, one gathers that the official policy of the PRC is to maintain its minority languages while at the same time encouraging the learning of Putonghua as a medium of communication with other citizens of the PRC. It would be premature, however, to draw any firm conclusions about the actual implementation and results of bilingual education in the PRC at this time.

SOME PSYCHOLOGICAL IMPLICATIONS

Comparing these four countries, then, one sees very different attitudes and approaches to bilingualism and bilingual education. The official position both in the U.S. and in the Soviet Union is that bilingualism is primarily a transitional stage in the process of assimilation into the dominant culture. The position in Canada and the PRC, on the other hand, is that bilingualism is a normal, everyday phenomenon and that the aim of bilingual education should be to enable citizens to function equally well in two languages.

The implementation of bilingual education likewise appears to have had rather different results at least for the U.S., the Soviet Union, and Canada.[5] In the U.S., for example, bilingual education programs have so far had mixed success (Cordes, 1985; McLaughlin, 1978; U.S. Department of Education, 1984). Although several programs have been extremely successful, with substantial gains being shown in school performance, others have shown lags in performance, which actually increase with time.

Critics of bilingual education in the U.S. argue that such varied results support the conclusion that bilingual education itself is not more effective than other types of remedial programs and that individual communities should be given more freedom to use whatever method they feel is most effective in helping minority-language children. Others insist, however, that these results may be due to a number of factors, including variations in the quality of teaching, in student background, and in the degree of community support.

Information about bilingual education in the Soviet Union is far less extensive than that available for the U.S. However, there are at least some indications that Soviet programs for teaching Russian to non-Russian minority children may be encountering similar difficulties. Kreindler (1982) has noted several published reports of a high incidence of school failures among the non-Russians.

Canada, on the other hand, appears to have had enormous success in implementing bilingual education successfully on a very large scale. The children who

---

[5]We feel that information available about the state of bilingual education in the PRC is so limited, we prefer not to make any further comments about it relative to the other countries which we are comparing.

emerge from the programs in Canada show academic performance at least the equivalent of that shown by children enrolled in monolingual classes (Lambert & Tucker, 1972; McLaughlin, 1978).

Beyond their social or political significance, these different policies undoubtedly have enormous psychological impact. Lambert (1977) has distinguished between additive and subtractive processes in bilingualism. With subtractive bilingualism, a second language replaces a first language. With additive bilingualism, the individual achieves and maintains a balanced proficiency in both languages.[6]

Lambert suggests that different psychological outcomes are associated with each of these processes. Children who undergo subtractive bilingualism (for example, when immigrant children were put into monolingual English language classes in the United States until the advent of bilingual education) are often prevented from using whatever language skills they acquired with the first language to learn the second language. These children, in comparison with monolingual children, may show deficits in performance because their general language processing skills have not been fully developed in either language. Also, the experience of being between two worlds, that is, between two different languages and cultures and, moreover, having to choose one over the other, may also be a source of emotional conflict for the child who undergoes a process of subtractive bilingualism.

On the other hand, children who experience additive bilingualism usually acquire both languages in an atmosphere wherein both languages are considered to be equally socially relevant. There is no pressure to give up one language for the other. Moreover, instruction in the second language often takes advantage of whatever skills children already possess in the first language. Those children will presumably do as well as monolingual children in their general scholastic performance and may even derive some secondary cognitive advantages from being proficient in two languages (see Palij & Homel, this volume).

Using Lambert's distinctions, we would classify Canada as a nation whose language policies promote additive bilingualism, whereas the U.S. and the Soviet Union are nations whose policies appear to promote subtractive bilingualism. Moreover, we feel that it is no mere coincidence that the pattern of success of bilingual education or lack of it, in each of these countries tends to agree with the predictions outlined by Lambert. It remains to be seen whether those who are concerned with evaluating the educational outcomes of bilingualism will consider the role of social context, even at the level of governmental policy, in the psychological development of the bilingual child.

---

[6]Lambert has also suggested a similar distinction for the phenomenon of biculturalism: additive biculturalism would be the process that allows a person to become knowledgeable about and an active participant in two cultures, subtractive biculturalism would be the process by which knowledge of and participation in one culture is exchanged for knowledge of and participation in another culture.

REFERENCES

Beaujot, R., & McQuillian, K. (1982). *Growth and dualism: The demographic development of Canadian society.* Toronto: Gage Press.

Bilingual Education Act of 1974, 20 U.S.C.A. 880b et. seq. (Supp. 1975). In United States Commission on Civil Rights (1974). *A better chance to Learn: Bilingual-bicultural education* (pp. 185–203). (Clearinghouse publication 51.) Washington, DC: U.S. Government Printing Office.

Bilinsky, Y. (1964). *The Second Soviet republic: the Ukraine after World War II.* New Brunswick, Rutgers University Press.

Brunner, E. (1981). *Soviet demographic trends and the ethnic composition of draft age males 1980-1995* (Rand note N-16541 Santa Monica, CA: Rand.

Comrie, B. (1981). *The languages of the Soviet Union.* London: Cambridge University Press.

Cordes, C. (1985, November). Studies dispute Bennet's attack on bilingualism. *APA Monitor, 16,* 6.

Dreyer, J. T. (1976). *China's forty millions.* Cambridge, MA: Harvard University Press.

Fishman, J. A. (1980a). Bilingualism and biculturalism as individual and as societal phenomena. *Journal of Multilingual and Multicultural Development, 1,* 3–15.

Fiske, E. B. (1985, September 26). Education department to alter bilingual efforts. *The New York Times,* pp. A1, B9.

Garcia, R. (1985, October 7). More new federalism [Letter to the editor]. *The New York Times,* p. A30.

Glazer, N., & Moynihan, D. P. (1970). *Beyond the melting pot: The Negroes, Puerto Ricans, Jews, Italians, and Irish of New York City* (2nd ed.). Cambridge, MA: MIT Press.

Greer, C. (1974). *Divided society: The ethnic experience in America.* New York: Basic Books.

Grosjean, F. (1982). *Life with two languages: An introduction to bilingualism.* Cambridge, MA: Harvard University Press.

Howe, H. (1985, October 7). Misguided tampering with bilingual education [Letter to the Editor]. *The New York Times,* p. A30.

Isayev, M. I. (1977) *National languages in the USSR: Problems and solutions.* Moscow: Progress Publishers.

Kaalt, J. (1977). A brief introduction to the census language data. In P. Lamy (Ed.), *Language maintainence and language shift in Canada: New dimensions in the use of census language data* (pp. 16–21). Ottawa: University of Ottawa Press.

Keefe, J. (1985, October 24). An alternative to bilingualism. *The New York Times,* p. A27.

Kreindler, I. (1982). The changing status of Russian in the Soviet Union. *International Journal of the Sociology of Language, 33,* 7–39.

Lambert, W. E. (1977). The effects of bilingualism on the individual: cognitive and sociocultural consequences. In P.A. Hornby (Ed.) *Bilingualism: Psychological, social, and educational implications* (pp. 15–27). New York: Academic Press.

Lambert, W. E., & Tucker, G. R. (1972). Bilingual education of children: The St. Lambert experiment. Rowley, MA: Newbury House.

Lau V. Nichols, No. 72–6520 (414 U.S. at 566, 1974).

Lehmann, W. P. (1975). *Language and linguistics in the People's Republic of China.* Austin: University of Texas Press.

Lewis, E. G. (1972). *Multilingualism in the Soviet Union.* The Hague: Mouton.

Luckyj, G. S. N. (1975). Socialist in content nationalist in form. In G. S. N. Luckyj (Ed.), *Discordant voices: The non-Russian Soviet literatures* (pp. 1–12). Oakville, Ont.: Mosaic Press.

Mathias, J. & Kennedy, T. L. (Eds.) (1980). *Computers, language reform, and lexicography in China: A report by the CETA delegation.* Seattle, WA: Washington State University Press.

McLaughlin, B. (1978). *Second language acquisition in childhood.* Hillsdale, NJ: Lawrence Erlbaum Associates.

Mei, J. Y. (1984). *Reading in China: Report of the U.S. reading study team to the People's Republic of China.* Washington, DC: National Committee on U.S.–China Relations.

Moser, L. J. (1985). *The Chinese mosiac: The peoples and provinces of China.* Boulder, CO: Westview Press.

Narodnoe khozjajstvo SSSR 1922-1982 [The national economy of the USSR 1922-1982]. (1982)- . Moscow: Financy i statistika.

Novak, M. (1977). *The rise of the unmeltable ethnics: Politics and culture in the seventies.* New York: Macmillan.

Savchenko, F. (1970). *Zaborona ukrajinstva 1876r* [The suppression of the Ukrainian activities] (Harvard Series in Ukrainian Studies vol. 14). Munich: Wilhelm Fink Verlag.

Simirenko, A. (1969). The development of soviet social science. In A. Simirenko (Ed.), *Social thought in the Soviet Union.* Chicago: Quadrangle.

Thernstrom, S., Orlov, A., & Handlin, O. (Eds.) (1980). *Harvard encyclopaedia of American ethnic minorities.* Cambridge, MA: Belnap Press of Harvard University.

U.S. Department of Commerce. Bureau of the Census. (1983). *1980 census: Detailed population characteristics; United States summary, part 1: section A:* United States (PC80-1-D1-A US Summary). Washington, DC: U.S. Government Printing Office.

U.S. Department of Education (1984). *The condition of bilingual education in the nation, 1984.* Rosslyn, VA: National Clearinghouse for Bilingual Education.

Whitaker, R. A. (1984). *The Quebec cauldron.* In M. S. Whittington and G. Williams (Eds.), *Canadian politics in the 1980's (pp. 33–57).* Toronto: Methuen.

II

LANGUAGE ACQUISITION AND PROCESSING

3

The Second-Language Learner in the Context of the Study of Language Acquisition

Kenji Hakuta
Yale University

How can the study of second language learners illuminate the fundamental issues of development? That is the central concern of this conference, one whose many-faceted responses will be slowly revealed through the papers presented. I would like to address specifically the problem of grammar in the acquisition of a second language after the primary language has been established. The problem can be put into the perspective presented by Lila Gleitman in the 10th Anniversary special issue of the journal *Cognition* (Gleitman, 1981). Essentially, Gleitman argues for the informative value of three different kinds of variations in investigating the differential roles of maturation and environment in determining language acquisition. First, there are variations in the quality of the language sample available to the child. These include the traditional variables used in the investigation of motherese. Second, there are variations in the interpretive information from the learner's perspective (for example, how does a blind child interpret the verb *see*?) And third, there are variations in the learner's endowment, specifically the ability to represent language. Although everyone would have their own pet variations to add to this list (my own being cross-linguistic variations, more to be said on this later), the framework is very useful in discussing where the study of second language acquisition fits in with respect to major issues in language acquisition.

With regard to the first point, there are probably more variations in linguistic environments for second language (L2) acquisition than for first language (L1) acquisition. Most L2 studies are concerned with "naturalistic" situations, that is, cases where the learners are not formally tutored in the second language. These studies bear the closest resemblance to the L1 input situation, although the source of input can vary from adults to peers. Then, there are cases where children and adults learn a second language through formally tutored classes. Such variations in the types of linguistic input to L2 learners can provide a rich source of data for assessing the role of the input. It is interesting that most L2 studies have been concerned with naturalistic acquisition, because tutored settings provide actually an ideal situation in which input data can be recorded accurately and experimentally manipulated.

Gleitman's second point, variations in interpretive information, can be well addressed by the study of L2 acquisition. A fact too obvious to dwell on at any length is that L2 learners are more cognitively advanced than the L1 learner, so that the usual confoundings of language and cognitive development can be separated out. By looking at the correlations between variations in the course of acquisition of L1 and L2 learners on the one hand and variations in their differences in interpretive capacities on the other, we can hypothesize what facts observed in L1 learners are "artifacts" of cognitive development. Likewise, similarities between L1 and L2 acquisition despite the vast cognitive differences would be strong evidence for language-specific processes. Leaving aside the problem of language transfer for the moment, one might even argue that L2 learners can reveal more about linguistic biases inherent in language acquisition than L1 learners (Gass & Ard, 1980). This brings us to the third point raised by Gleitman, on variations of the endowment of the learner.

Perhaps, as Gleitman puts it, "the early 'conceptual language' stage is not traversed during learning by these older children for they are capable of the mature representations of linguistic data" (p. 111). In addition to whether the first hypotheses by the L2 learner are represented linguistically rather than conceptually, there is much to be learned from language transfer. In the 1950s and 1960s, during the heyday of contrastive linguistics, language transfer was seen as evidence for the S-R view of language acquisition (see Hakuta & Cancino, 1977, for a historical review). However, more recently, transfer is seen as evidence for the learner's working hypotheses concerning the nature of the target language. By studying what types of linguistic rules transfer from the native language to the second language, we can garner a glimpse of the entrenchment of the native language in the child. The existence of transfer attests to the psychological reality of the linguistic rules in question. Another issue raised with regard to endowment in second language learners is that of the critical period. Does the capacity to represent language disappear with age (Lenneberg, 1967; Penfield & Roberts, 1959)? We can look at L2 learners varying in the age at which they begin acquisition.

First I would like to state the conclusions that can be drawn from the literature, and then provide the relevant evidence. Generally, it is not true that a second language learner, regardless of his–her age of learning, will perfectly mimic the developmental patterns displayed by a child learning the native language. In fact, more similarities are to be found between an adult and a 5-year-old second language learner than between a 5-year-old and a first language learner. However, there are also a large number of parallels between L1 and L2 acquisition that can be observed. Specifically, first, there are certain striking facts about L2 acquisition that can be best understood when cognitive-developmental factors are taken into account. That is to say, some of the differences between L1 and L2 acquisition are due to the fact that second language learners are cognitively more mature than their L1 counterparts. Second, there are also striking similarities between L1 and L2 learners. They reveal variation that can be attributed to the bureaucratic structure of the beast that all language learners, whether L1 or L2, must master. Regardless of the learner's endowment, certain structures are more difficult than others. This may be due to general cognitive factors, such as processing constraints imposed by configurational structure or memory, or it may be due to more abstract, language-specific factors. Third, the extent to which a human becomes entrenched in the native language can be seen in the effects of transfer from the native language to the second language. There is good evidence for the native language of the learner biasing L2 acquisition in different sorts of ways. And finally, there is good evidence to suggest that some time after puberty is a period when the capacity to acquire a second language deteriorates.

In support of these conclusions, I do not intend to review all of the available evidence. Rather, the discussion is intended to expose the newcomer to second language acquisition to the kinds of data that can be expected from such research. More extensive reviews of the literature can be found in McLaughlin (1976), Hakuta and Cancino (1977), Hatch (1978), Schumann and Stenson (1975), Oller and Richards (1973). The first section addresses the question of the effects of cognitive maturity. The second section reviews the effects of linguistic structure from the viewpoint of similarities between first and second language acquisition. The third section reviews evidence for transfer from the native language. The fourth section looks at the question of age effects. The fifth section proposes a framework for research from the viewpoint of language universals.

EFFECTS OF COGNITIVE MATURITY

A well-documented period in first language acquisition is the so-called two-word stage or Stage I speech in Brown's (1973) outline. It appears that a relatively small number of semantic relations characterize a large proportion of the two-word utterances that can be found in children during this period of development. Frequently found are relations such as agent-action, agent-object, attributive-entity, and so forth. Brown pointed to the correspondence between the semantic roles expressed during this period and the sensorimotor schemes outlined independently by Piaget, the conclusion being that early Stage I speech is constrained by the cognitive capacities of the child. Conspicuously missing are semantic relations such as if-then conditionals, sophisticated temporal and aspectual relations, and logical connectives. The obvious needed to be done. Lightbown (1977) looked at the acquisition of French by two 6-year-old children whose native language was English. She submitted the children's language in their initial stages of learning to the same kinds of analyses conducted for L1 learners. Essentially, Lightbown found that these children expressed all kinds of semantic relations from the very beginning. There was not the kind of orderly progression found with first language learners. She found relations expressed such as manner, intensifiers, and conjunctions. In short, L2 children, even when relatively young, do not seem to go through identical stages of development as L1 children.

It has been observed (Hakuta, 1975; Tiphine, personal communication) that L2 children use sentence coordination from quite early on in their development. In L1 children, this structure is relatively late in emerging (Brown, 1973; Hakuta, de Villiers, & Tager-Flusberg, 1982; Tager-Flusberg, de Villiers, & Hakuta, 1982), especially when used in the contexts corresponding to logical connectives (Beilin, 1976). An illustration of the early use of conjunctions appears in Table 3.1. The data are from a five-year-old Japanese girl, named Uguisu, learning English (Hakuta, 1975). Table 3.1 is frequency distribution of various conjunctions observed in her speech over time. The monthly samples were made equivalent in length at 200 utterances each. As can be seen, Uguisu used conjunctions from quite early on, in the case of *and* and *because,* from the very first sample. The usage was in most instances appropriate from the target language point of view.

Aside from the structure of their native language, second language learners most likely know certain facts about the functions of language, such as that it is used for conversations, that conversations involve turn taking, and so forth

TABLE 3.1
Distribution of Coordinating Conjunctions in
Uguisu's Speech Samples. Each Monthly
Sampling Period Contains 200 Utterances.

Month	and	but	because	so	if
1*	3	—	2	—	—
2	8	—	3	—	—
3	5	1	4	—	—
4	5	4	11	8	—
5	20	4	—	4	11
6	4	1	10	2	3
7	5	6	5	4	1
8	7	2	8	4	5
9	7	5	12	—	3
10	6	4	2	3	2

Note: *represents the first month when Uguisu started producing high frequency of utterances, which was 6 months after her initial exposure to English.
(Source: Hakuta, 1975)

(Keller-Cohen, 1979). This knowledge about the global properties of language, along with a more developed memory span for remembering whole sentences, has been hypothesized to account for the large number of prefabricated patterns observed commonly in second language learners (Hakuta, 1974b; Huang, 1971; Wong-Fillmore, 1976). Prefabricated patterns (or formulaic utterances, as Wong-Fillmore calls them) are characterized by lack of internal structure. It appears that second language learners memorize entire utterances without knowledge of underlying structure. This is not unheard of in L1 acquisition (Clark, 1974), but its preponderance in L2 acquisition is striking.

Huang (1971) studied a 5-year-old Taiwanese boy, Paul, learning English. He reports an excellent observation of Paul's first utterance in English:

> On February 4, only two days after the beginning of Paul's nursery school experience, the investigator heard him (Paul) muttering: *Get out of here.* On the way home from school the next morning, he asked me about the meaning of that utterance. When the investigator, instead of telling him the meaning, asked him to relate what had happened, he said that a boy who wanted to get away had said it. The Taiwanese translation he rendered means *Don't be–stay here,* which is very close to *Get out of here* in meaning. An incident in the nursery school the next day proved Paul's capacity not only to understand this utterance but to use it appropriately as well.
> (Paul was on a tricycle while Michele holding on to the handle bar, kept on bothering him. Obviously, he wanted her to leave him alone.)
> Paul: Get out of here.
> (Michele walked away, somewhat embarrassed.) (pp. 12-13)

Wong-Fillmore (1976), in her study of five Spanish-speaking children learning English, reported that over half of the children's utterances contained prefabricated forms. She argued that through the gradual analysis of such forms, later linguistic structure developed: "All of the constitutents of the formula become freed from the original construction, [and] what the learner has left is an abstract structure consisting of a pattern or rule by which he can construct like utterances" (p. 645).

It is not clear, however, whether such abstract structure can emerge through brute force. That is the traditional problem associated with the emergence of grammar. Nevertheless, what is clear is that second language learners have been observed to begin with whole sentences, and that if the same form is followed over time, the emergence of structure can be observed. A striking example of this can be illustrated in Uguisu's use of embedded "how" questions (Hakuta, 1976). During the third month of observation, Uguisu made the following set of utterances:

- I know how to do it.
- I know how to do read it this.

- I know how to read it this.
- I know how to make.
- I know how to draw it cat.
- I know how to draw (it) butterfly.
- I know how to draw it boy.

These can be characterized by a prefabricated pattern, *I know how to + VP*. This apparently correct form changed over time into forms such as the following, which were observed in her 15th month.

- First I gotta write it and show you how do you spell 'Debra'.
- I know how do you spell Vino.
- We only know how do you make it like that.
- I know how do you write this.

Figure 3.1 plots the proportion of forms using "how to" over the total number of how-questions, showing that the decline in performance is a gradual one. I have argued elsewhere that this change is in fact reflective of her other uses of indirect wh- questions, where forms were first used with subject-aux inversion (Hakuta, 1976). At any rate, prefabricated patterns are quite predominant in early second

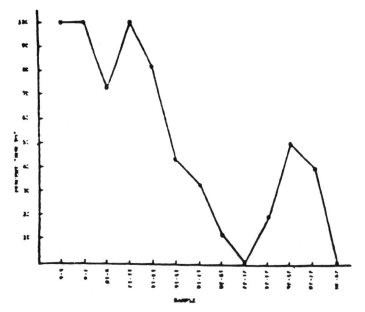

Fig. 3.1. Proportion of correct how-embeddings (how to) over total how-embeddings. Biweekly samples are paired. Source: Hakuta, 1976.

language speech, but it is clear that gradually they are analyzed into more flexible form. Although prefabricated patterns may be a good place to start, and may provide the linguistic data upon which the language acquisition mechanism might work, the problem of what the analytic process consists of is a mystery, just as it is in first language acquisition.

Perhaps a longer processing span would imply that the second language learner would not show effects of length (such as would be reflected in M. L. U. upper bounds). One indication of this can be found in Uguisu's use of the English possessive inflection 's. Cazden (1968) reported differential use of the possessive in Adam, Eve, and Sarah, depending on whether they were used in noun-noun contexts (e.g., Mom's pie) or in elliptic contexts (e.g., Mom's). For all three children, there was a large difference in the percentage to which the morpheme was supplied in obligatory context, with greater proportion being supplied in elliptic contexts than in noun-noun. Uguisu, on the other hand, performed equally in both contexts (see Hakuta, 1976). Because the elliptic context requires only one noun, while the noun-noun context two, it is possible that this difference reflects the larger processing space available to second language learners. In turn, this provides an explanation for the otherwise perplexing differential use in L1 children. First language learners, having a more limited processing span, may omit the morpheme when they have to process two nouns for the non-elliptic form, but in the elliptic form may find it possible to "fit in" the morpheme because there is only one noun to process. The phenomenon found in first language learners, then, may be a simple performance factor.

Finally, with regard to the manifestations of cognitive maturity, it is worth pointing to vocabulary development as an under-investigated issue. All indications are that lexical development in second language learners is extremely rapid. Gillis (1975), in her study of 3 seven-year-old Japanese children learning English, reported PPVT (Peabody Picture Vocabulary Test) increases in mental score equivalents of 6 months to 1 year in a period of just 1 month. Snow and Hoefnagel–Hohle (1978) report that age is positively correlated with vocabulary development in American children learning Dutch, suggesting that older learners, with more cognitive capacity, pick up vocabulary faster. What is needed is a study of the organization of the lexicon in bilingual children, a promising area for future investigation.

EFFECTS OF LINGUISTIC STRUCTURE: L1 AND L2 SIMILARITIES

An active research tradition in applied linguistics is one commonly called "error analysis" (Corder, 1971; Nemser, 1971; Oller & Richards, 1973; Schumann & Stenson, 1975; Selinker, 1972; Svartvik, 1973). Typically, error analysis looks at the kinds of systematic deviations from the target language grammar observed in language learners, and the errors are classified with respect to their hypothesized source. Usual categories for classification are *transfer, simplification,* and *overgeneralization.* Transfer errors refer to those errors whose source is clearly identifiable as the native language grammar. For example, a native speaker of Spanish saying "He no have happiness" is considered to have constructed an English utterance based on his native language. Simplification usually refers to errors of omission, particularly inflections and auxiliary verbs. The utterance "Reagan always sleep" is considered an example of omission, where the third person singular indicative marker is missing. Overgeneralization errors are most striking, and usually involve the learner "ironing out" irregularities common to language. For example, "Cooney fighted poorly" shows overgeneralization of the regular past tense marker *-ed* to irregular instances. Simplification and overgeneralization are errors well known to the student of language acquisition.

Studies employing error analysis typically show a relatively small number of transfer errors, with simplification being the most frequent (Cohen, 1975; Dulay & Burt, 1973; Duskova, 1969; Politzer & Ramirez, 1973; Selinker, Swain, & Dumas, 1975). For example, Dulay and Burt (1974a) looked at the errors produced by 179 Spanish-speaking children learning English. Out of 513 errors that they considered, 5% were classified as interference, whereas 87% were either simplification or overgeneralization errors. However, the classificatory system differs somewhat from study to study, and it is difficult to know how to interpret the results (Hakuta & Cancino, 1977). It is not a simple matter to classify errors. Japanese does not have articles, so should the omission of errors by a Japanese child learning English be considered an interference error or a simplification error? Also, it is not clear that the different types of errors are comparable, since their opportunities for occurrence are uncontrolled for. These studies in error analysis, however, do suggest commonalities between first and second language learners even when error proportion are left aside. Similar kinds of errors can be found in both kind of learners and across second language learners of different language backgrounds.

With regard to specific structures, there is some indication of similarities. Ervin-Tripp (1974) reports a study in which she looked at the comprehension of French passives in American children learning French. She found systematic misinterpretation of passives similar to those reported for French L1 children by Sinclair-de Zwart (1973). Interestingly enough, the children who misinterpreted the passives were at the same time correctly interpreting passives in English. Gass and Ard (1980) report a study of English relative clause comprehension by adult second language learners from different native language backgrounds. Their results (though not their interpretation of the data) are similar to those obtained for the same structures in English L1 children (for reviews of the English L1 literature, see de Villiers, Tager-Flusberg, Hakuta, & Cohen, 1979; Hakuta, 1981). Finally, D'Anglejan and Tucker (1975) administered to adult L2 learners English complementizer structures similar to those used by Carol Chomsky (1969) for older L1 children, and obtained similar results. The tentative generalization emerging from these three studies seems to be that at least when comprehension procedures are employed to investigate particular syntactic structures, L2 learners perform similarly to L1 learners.

Ever since Brown's (1973) report on the order of acquisition of "grammatical morphemes" appeared, researchers in second language acquisition have concerned themselves with whether the same order can be observed in second language learners (Cancino, 1976; Dulay & Burt, 1973, 1974b; Gillis, 1975; Hakuta, 1974a, 1976; Bailey, Madden, & Krashen, 1974; Larsen-Freeman, 1976; Rosansky, 1976). The answer is relatively straightforward: it is not. However, there has emerged a striking similarity in order of acquisition across second language learners, regardless of their native language. To be sure, there are influences of the native language (to be discussed in the next section), but the differences seem to be overshadowed by the similarities. This is taken as evidence that the native language exerts minimal influence on the order of acquisition of grammatical morphemes (see Hakuta & Cancino, 1977). The inference from here to the conclusion that first and second language acquisitions are similar is a somewhat difficult one, although it is one commonly made. On the one hand, there is no reason to expect, even if the two processes were the same, that the linguistic product would be the same. On the other hand, without some explanation for the differences, one is left skeptical. Compounding this problem is the commonly held misconception that "cognition equals semantics." For example, Dulay and Burt (1974b), in explaining the difference found in the order in first and second language learners, state: "It seems intuitive that children who are acquiring their first language have to deal with both semantic and syntactic information. However, six, seven, and eight-year old children learning a second language need not struggle with semantic concepts they already acquired, such as concepts of immediate past, possession, or progressive action" (p. 74).

The problem with this reasoning, as Schlesinger (1974) points out, is that cognition does not equal the semantics of a language. If they were the same, there would have to be no distinction between the two. The best demonstration of this complex relationship is through the fact that the cognitive categories from which languages draw are not uniform across language. For example, although many languages observe the distinction between alienable and inalienable possessions, English does not. Gender is another cognitive category that is expressed to widely varying degrees in different languages. Although cognitive development may be a pacesetter for cognitive categories available to the learner, the semantics of each particular language (one aspect of the formal complexity of the language) is often specific to that language (Slobin, 1973). As I argue later, the semantic distinction drawn in English between definite and indefinite articles presents precisely such a stumbling block for learners from languages that do not draw upon this distinction.

One explanation for the morpheme ordering has been provided by Larsen-Freeman(1976), who suggests frequency (although frequency itself should be explained). Larsen-Freeman correlated the L2 orderings with the frequencies reported by Brown for the mothers of Adam, Eve, and Sarah. Although Brown found no correlation between maternal frequency and the order of acquisition for the children, Larsen-Freeman found rank order correlations of roughly .80 (depending on the study). Should we accept this conclusion, that L2 learners are sensitive to frequency whereas L1 learners are not, at least for closed class items, what are we to conclude about the similarities and differences? Gleitman (1981) suggests that L1 children can be influenced by differential use of closed class items in maternal input. Perhaps this would force a reexamination of the issue of frequency in L1 acquisition as well, as a "modified frequency" hypothesis.

EFFECTS OF LINGUISTIC STRUCTURE: NATIVE LANGUAGE TRANSFER

Just as language contact in society was seen as a reliable indicator of the dynamic interaction between cultures by the great sociolinguist Weinreich (1953), the interplay of the two linguistic systems in the individual can be seen as reliable indicators of interplay between mental structures. This effect is best seen in language transfer. What better indicator is there for the psychological reality of a linguistic structure than the fact that it can transfer to another language in the course of L2 acquisition?

A constant thorn in the side of those who want to argue for the similarity in the order of acquisition of grammatical morphemes is the English article system. As mentioned above, children learning English with Japanese (Hakuta, 1976) and Korean (Fathman, 1975; Kang, 1982) as their native language (neither of which has an article system) had difficulty in learning the English article system. This compares, for example, to Frauenfelder's (1974) study of English-speaking children in a French immersion program in Canada, in which he found that although the children made many errors in gender on articles, they never confused the definite–indefinite contrast. Notice how this exemplifies the distinction between semantic development and cognitive development. It certainly cannot be that the Japanese and Korean children were unable to conceptualize the difference between definite and indefinite reference. Rather, it was that the distinction was not marked in the semantic system of their native language. It appears that the semantic structure of the native language guides the formulation of specific hypotheses about the target language, not the cognitive system.

Negation has been investigated by a number of researchers in both children and adults (Adams, 1974; Butterworth, 1972; Cazden, Cancino, Rosansky, & Schumann, 1975; Wong-Fillmore, 1976). The general finding seems to be that native speakers of Spanish have a characteristic stage of preverbal *no,* such as *Carolina no go to play.* This structure is seen as deriving from the Spanish structure, where in fact a morpheme of very similar sound as the English form is used. Both children and adults use such structures in their early stages of acquiring English. Recently, Herlinda Cancino and I completed a large study of 59 adult speakers of Spanish, all of whom had arrived in the United States after adolescence. One of the structures we investigaged was negation. In an imitation task, we asked subjects to repeat sentences where the third person singular negative auxiliary was required (e.g., "The man does not like cheese"). Responses were scored as follows: 1 point for *no + Verb* responses; 2 points for *not + Verb* responses; 3 points for *don't + Verb* responses; and 4 points for *doesn't + Verb* responses. They corresponded to the rough order of development in the case studies. Figure 3.2 shows the scatterplot of the mean response score against an independent measure of grammatical ability based on ratings and a vocabulary test. The systematicity in their development is remarkable, despite the large range of variation with respect to the subjects' length of residence in the United States and educational status. These findings seem to support the conclusion that the first hypothesis the second language learner entertains is that "this language is mine unless proven otherwise."

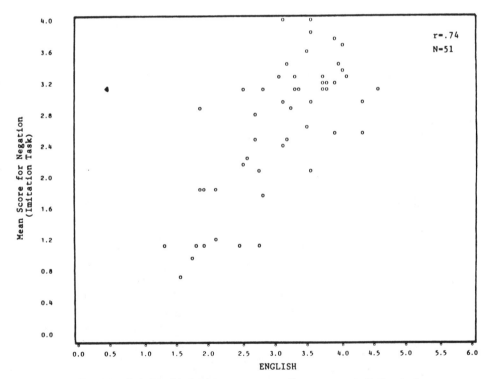

Fig. 3.2. Relationship between mean negation score on imitation task and global measure of English fluency in adult Puerto Ricans learning English.

Lest we mistakenly conclude that all language transfer occurs during the initial phases of L2 acquisition, two specific examples indicating otherwise will be mentioned. The first case involves Uguisu's use of English reflexives (reported in Hakuta, 1976). Some time between the 5th and 6th month after she started speaking English, Uguisu began using reflexives in utterances such as *You have to do self, because remember I do self?* (meaning You have to do it by yourself, because remember I did it by myself?) Although such use of the reflexive has not been reported (to my knowledge) for L1 learners, it is certainly something that might be expected. Around the 10th month, she began placing a pronoun in front of *self*, but in addition, she began using the English preposition *with*, resulting in utterances such as *They have to do it with theirselfs,* and *I can make toast with myself.* In Japanese, the instrumental preposition is used with reflexive pronouns, and Uguisu apparently came to put the two together, resulting in the transfer error. What a clever child. In her native language knowledge, reflexivity was paired with the instrumental case, presumably at the semantic level.

The other case involves a Spanish-speaking five-year-old girl, named Marta (Cancino, 1976). Marta began using the possessive in contexts determined to require *'s* using the Spanish-derived form and word order *de,* as in *book de Marta.* Notice that the order, possessed-possessor, reverses the usual English order. Then, she reversed the nouns, but omitted the *'s,* as in *Marta book.* Now, her forms were just like one would find in an L1 learner. Four samples later, she picked up on the English preposition *of,* as in *frog of Freddie,* and for two samples she used both this form and the earlier form in apparently free variation. Shortly following this period, she gradually began supplying the *'s* in obligatory contexts. Essentially, there were two levels at which language transfer occurred, one at a gross level of actually using the native language form, then a more sophisticated transfer once the relevant English form was acquired.

Another error of potential interest in inferring the organization of the native language occurs when the native language and the target language differ with respect to the form class representing specific concepts. One example of this can be seen in Uguisu's use of the word *mistake* in English (Hakuta, 1976). In Japanese, it is a verb, whereas in English, it is commonly a noun. Uguisu, until the last few samples, used *mistake* as a verb, resulting in utterances such as *Not there, I mustake; Don't give me more because you're mustaking; I just mustake, and I just skipped.* Such errors give an indication that Uguisu was transferring at the unit of the form class, and that individual lexical items in her native language were tagged with the particular privileges of occurrence that define membership in form classes (Maratsos & Chalkley, 1980).

Finally, it should be pointed out that transfer does not manifest itself only as errors. Schachter (1974) showed that in written English compositions by native speakers of different languages, the native language made an important difference in the frequency with which they used relative clause structures. English is a "right-branching" language, that is, the relative clause comes to the right of the head noun, such as in

the bottle [that fell on the floor].

The direction of branching, left or right, has been considered an important variable in the study of language typology (Lehmann, 1973). It turns out that in Schachter's study, subjects who came from right-branching languages (Arabic, Spanish) used more relative clauses than those from left-branching languages (Japanese and Chinese). It is important that there were no differences between these two groups in terms of error rates, that is, the degree to which they correctly used relative clause structure when it was in fact used. Thus, the data can be interpreted as avoidance of the structure, rather than inability. In a comparison of Uguisu and Marta's speech samples, Hakuta (1976) found, albeit tentatively because of the difficulty in comparability, that Marta, whose native language is Spanish, used more relative clauses than Uguisu, extending Schachter's important finding to children. Thus, it is important in considering transfer to look at the overall *pattern* of development.

EFFECTS OF AGE

I finally turn now to a discussion of whether there is a critical period for second language acquisition. It is assumed that this question bears on the more general issue of concern, that of capacity for language. Much speculation has been made about the age at puberty (roughly 13 to 14) as the pivotal point beyond which second language acquisition becomes difficult (Lenneberg, 1967). Hence, it is not surprising that most studies have attempted to span that age period.

Williams (1974) looked at a very specific aspect of speech perception in investigating the problem. She chose the Voice Onset Time (VOT) parameter differentiating /pa/ from /ba/. In Spanish, the boundary falls at the 0 msec. VOT, whereas for English, the boundary is at +25 msec. Capitalizing on this contrast, Williams tested Puerto Rican subjects who varied along two background variables: age of arrival in the United States (from 8 years old to 16 years old) and length of exposure to English (from 0 years to 3 ½ years). She used both discrimination and labeling paradigms to determine the boundary in the English /pa/ and /ba/. Williams found main effects for both length of exposure and for age of arrival, with closer approximation to the English + 25 msec. boundary associated with longer exposure and with younger age of arrival. She also was able to obtain production of the sounds from the same subjects, and showed through spectographic analysis a close correspondence to the perception results.

Oyama (1976) used a more global measure of rated degree of accentedness in the speech of adult Italian immigrants to the United States. Her subjects varied in age of arrival from 6 years old to 20 years old, and for her length of exposure variable, she took the range far exceeding William's range: 5 years to 18 years. Oyama found that age of arrival was an important predictor of rated pronunciation, but length of exposure had no predictive power. The latter result does not conflict with Williams because of the differences in range. Oyama (1978) reported the results of a sentence comprehension task with the same subjects, and reported essentially the same results.

A recent study by Patkowski (1980) looked at syntactic ability in adults as rated by judges. Subjects came from a variety of language backgrounds. Age of arrival ranged from 6 years old to 61 years old, and although length of stay was not controlled strictly, all subjects had been in the United States for longer than 5 years. Patkowski reports that age of arrival was correlated -.74 with syntactic rating. Neither length of stay nor amount of formal instruction in English made a difference. Thus, in all three studies, there is substantial support for a negative relationship between age and degree of success in second language acquisition.

One study, in which the age of subjects ranged down from 3 years old up to 15 years old, reports a positive relationship with age (Snow & Hoefnagel-Hohle, 1978). Subjects were American children learning Dutch, and they were tested on a variety of measures including pronunciation, auditory discrimination, and morphology. The fact that they found that learning increased with age is interesting, especially in light of our earlier discussion of the advantages of having a more cognitively mature system to work with. Perhaps up until somewhere around a "critical" period, there is a positive relationship. On the other hand, it is entirely possible that the older children were performing better on the tasks because they are better test takers.

The evidence previously summarized looks fairly strong in support of a negative relationship of language learning ability with age, but that is only a beginning. It will be recalled that there were many pieces of evidence suggesting similarities between child and adult second language learning. What accounts for these similarities? Without specification of what capacity it is that deteriorates, statements regarding age effects are bound to be misleading and uninterpretable. In addition, there are many successful adult second language learners. Even in Patkowski's distribution, which was fortunately published, there were overlaps in the distributions. The critical period is hardly likely to be even an absolute boundary. Further linguistic studies that shed light on the nature of the acquisition process can help sharpen the problem.

LANGUAGE UNIVERSALS AS AN INTEGRATED PERSPECTIVE

How are we to understand the maze of data from second language acquisition, and its relationship to first language acquisition? In an earlier paper (Hakuta, 1982), I argued for the use of research in language universals and language typology as a framework.

Any particular human language can be specified by its location within an *n*-dimensional space that defines the limits of variation of all human languages. As a psycholinguist, I understand the study of language typology and language universals to be an attempt to determine what the relevant dimensions are, and to determine how many meaningful dimensions exist. I assume as a working hypothesis that the *n*-dimensional space bears some relevance to the facts of human language learning. Perhaps there is some isomorphism between the *n*-dimensional space defined by language typologists and the hypothesis space of the language learner.

On a conceptual level, the goal of language typologists can be seen as similar to the factor-analytic personality psychologist (e.g., Cattell, 1965), with languages being used instead of people as random variables. Unlike psychologists, however, linguists do not go around asking raters to a rate a large number of languages along various linguistic dimensions. In addition, the types of data, or scales of measurement, used in language typology are different. The linguistic dimensions are most frequently considered to be categorical (Greenberg, 1978), whereas personality dimensions are interval scale data, and assumed to be continuous. But these differences constitute differences in statistical treatment. The working assumption seems to be that once enough typological dimensions have been formulated and investigated with respect to a large number of languages, these variables can be collapsed through statistical techniques to a smaller number of underlying dimensions, the essence of human language. As Greenberg recently put it, "A theoretical analysis of basic typological concepts helps us to broaden our conception of cross-linguistic generalizations, while its application provides a useful methodology for discovering such generalizations at the lower empirical levels and thus providing the materials for broader and deeper conclusions about the nature of human language" (p. 58).

Linguists have typically kept away from providing hypotheses as to the reasons for the existence of cross-linguistic generalizations (with notable exceptions such as Kuno, 1974, and Givon, 1979. For example, Downing (1978), in formulating universal characteristics of relative clause structures, writes: "In their present form they may serve as a summary of observations on the nature of relative clauses across languages, with which the data of additional languages may be compared. As such generalizations are refined, they afford an increasingly solid empirical basis for the formulation of explanatory principles in functional and psychological terms" (p. 411). Along similar lines, Steele (1978) formulates constraints to account for word order variation, such as the following: "A variation on basic word order in which the object precedes and the subject follows the verb is to be avoided" (p. 604). Although such constraints serve to explain at one level the observed data on word order variation, she writes in a footnote that "I am not offering explanations for the constraints" (p. 604, footnote 15).

Given this tendency, the developed product of language-typological research will be essentially a set of factors with loadings on different linguistic variables (e.g., direction of branching, order of verb and object, etc.). These *n* factors will constitute the *n*-dimensional space of human languages. My understanding of language typological research in its present state is that it is not yet at this stage, but it is perhaps not too early to discuss at the abstract level the psychological question, "In what ways is the *n*-dimensional space psychologically real, and how can we understand changes in the relationship under different psychological conditions of language acquisition?" I use the term *psychological correspondence* to refer to an empirical correspondence between the linguist's dimensions and psychological data obtained from studies of language learners.

For discussion's sake, consider the following variables along which languages are known to be distributed:

1. POSITION (postposition/preposition)
2. BRANCHING DIRECTION (left-branching/right-branching)
3. WORD ORDER VARIABILITY (rigid word order/free word order)
4. DUMMY SUBJECT (has no dummy subjects/has dummy subjects)
5. OBJECT-VERB ORDER (verb-object/object-verb)
6. AGREEMENT (has no subject-verb agreement/has agreement)
7. PASSIVIZATION (has no passives/has passives)

Table 3.2 presents raw data for 20 hypothetical languages (fabricated from my imagination with a little help from the intuition of several colleagues about some real languages) with values on each of the variables. A value of "0" is entered where the language exhibits properties of the first level of the variable, and "1" is entered where the second level is exhibited. The relationship between the variables across languages can be expressed in a correlation matrix, which appears in Table 3.2. A casual inspection of Table 3.3 reveals that there are many variables that are well correlated. For example, OBJECT-VERB AND BRANCHINGNESS are correlated -1.00, a perfect negative relationship revealing that all OV languages are left-branching, and all VO languages are right-branching. AGREEMENT is correlated .70 with DUMMY SUBJECT, indicating that languages with subject-verb agreement also tend to have dummy subjects. An underlying structure of the intercorrelations between the variables can be revealed strikingly through factor analysis, the results of which appear in Table 3.4. Factor 1 is "saturated" with the variables of branchingness, object-verb, and position. This may be interpreted as follows: languages that are left-branching tend to be object-verb and have postpositions, whereas right-branching languages tend to be verb-object and have prepositions. Factor 2 is saturated with the variables dummy subject, agreement, and passive. The interpretation is that languages with dummy subjects also tend to have subject-verb agreement and passivization. When I fabricated the data for Table 3.1, I had in mind two clusters of variables that have been suggested in the literature, one related to the

TABLE 3.2
Distribution of 20 Fabricated Languages with Respect to Language Variables.

			Language Variables				
	Position	Branching	Word Order	Dummy Subject	Object Verb	Agreement	Passive
Language							
1	0	1	1	0	0	0	0
2	1	1	1	0	0	0	0
3	0	1	1	1	0	1	1
4	1	1	1	1	0	1	0
5	0	1	0	0	0	0	0
6	1	1	0	0	0	0	1
7	0	1	0	1	0	1	1
8	1	1	0	1	0	1	1
9	0	0	1	0	1	0	0
10	0	0	1	0	1	0	0
11	0	0	1	1	1	1	1
12	1	1	1	0	0	1	1
13	0	0	1	0	1	0	0
14	1	1	0	1	0	1	1
15	1	1	0	1	0	1	1
16	1	1	1	1	0	1	1
17	0	0	1	0	1	0	0
18	1	1	1	0	0	1	1
19	0	0	1	0	1	0	1
20	0	0	0	1	1	0	1

Variable labels: Position (0 = postposition; 1 = preposition)
Branching (0 = left-branching; 1 = right-branching)
Word Order (0 = rigid word order; 1 = free word order)
Dummy Subject (0 = has no dummy subject; 1 = has dummy subject)
Object-Verb (0 = verb-object order; 1 = object-verb order)
Agreement (0 = has no subj-verb agrmnt; 1 = has subj-verb agrmnt)
Passive (0 = has no passives; 1 = has passives)

TABLE 3.3
Correlation Matrix of Language Variables Across 20 Fabricated Languages.

	Position	Branch	Word Order	Dummy Subj.	Object Verb	Agreement	Passive
Position	1.00	0.66	−0.17	0.19	−0.66	0.50	.32
Branching	0.66	1.00	−0.31	0.24	−1.00	0.52	.25
Word order	−0.17	−0.31	1.00	−0.38	0.31	−0.10	−.38
Dummy subject	0.19	0.24	−0.38	1.00	−0.24	0.70	.53
Object Verb	−0.66	−1.00	0.31	−0.24	1.00	−0.52	−.25
Agreement	0.50	0.52	−0.10	0.70	−0.52	1.00	.61
Passive	0.32	0.25	−0.38	0.53	−0.25	0.61	1.00

TABLE 3.4
Factor Analysis Solution with
Varimax Rotation for 20
Fabricated Languages.

	Factor 1	Factor 2
Position	0.63	0.26
Branching	0.98	0.19
Word order	−0.21	−0.33
Dummy subject	0.07	0.84
Object verb	−0.98	−0.19
Agreement	0.38	0.74
Passive	0.15	0.70

order of elements in sentences (e.g., Greenberg, 1963; Lehmann, 1973) and the other related to the subject-topic typological dimension suggested by Li and Thompson (1976). The factor structures in Table 3.4 reflect these dimensions, although I should point out that, for purposes of the present paper, the actual variables that load on the factors are irrelevant. What's important is simply the fact that this is the kind of way in which the ultimate outcome of the current thrust of language typology might be represented. In subsequent discussion of the factor structure of languages, I simply label the factors Factor A and B, and the individual variables that load on the factors Variables 1, 2, and so forth, so that our discussion is uncluttered by the truth value of linguistic statements and concentrate on the logic of inquiry.

IN SEARCH OF PSYCHOLOGICAL CORRESPONDENCE

As Stephen Jay Gould points out in his elegantly written book on intelligence testing (Gould, 1981), we human consumers of statistics have an inherent bias towards reifying factors derived through factor analysis. This is a higher order bias similar to the bias of inferring causality from correlation, against which we are warned repeatedly in elementary statistics classes. Language factors are no more than statements about the distribution of the world's languages. We should be wary of using observed language factors as explanations for psychological data. Rather, the question should be "What are the principles that determine the observed factor structure?"

The observation of the language learner can constrain the psychological plausibility of the n-dimensional space. We can look for the preservation or fragmentation of the factor structure in the language learner, under different circumstances, i.e., in L1 and L2 learners. If it can be observed in some circumstances, but not others, then we might be able to formulate hypotheses about its governing principles. If we consider the *n*-dimensional space defined by language factors to be a good candidate as a psychologically real hypothesis about the target language on the part of the langage learner, we expect there to be some correspondence between the language factor and data obtained from language learners. In this section, I sketch out some considerations that must go into the search for psychological correspondence.

The task for the learner can be defined as a process of determination of the factor score for the particular target language. Having determined the factor score, the learner can be guided in the search for the particular realizations of the individual variables that go with the factor. Consider the situation in Table 3.5. A language with a high positive score on Factor A will have a value of "1" on Variables 1–3, and a value of "0" on Variables 4 and 5, as in LANGUAGE X. A language with a high negative score on Factor A will have values of "0" on Variables 1–3, and values of "1" on Variables 4 and 5, a situation reflected in LANGUAGE Z. The two hypothetical languages are mirror images of each other with respect to Factor A. Although it would be highly interesting if all languages were of the types X and Z above, it would be difficult to test for psychological correspondence, since there would be no variance across languages. However, such a situation is unlikely and is certainly inconsistent with current knowledge about cross-linguistic variation. Then, variations across languages with respect to their language factor scores (i.e., the extent to which they reflect the ideal factor structure) can be used to test the psychological coherence of the factor. Take for example LANGUAGE Y in Table 3.5, conveniently created for our purposes. The values on the variables mostly reflect a high positive loading on Factor A, with the exception of Variable 3. The structure of Variable 3 for LANGUAGE Y in fact matches that for LANGUAGE Z, which is the ideal language with negative loading on Factor A. There are several predictions that can be made, and empirically tested, given such a situation. One would expect that the learner of LANGUAGE Y would have fewer cues than the learner of LANGUAGE X, due to the mismatch on Variable 3. If the determination of the factor score is a psychologically real process, then one can predict differences in

TABLE 3.5
Distribution of Values on Variables for Three
Hypothetical Languages.

	VAR1	VAR2	VAR3	VAR4	VAR5	VAR6
Loading on Factor A	+	+	+	−	−	0
Language X	1	1	1	0	0	1
Language Y	1	1	0	0	0	1
Language Z	0	0	0	1	1	1

the ease of acquisition of structures that reflect variables with the same values for both languages, assuming that other sources of differences, such as frequency, can be controlled. Thus, for Variables 1, 2, 4, and 5, the learner of LANGUAGE X is at an advantage over the learner of LANGUAGE Y. In Table 3.5, I have also inserted Variable 6, which has no loading on Factor A. This might be considered a control variable, for which no difference would be predicted between the two languages.

If we had LANGUAGE Z for comparison, we can make further predictions, since the values on Variable 3 are similar for both LANGUAGES Y and Z. Since the value for LANGUAGE Z is consonant with the factor structure, while it is not for LANGUAGE Y, we would predict that the structure for Variable 3 would be easier for the learner of LANGUAGE Z than for the learner of LANGUAGE Y. Furthermore, we can make predictions about the frequency and kinds of errors that might be expected in the course of learning. Learners of LANGUAGE X will be likely to make errors on structures reflecting Variable 3 that deviate toward the value of "1." This can be compared to the likelihood of such errors for learners of LANGUAGE Z.

Whether the psychological correspondence can be determined or not is an empirical question. Ideally, one should be able to iterate the above process across each of the variables, finding strategically located languages. If we find that certain variables consistently do not affect the acquisition of its *related variables* (i.e., variables with which it is related through the factor structure), we can weed them out from our mapping of psychological correspondence. The end result would be a psychologically real hypothesis space of language learners, which can be used in the further, and necessary, investigations into the nature of the task-specificity and species-specificity of language.

In the discussion above, I have simplistically reduced the study of language typology and universals to factor analysis, and glossed over many of the technical difficulties that the researcher would encounter in searching for psychological correspondence for language factors. I undertook this exercise because I wanted to emphasize the viewpoint toward first and second language acquisition that is implicit in an approach that incorporates language typology and universals, a viewpoint that I believe at present to be potentially the most productive. In sum, in this approach, we do not treat each linguistic variable as an isolated entity, but rather as one of a constellation of variables related to each other, concretized for the researcher through factor structures.

My current analogy can be found in a recent article in the *American Scientist* that reviewed some recent research in developmental biology (Tickle, 1981). In particular, the article was concerned with similarities and differences between the growth of limbs during ontogeny on the one hand, and the regeneration of severed limbs (in certain species) on the other. Essentially, the problems faced by the cells in these two processes are similar: how does a growing cell know what part of the limb it is ultimately to become? To make a long story short, there are marked differences between the two, which can be characterized by the degree to which developing cells are sensitive to, and interact with, positional specifications of neighboring cells. In development, the positional specifications are developed in cell generation, whereas in limb regeneration, the positional specifications of the new growth interacts with the already established positional specifications of its neighbors. This is an interesting statement about the relationship between the two processes that could not have been possible without a system for specifying position (it turns out that position can be specified by three dimensions: anterior–posterior, dorsal–ventral, and proximal–distal, and some promising mechanisms for how this information is signaled have been proposed).

The relationship between first and second language acquisition and language typology might be regarded in a similar way. The n-dimensional space hypothesized by language typologists, whose psychological correspondence is verified, can become a tool similar to the positional specification of the developmental biologist concerned with limb growth. It defines the problem, and the problem for the language acquisition researcher then becomes to observe and explain the role that this n-dimensional space might play in the different conditions under which language is learned. Although we are still uncertain as to the nature of this n-dimensional space, I believe that it is not too early to begin speculating and formulating our research questions with respect to its manifestations under different psychological contexts.

CONCLUSIONS

Conclusions need not be stated since they were listed in the introductory remarks. I only hope that the evidence presented was tantalizing to the newcomer to second language acquisition. There has always been a kind of unstated snobbery among psychologists and linguists toward applied linguistics and its interest in the applied problem of second language acquisition. Some of it may be justified. Applied linguists are not trained in conducting sound research from an empirical perspective. However, much of the denigration of studying second language learners most likely comes from lack of knowledge and from artificial dean's boundaries in the academic world. Once we admit that second language acquisition can shed light on the nature of our capacity to learn language, the door swings wide open for adding numerous variations that can shed light on the beast. I have argued that the study of language typology and universals can be a working framework around which L1 and L2 acquisition can be unified. They are, after all, the same problem. And given the lack of progress we have made in the past few years toward understanding our ability to learn language, who can turn away such an interesting source of variation on the problem? John Macnamara (1976) was right when he said, "When an infant, a ten year old child, and an adult learn Russian, the most striking outcome is Russian" (p. 175).

ACKNOWLEDGMENT

Preparation of this paper was supported in part by Grant G-81-0123 from the National Institute of Education.

REFERENCES

Adams, M. (1974). *Second language acquisition in children: A study in experimental methods: Observations of spontaneous speech and controlled production tests.* Unpublished master's thesis, English Department, University of California at Los Angeles.

Bailey, N., Madden, C., & Krashen, S. (1974). Is there a "natural sequence" in adult second language learning? *Language Learning, 21,* 235–243.

Beilin, H. (1976). *The Cognitive Basis of Language Development.* New York: Academic Press.

Brown, R. (1973). *A First Language: The Early Stages.* Cambridge, MA: Harvard University Press.

Butterworth, G. (1972). *A Spanish-speaking adolescent's acquisition of English syntax.* Unpublished master's thesis, English Department, University of California at Los Angeles.

Cancino, H. (1976). *Grammatical morphemes in second language acquisition-Marta.* Unpublished qualifying paper, Harvard Graduate School of Education.

Cattell, R. (1965). *The Scientific Analysis of Personality.* Chicago: Aldine.

Cazden, C. B. (1968). The acquisition of noun and verb inflections. *Child Development, 39,* 433-448.

Cazden, C., Cancino, H., Rosansky, E. & Schumann, J. (1975). *Second language acquisition sequences in children, adolescents, and adults.* Cambridge, MA: Harvard Graduate School of Education. (ERIC Document Reproduction Service No. ED 123 873.)

Chomsky, C. (1969). *The acquisition of syntax in children from 5 to 10.* Cambridge, MA: M. I. T. Press.

Clark, R. (1974). Performing without competence. *Journal of Child Language, 1,* 1-10.

Cohen, A. D., (1975). *A sociolinguistic approach to bilingual education: Experiments in the American Southwest.* Rowley, MA: Newbury House.

Corder, S. P. (1971). Idiosyncratic dialects and error analysis. *International Review of Applied Linguistics, 9,* 147-160.

d'Anglejan, A., & Tucker, G. R. (1975). The acquisition of complex English structures by adult learners. *Language Learning, 25,* 281–196.

de Villiers, J., Tager-Flusberg, H., Hakuta, K., & Cohen, M. (1979). Children's comprehension of relative clauses. *Journal of Psycholinguistic Research, 8,* 499-518.

Downing, B. (1978). Some universals of relative clause structure. In J. H. Greenberg (Ed.), *Universals of human language: Vol. 4, Syntax.* Stanford, CA: Stanford University Press.

Dulay, H., & Burt, M. (1973). Should we teach children syntax? *Language Learning, 23,* 245–258.

Dulay, H., & Burt, M. (1974a). Natural sequences in child second language acquisition. *Language Learning, 24,* 37–53.

Dulay, H., & Burt, M. (1974b). A new perspective on the creative construction process in child second language acquisition. *Working Papers on Bilingualism, 4,* 71–98.

Duskova, L. (1969). On sources of errors in foreign languages. *International Review of Applied Linguistics, 7,* 11–36.

Ervin-Tripp, S. (1974). Is second language learning like the first? *TESOL Quarterly, 8,* 111–127.

Fathman, A. (1975). *Language background, age, and the order of English structures.* Paper presented at the TESOL Convention, Los Angeles.

Frauenfelder, U. (1974). The acquisition of French gender in Toronto French Immersion school children. Unpublished senior honors thesis, University of Washington.

Gass, S., & Ard, J. (1980). *L2 data: Their relevance for language universals.* Paper presented at the TESOL (Teachers of English to Speakers of Other Languages) Convention, San Francisco.

Gillis, M. (1975). *The acquisition of the English verbal system by two Japanese children in a natural setting.* Unpublished master's thesis, McGill University.

Givon, T. (1979). *On understanding grammar.* New York: Academic Press.

Gleitman, L. R. (1981). Maturational determinants of language growth. *Cognition, 10,* 103–114.

Gould, S. J. (1981). *The mismeasure of man.* New York: Norton.

Greenberg, J. H. (1963). Some universals of grammar with particular reference to the order of meaningful elements. In J. J. Greenberg (Ed.), *Universals of language.* Cambridge, MA: M. I. T. Press.

Greenberg, J. H. (1978). Typology and cross-linguistic generalizations. In J. H. Greenberg (Ed.), *Universals of human language: Vol. 1, Method and Theory,* (pp. 33–60). Stanford, CA: Stanford University Press.

Hakuta, K. (1974a). A preliminary report on the development of grammatical morphemes in a Japanese girl learning English as a second language. *Working Papers on Bilingualism, 3,* 18–43.

Hakuta, K. (1974b). Prefabricated patterns and the emergence of structure in second language acquisition. *Language Learning, 24,* 287–297.

Hakuta, K. (1975). *Becoming bilingual at age five: The story of Uguisu.* Unpublished senior honors thesis, Department of Psychology and Social Relations, Harvard University.

Hakuta, K. (1976). A case study of a Japanese child learning English. *Language Learning, 26,* 321–351.

Hakuta, K. (1981). Grammatical description versus configurational arrangement in language acquisition: The case of relative clauses in Japanese. *Cognition, 9,* 197–236.

Hakuta, K. (1982). *In what ways are language universals psychologically real?* Paper presented at the conference on Language Universals and Second Language Acquisition, University of Southern California.

Hakuta, K. (in press). Theoretical issues and future directions in second language acquisition research, with special reference to Asian-Americans. In M. Chu-Chang (Ed.), *Comparative research in bilingual education: Asian-Pacific-American perspectives.* (pp. 31–55) New York: Teachers College Press.

Hakuta, K., & Cancino, H. (1977). Trends in second language acquisition research. *Harvard Educational Review, 47,* 294–316.

Hakuta, K., de Villiers, J., & Tager-Flusberg, H. (1982). Sentence coordination in Japanese and English. *Journal of Child Language, 9,* 193–207.

Hatch, E. M. (Ed.) (1978). *Second language acquisition: A book of readings.* Rowley, MA: Newbury House.

Huang, J. (1971). *A Chinese child's acquisition of English syntax.* Unpublished master's thesis, University of California at Los Angeles.

Kang, H. (1982). *The contexts in which errors of article usage occur and their implication for native-language transference.* Unpublished senior essay, Department of Psychology, Yale University.

Keller-Cohen, D. (1979). Systematicity and variation in the non-native child's acquisition of conversational skills. *Language Learning, 29,* 27–44.

Kuno, S. (1974). The position of relative clauses and conjunction. *Linguistic Inquiry, 5,* 117–136.

Larsen-Freeman, D. (1976). An explanation for the morpheme acquisition order of second language learners. *Language Learning, 26,* 125–134.

Lehmann, W. (1973). A structural principle of language and its implications. *Language, 49,* 47–66.

Lenneberg, E. H. (1967). *Biological foundations of language*. New York: Wiley.

Li, C., & Thompson, S. (1976). Subject and topic: A new typology of language. In C. Li (Ed.), *Subject and topic*. New York: Academic Press.

Lightbown, P. (1977). *French L2 learners: What they're talking about*. Paper presented at the first Los Angeles Second Language Research Forum, UCLA.

Macnamara, J. (1976). Comparison between first and second language learning. *Die Neueren Sprachen, 2*, 175–188.

Maratsos, M. P., & Chalkley, M. A. (1980). The internal language of children's syntax: The ontogenesis and representation of syntactic categories. In K. E. Nelson (Ed.), *Child language* (Vol. 2, pp. 127–214). New York: Gardner Press.

McLaughlin, B. (1976). *Second language acquisition in childhood*. Hillsdale, NJ: Lawrence Erlbaum Associates.

Nemser, W. (1977). Approximative systems of foreign language learners. *International Review of Applied Linguistics, 9*, 115–123.

Oller, J., & Richards, J. (Eds.). (1973). *Focus on the learner: Pragmatic perspectives for the language teacher*. Rowley, MA: Newbury House.

Oyama, S. (1976). A sensitive period for the acquisition of a non-native phonological system. *Journal of Psycholinguistic Research, 5*, 261–185.

Oyama, S. (1978). The sensitive period and comprehension of speech. *Working Papers on Bilingualism, 16*, 1–17.

Patkowski, M. (1980). The sensitive period for the acquisition of syntax in a second language. *Language Learning, 3*, 449–472.

Penfield, W., & Roberts, L. (1959). *Speech and brain-mechanisms*. Princeton: Princeton University Press.

Politzer, R., & Ramirez A. (1973). An error analysis of the spoken English of Mexican-American pupils in a bilingual school and a monolingual school. *Language Learning, 23*, 39–61.

Rosansky, E. (1976). *Second language acquisition research: A question of methods*. Doctoral dissertation, Harvard Graduate School of Education.

Schachter, J. (1974). An error in error analysis. *Language Learning, 24*, 205–214.

Schlesinger, I. M. (1974). Relational concepts underlying language. In R. L. Schiefelbusch & L. L. Lloyd (Eds.), *Language perspectives: Acquisition, retardation and intervention* (pp. 129–151). Baltimore: University Park Press.

Schumann, J., & Stenson, N. (Eds.). (1975). *New frontiers in second language learning*. Rowley, MA: Newbury House.

Selinker, L. (1972). Interlanguage. *International Review of Applied Linguistics, 10*, 219–231.

Selinker, L., Swain, M., & Dumas, G. (1975). The interlanguage hypothesis extended to children. *Language Learning, 25*, 139-152

Sinclair-de-Zwart, H. (1973). Language acquisition and cognitive development. In T. Moore (Ed.), *Cognitive development and the acquisition of language* (pp. 9–25). New York: Academic Press.

Slobin, D. I. (1973). Cognitive prerequisites for the development of grammar. In C. A. Ferguson & D. I. Slobin (Eds.), *Studies of child language development*. New York: Holt, Rinehart & Winston.

Snow, C., & Hoefnagel-Hohle, M. (1978). The critical period for language acquisition: Evidence from second language learning. *Child Development, 49*, 1114–1128.

Steele, S. (1978). Word order variation: A typological study. In J. H. Greensbert (Ed.), *Universals of human language: Vol. 4, Syntax* (pp. 585–623). Stanford, CA: Stanford University Press.

Svartvik, J. (1973). *Errata: Papers in error analysis*. Lund, Sweden; Gleerup.

Tager-Flusberg, H., de Villiers, J., & Hakuta, K. (1982). The development of sentence coordination. In S. A. Kuczaj (Ed.), *Language development: Vol. 1, Syntax and semantics* (pp. 201–243). Hillsdale, NJ: Lawrence Erlbaum Associates.

Tickle, C. (1981). Limb regeneration. *American Scientist, 69,* 634–646.

Weinreich, U. (1953). *Languages in contact.* New York: Linguistic Circle of New York.

Williams, L. (1974). *Speech perception and production as a function of exposure to a second language.* Unpublished doctoral dissertation, Harvard University.

Wong-Fillmore, L. (1976). *The second time around: Cognitive and social strategies in second language acquisition.* Unpublished doctoral dissertation, Stanford University.

Bilingualism, Language Profiency, and Metalinguistic Development

Jim Cummins
Ontario Institute for Studies in Education

By ''metalinguistic development'' I refer to both the development of children's awareness of certain properties of language and their ability to analyze linguistic input, i.e., to make the language forms the objects of focal attention and to look at language rather than through it to the intended meaning. Early investigators of children's language development have speculated that access to two languages in early childhood might promote an awareness of linguistic operations and a more analytic orientation to linguistic input. Vygotsky (1935, 1962), for example, argued that being able to express the same thought in different languages enables the child to ''see his language as one particular system among many, to view its phenomena under more general categories, and this leads to awareness of his linguistic operations'' (1962, p. 110). In an earlier work directly concerned with multilingualism in children, Vygotsky (1935) suggested that when the application of sound pedagogical principles ensured that each language had an independent sphere of influence, bilingualism could orient the child toward more abstract thought processes ''from the prison of concrete language forms and phenomena'' (p. 14). Leopold (1949) and Imedadze (1960) have both argued on the basis of observational studies of children's simultaneous acquisition of two languages that bilingualism can accelerate the separation of name and object and can focus the child's attention on certain aspects of language. In more recent years, Lambert and Tucker (1972) suggested that the experimental group in the St. Lambert bilingual education project had learned to engage in a form of contrastive linguistics by comparing similarities and differences in their two languages.

Thus, the hypothesis that access to two languages in early childhood should affect the development of children's metalinguistic skills appears plausible both to theorists of cognitive development and to those who have made detailed systematic observations of bilingual children's language acquisition. Before examining the research studies that have formally compared bilingual and unilingual children on metalinguistic tasks, it is useful to place the two constructs we are considering, bilingualism and metalinguistic development, into a broader theoretical framework. Many of the limitations of the research studies and the difficulty of interpreting the results derive from the fact that they have been carried out with a very crude conception of the nature of bilingualism and in a theoretical vacuum as far as metalinguistic development is concerned.

THE CONSTRUCT OF BILINGUALISM

An extremely large number of types of bilingualism and bilingual learning situations have been suggested (see Baetens Beardsmore, 1981, for a review) but for present purposes, only two refinements that appear directly related to interpreting research on the effects of bilingualism are considered. These refinements are closely related to one another—the first dealing with the additive-subtractive nature of the bilingualism and the second with the levels of bilingual proficiency attained. Both sets of constructs derive from attempts to reconcile apparently contradictory findings relating to the effects of bilingualism on cognition, specifically, the finding from many early studies (1920–1960) that bilinguals performed poorly on verbal-academic tasks whereas more recent research has reported cognitive and linguistic advantages for bilinguals (see Cummins, 1978a, for a detailed review). In addition, a distinction between short-term and long-term effects of bilingual experiences is made.

Additive and Subtractive Bilingualism

Lambert (1975) has pointed out that a large majority of early studies were carried out with immigrant or minority language children whose first language (L1) was gradually being replaced by a more dominant and prestigious second language (L2). He terms the resulting form of bilingualism *subtractive* in that bilingual children's proficiency in their two languages at any point in time is likely to reflect some stage in the subtraction of L1 and its replacement by L2.

Lambert contrasts the subtractive bilingualism of many minority language children with the additive bilingualism generally achieved by children whose L1 is dominant and prestigious and in no danger of replacement by L2. This is the situation of anglophone children in French immersion programs. The bilingualism of these children is termed *additive* because another socially relevant language is being added to the bilingual's repertory of skills at no cost to proficiency in L1. The majority of studies reporting cognitive advantages associated with bilingualism have been carried out in contexts where children have attained an additive form of bilingualism, that is, relatively high levels of proficiency in both languages.

This analysis suggests that the level of proficiency bilingual children achieve in their two languages may be an important factor in determining the cognitive effects of bilingualism. This idea is elaborated in the "threshold" hypothesis (Cummins, 1976).

The Threshold Hypothesis

The threshold hypothesis proposes that there may be threshold levels of linguistic proficiency that bilingual children must attain in order to avoid cognitive disadvantages and to allow the potentially beneficial aspects of becoming

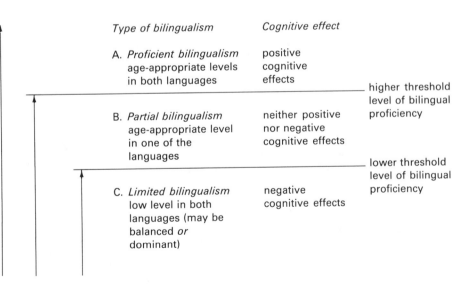

FIGURE 4.1. Cognitive Effects of Different Types of Bilingualism (adapted from Toukomaa & Skutnaab-Kangas, 1977).

bilingual to influence cognitive growth. This hypothesis assumes that those aspects of bilingualism that might positively influence cognitive growth are unlikely to exert a significant long-term effect until the child has attained a certain minimum or threshold level of proficiency in both languages. Conversely, if bilingual children attain only a very low level of proficiency in L2 or L1, the range of potential interaction with the environment through that language is likely to be limited.

The form of the threshold hypothesis that seems to be most consistent with the available data is that there is not one, but two, thresholds (Cummins, 1976; Toukomaa & Skutnabb-Kangas, 1977). The attainment of a lower threshold level of bilingual proficiency would be sufficient to avoid any negative cognitive effects, but the attainment of a second, higher level of bilingual proficiency may be necessary to lead to long-term cognitive benefits. Essentially, the hypothesis of a lower threshold level of bilingual proficiency proposes that bilingual children's proficiency in a language can be sufficiently weak to impair the quality of their interaction with their educational environment through that language. Thus, the early findings of negative cognitive effects associated with bilingualism would be explained by the fact that the minority language children in these studies often failed to develop a sufficiently high level of proficiency in the school language to benefit fully from their educational experience.

The rapid cognitive and academic progress of bilinguals reported in recent studies is explained by the fact that these children had attained the upper threshold level of bilingual proficiency, that is, high levels of both L1 and L2 skills. The threshold hypothesis would predict that neither positive nor negative cognitive effects would result from dominant bilingualism where children develop native-like proficiency in their dominant language but achieve only intermediate levels of proficiency in their weaker language.

Note here, however, that the relevance of this hypothesis for interpreting the data regarding the effects of bilingualism on metalinguistic development represents only a relatively crude refinement to the construct of bilingualism because the nature of the language proficiency involved in the thresholds is left largely undefined. The issue of what constitutes language proficiency and metalinguistic proficiency is considered in a later section.

Short-Term and Long-Term Effects of Bilingualism

The threshold hypothesis is primarily relevant only to long-term effects of bilingualism, i.e., effects that result from actually functioning bilingually over a prolonged period of time. Proficiency in L1 and–or L2 becomes important for cognitive development only when it is necessary to use L1 and–or L2 to interact with the environment over a prolonged period. This type of prolonged bilingual interaction will result in relatively fixed patterns of orientation or proficiency.

However, it is possible to distinguish these long-term effects of bilingual functioning from short-term effects that may result from the second language learning experience itself. The defining characteristic of a short-term effect is that it results from the process of acquiring proficiency in L2 and it does not effect a fundamental or permanent change in an individual's cognitive functioning or development. Whether or not short-term effects will exert a more permanent long-term influence may depend on the type of bilingual proficiency attained. The distinction between short-term and long-term effects is illustrated with reference to the research findings to be considered in a later section.

In summary, I have suggested some refinements to the construct of bilingualism that may be helpful in interpreting the research findings. These refinements come from examining patterns of associations that emerge in studies relating bilingualism and cognition. What is suggested by these hypotheses is that the language acquisition context will effect the type of bilingualism attained, which in turn will strongly influence the long-term consequences of that bilingualism for overall cognitive and linguistic functioning. However, more transient effects on cognitive functioning may result from the actual second language acquisition process.

Obviously in any discussion of the effects of bilingual proficiency there is some implicit notion of language proficiency. The theoretical framework presented next is intended to permit the constructs of language proficiency and metalinguistic skills to be related to overall cognitive and academic functioning.

THE CONSTRUCTS OF LINGUISTIC
AND METALINGUISTIC PROFICIENCY

Much of the confusion surrounding the measurement of bilingual proficiency and the effects of bilingual education on children's development (e.g., Baker & de Kantor, 1981) derives from a failure to adequately conceptualize the nature of language proficiency and its cross-lingual dimensions (Cummins, 1981). Similarly, the construct of metalinguistic development has not been integrated into an overall framework of cognitive and academic functioning. The framework outlined has been applied to a variety of issues (e.g., second language acquisition, measurement of language proficiency and communicative competence, language pedagogy, learning disability and psychological assessment, and the nature of bilingual proficiency) (Cummins, 1983).

The framework presented in Fig. 4.2 proposes that language proficiency can be conceptualized along two continua. First is a continuum relating to the range of contextual support available for expressing or receiving meaning. The ex-

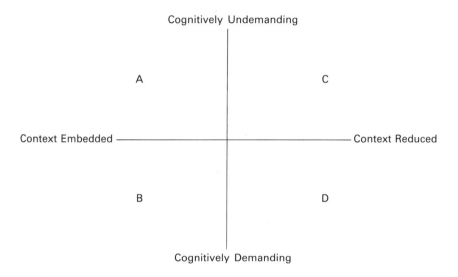

FIGURE 4.2.   Range of Contextual Support and Degree of Cognitive Involvement in Communicative Activities.

tremes of this continuum are described in terms of context-embedded versus context-reduced communication. They are distinguished by the fact that in context-embedded communication the participants can actively negotiate meaning (e.g., by providing feedback that the message has not been understood) and the language is supported by a wide range of meaningful paralinguistic and situational cues; context-reduced communication, on the other hand, relies primarily (or at the extreme of the continuum, exclusively) on linguistic cues to meaning and may in some cases involve suspending knowledge of the "real" world in order to interpret (or manipulate) the logic of the communication appropriately.

In general, context-embedded communication derives from interpersonal involvement in a shared reality that obviates the need for explicit linguistic elaboration of the message. Context-reduced communication, on the other hand, derives from the fact that this shared reality cannot be assumed, and thus linguistic messages must be elaborated precisely and explicitly so that the risk of misinterpretation is minimized. It is important to emphasize that this is a continuum and not a dichotomy. Thus, examples of communicative behaviors going from left to right along the continuum might be engaging in a discussion, writing a letter to a close friend, writing (or reading) an academic article. Clearly, context-embedded communication is more typical of the everyday world outside the classroom, whereas many of the linguistic demands of the classroom reflect communication that is closer to the context-reduced end of the continuum.

The vertical continuum is intended to address the developmental aspects of communicative proficiency in terms of the degree of active cognitive involvement in the task of activity. Cognitive involvement can be conceptualized in terms of the amount of information that must be processed simultaneously or in close succession by the individual in order to carry out the activity.

This continuum incorporates a developmental perspective in that some language subskills (e.g., L1 phonology and syntax) quickly reach plateau levels at which there are no longer significant differences in mastery between individuals (at lease in context-embedded situations). Other subskills continue to develop throughout the school years and beyond, depending on the individual's communicative needs in particular cultural and institutional milieu.

The upper parts of the vertical continuum consist of communicative tasks and activities in which the linguistic tools have become largely automatized (mastered) and thus require little active cognitive involvement for appropriate performance. At the lower end of the continuum are tasks and activities in which the communicative tools have not become automatized and therefore require active cognitive involvement. Persuading another individual that your point of view rather than hers or his is correct, or writing an essay on a complex theme are examples of such activities. In these situations, it is necessary to stretch one's linguistic resources to the limit in order to achieve one's communicative goals. Cognitive involvement, in the sense of amount of information processing, can be just as intense in context-embedded as in context-reduced activities.

As mastery is developed, specific linguistic tasks and skills travel from the bottom toward the top of the vertical continuum. There tends to be a high level of cognitive involvement in task or activity performance until mastery has been achieved or, alternately, until a plateau level at less than mastery levels has been reached (e.g., L2 pronunciation in many adult immigrants, "fossilization" of certain grammatical features among French immersion students, etc.). Thus, acquiring the phonology and syntax of L1 requires considerable cognitive involvement for the two-and three-year-old child, and therefore these tasks would be placed in quadrant B (context-embedded, cognitively demanding). However, as mastery of these skills develops, tasks involving them would move from quadrant B to quadrant A because performance becomes increasingly automatized and cognitively undemanding. In a second language context the same type of developmental progression occurs.

The framework is related to theoretical constructs elaborated by Donaldson, 1978 (embedded-disembedded thought), Olson, 1977 (utterance-text), Bruner (communicative-analytic competence), Bereiter and Scardamelia, 1982 (conversation-composition). In addition, depth of cognitive processing is a construct employed by many psychologists and applied linguists (e.g., Oller, 1980).

Where the present framework differs from others is in positing two independent continua and in applying them to interpreting (and synthesizing) data from a wide variety of research areas.

By definition metalinguistic skills are clearly at the extreme context-reduced end of the horizontal continuum. However, the location of any particular metalinguistic task on the vertical continuum will depend on a variety of factors, primarily degree of difficulty of task in relation to child's cognitive developmental level and degree of practice or exposure to similar tasks or situations. Thus, in terms of the definition of metalinguistic development (provided at the beginning of the chapter) it is clear that tasks can require metalinguistic skills (insofar as they require individuals to look at language rather than through it) at very different cognitive levels. Both these dimensions (cognitive level and degree of context-reduction) must be kept in mind when considering the relationships among metalinguistic tasks or between metalinguistic and cognitive–academic tasks. Based on the location in quadrant D of metalinguistic tasks on which degree of mastery varies among students, we would expect strong relationships between such tasks and other quadrant D tasks (e.g., reading proficiency, verbal intellectual skills, etc.). There is considerable evidence for such relationships (see Ryan & Ledger, 1978).

Bilingualism and Metalinguistic Skills: Research Evidence

There is a considerable body of research (see Cummins, 1981) which shows that cognitive–academic (quadrant D) skills transfer across languages given sufficient exposure and motivation to acquire both. Thus, in French immersion programs, English-background students who have not been exposed to English language instruction prior to Grade 2 or 3 catch up to equivalent students in all-English programs within a relatively short time of the introduction of formal English language arts. This transfer of underlying cognitive–academic proficiencies occurs even across languages that have no surface similarities, for example, Japanese and English (Cummins et al., 1984).

An implication of this general finding is that metalinguistic skills will also transfer across languages and, in fact, the presence and use of two codes may prompt greater monitoring and inspection of each such that metalinguistic awareness is enhanced. Many of the research findings suggest that bilingualism may exert some subtle effects on children's orientation to linguistic and perceptual structures.

One of the first studies to report data relating to bilingualism and metalinguistic development is that conducted by Feldman and Shen (1971) who found that five-year-old Head Start bilingual children were superior to unilinguals in their ability to switch names and in their use of common names and nonsense names in relational statements. Bilingual and unilingual groups, however, were not matched on IQ or other cognitive measures and thus the results must be considered tentative.

Ianco-Worrall (1972), in a study conducted in South Africa, reported that bilingual children, brought up in a one-person, one-language home environment, were significantly more sensitive than unilingual children matched on IQ, to semantic relations between words and were also more advanced in realizing the arbitrary assignment of names to referents. Unilingual children were more likely to interpret similarity between words in terms of an acoustic rather than a semantic dimension (e.g., cap-can rather than cap-hat) and felt that the names of objects could not be inter-changed.

The fact that in Ianco-Worrall's study bilinguals agreed more often that names of objects could be interchanged is capable of another interpretation. There were three pairs of names: dog, cow; chair, jam; book, water. Children were first asked, "could you call a dog 'cow' and a cow 'dog'?" High school children tended to answer no to this question because they felt there were social and linguistic conventions regarding names that could not be broken, therefore a second question was added. This question was, "suppose you were making up names for things, could you then call a cow 'dog' and a dog 'cow'?" High school children invariably agreed that, in principle, this could be done. Ianco-Worrall's assertion that bilinguals were more aware of the arbitrary nature of word-referent relationships is based on the fact that at both the 4–6 and 7–9 age levels a significantly higher proportion of bilinguals fell into this "no-yes" category. However, there is evidence (see Cummins, 1978a, for a review) that bilingual children are more sensitive to feedback cues. The change in the form of the question may have provided cues to children that would cause them to change their response from no to yes and bilingual children may have been more sensitive to these cues. Thus, because children were not required to justify their responses, Ianco-Worrall's findings are inconclusive as to whether the bilingual children in her sample were in fact more aware of the arbitrary nature of word-referent relationships or whether they were just more sensitive to feedback cues.

Examples of both short-term and long-term effects of bilingualism as well as the possible consequences of level of bilingual proficiency come from a study by Cummins and Mulcahy (1978) in the context of the Ukrainian-English bilingual program (50% Ukrainian, K-6) in Edmonton, Alberta. Three groups of children were compared on a variety of language processing tasks. One group of children in the program spoke extensive Ukrainian at home and were judged by their teachers to be relatively fluent in Ukrainian (Bilingual Group). A second group spoke little Ukrainian at home and were judged by teachers to have relatively little fluency in Ukrainian (L2 Learners). The third group was a unilingual group attending regular classes in the same schools as the bilingual program students.

All three groups were matched on nonverbal IQ and SES and were also equivalent in English reading skills. Among the measures administered were the Semantic-Phonetic Preference Test, a Word Association Test, and an Ambiguities Test.

The Semantic-Phonetic Preference Test was developed by Purbhoo and Shapson (1975) on the basis of a similar task used by Ianco-Worrall (1972). Children were asked 16 questions of the type "Which word is more like ARM, is it HAND, or is it ART?" Semantic and phonetic choices occupied each position 50% of the time. Children were classified as semantically oriented if they made at least 12 semantic choices. The Word Association Test consisted of 20 stimulus words read to each subject individually. Subjects were required to give one association for each stimulus word and their responses were tape recorded and later timed. The Ambiguities test was taken from Kessel (1970) and assessed children's sensitivity to lexical, surface structure and underlying structure ambiguities. The test consisted of four items of each type randomly ordered. Children were shown four line drawings, two of which depicted different meanings of a sentence that was read aloud by the experimenter. The following are examples of each type of ambiguous sentence: L - "The boy picked up the bat" (baseball bat, flying bat); SS - "He told her baby stories." US - "She hit the man with glasses." Children were given a score of 2 if they gave the two meanings and correct justifications spontaneously, 1 if they gave the two meanings and justifications after probing, and 0 if they chose the wrong pictures or only one correct picture or if their justifications showed they had not grasped the two meanings.

The results of the Semantic-Phonetic test are not consistent with Ianco-Worrall's finding that bilingual children were more semantically oriented than unilingual children. In fact, at the Grade 1 level, the L2 learners were significantly more acoustically (and less semantically) oriented than the unilingual group. This difference disappears by Grade 3 and is probably due to the necessity to "train one's ear" and pay attention to phonetic similarities and dissimilarities in the initial stages of the bilingual program. It would thus be classified as a short-term effect of bilingual experiences.

The pattern of results on the Ambiguities test provides direct support for the threshold hypothesis in that fluent bilinguals performed better than L2 learners who, in turn, performed better than unilinguals.

Consideration of the Semantic-Phonetic Preference results, in relation to the Ambiguities results, suggests a general hypothesis regarding the development of an analytic orientation to language among bilingual children. Realization of sentence ambiguities involves analysis of both semantic and syntactic aspects of the sentence and thus this result could be interpreted as evidence of greater semantic orientation among bilinguals. However, this orientation does not emerge on the Semantic-Phonetic Preference task because of the necessity for a forced choice between semantic and phonetic similarities between words. An equally strong case can be made that bilingualism should lead to greater sensitivity to phonetic patterns and several studies support this general hypothesis (see, e.g., Cohen, Tucker, & Lambert, 1967). The greater phonetic orientation of the Grade 1 L2 learners suggests that in the initial stages of exposure to the second language, phonetic features of words are more salient than semantic features. In fact, phonetic discrimination is probably a necessary condition for semantic understanding. With increasing competence in the second language, phonetic discrimination becomes less problematic and semantic and syntactic analysis more necessary to understand the linguistic input.

Because Ianco-Worrall's sample had been exposed to both languages in the home since infancy, phonetic features of their languages were no longer problematic, whereas the same may not have been true for many of the fluent bilingual and certainly not for the nonfluent Grade 1 bilingual children in the Ukrainian study.

In contrast to the Semantic-Phonetic test results, the differences between the Bilingual and other groups in Table 4.2 represent long-term effects since the bilingual children have been functioning bilingually for a considerable period of time. The finding that the bilinguals at both grade levels take longer to respond on the word association task agrees with Ben Zeev's (1977a) finding and suggests that bilinguals may process the semantic information more deeply than the other groups. It is also possible that generation of a response is more difficult for the bilinguals as a result of linguistic interference (Torrance, Gowan, Wu, & Aliotti, 1970).

Ianco-Worrall's finding that bilinguals were more aware of the arbitrary nature of the word-referent relationships was further investigated in studies conducted with Irish-English bilingual children (Cummins, 1978a) and with the Ukrainian-English bilingual group (Cummins & Mulcahy, 1978). Unlike Ianco-Worrall's procedure, children were required to justify their responses, and justifications rather than the actual responses were scored correct or incorrect. In the Irish study there were significant differences between bilingual and unilingual groups in favor of the bilinguals at both Grades 3 and 6, but the Ukrainian study found no group differences either at Grade 1 or Grade 3. The equivocal nature of the findings may be a reflection of the relative crudeness of the measurement instruments. The phenomenon of metalinguistic awareness is still inadequately understood and the literature is devoid of instruments whose construct validity has been demonstrated.

The Irish study also reported that Grades 3 and 6 bilingual children were better able than unilingual children matched for IQ, SES, and age to evaluate nonempirical contradictory statements; e.g., "The poker chip (hidden) in my hand is blue and it is not blue—True, False or Can't Tell?" Children were required to justify their responses and, as in the Arbitrariness of Language task, justifications rather than actual responses were scored correct or incorrect. These findings are consistent with the findings of the Ukrainian study and suggest that bilingualism can promote an analytic orientation to linguistic input.

The results of two studies conducted by Ben-Zeev (1977a, 1977b) are also consistent with this hypothesis. Ben-Zeev argues that in order to overcome interlingual interference, bilinguals develop strategies of linguistic processing that can promote cognitive growth. She proposes four different mechanisms by means of which the bilingual child attempts to resolve the interference between his languages. These mechanisms are (a) analysis of language; (b) sensitivity to feedback cues; (c) maximization of structural differences between languages; and (d) neutralization of structure within a language. The first two mechanisms are supported by Ben-Zeev's studies of middle-class Hebrew-English bilinguals and lower class Spanish-English bilinguals. In both studies IQ differences between bilingual and unilingual groups were controlled.

Ben-Zeev used a symbol substitution task to investigate children's ability to play with words. For example, children were asked, "How do we say 'They are good children'?" substituting "Spaghetti" for "They." The Hebrew-English bilinguals were significantly superior on this task than their unilingual controls. There were no differences between the Spanish-English bilinguals and their controls on this task. However, Ben-Zeev reports that the Spanish-English bilinguals made significantly fewer errors of a global, primitive type, i.e., simply uttering the substitute word in place of the entire sentence. This type of error, she argues, is indicative of inability to treat the sentence analytically. This interpretation should be treated cautiously because the symbol substitution is subject to the same limitations as many of the metalinguistic tasks used in other studies, i.e., uncertain construct validity.

Although Ben-Zeev reports that bilinguals were better able to treat sentence structure analytically, in both studies they had significantly lower vocabulary scores and the Spanish-English bilinguals made significantly more grammatical mistakes on a story-telling task. Doyle, Champagne, and Segalowitz (1977) have also reported lower levels of vocabulary among preschool bilingual children in Montreal. Ben-Zeev suggests that the relative lack of experience with each language probably has some limiting effect on both vocabulary and knowledge of standard grammatical rules.

Ben Zeev interprets findings of bilingual-unilingual differences on several aspects of nonverbal tasks as evidence for the generalization of bilinguals' analytic strategy toward languages to other kinds of structures. The responses of the Spanish-English bilinguals were characterized by attention to structure on classification, matrix transposition and picture completion tasks. In the Hebrew-English study the same strategy was evident on the matrix transposition task. On many of the tasks in the Ben-Zeev studies, the overall performance of bilingual and unilingual groups did not differ but the response strategies of the bilinguals were characterized by attention to structure and readiness to reorganize cognitive schemata.

Superior performance by bilinguals on tasks involving an ability to restructure linguistic and perceptual schemata has also been reported by Balkan (1970). In a study conducted in Switzerland, Balkan matched balanced bilinguals and unilinguals on nonverbal intelligence and found that the bilingual group performed significantly better on two variables that he claims measure cognitive flexibility. One of these tests was similar to the Embedded Figures Test, and involved an ability to restructure a perceptual situation (Figures Cachées). The other test required a sensitivity to the different meanings of words (Histoires). Balkan also divided his bilingual group into early (those who learned their second language before the age of four) and late (those who learned their second language between four and eight) bilinguals and found that the superiority of the early bilinguals over their matched unilingual counterparts on these tests was much more pronounced than the superiority of the late bilinguals. Balkan suggests that the habit of switching from one language to another leads to a greater degree of cognitive flexibility in bilingual children. It is worth noting that Bruck, Lambert, and Tucker (1978) found large differences between experimental and control groups in the St. Lambert project at the Grade 6 level on the Embedded Figures Test.

Starck, Genesee, Lambert, and Seitz (1977) tested the hypothesis that children who have had a linguistically enriched schooling may develop a more lateralized verbal processing system than comparable children without that form of linguistic enrichment. Starck et al. compared native speakers of English from Kindergarten, and Grades 1 and 2 attending a Hebrew-French immersion school with unilingual English speakers whose instruction was totally in English on a dichotic listening measure of ear asymmetry. Groups were matched on IQ and SES. In the first study, the trilingual group demonstrated a right-ear advantage on both accuracy and order of recall whereas the unilingual group did not. The second study failed to replicate the first in that the trilinguals did not show a greater right-ear advantage than the unilinguals. However, their recall was significantly more accurate than that of the unilinguals. Starck et al. conclude that ``bi- or multilingual experiences do seem to help establish more reliable ear asymmetry effects, which are thought to reflect enhanced cerebral asymmetry'' (pp. 53–54). The relationship between this finding and findings of greater ability to analyze structure among bilinguals is that right-ear advantage on dichotic listening tasks reflects greater development of the more analytic left hemisphere functions in comparison to right hemisphere functions.

Several other studies add to the evidence that bilingualism promotes some subtle forms of metalinguistic awareness. Diaz and Hakuta (1981) compared a group of Spanish-English balanced bilingual children to a group of Spanish-speaking children who were just beginning to learn English as a second language at school; the comparison group could be considered, therefore, relatively monolingual children who were at beginning stages of second-language learning. The two groups of children were equivalent in their Spanish ability, lived in the same neighborhoods, and attended the same kindergarten and first-grade bilingual classes.

The metalinguistic awareness tasks consisted of eight ungrammatical Spanish sentences and eight Spanish sentences with one English word in each (e.g., La *teacher* esta en la clase or El dog es grande); several correct Spanish sentences were intermixed within each set of wrong sentences. For the first set of sentences, children were asked to give a correct or grammatical version of the sentences presented. The results showed no differences between the two groups of children in their ability to detect grammatical errors in their native language. However, balanced bilinguals showed a greater ability to make grammatical corrections and to detect confusions between their two languages. Diaz and Hakuta conclude that the balanced bilingual children showed an awareness of the independence and appropriate separate usage of their two languages.

Mohanty (1982) carried out two studies in India that support the notion that bilingualism confers metalinguistic (and general cognitive) advantages on children. The first study examined the metalinguistic development of 300 Grades 6, 8, and 10 bilingual and unilingual children from urban and tribal cultures matched for SES. A significant main effect was found for bilingualism and an interaction between language and culture was also found indicating that bilingualism had a somewhat more positive effect on metalinguistic skills in urban culture than among tribals.

The second study was carried out among 180 Grades 6, 8, and 10 tribals, some of whom were bilingual in Kui and Oriya and others unilingual in Oriya. Detailed sociocultural background analysis revealed that culturally, racially, and in terms of socioeconomic differences the Konds are very similar regardless of language differences. Mohanty (1982) found that "in comparison to the unilingual controls the Kui-Oriya bilingual Kond children perform better in tests of cognitive information processing ability, have a more objective and analytic orientation to language, and demonstrate a level of linguistic development in their second language at par with the development of the only language of the unilinguals" (p.7).

In summary, the studies discussed in this section tend to support the hypothesis that bilingualism promotes an analytic orientation to both linguistic and perceptual structures. However,the evidence that bilinguals are more semantically oriented than unilinguals and have a greater awareness of certain properties of language is equivocal. There was also evidence in two studies that bilinguals had longer response latencies on a word association task than unilinguals. This might be due to either linguistic interference in response generation or deeper semantic processing (or both of these hypotheses).

A major difficulty in interpreting these studies (apart from the usual bilingual-unilingual control problems) is that the measures used to assess metalinguistic skills usually only have face validity. Where correlations between tasks are reported (e.g., Cummins, 1978b) they tend to be low, thus raising not only the empirical validity question but also the theoretical question of what the dimensions are of the construct of metalinguistic awareness or skill and what developmental stages it goes through. Some promising work directed toward answering these questions has recently started (Bialystok & Ryan, 1985). Until the theoretical issues relating to the construct of metalinguistic development are tackled, little further empirical progress is likely to be made in elucidating its relationship to bilingualism.

REFERENCES

Baetens Beardsmore, H. (1981). *Bilingualism*. Clevedon, Avon: Tieto.

Baker, K. A., & de Kanter, A. A. (1981). *Effectiveness of bilingual education: A review of the literature*. Final draft report, Office of Technical and Analytic Systems, Office of Planning and Budget, U.S. Dept. of Education.

Balkan, L. (1970). *Les effets du bilinguisme francais-anglais sur les aptitudes intellectuelles*. Bruxelles: Aimav.

Ben-Zeev, S. (1977a). The effect of Spanish-English bilingualism in children from less privileged neighbourhoods on cognitive development and cognitive strategy. *Working Papers on Bilingualism, 14*, 83–122.

Ben-Zeev, S. (1977b). The influence of bilingualism on cognitive development and cognitive strategy. *Child Development, 48*, 1009–1018.

Bereiter, C., & Scardamelia, M. (1982). From conversation to composition: the role of instruction in a developmental process. In R. Glasser (Ed.) *Advances in instructional psychology, Volume 2*. Hillsdale NJ: Lawrence Erlbaum Associates.

Bialystok, E. & Ryan, E. B. (1985). A metacognitive framework for the development of first and second language skills. In D. L. Forrest-Pressley, G. E. Mackinnon, & T. G. Walles (Eds.)., *Meta-cognition, cognition and human performance*. New York: Academic Press.

Bruck, M., Lambert, W. E., & Tucker, G. R. (1976). Cognitive and attitudinal consequences of bilingual schooling: The St. Lambert project through grade six. *International Journal of Psycholinguistics, 6*, 13–33.

Cohen, S. P., Tucker, G. R., & Lambert, W. E. (1967). The comparative skills of monolinguals and bilinguals in perceiving phoneme sequences. *Language and Speech, 10*, 159–168.

Cummins, J. (1976). The influence of bilingualism on cognitive growth: A synthesis of research findings and explanatory hypotheses. *Working Papers on Bilingualism*, No. 9, 1–43.

Cummins, J. (1978a). The cognitive development of children in immersion programs. *The Canadian Modern Language Review, 34*, 855–883. (a)

Cummins, J. (1978b). Language and children's ability to evaluate contradictions and tautologies: A critique of Osherson and Markman's findings. *Child Development, 49*, 895–897.

Cummins, J. (1981). The role of primary language development in promoting educational success for language minority students. In California State Dept. of Education, *Schooling and language minority students: A theoretical framework*. Los Angeles: National Dissemination and Assessment Center.

Cummins, J. (1983). Language proficiency and academic achievement. In J. W. Oller Jr. (Ed.), *Current issues in language testing research*. Rowley, MA: Newbury House.

Cummins, J., & Mulcahy, R. (1978). Orientation to language in Ukrainian-English bilingual children. *Child Development, 49,* 1239–1242.

Cummins, J., Swain, M., Nakajima, K., Hanuscombe, J., Green, D., & Tran, C. (1984). *Linguistic interdependence among Japanese and Vietnamese immigrant students.* In C. Rivera (Ed.), *Communicative competence approaches to language proficiency assessment: research and application.*. Clevedon, England: Multilingual matters.

Diaz, R. M., & Hakuta, K. (1981, April). *Bilingualism and cognitive development: A comparison of balanced and non-balanced bilinguals.* Paper presented at the meetings of the Society for Research in Child Development, Boston, MA.

Donaldson, M. (1978). *Children's minds.* Glasgow: Collins

Doyle, A. B., Champagne, M., & Segalowitz, N. (1977). Some issues in the assessment of linguistic consequences of early bilingualism. *Working Papers on Bilingualism,* No. 14, 21–30.

Feldman, C., & Shen, M. (1971). Some language-related cognitive advantages of bilingual five-year-olds. *Journal of Genetic Psychology, 118,* 234–235.

Ianco-Worrall, A. (1972). Bilingualism and cognitive development. *Child Development, 43,* 1390–1400.

Imedadze, N. V. (1960). K psikhologichoskoy priorode rannego dvuyazyehiya (on the psychological nature of early bilingualism). *Voprosy Psikhologii, 6,* 60–68.

Kessel, F. (1970). The role of syntax in children's comprehension from ages six to twelve. *Monographs of the Society for Research in Child Development, 35,*

Leopold, W. F. (1949). *Speech development of a bilingual child.* (Vol. 3). Evanston: Northwestern University Press.

Lambert, W. E. (1975). Culture and language as factors in learning and education. In A. Wolfgang (Ed.), *Education of immigrant students.* Toronto: Ontario Institute for Studies in Education.

(Ed.), *Education of immigrant students.* Toronto: Ontario Institute for Studies in Education.

Lambert, W. E., & Tucker, G. R. (1972). *Bilingual education of children: The St. Lambert experiment.* Rowley, MA: Newbury House.

Mohanty, A. K. (1982). *Bilingualism among Kond Tribals in Orissa (India): Consequences, issues and implications.* Unpublished manuscript, Uktal University.

Oller, J. W., Jr. (1980). A language factor deeper than speech: More data and theory for bilingual assessment. In J. Alatis (Ed.), *31st Annual Georgetown University Round Table on Languages and Linguistics.* Washington, DC: Georgetown University Press.

Olson, D. R. (1977). From utterance to text. The bias of language in speech and writing. *Harvard Educational Review, 47,* 257–281.

Purbhoo, M., & Shapson, S. (1975). *Transition from Italian.* Toronto: Toronto Board of Education.

Ryan, E. B., & Ledger, (1979). *Differences in syntactic skills between good and poor readers in the first grade.* Paper presented at the meeting of the Midwestern Psychological Association, Chicago.

Starck, R., Genesee, F., Lambert, W. E., & Seitz, M. (1977). Multiple language experience and the development of cerebral dominance. In S. J. Segalowitz & F. A. Gruber (Eds.), *Language development and neurological theory,* (pp.). New York: Academic Press.

Torrance, E. P., Gowan, J. C., Wu, J. M., & Aliotti, N. C. (1970). Creative functioning of monolingual and bilingual children in Singapore. *Journal of Educational Psychology, 61,* 72–75.

Toukomaa, P., & Skutnabb-Kangas, T. (1977). *The intensive teaching of the mother tongue to migrant children of pre-school age and children in the lower level of comprehensive school.* Helsinki: The Finnish National Commission for UNESCO.

Vygotsky, L. S. (1935). Multilingualism in children. Translated by Metro Gulutsan and Irene Arki, Centre for East European & Soviet Studies, the University of Alberta, mimeo, 1975. The essay appears in a collection of essays written by Vygotsky and edited by L. V. Zankov, Zh. 1. Shif, & D. B. El konin, *Umstvennoe razvitie detei v protesesse obucheniia, spornik statei* (Mental *development of children in the process of education,* a collection of essays). Moscow & Leningrade: State Pedagogical Publishing House.

Vygotsky, L. S. (1962). *Thought and language.* Cambridge, MA: MIT. Press.

5

The Impact of Language Differences on Language Processing: An Example from Chinese-English Bilingualism

Doris Aaronson
Steven Ferres
New York University

In this chapter we compare the processing of English by Chinese-English bilinguals with that of monolingual English speakers. We have selected Chinese-English bilinguals (whom we often call ''Chinese'') for comparison to monolingual English speakers (whom we often call ''Americans'') for three interrelated reasons. (a) First, the Chinese and English languages differ on important linguistic dimensions, some of which question theories about linguistic universals. In contrast, most of the past bilingual research has focused on either Spanish/English or French/English speakers. Focusing on a non-Indo-European language may reveal differences that do not emerge when comparing two members of the same language family.

(b) Second, most of the past bilingual research within the framework of cognitive psychology is of a general nature, dealing with the possibility of dual semantic coding, of extra processing time for mental translation, or of performance decrements due to capacity limitations when *any* two languages must share attention or memory space (Hatch, 1978; Spolsky & Cooper, 1978). Instead we focus here on *language specific* effects, i.e., on performance differences attributable to particular semantic and syntactic differences between Chinese and English.

(c) From an applied standpoint, the determination of specific linguistic differences that have psychological correlates has implications for understanding second language acquisition and performance of language-based cognitive tasks by bilinguals. There are probably over 2 million Chinese immigrants or immediate descendants of those immigrants now living in countries speaking Indo-European languages (Cheng, 1978). Relatively little has been done to develop high quality bilingual education in those countries, or to deal with other sociocultural differences that may stem in part from linguistic differences. A more detailed understanding of those differences is a necessary precursor to developing effective programs.

THE STRUCTURE AND MEANING OF LEXICAL CATEGORIES IN ENGLISH

This chapter deals largely with properties of words because they are an important linguistic and cognitive unit in English. Linguistically, a word can be defined as a "minimum free form" which is the union of a particular complex of sounds (phonology) with a particular meaning (semantics) capable of a particular grammatical employment (syntax) (Lyons, 1979). Cognitively, words are an important unit in the perception, comprehension, and memory of text (Clark & Clark, 1977; Miller & Johnson-Laird, 1976). This chapter focuses on the lexical category or form class of words as defined in dictionaries (e.g., noun, verb), because that is an organizational level which is relatively word-specific. However, we will see later that Chinese raises difficulties for such definitions of words and of lexical categories, which are based on Indo-European languages.

Traditionally, the lexical categories have been divided into content words and function words. In addition we consider the *psychological* attributes of "meaning" and "structure" that cut across the content and function words, as all words contribute both meaning and structure to a sentence. A person's coding of meaning and structure from the various lexical categories may be based on both "linguistic" and "verbal" information. For example, the cognitive processing of *structural* information from words may be based on properties such as their *syntactic* (functional) role within the surface phrase structure, their form class, their length in letters or syllables (e.g., function words are often shorter than content words), or their rhythmic value within the text based on coding time, stress, and intonation patterns. Processing *meaning* information from words may include processing their *semantic* attributes, their referential relation to other text components and to worldly entities, their propositional involvement, their word frequency (words with more selective or specific meaning often have lower frequency in the vocabulary), or their stress value within a covert acoustic representation (words that convey more meaning within a context often carry a heavier stress value).

Throughout much of this chapter we are concerned with differences in the ways Chinese-English bilinguals and monolingual English speakers process the meaning and structure of words, and of sentences as a whole. The next section suggests some specific differences between the Chinese and English languages that should lead to differences in processing meaning and structure between the two language groups.

AN OVERVIEW OF CHINESE-ENGLISH DIFFERENCES

Although most of the information in this paper is general enough to apply to all Chinese dialects, specific examples are primarily taken from what is termed Modern Standard Chinese (for the most part, the Biejing dialect of Mandarin). Since 1966, the Chinese government has encouraged the development of MSC as a single unifying language throughout the mainland and 70% of the people now use it (Fincher, 1978; Li & Thompson, 1981; Mathias & Kennedy, 1980). MSC is also an important language in Taiwan. Although many Chinese-Americans speak Cantonese, the *written forms* of the various Chinese dialects are very similar.

As is generally well known, the minimum free form in Chinese is the single character ideogram or pictogram, as opposed to the word (Lyons, 1979; Sapir, 1921; Venezky, 1984). In contrast to words, there are no regular or systematic relationships between Chinese orthography and phonology (Henne, Rongen & Hansen, 1977). Further, the acoustic representation of a given character may vary with context. As Chinese dictionaries are often organized in terms of number of strokes in a written character (or in the root of a family of characters), a person who wants to learn how to write a character he heard will have difficulty locating it in the dictionary.

The Chinese character is a monosyllabic morpheme. Sentences consist of morphemic strings. In most cases a single morpheme is a conceptual and semantic "unit." However, Chinese has three ways to form multimorphemic units (Henne et al., 1977; Li & Thompson, 1981). First, *compounds* consist of two adjacent characters (e.g., feng-che = wind-vehicle = windmill; re-xin = hot-heart = enthusiastic). Second, *reduplication* involves repeating a character such that the double forms a new semantic and/or syntactic entity (e.g., xie = rest; xie-xie = rest a little, i.e., nap; man = slow; man-man = slowly). Finally, Chinese has some *affixes* (although they are few compared to Indo-European languages) that can indicate grammatical or semantic attributes. The multimorphemic entities appear to vary along a continuum from strongly bound, to loosely concatenated, to free but linguistically related pairs. Occasionally more than two characters may be "combined." As there is often no clear agreement on the strength of a paired relationship, an open linguistic question regards the nature of "words" in Chinese (Halliday, 1956; Henne et al., 1977; Simon, 1937). When written, there is no spacing difference between two mono-morphemic and one compound morphemic entity. The ratio of morphemes to words (including compounds) is respectively 1.2 in Chinese (based on Chen, 1982, and Liu, Chaung, & Wang, 1975), and 1.7 in English (Lyons, 1979).

In this chapter we are making the *psychological* assumption that Chinese monomorphemic characters are important perceptual and cognitive units that may function as coding units in ways somewhat analogous to those of English words. (Ideograms and words are the minimum free forms in their respective languages.) However, the differences between Chinese characters and English words may lead Chinese-English bilinguals to perceive English words differently than monolingual English speakers do. Throughout this chapter, we loosely use the term "Chinese word" to refer to either a single morpheme or a combination, with the understanding that the single character is the basic unit.

Not only the nature of Chinese words, but also the nature of lexical categories is questioned (Halliday, 1956; Simon, 1937). Sinologists have divided morphemes into "full" words having semantic content and "empty" words, which are grammatical markers devoid of substance (e.g., a morpheme to indicate that prior characters modify a subsequent character; a morpheme to indicate that the previous string is a question or a warning). Recent linguistic research has further divided the Chinese "full" words into two families, "verbals" and "nominals," which together contain almost everything characterized as a content word in English, and also some of the function words.

These differences between languages are further increased by the fact that the exact same Chinese character can represent many different lexical categories (e.g., the same character can mean the noun happiness, the adjective happy, the adverb happily, or the stative verb is-happy). This situation arises in part because Chinese words generally have no grammatical inflections to indicate case, number, gender, tense, or degree (Henne et al., 1977; Li & Thompson, 1981). Further, even sentential position is not a fully reliable cue to a word's functional role (e.g., subject, object) in a sentence. This is partly because Chinese is a "topic-prominent" language (Li & Thompson, 1981). That is, the semantic topic (rather than the syntactic subject) of a sentence generally comes first (e.g., This tree, [its] leaves are very big. Yesterday, [I] read for two hours).

In the above examples, some of the function words are in parentheses. In illustrative examples throughout this chapter, words in parentheses are to be understood as instances where Chinese would omit the word entirely. In contrast to English, most Chinese "function" words are optional and are suppressed when that would not lead to ambiguity.

In sum, we see major differences between Chinese and English that could affect the cognitive and linguistic processing of English words by bilinguals. The nature of Chinese and English words and lexical categories appear to differ. As considered later in this paper, Chinese full and empty words do not systematically map into English content and function words. A given Chinese substantive can represent many different English lexical categories (including function words), and empty words (as well as some substantives) are suppressed whenever possible. As we see in the next section, processing the "structure" and "meaning" of words in English sentences differs between bilinguals and monolinguals. We argue that those differences between language populations in psychological performance tasks are consistent with the specific linguistic differences between Chinese and English.

LINGUISTIC PERFORMANCE BY CHINESE-ENGLISH BILINGUALS

The specific syntactic and semantic differences between Chinese and English may lead to differences in the processing of English words in various linguistic performance tasks. In this section, we consider several different types of data to provide evidence on performance effects. First, we present some case study data on the English writing of Chinese-English bilinguals. Next, we review some research by A. Bloom (1981) showing that linguistic differences between Chinese and English in dealing with abstraction lead to cognitive performance differences between the two populations. Finally, we present data from a sentence perception experiment that compares Chinese-English bilinguals with monolingual English speakers. These data are considered in some detail, because (a) they illustrate many of the language-specific differences mentioned in the overview, and (b) they have implications for reading differences between the two language populations. We suggest that the linguistic performance data to be considered support two general hypotheses about Chinese-English bilinguals.

B1. *The Comparison Hypothesis.* Bilinguals perceive English in relation to their past combined linguistic experience in both languages.

B2. *The Cognition Hypothesis.* Language-specific differences can lead to associated cognitive performance differences between bilinguals and monolinguals in processing the meaning and structure of sentences.

Writing Performance: Chinese-American University Students

We examined the written course work of two Chinese-American NYU students for writing problems (both errors and nontraditional style). It appears that almost all of these would be consistent with the Chinese/English differences indicated above. JC is 21 years old, was born in Hong Kong, and immigrated to the U.S. at age 5. She attended the New York City public school system and she also attended a Chinese language school for 8 years. She is a senior psychobiology (pre-med) major, probably in the top 10% of her class in terms of grades, and is doing independent research on the role of the lateral hypothalamus in feeding. The data base for our evaluation was her 10-page typed report on that research (graded A-). JC's rather discrepant SAT scores, 620 math, 420 verbal, along with her high GPA (about 3.5) suggest specific language problems.

The second student, JY, is 21 years old and was born in the U.S. Like JC, Chinese (Cantonese dialect) is the primary home language. She attended the New York City public schools, a Chinese language school for 10 years, and took Mandarin courses at NYU. JY is a junior and in about the top 30% of her class. Her GPA is 3.0, and she has verbal and quantitative SAT scores of 510 and 520 respectively. The data base for our evaluation in her case is a 4-page typed research proposal (graded A-) designed to test the hypothesis that certain types of educational TV programs can increase the vocabulary of preschoolers.

Table 5.1 presents data on the types of linguistic problems exhibited by the two bilingual students. In reality, a given problem cannot be classified as exclusively affecting structure/syntax versus meaning/semantics or content versus function words, as neither the categories nor the problems are dichotomous. However, the predominant focus (in our opinion) is indicated in the table, along with the frequency with which the problems occurred. These data suggest that more of the problems center on content than function words, and more concern structure than meaning.

1. Content Words.   The major problems for both students may be related to the fact that English content words are often inflected to indicate syntactic information, whereas Chinese words are not. This language difference appears to underlie three types of writing errors. The most frequent problem appears to be lack of agreement between words in number (i.e., singular/plural) for noun/-verb, noun/noun, and noun/pronoun relationships. A second content-word problem for both students involved the use of incorrect verb forms, including tense, aspect, and modal information. For example, lexical verbs had incorrect inflections and were accompanied by incorrect auxiliary verbs. A third problem for both students involved incorrect inflections on adjectival and adverbial modifiers that yielded the wrong lexical category (e.g., random vs. randomly) or the wrong degree (e.g., larger vs. largest).

At this point, let us give a word of caution regarding overinterpreting the data. The above examples from both students are indeed *consistent* with the inflection differences between Chinese and English. But most teachers have also seen such errors on the part of monolingual English-speaking students. However, the large number of linguistic errors in conjunction with the otherwise high quality of these students' academic performance is striking, and is certainly suggestive of problems specific to Chinese/English differences.

2. Function Words.   ·Both students had difficulties with English function words that appear to be consistent with some of the Chinese/English differences mentioned in the overview. First, both students used function words that didn't have precisely the correct meaning. JC frequently selected prepositions that were not quite appropriate within her sentence context, as illustrated in Table 5.1. She also invented verb-preposition compounds, with no nominal objects for the prepositions (e.g., coded-for). Her use of these compounds often gave the feeling of Chinese co-verbs (discussed later). JY used "that" as a universal relative pronoun, when wh-words would have been semantically more appropriate (see the discussion below of the Chinese "universal" subordinating morpheme "-de"). As discussed below, many Chinese function words, including prepositions and relative pronouns, can be used in a broader range of semantic contexts than the

TABLE 5.1
Writing Errors of Chinese-English Bilinguals

Type of Error	Frequency	Examples[a]
A. Student JC		
Content categories		
Singular/plural	16	bites was; stimulation were
Verb form	5	The latency increased while the duration of eating is shortened
Word order	3	the amount (of food) eaten per bite of food
Adjective inflection	1	The electrode designated as more (most) effective
Function categories		
Preposition	9	The latency was coded for in the following manner
Classifier	5	converted into time in the unit of seconds
Article	4	If (the) mouth is in contact with (the) food
B. Student JY		
Content categories		
Verb form	6	The children will be tested. . .they had (will); I would want. . .so that I can (could)
Singular/plural	5	TV is one of the form of media; the experiment were
Lexical category	5	sample to be selected random(ly)
Function categories		
That/who	4	the children that played; the ones that watched
Missing function word	4	(On) the first day; It helps (them) to improve
C. Szechuan menu		
Content categories		
Singular/plural	25	Cold noodle with sesame sauce
Lexical category	11	Tenderly chicken breast; Choiced jumbo shrimps; a nature flavor
Semantic errors	11	Lotus stems keep turnover averagely in the wok
Verb form	6	Deep fried and sprinkle with scallions
Word order	4	Watermouthing ginger sauce
Function categories		
Preposition	5	Shrimps are combined to match (with) broccoli
Article	4	We offer the (a) reasonable price

[a]Errors are underlined. Words that should have been included are in parentheses.

English functors. In addition, both students entirely omitted function words (articles, prepositions, pronouns) to yield grammatically questionable or erroneous constructions. In the equivalent Chinese sentences, these function words would be optional and unnecessary.

Finally, both students used English constructions (involving both content and function words) that were stylistically unusual, but appropriate for Chinese sentences. For example, Chinese permits nonstandard word order for the purposes of emphasis to a greater extent than English does. In addition, JC used prepositional phrases as "classifiers"[1] in contexts that were stylistically unnecessary or unusual for English.

In sum, almost all of the writing difficulties exhibited by JC and JY appear to be consistent with linguistic differences between Chinese and English, and may be attributable in part to their bilingual abilities, supporting both hypotheses B1 and B2. Hakuta's chapter in this volume provides evidence for similar trends in Japanese-English bilinguals. He suggests causal mechanisms of inter-language transfer and linguistic simplification.

Writing Performance: Commercial Business

As a last example of written performance by Chinese-American bilinguals, we examined the two-page menu of a neighborhood Szechuan restaurant. The content and function word errors were similar to those of the students, but occurred much more frequently. The major types of errors, along with specific examples, are illustrated in Table 5.1c.

1. Content Words. As with the students, the most frequent error was a confusion of singular and plural designations, mostly for nouns, as Chinese does not discriminate between these forms syntactically. Second, almost all content word lexical categories were incorrectly substituted for each other at one point or another on the menu, consistent with the lack of inherent specific markers (e.g., inflections) in Chinese words. Analogously, Hakuta (this volume) mentions a bilingual child who regularly used the noun "mistake" as a verb, consistent with its usage in Japanese. Third, the menu had a fairly high number of semantic errors, not shown by the students. But, consistent with the students, frequent errors involved incorrect verb forms. These were mostly tense inflections in accord with the lack of such inflections in Chinese.

2. Function Words. The most frequent function word errors involved prepositions, including missing, extra, and semantically incorrect words. Also, errors

---

[1]Chinese classifiers are somewhere between articles, quantifiers and adjectives. Examples of their analogues in English would be: *bunch of* bananas, *sheet of* paper, *heard of* cattle, *pack of* wolves, *squad of* soldiers.

with articles included incorrect substitutions of "the" for "a" and vice versa, as well as missing and extra articles. These errors are consistent with the lack of articles in Chinese, with the lack of some of the usual Indo-European prepositions in Chinese, and with the general suppression of Chinese prepositions in sentences where their absence would not cause ambiguity within the total context.

In the case of a restaurant menu, the linguistic errors may indeed have a positive impact on business. They suggest that we will be provided with authentic Chinese cuisine, as advertised, rather than an American imitation. However, in other business contexts, these types of errors could lead to financial losses.

Abstract Thinking in Chinese-English Bilinguals

In accord with other linguists and with anecdotal comments by Chinese-English bilinguals, Bloom (1981) maintains that Chinese does not have some linguistic markers, inherent in words of Western languages, that are used to express abstract ideas. He hypothesizes that the absence of such markers leads (a) to a relative inability to do certain types of abstract thinking and (b) to difficulties in communicating with Westerners. A series of experiments with monolingual and bilingual speakers provides evidence to support his points.

1. Counterfactuals.   English has specific structures, using subjunctive verb forms plus function words, that linguistically mark the counterfactual realm. Some examples are: "If I were he, I would respond to the letter"; "If John had come, he could have seen Mary." Instead of counterfactuals, the Chinese use descriptive or implicational statements that convey a concrete or factual sense, rather than an abstract theoretical or hypothetical sense. The English counterfactual "If the lecture had ended earlier, Bill would have had time to prepare for the exam" would more likely be expressed in Chinese (or in English by bilinguals) as "The lecture ended too late, so Bill did not have time to prepare for the exam." Thus, a hypothetical statement would be turned into a factual statement.

Bloom hypothesized that the lack of a linguistically marked or natural counterfactual structure would lead to difficulties in the cognitive processing of such information. To test that hypothesis, he developed Chinese and English stories including counterfactual information. The linguistic structure of the stimulus was modified to enable somewhat similar expressions in both languages: "X was not the case, but if X had been the case, then Y would have been the case." Based on comprehension questions, 97% of the monolingual Americans understood the English stories, but only 29% of the Chinese understood the Chinese stories. Further, Chinese comprehension of Chinese stories correlated significantly with their English ability. Finally, a group of Chinese who used English every day in business were first tested on Chinese stories, and a month later on matched English stories. Their comprehension was 6% on the Chinese and 94% on the

English stories. This striking difference in the *same* subjects suggests to us that there are language-specific differences in verbal processing *strategies,* rather than differences in general thought processes between the two populations.

We should note that Au (1983, 1984) failed to replicate some of Bloom's results and questions some of his methodology. Although she found differences between English and Chinese people in representing and producing counterfactuals linguistically (in either language), she did not find failures in Chinese students' abilities to understand counterfactual reasoning. However, according to Bloom (1984) differences between the studies might be attributed to differences in the abstractness of the text materials (Bloom's were more abstract), and in the English abilities of the subjects (Bloom's knew less English).

Bloom goes on to cite numerous examples of cross-cultural conversations where counterfactual statements caused miscommunications, confusions, and the perception that American speakers were out to mislead the Chinese listeners, or to impose Western ideas on them. One socially and politically embarrassing situation involved an American judge in a customs case against a Chinese man. Even with an experienced Chinese translator present, the man could not understand that the judge was raising hypothetical situations to test whether he understood the laws, rather than making realistic threats. In a content analysis of a Taiwan newspaper, in 3 weeks of issues Bloom found only one example of what might be called counterfactual argument—in the translation of a speech by Henry Kissinger! Bloom's work is consistent with our own notions in two important ways. (1) English is interpreted by Chinese-English bilinguals in relation to their combined past experience in both languages. Chinese bilinguals, quite fluent in English, still perceive English sentences differently than monolingual English speakers do (hypothesis B1). (2) Linguistic differences in syntax and semantics lead to cognitive performance differences in processing structure and meaning by Chinese-English bilinguals (hypothesis B2).

2. Definite "Generic" Articles.   English uses the article "the" in two different ways. First, it is used to introduce an anaphoric referent to a particular noun in the recent shared experience of the speaker and the listener (e.g., A buffalo was drinking fresh rain water. *The* buffalo stopped suddenly when a coyote approached). Second, it is used to refer to a generic nominal concept, with no particular instance at hand (e.g., *The* buffalo is becoming extinct). Although Chinese does not have definite articles, the demonstrative adjectives "this, that, these, those" are sometimes used to fulfill the first usage. However, there is no linguistic device to communicate the second notion of "generic the." Bloom maintains that the lack of such function words is another example of the lack of a verbal paradigm to express abstract ideas. Even when explicitly told that the example above refers to "a conceptual" buffalo, Chinese-English bilinguals will not accept the notion. They will respond with statements like

"What do you mean by 'conceptual' buffalo? Either you are talking about a single buffalo or about all buffaloes. What else is there?" (Remember that Chinese has no reliable syntactic inflections for singular/plural.) In an experiment in which Chinese-English bilinguals were given generic explanations of Chinese sentences, only 37% were willing to respond *yes* that the sentences could refer to conceptual entities, and most of those 37% had had extensive experience with English.

3. Entification of Properties, Actions, and Conditions. Chinese does not have general affixes (or other linguistic devices) to convert concrete content words into abstract entities (e.g., red, red*ness*; to accept, the accept*ance* of; capital, capital*ism*; modern, modern*ize*). Not only can English entify individual content words, but syntactic transformations exist to convert entire sentences to abstract nominals (e.g., "Interest rates rose"; "The rise of interest rates"). Bloom notes (p. 40) that "when the English speaker shifts from 'That measure will be approved by Congress' to 'The approval of that measure by Congress,' he not only converts a completed sentence into a noun phrase, but on a semantic level he moves from the description of an event that has happened, is happening, or will happen to an abstraction of the idea or the event as a purely theoretical notion," (e.g., "The approval of that measure by Congress will depend on the subcommittee's report.")

In some cases, Chinese can express entification in terms of subordination, with the marker *de*. However, the use of "de" requires that the modifiers precede the nominal, yielding chains of left-embedded structures which rapidly exceed the listener's memory span. For example, English speakers had no trouble understanding sentences like "we will put off to next week discussion of the further implications of the new method for calculating the relationships between the rate of economic development and the individual standard of living." But only 58% of Taiwan university students knew what would be discussed when given an appropriate Chinese translation with "de" yielding something like "We will put off discussing until next week calculate economic development 'de' rate and individual standard of living 'de' relationship 'de' new method 'de' further implications."

In a related experiment, Chinese and Americans were given several simple examples of entification transformations in their *native languages* (e.g., John and Mary got married—The marriage of John and Mary; This thing is important—The importance of this thing) and were asked to generalize to similarly constructed new strings. Bloom found that 87% of the Americans, but only 11% of the Chinese, could do the task consistently and accurately. Bloom suggests that the syntactic structure in English makes the abstract semantic *relationship* between events predominate over the individual conditions or events being related, and also makes it take on a reality of its own. In contrast, Chinese sentences call attention to the two individual conditions, and then in addition, stipulate their relationship. When subjects were given complex stories in their *native* language including such entification, response accuracy for comprehension questions was 59% and 79% respectively for Chinese and Americans.

Bloom maintains that difficulties in using entification, the counterfactual, and the generic "the" illustrate that Chinese do not have cognitive strategies for many types of abstractions. He suggests that the lack of linguistic structures can often lead to children developing without the associated cognitive schema, and to adults lacking the associated performance ability. However, Bloom has not provided evidence on the extent to which the difficulties are related to language processing as opposed to more general thought processes.

A COMPARISON OF SENTENCE PROCESSING
IN BILINGUALS AND MONOLINGUALS

In the study reported here, we examine the differences between monolinguals and bilinguals who evaluate the contributions of content words (nouns, verbs, adjectives, adverbs) and function words (prepositions, conjunctions, articles, pronouns) to the structure and meaning of English sentences. Lexical categories can be conceptualized based on their relative contribution to structure and meaning (Aaronson & Ferres, 1983a, 1983b, 1984a). The primary importance of function words is in signaling structure and that of content words is in conveying meaning. However, within both major divisions, the subcategories vary in their emphasis on structure or meaning. For example, *within* the content words, verbs are more important for the structural organization of the text, whereas nouns (and their adjectives) are more critical for its meaning. *Within* the function words, prepositions and conjunctions are more important for structure, whereas pronouns and articles are more important for meaning.

Empirical evidence shows that people can use the "structure-oriented" lexical categories as cues to initiate phrase-unit coding in a sentence. The *verb* is scored as the most important sentential division in cluster analyses of recall data (Levelt, 1970) and in subjective parsing data (Bond & Gray, 1973). *Conjunctions* are coded differently in contexts where they conjoin sentences as opposed to phrases (Jeremy, 1978). Clark and Clark (1977) highlight *prepositions* as structural cues in their list of syntactic coding strategies: "Whenever you find a preposition, begin a new prepositional phrase" (p. 59); "After identifying a preposition, look for a noun phrase which closes out the prepositional phrase" (p. 62). When the performance task requires extensive memory, silent reading shows selective increases both in eye fixations (Gibson & Levin, 1975) and in key-press RTs at the structurally oriented categories that initiate phrases (Aaronson & Ferres, 1983a, 1983b; Aaronson & Scarborough, 1976, 1977).

In contrast, empirical evidence suggests that people rely more on the "meaning-oriented" lexical categories when the performance task emphasizes comprehension. When *nouns* are deleted, sentence comprehensibility drops markedly (Healy & Miller, 1971). The use of *determiners* such as "a" and "the" influences whether or not people integrate the semantic information from one sentence to the next (de Villiers, 1974). Anaphoric *pronouns* play an important role in aiding the semantic integration of sentence components (Caramazza, Grober, & Garvey, 1977). *Adjectives* set up expectancies that facilitate the processing of related nouns (Foss, Cirilo, & Blank, 1979).

To provide detailed information about the differences between bilinguals and monolinguals in coding lexical categories in English sentences, we have taken two approaches. First, we asked these groups of people to indicate the contributions of words from the various categories to the meaning and structure of their sentences on each of two 5-point rating scales. Second, we reviewed a substantial amount of literature on the Chinese language and its usage, in order to make comparisons to English usage. Thus, we first present the rating study, which then serves as an organizational framework for a theoretical analysis of the past literature.

METHODS FOR THE RATING STUDY

Stimulus Sentences

The 90 English stimulus sentences ranged in length from 9 to 19 words, and had a mean of 14.4 words. The sentences were varied widely in syntactic structure, including clauses and phrases that varied in number, length, location, and subject-rated complexity. The semantic content was not constrained by any specific rules and was obtained primarily from newspapers and magazines. Example sentences are in Table 5.2. Table 5.3 contains the sample sizes for words rated in each lexical category.

TABLE 5.2
Sample Stimulus Sentences

1. Only the lower economic section of Washington was burned by the militants.
2. In a meeting with the cabinet the President made known his feelings about foreign policy.
3. Because of the doctor's new cure the patient was able to continue his work.
4. After many long hours of debate the housing bill was approved by the legislature.
5. Within all of the government only the office of the President issued a statement about the arms treaty.

TABLE 5.3
Sampling of Lexical Categories

Lexical category	N for All Stimuli	N for S,M Ratings	Lexical category	N for All Stimuli	N for S,M Ratings
Content words	662	93	Function words	300	161
Verb set	172	45	Organizational set	107	61
Lexical verbs	89	15	Conjuctions	17	17
Auxiliary verbs	60	15	Prepositions	90	44
Adverbs for verbs	23	15			
Noun set	490	48	Definiteness set	193	100
Nouns	302	15	A, an	33	17
Adjectives	167	18	The	109	36
Adverbs for adjec.	21	15	Absolute pronouns	36	33
			Relative pronouns	15	14

Subjects

Sixteen NYU undergraduates provided 5-point judgments of structure and meaning for sets of three underlined words in each sentence, generally one content and
two function words as indicated in Table 5.2. All subjects spoke English from
birth. The bilinguals also spoke Chinese from birth, as both English and Chinese
were spoken in their homes. Most of their parents were immigrants from mainland China or Taiwan and are currently middle-class families living in New York
City. Most of these students attended New York public schools. Many also
attended Chinese language school for several years and some are enrolled in
NYU Chinese courses.

As the subjects in this study were 18–20 years of age, they are at the far end
of a language and cognitive development scale. Continued syntactic and semantic development occurs for students having English as either a first or second
language, according to teachers for the required NYU Writing Workshop
Course. Our data provide evidence that differences in childhood language background systematically influence sentence processing in these young adults.

Rating Procedures

The subjects rated each underlined word separately for its contribution (1) to the
structure and (2) to the meaning of its sentence. The rating instructions were
designed to be unrestrictive and theoretically neutral, as illustrated by the following excerpt: "Words in sentences play two roles in helping you understand the
sentence. They contribute to the meaning and they provide structural information
to help you organize the context into ideas. Most words contribute to both
meaning and structural aspects. But any particular word might contribute more or

less to either type of information than other words do. How much a particular word contributes to structure or to meaning depends on many things, including: (a) the particular *word* itself; (b) its local and total sentence *context*; as well as (c) the knowledge or orientation of the *reader*. We would like you to rate some of the words in 90 sentences according to how much you think each particular word contributes to structure and to meaning. You will have a five-point scale for indicating each of these attributes separately for each word in its particular context. There are no right or wrong answers.''

In further instructions, subjects were asked to use as a framework for their structure and meaning ratings the contributions of words encountered in their general past language experience. Their ratings were based on the following scale: (1) very low contribution; (2) moderately low contribution; (3) medium contribution; (4) moderately high contribution; and (5) very high contribution. Subjects were given example sentences and were encouraged to ask questions if the written instructions were not clear to them.

RESULTS OF THE RATING STUDY

Meaning Ratings

Three trends in the meaning ratings are of interest. First, Fig. 5.1 shows that the ratings are consistently higher for the bilinguals than the monolinguals (*t* test: $p < .05$) for every lexical category. The ''Chinese'' may perceive English words to be semantically richer than do the ''Americans.'' Second, Fig. 5.1 shows that both the bilinguals and monolinguals give higher meaning ratings to the content words than to the function words (*t* test: $p < .05$). This would be expected based on the differential contributions of content and function words to the semantics of English sentences.

Third, for the meaning ratings, there is an interaction between language background and lexical category. The rating *differences* between the two subject groups are greater for function than content words (ANOVA: $p < .05$). This is observed in Fig. 5.1, and more explicitly in Figs. 5.2a-5.2d. The four panels of Fig. 5.2 compare pairs of content and function categories that have related functional roles in English sentences but that differ in semantic value. Fig. 5.2a compares nouns (e.g., friends, engine) with ''absolute'' pronouns (e.g., she, it, his, their) that can substitute for nouns. (Relative pronouns were not used in this panel because they have a subordinate as well as a nominal feature.) Fig. 5.2b compares lexical verbs (e.g., hunting, run) with auxiliary verbs (e.g., had, can) that provide aspect or modal information. Fig. 5.2c compares adjectives and indefinite articles, which both modify nouns. Fig. 5.2d compares adverbial modifiers (e.g., rapidly) with prepositions introducing adverbial modifier phrases (e.g., swam *with* great speed). All four panels show larger meaning

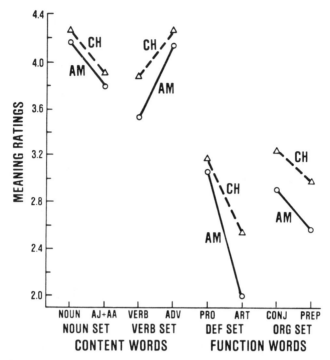

FIGURE 5.1   Meaning ratings of monolingual English speakers and bilingual Chinese-Americans for eight lexical categories. Abbreviations: AM = American, CH = Chinese, AJ = adjectives, AA = adverbs that modify adjectives; ADV = adverbs that modify verbs; PRO = pronouns; ART = articles; CONJ = conjunctions; PREP = prepositions; DEF = definiteness; ORG = organization

differences between Chinese and Americans for function words than for their related content word categories, illustrating the above interaction.

Structure Ratings

Two trends in the structure ratings are of interest. First, Fig. 5.3 shows that the ratings are generally higher for the bilinguals than the monolinguals (*t* test: $p < .05$). The reversal for verbs is important and is considered later. The subject effects in Fig. 5.3 are consistent with those in Fig. 5.1, with Chinese ratings exceeding those of Americans for both structure and meaning.

Figures 5.2 and 5.3 suggest an interaction for structure ratings between language background and lexical category that is opposite to the interaction observed for meaning ratings. In general, structure *differences* between the two subject groups are greater for content than function words. This is observed for

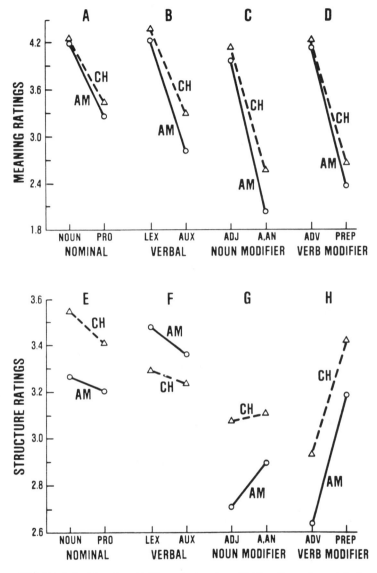

FIGURE 5.2 Meaning (A-D) and structure (E-H) ratings for related pairs of content and function words for monolinguals (AM) and bilinguals (CH). Abbreviations: LEX = lexical verbs; AUX = auxiliary verbs; AV PREP = adverbial prepositions (introducing phrases that modify verbs); for other abbreviations, see Fig. 5.1.

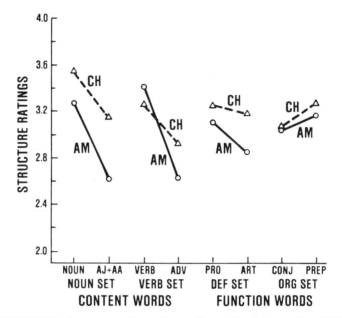

FIGURE 5.3 Structure ratings of monolingual English speakers (AM) and bilingual Chinese-Americans (CH) for eight lexical categories. Abbreviations: see Fig. 5.1.

the functionally related pairs of lexical categories in Figs. 5.2e, g, and h. (Note the reversal of subject effects for verbs in Fig. 5.2f.)

Comparison of Structure and Meaning

In comparing structure and meaning ratings, the data show two types of effects that are of interest: (a) a lexical category effect and (b) a subject group effect.

Figures 5.4a and 5.4b show that the ratings are higher for meaning than structure for content words, but that the reverse holds for function words. This interaction between lexical categories and rating types holds for both monolingual and bilingual subjects (F test: $p < .05$). The data in Fig. 5.5 are the proportions of the total meaning (M) plus structure (S) values that are assigned to structure for each lexical category, i.e., $S/(S + M)$. A graph of $M/(S + M)$ would obviously show complementary results. The Fig. 5.5 data are consistent with those in Fig. 5.4. Namely, both subject groups show higher values of $S/(S + M)$ for function than content words. Thus, higher values of $M/(S + M)$ would occur for content than function words. One would expect these trends based on the relative contributions of function and content words to the syntax and semantics of English sentences.

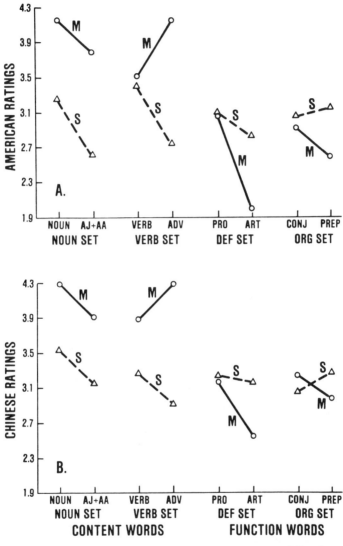

FIGURE 5.4   A comparison of structure (S) and meaning (M) ratings for monolinguals (top graph) and bilinguals (bottom graph). Abbreviations: S = structure ratings, M = meaning ratings; for other abbreviations, see Fig. 5.1.

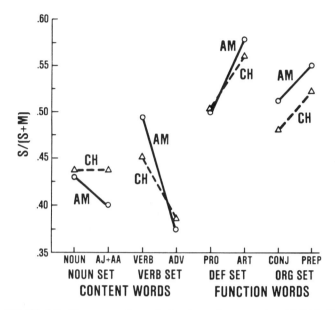

FIGURE 5.5   The proportion of structure plus meaning (S $ PL M) assigned to structure (S) for monolinguals (AM) and bilinguals (CH). Abbreviations: see Fig. 5.1.

Figure 5.5 also shows an interaction between subject groups and lexical categories (*F* test: *p*<.05). (Again, verbs are an important exception.) For *function* words, a greater proportion of the total rating value is devoted to *meaning* by Chinese than by Americans. In contrast, for *content* words, a greater proportion of the total rating value is devoted to *structure* by Chinese than by Americans. This interaction is consistent with the interaction between subject groups and lexical categories observed in Fig. 5.2.

A THEORY OF SENTENCE PERCEPTION IN CHINESE-ENGLISH BILINGUALS

This section focuses on reasons for the differences in the ratings between the two language groups. The rating differences are considered in the context of semantic and syntactic differences between the Chinese and English languages, as discussed in the linguistics literature. In particular, we focus on an expansion of the *Comparison Hypothesis:* (a) In rating any particular English word's linguistic contribution to its sentence, monolingual Americans compare its role to that of many other English words in many other English sentences that they have experienced in the past. (b) In contrast, the bilingual Chinese compare its role, in part,

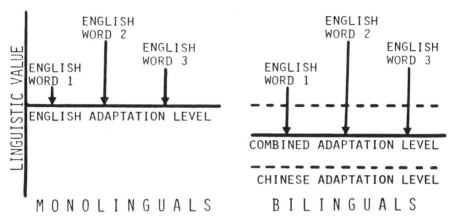

FIGURE 5.6   Schematic illustration of the Comparison Hypothesis.

to that of Chinese "words" in Chinese sentences that they have experienced.

In essence this is an *"adaptation level"* theory, as illustrated in Fig. 5.6. The college-aged subjects have about 20 years of language experience, and are presumed to compare any particular stimulus to some kind of averaged baseline, perhaps weighted by recency, as well as frequency of language experience. Thus, American and Chinese ratings of the same English stimuli should differ to the extent that the adaptation levels of these two subject groups differ. If the English stimuli are *perceived* to carry more (or less) linguistic information than broadly analogous Chinese "words" comprising part of a bilingual's adaptation level, then those stimuli should be assigned correspondingly higher (or lower) ratings. In Fig. 5.6, these perceptions are indicated by the distances between words and the relevant adaptation level for each group.

We argue that, in general, Chinese "words" carry less linguistic information than analogous English words, producing a lower (combined) adaptation level for the bilingual than the monolingual subjects. This would yield higher ratings for English words by the Chinese than the Americans, in contrast or comparison to their particular adaption level. Table 5.4 contains an outline of linguistic differences between English and Chinese that could possibly lead to different perceptions, and thus to different ratings, between the two language populations. These linguistic factors are discussed in detail below. As a fair amount of information is covered, the summary in Table 5.4 might be a useful organizational aid to the reader.

The next sections are organized as follows. First we consider the meaning ratings, second, the structure ratings, with a separate part on verbs, and third, a comparison of meaning and structure. Each main section contains subsections on content and function words.

TABLE 5.4
Linguistic Differences Between English and Chinese Which
Could Lead to the Rating Differences Between Bilinguals and
Monolinguals

Meaning ratings: bilinguals <monolinguals

For content and function words, on the average:
1. English words have more meaning per unit than Chinese.
2. English words are less contextually dependent than Chinese.
3. English words are more abstract than Chinese.

Structure ratings: bilinguals <monolinguals
For content words, on the average:
1. English words have less overlap among grammatical categories than Chinese.
2. English words have grammatical inflections more often than Chinese.
For function words, on the average:
1. English words serve multiple syntactic functions less often than Chinese.
2. English words are optional (vs. obligatory) less often than Chinese.

MEANING RATINGS

Content Words

Figure 5.1 shows that bilinguals give higher meaning ratings than monolinguals for all four categories of content words. Let us compare Chinese and English to gain some insight on why these trends might have occurred.

As suggested earlier a psychological assumption underlying the Comparison Hypothesis is that the perceived comparison unit for the written English word is generally the single Chinese character or morpheme, or perhaps a root morpheme plus an occasional second character (Kratochvil, 1968). This is reasonable, because (a) formal unit boundaries (i.e., spaces) in written Chinese are between individual characters (Henne et al., 1977), (b) pauses are permissible between spoken characters (Brandt, 1943), and (c) Chinese morphemes are the minimal free-standing unit of meaning (Halliday, 1956). Given the above "morpheme/word" assumption, three differences between English and Chinese "content words" would support the Comparison Hypothesis.

1. Amount of Meaning per Unit.   English content words in newspapers (e.g., the *Southampton Press*) and magazines (e.g., *The Readers Digest*) average about 2 syllables. The content words rated in the present study averaged 2.1 syllables and 1.8 morphemes. Because Chinese "content words" average closer to one morpheme (Chen, 1982; Karlgren, 1962; Liu et al., 1975), the present stimuli should be perceived as having more meaning than a bilingual adaptation level. Even if the bilingual subjects had an adaptation level that was a weighted average of the two languages (perhaps with English weighted more heavily), pure English words should still be perceived as conveying more meaning than the bilingual baseline.

The following is just one illustration of the above language difference. As Chinese "words" generally consist of a single root morpheme, with no inflections to indicate case, tense, and so forth, what linguists term "grammatical meaning" is often not *inherent* in *individual* content words. For example, adjectives contain no features to distinguish degrees of comparison or gradations of intensity in their meaning (e.g., great, greater, greatest; hot, hotter, hottest). Instead, an entire phrase must be used, e.g., "great compared (with) me," or "great surpass(ing) me." Thus, the amount of meaning generally associated with a single English content word is often spread over several Chinese "words," resulting in less meaning per word (Forrest, 1973).

2. Context Dependency of the Unit.   English words generally, but not always, have a fairly well defined meaning associated with a particular orthographic representation. In contrast, the meaning of a Chinese character is often less precise and highly variable. It may have several meanings (homographs) that are context-dependent, and that are not completely disambiguated by context. Some examples of homographs in "standard" Chinese (Mandarin) are the following: yang = ocean, foreign; ken = the heel, to follow, with, and; ts'ai = to cut cloth, to decide; ho = to shut, harmonious; ching = clean, only; keng = more, to alter, a night-watch (Brandt, 1943). Far more frequent than such distinctly different meanings are sets of related meanings that correspond to a single character. Some examples are the following: tien = lightning, electricity; chu = host, master, ruler; hsia = blind, reckless, heedless; t'ung = together, with, alike, identical; p'ai = hit, clap, pat; wen = hear, smell, news; shu = a number, some, several, to count, to calculate; ming = a name, fame, reputation (Brandt, 1943).

Two kinds of empirical data support the above illustrations, based on (a) types and (b) tokens in the language. First, Karlgren (1962) reports an average of 10 different meanings per word in a small Chinese dictionary of 4,200 words, with some words having 30–70 different meanings. Second, 2,460 different characters account for 99% of the total corpus of a 1 million-word Chinese frequency count. If we consider words, rather than characters, including the multimorphemic compounds, about 15,000 words account for 99% of the text (Chen, 1982; Liu et al., 1975). In comparison, 40,000 words account for 99% of the 1 million-word Kučera-Francis (1967) English-word-frequency dictionary. If we assume that these two very large corpuses contain about the same amount of meaning, we see that Chinese expresses that meaning in far fewer units, and thus far more meanings per unit than English. Thus, the extent to which context determines the exact meaning will be much greater in Chinese than in English.

Because Chinese content words have multiple shades of meaning, as well as multiple meanings, and because many content words can serve as noun, verb, adjective, or adverb (without orthographic modifications) depending on the context, a national "language game" has developed that makes use of these attributes (Herdan, 1964). The game is a kind of sentence-level anagrams, and is "played" rather seriously by both poets and mathematicians. For example, poems might be written in matrix format with each row and column having four sentences, each composed of four words. The words are selected so that various permutations of the rows and/or columns will result in a new and meaningful poem. For the poet, the "game" is to write in this format with high literary quality. For the mathematician, the game goes beyond a simple two-dimensional matrix, and involves topological structures with a wide variety of mathematical constraints.

In light of the above, if the meanings of individual English words are more precise, well-defined, reliable, or unambiguous than those of Chinese words, both in isolation and within a sentential context, then one should rate those English words higher in relation to a bilingual adaptation level. However, there is no reason that the stimulus words should differ in amount or precision of meaning from what the American subjects are used to reading in their daily lives.

3. Quality of Meaning: Abstractness and Frequency of Unit.   Past research has shown that subjects give higher ratings of "meaningfulness" and "importance," and that they spend more time when reading words (a) that are more *abstract* (as opposed to concrete), and (b) that are *lower frequency* or rarer in the vocabulary (Aaronson & Ferres, 1984a; Ferres, 1981). Both of these attributes should be related to the rating differences between Chinese and American subjects as follows.

Regarding abstractness, it is widely believed that, on the average, Chinese "words" are not as abstract as the words of English and other Western languages. In part this is because Chinese makes little use of affixes to build abstract words (e.g., poly-, super-, anti-; -tion, -ment, -ist), as is done in many other languages (Forrest, 1973). In addition, the lack of abstraction may stem in part from the early development of Chinese orthography as "pictograms." Today, however, less than 10% of the characters might be considered to embody some visual representation of their semantic content (Karlgren, 1962; Venezky, 1984).

To express abstract concepts in modern standard Chinese, one can use a combination of characters that, in and of themselves, have more concrete meanings. For example, the English word "truth" corresponds to the Chinese string meaning "say true words;" "sincerity" corresponds to "true heart" (Forrest, 1973); "emancipate" corresponds to "turn over one's body," and "youthful" corresponds to "years are light" (Henne et al., 1977). Some abstract concepts are formed by compounding or concatenating two more concrete morpheme pairs. Examples of this are: dawn (tian liang) = day + brighten; adult (da ren) =

big + person; algebra (dai shu) = to substitute + numbers; traffic (che ma) = vehicles + horses; language (yu yan) = words + speech; landscape (shan shui) = mountains + waters; length (chang duan) = long + short; analysis (fen xi) = divide + separate; tailor (cai feng) = cut + sew; start (dong shen) = move + body (Henne et al., 1977).

Finally, there are many cases where Chinese lacks the word for an abstract class name (or superordinate), but does have a wide variety of words for the simple concrete instances of the class. For example, Chinese has no general word for "orange," but does have words for "thin-skinned orange," "orange with thick loose skin," and for a kind of small tangerine. There is no general word for "carry," but there are words for "carry on a pole," "carry on the shoulders," "carry between two men," or "carry in the arms" (Forrest, 1973).

Thus, relative to Chinese, many English words would attain a high meaning rating either because they are conceptually more abstract than the Chinese equivalent, or because one English word is worth two Chinese characters. A small percentage of pictograms still have some resemblance to a concrete image (Kratochvil, 1968), whereas English letters and words have absolutely no correspondence to their meaning or to any real-world image.

Regarding frequency, the equivalents of rare words in the Chinese vocabulary are often expressed as combinations of more frequently occurring morphemes. An educated adult may have a vocabulary of over 50,000 concepts, but these may be represented by combinations of far fewer monomorphemic characters. Chinese printing houses may have about 6,000 characters and the Bible was printed with only 2,000 characters (Brandt, 1943). Frequent words may be rated as less meaningful than rare words (a) in part because their high frequency of occurrence gains them more links or associations to other words, and thus more contextual redundancy, and (b) in part due to their lack of novelty.

As noted earlier, some Chinese concepts are formed as reduplications of individual characters, thus yielding an even higher frequency of occurrence for those characters. For example, reduplication is done to indicate a distributive meaning: ren ren = everybody (ren = person). Reduplication is also done to indicate an intensification of quality: Hao hao xuexi = study really well! (hao = well). Finally, reduplication of modifiers is used for itemization (as is done in English) yiju yiju de jieshi = explain sentence by sentence; yici yici de lai = come time and again; yige yige de naqilai = pick up one by one. Thus, Chinese forms many verbal concepts from far fewer, but more frequently used, single characters. English also does this on a *syllable* level (e.g., carefree, mailman, sometimes), but it appears that Chinese uses combinations more often.

In sum, the linguistics literature provides three reasons why English content words should be perceived as containing more meaning than Chinese morphemes. On the average, (a) English words contain more meaning per unit, (b) they have meanings that are less contextually dependent, and (c) the words are sometimes more abstract and occur less frequently. These linguistic differences should yield higher meaning ratings by the bilinguals than the monolingual subjects, supporting the Comparison Hypothesis. Note, however, we are *not* suggesting that Chinese sentences or paragraphs carry less meaning than English ones do. Linguistic information inherent in *individual* English words may be carried at higher levels in Chinese. Chinese appears to be a more context-dependent language than English.

Function Words

As graphed in Fig. 5.1, function words, also, are given higher meaning ratings by bilingual than monolingual subjects. Explanations analogous to those suggested for the content word effects appear to hold for the function words.

1. Amount of Meaning per Unit.   The equivalents of English function words sometimes don't exist in Chinese. Further, to serve some of the purposes of English function words, Chinese has syntactic markers[2] classified by Chinese linguists as "empty" or "vacuum" words (i.e., devoid of substantive meaning) and particles, which may have less meaning than the approximate English equivalent.

The first illustration of the above English-Chinese difference is that Chinese really has no exact analogues for English *articles* (Forrest, 1973; Henne et al., 1977). Words functioning in sentences as nominals are not accompanied by "a" or "the." The definite or indefinite status of a noun is generally inferred, based on context. However, if it is desired, for clarity or emphasis, the cardinal number "one" (yiben) and the demonstrative adjective "this, that" (i.e., endbound morphemes "zhei-" and "nei-") are sometimes used respectively to function as indefinite and definite articles. Thus, relative to the general absence of articles in Chinese, the English articles should be perceived to have a fair amount of meaning by the bilingual subjects.

Second, Chinese has fewer *pronouns* than English, because separate forms generally do not exist or are not used to discriminate among the fine-grain meaning attributes of gender and, to some extent, case. For example, he, him, she, her, and it are all translated as "ta"; I, me, and my are all translated as "wo" (Henne et al., 1977). Thus, many Chinese pronouns serve as general noun substitutes and have less *specific* meaning than English pronouns. Further, even the semantically general pronouns are suppressed whenever possible as indicated below by parentheses. For example, it would be semantically appropriate and syntactically correct for one person to answer a question "(I) don't know," and for another to repeat "He says (he) doesn't know." In neither case is the subject

---

[2]English has no words serving as pure syntactic markers. For readers familiar with Hebrew, the word pronounced "et," which is obligatory before a definite direct object, provides an example of a syntactic marker.

of the verb "know" expressed (the pronouns are suppressed and the verb is not inflected), and the communication is perfectly intelligible without such explicit semantic information (Forrest, 1973).

Although Chinese does have some real *prepositions* (and their associated locative adverbs) which indicate relationships among content words, they are often not used, as the relationship is deduced from context. Further, Chinese equivalents of many Indo-European prepositions are supplied by nouns and verbs placed before, after, or compounded with other substantives. For example, "in the sea" would occur in Chinese as the noun pair "(the) *midst* (of the) sea." Instead of saying "eats *with* chopsticks," one would use the verb pair "*eats using* chopsticks." Other verb-like substitutes for prepositions are "enter" for "into," and "arrive at" for "until" (Forrest, 1973). Thus, semantic attributes carried by English function words are carried, in part, by Chinese content words. Prepositions provide yet another lexical category where bilingual subjects would compare English words to a general paucity of the given form class in Chinese.

Conjunctions also appear to play a weaker semantic role in Chinese than in English (Henne et al., 1977). The coordinate conjunctions "and" and "but" are often omitted from context. Their functional role might be indicated by punctuation (or by pauses in speech). The "universal" subordinate marker "-de" indicates that words, phrases, or clause-like strings preceding it are modifiers. Other than its grammatical function, "-de" carries little lexical meaning. Depending on context, it substitutes for that, which, who, whose, to whom, how, what, of, and the possessive case for nouns. Further, it is often omitted, yielding unmarked subordination, where the modifying word or string immediately precedes the substantive.

The frequent omission of function words in Chinese results in sentences whose meaning must be inferred from *non*-linguistic as well as linguistic context. For example, the character string "Ji bu chi le" (literally, chicken(s) not eat [perfective]) is interpreted to mean either "The chickens are not eating any more" or "As for chicken, I am not going to eat any more," depending on whether the communication context is that of farms or restaurants (Li, 1971). Likewise, omission of function words results in the same character string meaning "I am going to cut his hair" or "I am going to get a hair cut," depending on whether the speaker is a barber or a customer (Forrest, 1973). Such omissions of function words would seemingly imply that they add little or no additional meaning to a presumably over-redundant communication context. Hence, they are aptly classified as "empty" words (Forrest, 1973; Kratochvil, 1968).

In sum, although Chinese does have function words, (a) they primarily serve as syntactic markers with little lexical meaning, (b) the semantics that they do carry is general in nature, and (c) much of the time they are omitted, leaving unmarked relationships to be inferred from context. Thus, by comparison, bilinguals should view English function words as having more meaning than their monolingual cohorts.

2. Context Dependency of the Unit.   As with content words, many of the Chinese function words have multiple meanings, as well as multiple syntactic functions, so that their exact sense is heavily context dependent. For example, depending on the context, the same character "gen" can mean "with" (i.e., instrumental case) "together with," "and," "using," "following," and in comparative constructions "as" or "from" (the same length as; different from) (Henne et al., 1977; Tewksbury, 1948). As the character "gen" (a) is often used in combination with verbs, (b) often serves in linguistic units that would be adverbial prepositional phrases[3] in Western languages, and (c) often has verb-like semantics (e.g., "using" and "following" are features of gen), it is termed a "co-verb" by sinologists.

Some characters serving prepositional functions are context dependent in a different way. The relative "place" and "time" words are often not free-standing function words, but are relegated to being suffixes of, or compounded with nouns. Thus, sinologists do not classify them as a separate form class, but term the combined unit a place or time nominal, i.e., a content "word." For example, the start-bound morpheme "-li" meaning "in, on, during, inside of" occurs with nouns as follows: jiang*li* (in the river), woche*li* (inside the sleeping car), chuntian*li* (during the spring) (Henne et al., 1977). The morpheme "t'ou" forms adverbs or prepositions of locality such as li*t'ou* (inside), shang*t'ou* (on the top, i.e., topside), wai*t'ou* (outside), hsia*t'ou* (below, i.e., underside). It should again be noted that such morphemes may serve rather different linguistic functions in other contexts. For example, the same character *t'ou* also serves as a totally meaningless syntactic marker to indicate that another character is being used as a noun (e.g., jih*t'ou*, the sun; shih*t'ou*, a stone; chih*t'ou*, a finger) (Brandt, 1943). In sum, many Chinese function characters have general or multiple meanings that are determined in part by the context rather than being inherent in the lexical item itself, or that are nominal suffixes rather than being independent function words.

3. Quality of Meaning: Abstractness and Frequency.   The comparison of Chinese and English "function words" in terms of quality of meaning is not as straightforward as it was for content words. First, consider the *perceived* abstractness of Chinese function words. On the one hand, many of them (e.g., the subordinate -de, and the time and place "prepositions") may be perceived as more concrete than the English equivalents. This is because they are often (or always) bound morphemes that occur in combination with nominals (and other content words), and such content words are generally far more concrete than function words. On the other hand, the fact that many Chinese function words

---

[3]Indeed the adverbial prepositional phrases "paints *with* a brush" and "walks *with* his friends" can be closely paraphrased using verbals: "paints using a brush" and "walks accompanying his friends."

are almost pure syntactic markers, devoid of semantic content, could mean that they are perceived to be more abstract than their English analogue.

If one considers perceived word frequency, a comparison of English and Chinese function words might also yield either ordering. On the one hand, the fact (a) that many of the Chinese function characters serve multiple purposes and (b) that many of them at once correspond to several English words, should cause Chinese functors to have higher perceived word frequency than English functors. Alternatively, the fact that many Chinese functors are often omitted, leaving their role to be inferred from context, may yield lower perceived frequency values.

In sum, although the evaluations of abstractness and frequency attributes are equivocal, the above evaluations of (a) meaning per unit and (b) context dependency provide an accounting that is consistent with the meaning ratings for function words in Fig. 5.1. In comparison to English, Chinese functors appear to have less meaning and to be more heavily context dependent. Thus, in line with the Comparison Hypothesis, this should lead to higher meaning ratings for English functors by the bilingual than the monolingual subjects.

STRUCTURE RATINGS

Content Words

Figure 5.3 shows higher structure ratings for bilinguals than monolinguals for three of the four classes of content words. Below, we consider some possible reasons for the dominant trend. The exception category, verbs, is discussed later. There are two important differences between Chinese and English that could yield a perception of less structure or syntax, and thus a lower adaptation level, for Chinese content words: Chinese has extensive overlap among grammatical categories, and a lack of grammatical inflections to designate categories.

1. Overlap Among Grammatical Categories. In English (and other Indo-European languages) a reliable property of most words is their grammatical or lexical category. Although a small percentage of the words may belong to more than one category (e.g., to plant, the plant), this is so unusual that school children are taught to label and to learn the particular "parts of speech" associated with each word (e.g., "Nouns are the names of persons, places and things"). By and large, linguists agree on the major lexical categories and on which words should be classified into which categories, and dictionaries indicate those categories. The category structure has so much commonality across major families of languages that linguists have hypothesized it to be a linguistic universal (Halliday, 1956; Kratochvil, 1968).

In sharp contrast, classical sinologists did not classify ideograms into lexical categories. As noted earlier, only a distinction between "full words" and "empty words" was made. The recent subdivision of the substantives into nominals and verbals is based more on the behavior or function of words in their sentence contexts than on any *inherent* properties of the word itself. To this day, there is little agreement on such matters within national Chinese linguistic committees that are revising, simplifying, and standardizing the language (Mathias & Kennedy, 1980). Chinese children are not taught lexical categories and do not make syntactic tree diagrams of sentences (according to recent immigrant students at NYU).

Western linguists have written papers illustrating how the Indo-European grammatical categories can also provide a conceptual framework for Chinese (Halliday, 1956; Simon, 1937). Their analyses are *not* based on *inherent* lexical attributes, but rather on the *functioning* of characters within strings. However, even a functional analysis is often controversial, because so many words can serve multiple functions. For example, the string "baba xie de hao" has two translations into English (Kratochvil, 1968). (1) "Father writes well," where baba (father) is a noun, xie (to write) is a verb, hao (well) is an adverb, and the marker de denotes the relationship between the verb and the adverb. (2) "What father writes is good," where baba xie (father writes or father's writings) is a substantive, the marker de denotes that the word group or character compound is used instead of a noun, and hao is an adjective. Kratochvil makes the points (a) that the semantics of the string are not sufficient to determine the grammatical categories, (b) that the functioning of characters within the string as a whole are not sufficient, and (c) that examples like this question some supposed universals of both syntax and semantics.

In further support of the notion that Chinese "words" do not have *inherent* grammatical categories are the examples in Herdan's (1964) mathematical "language games." In one set of sentential anagrams, he states that there are 108 ways of selecting sets of three characters from nine to make coherent sentences that satisfy severe topological constraints specified in one of Pascal's theorems. (These constraints are the type that crossword puzzles place on rows and columns, but at the syntactic and semantic levels.) As mentioned earlier, this can be done in Chinese because almost any substantive character can occupy almost any "content-word" category. From his example, here are three characters that can each serve multiple grammatical categories.

sheng: life (noun); living, growing (adjective); to live, produce, grow (verb)
hsi: happiness (noun); happy (adjective); to rejoice (verb); happily (adverb)
chang: length, seniority (noun); long, elderly (adjective); prolong, grow (verb)

In English it is also possible to create syntactically ambiguous constructions based on multiple grammatical categories for some words, but they are the exception rather than the rule. Indeed, psychologists have devoted a lot of discussion to structures having the two parsings "they are (eating-apples)" and "they (are eating) apples." This ambiguity is possible because the same -*ing* inflection both (a) denotes the present progressive verb form and (b) converts some verb classes to adjectival form. There are few (if any) other types of syntactic ambiguity discussed in the literature on English. In contrast, as indicated above, both Chinese poetry and word games are based on the very high frequency of words with multiple syntactic roles. Standard Chinese grammar books have entire chapters devoted to such syntactically ambiguous structures. For example, the "complex stative construction" is illustrated by the sentence "women chi de hen kaixin," literally meaning "we eat (marker) very happy." Depending on the context, Chinese would interpret this as either "We ate very happily" (happily = adverb) or "we ate to the point of being very happy" (happy = adjective) (Li & Thompson, 1981). Syntactic ambiguity based on multi-category words is not unique to Chinese, but it is certainly more prevalent than in English.

Although there is enormous syntactic flexibility within Chinese, there are several linguistic devices that are used together to convey structure for a sentence. Thus, in accord with Halliday's and Simon's views that Chinese does have at least functional grammatical categories within a sentence, one finds the following types of partially reliable cues to syntax: (a) the semantics of the words and (b) of the string, (c) grammatical markers and particles (which are often optional), (d) syntactic affixes (again optional), (e) positions of words relative to each other (Chinese often has subject-verb-object strings with modifiers generally preceding their major substantives), (f) extra content words to indicate conjugation and declension information (e.g., yesterday and tomorrow indicate past and future tense for verbals), (g) tone/stress patterns for individual words, and (h) suprasegmental intonation contours.

Granted the above syntactic cues, the Comparison Hypothesis concerns the contribution to sentence structure from *individual* English words. To the extent that structural information in Chinese is embodied heavily in the sentence as a whole, rather than inherent in the individual words, a word-based adaptation level should be lower for the bilingual than the monolingual subjects.

2. Paucity of Grammatical Inflections. An important part of a word's syntactic contribution to the sentence lies in its grammatical inflections. In English the inflections signal the word's lexical category (e.g., noun), functional role (e.g., subject), and grammatical relations to other words in the sentence. Kratochvil makes an important point that affixes in English have a kind of binary significance, with the absence of the affix being as significant as its presence. Thus, if an English noun can occur with a plural suffix (e.g., students), its occurrence in the singular immediately provides grammatical information about number. That is not the case for Chinese. Occasionally there are grammatical affixes (e.g., -men, to denote plural), but the absence of the affix does not imply the absence of the corresponding grammatical feature (e.g., dropping -men leaves words that could be either singular or plural).

For the most part, Chinese words have no inflections. "Nouns" generally have no number, gender, or case features. "Verbs" have no conjugations to indicate past, present, or future tense. "Adjectives" have no comparative or superlative forms, and frequently cannot be discriminated from "adverbs" (e.g., hao means both well and good, and is often considered to be a stative verb "is good," Brandt, 1943). However, this is an extreme view, as all Western languages have "exception" or "irregular" words that lack the standard inflection or, occasionally, any inflection. Further, as suggested in subsection (1) above, Chinese has other linguistic devices to communicate the syntactic information carried by inflections in Western languages. But, as we indicated earlier, these devices are optional and appear to be less reliable cues to the syntactic structure of a sentence, or of its words, than are most syntactic coding devices in Western languages.

In sum, the paucity of grammatical inflections for individual content words is yet another reason why bilinguals may perceive English content words to contribute more structural information to the sentence than Chinese words do. Consequently, the bilinguals' rating of English content words relative to their overall adaptation level, should exceed those of the monolingual subjects.

Function Words

Figure 5.3 shows that bilinguals also rate English function words as contributing more to sentential structure than do monolinguals. There are three attributes of Chinese that would provide explanations for this trend.

1. Multiple Syntactic Functions.   First, as was the case for content words, Chinese "function words" can often play more than one syntactic role, whether these functors be affixes, free or bound markers, particles, or true words. For example, as indicated earlier, t'ou is a marker to designate nouns, as well as being an adverb/preposition of locality. It is also a "classifier" (see footnote 1) of mules, oxen, and donkeys! Another example of multiple roles served by functors is provided by the particle ti or its variant te (Brandt, 1943). (a) In combination with a verb, and prior to a noun, ti serves as a relative pronoun (shuo hua ti jen; the person *who* speaks). (b) It serves as a semantically empty marker that a verb is being modified by an adverb (ni shuo ti t'ai k'uai; you speak too fast). (c) It indicates the possessive or genitive case (wo ti shu; my book, the book *of* me). (d) It indicates adjectives when they are not followed by substantives (wo yao mai hao ti; I want to buy good *ones*). (e) It often follows a verb to indicate past tense (t'a tso t'ien hui hai ti; he came back yesterday). (f) Ti following yu forms a kind of adjective clause (there are those which/who . . . .). (g) In combination with reduplicated adjectives, ti forms adverbs (hao hao ti; diligently, properly). (h) Combined with substantives, ti indicates occupations or professions (beggar, merchant, gate-keeper, etc.). (i) It is used with the names of materials (che shih mu t'ou ti; this is made *of* wood). As many Chinese functors play multiple roles, their reliability as psychological cues in signaling any one syntactic attribute is low.

2. Optionality.   In addition to the multiple roles played by Chinese functors, even their presence in sentences is optional. As discussed earlier, when there is little chance of ambiguity, characters indicating syntactic functions in Chinese are generally dropped. From an information standpoint, this makes Chinese an efficient and low-redundancy code, but from an information *processing* standpoint, it can yield unreliable cues to syntactic structure. As an example of the optionality or non-reliability of some Chinese functors as linguistic cues, it is instructive to read the key sentence in a standard grammar lesson on the particles ma, a, na, ni, and yi, used to indicate interrogative form, sentence termination, and assertion (i.e., strong declarative): "No rules are given for their usage, and their proper usage can only be acquired by close attention to the manner in which the Chinese use them" (Brandt, 1943, p. 133).

3. Affixes.   Finally, some Chinese functors are in reality affixes or bound morphemes, as opposed to independent words. For example, as suggested earlier, some words that would be free-standing prepositions in English occur as noun suffixes for time and place words. If those "affixes" are not viewed as full words, they may lower the bilingual's adaptation level for the contribution of functors to the structure of a sentence.

THE ROLE OF VERBS IN SENTENCE STRUCTURE

Figures 5.2, 5.3, and 5.5 show that verbs are an exception to the trends for structure ratings of content words. For the other three categories bilingual ratings exceed those of monolinguals. But for verbs, the reverse occurs (t test: $p<.05$). In terms of the Comparison Hypothesis, if the syntactic attributes (and thus the subjective perceptions) of Chinese verbs *exceed* those of English verbs, a higher bilingual adaptation level would result. This would yield a lower structural rating for English verbs in comparison to the monolinguals. The linguistic literature supports these ideas, as indicated below.

1. Grammatical Affixes.   Although Chinese content words have no *inherent* grammatical inflections, "verbals" do have an extensive set of bound particles to convey aspectual and modal information, and possibly tense[4] (but recent work questions tense). Thus, a standard introductory text on Chinese (Brandt, 1943)

---

[4]In contrast to earlier linguists, Li and Thompson (1981) maintain that Chinese has aspect but *not* tense markers. They define tense (i.e., past, present, future) as the time of a reported event relative to the time of speaking, and aspect as time relative to the internal make up of the event itself (e.g., progressive: read*ing*), or to other events.

contains grammatical lessons on markers and particles at the ends of 20 chapters, and 16 of those are devoted primarily to verb-related particles. For example, chiu indicates immediate action (wo chiu ch'u, I shall go now); cho can indicate an action or state in progress (e.g., sitt*ing*); lai + cho indicates past tense; tao indicates completion of action; ch'i can indicate either the beginning or completion of action; chao+pu can indicate the impossibility or failure of action (e.g., can't); pei indicates passive voice.

2. Multiple Grammatical Categories.   The other lexical categories have substantial overlap of words, and that is also true for "verbal" characters. However, linguists have recently itemized a large number of distinct subcategories for verbs alone, based on both syntactic and semantic features. Further, the linguists are in moderate agreement on the definitions of many of these categories. All of these categories meet the general syntactic definitions of "verbals," as discussed below (e.g., can serve as a sentence nucleus [except coverbs], and can be negated). This wide variety of subcategories permits "verbs" to handle a broad range of syntactic functions, some of which are served in English by adjectives, prepositions, and adverbs.

Standard texts describe the verb categories as follows (Henne et al., 1977). Verbs are divided into two main categories: description verbs and relational verbs. *Description* verbs are of two kinds: (a) *action* verbs (e.g., xie = write; yan = perform; dai = wear) and (b) *quality* verbs (e.g., hao = is-good; qingchu = is-clear; note that these would be represented as a copula plus a predicate adjective in English). *Relational* verbs are of four kinds: (a) *existential* verbs (e.g., you = to exist, to be, to have); (b) *classificatory* verbs (e.g., shi = to be equal to; xing = to be named); (c) *coverbs* (e.g., yong = using; xiang = facing; note that these would substitute for the English prepositions "with" and "toward"); (d) *modals* (e.g., hui = can). Thus, the Chinese verbals, as a large and somewhat cohesive group, may be perceived as comprising a more powerful and wide range of linguistic features than other "lexical categories."

3. Sentential Nucleus or Central.   The most important syntactic attribute of the Chinese verb is that it can serve as the "central" of a sentence. Everything else in the sentence ultimately depends on the verb, and no other "lexical category" can serve this nuclear syntactic function (Henne et al., 1977). Kratochvil (1968) presents a scheme for sentential parsing or analysis whereby all words form a kind of tree diagram as a function of their "linguistic" distance from the central. This is a kind of deep-structure analysis, as reduced sentences can be formed by successively dropping words that are syntactically (and simultaneously semantically) most remote from the central. In any Chinese sentence a predicate is *required*, and the verb is both the linguistic (and psychological) center or focus of the predicate and of the sentence. In forming reduced sentences from the original, i.e., all possible sentences derived from the original string, the central must be a part of each. Further, the verb itself is the minimal sentence that can be derived from the original. In fact, in Chinese, single-verb sentences are quite frequent and normal. Some examples from Henne et al. (1977) are the following: Jide = (I) remember; Pianyi = (It) is cheap; Shuizhe = (someone) is sleeping; Nianwanle = (I) have finished reading (it); Chiguo = (He) has (in the past) tasted (it).

In contrast, English rarely has single-verb sentences (except in unusual situations, e.g., the command: Run!) because subject and object pronouns, auxiliary verbs, and so on, are obligatory rather than optional in a grammatically well-formed string. Thus, "minimal" English sentences are generally three words: subject, verb, object. As complete Chinese sentences do not require an explicit subject and/or object, the verbal gains a much higher syntactic status than any other lexical category. The Chinese verb is not only a word; it is *often* an entire sentence! This is probably the most important reason why the trends for structure ratings of verbs differ from those of other content words in Figs. 5.2, 5.3 and 5.5 (S/S + M). The bilingual adaptation level for verbs is higher than the perceived structural role of the English verb.

COMPARISON OF STRUCTURE AND MEANING

The type of rating (structure/meaning) interacts with the lexical categories and with the subject groups. For both bilingual and monolingual subjects the meaning ratings exceed the structure ratings for content words, but are less than the structure ratings for function words (Figs. 5.4 and 5.5). These trends are expected if the subjective meaning and structure ratings are determined in large part by the semantic and syntactic attributes of the content and function words. As such "language determined" effects for 18 lexical categories are discussed by Aaronson and Ferres (1984a), we do not consider them here. Instead, we will focus on the interactions with the language background of the subjects.

In relation to the total "linguistic value" (S + M), the perceived emphasis of the various lexical categories on structure versus meaning differs for the two subject groups. In Fig. 5.5 bilinguals, in comparison to monolinguals, indicate function words as conveying relatively more meaning (M/(S + M)), and content words as conveying relatively more structure (S/(S + M)). The top of Fig. 5.7 shows these trends averaged for function and content categories.[5] The left graph shows that Chinese perceive English *function* words as contributing relatively more to *meaning* than Americans do. But the reverse is true for content words. The right graph shows that Chinese perceive the *content* words as contributing relatively more to *structure* than Americans do. Again, the reverse is true for

---

[5]Verbs have been omitted, based on their reversal in structural attributes discussed earlier. The interactions in the top and bottom of Fig. 5.7 are statistically significant both with and without verbs.

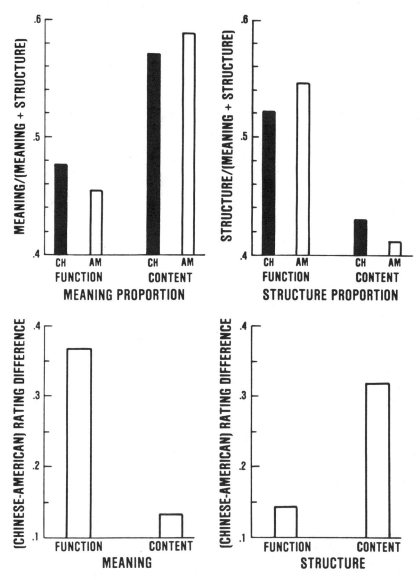

FIGURE 5.7 Interactions between language populations and lexical categories. Top panels: The proportion of "linguistic value" devoted to meaning (left) and structure (right). Bottom panels: Chinese-American rating differences for meaning (left) and structure (right).

function words. These graphs, normalized for total linguistic value, provide evidence that the data can*not* be attributed simply to a response bias toward higher overall ratings for Chinese.

A comparison of Figs. 5.2a-d with 5.2e-h provides another way of examining the interactions between subject group and lexical category that are illustrated in Figs. 5.5 and 5.7 (top). Figs. 5.2a-d show greater Chinese/American *meaning* differences for *function* than content words. In contrast, Figs. 5.2e-h show greater Chinese/American *structure* differences for *content* than function words. This interaction is shown more simply on the bottom of Fig. 5.7. These graphs show the rating *difference* between Chinese and Americans, averaged for each of the two word groups (left panel). The difference in meaning is greater for function than content words (right panel). In contrast, the difference in structure is greater for content than function words. These rating differences would correspond to differences in adaptation levels in the theoretical model of Fig. 5.6. The interactions are reasonable in light of the relative magnitudes of the various linguistic differences between Chinese and English, as discussed later in this chapter.

Function Words

The function word differences between subject groups were greater for the meaning than the structure ratings. Although function words in both languages provide syntactic cues, Chinese functors have less semantic value in part because they play multiple semantic roles, and their use is often optional semantically. However, for many function words in many contexts there is little point in even discussing such considerations, as these "empty" words have virtually no semantic attributes (Forrest, 1973; Kratochvil, 1968; personal communication with NYU students).

Content Words

A consideration of content words shows the opposite trends. With the exception of verbs, content word differences between subject groups were greater for the structure than the meaning ratings. Although content words in both languages are semantically important, syntactic differences between Chinese and English content words are large. As discussed earlier, Chinese content characters have no inherent grammatical categories, and they also have no inflections to indicate case, number, gender, or syntactic agreement with other words in their sentences (Forrest, 1973; Kratochvil, 1968; Simon, 1937). Kratochvil states that Chinese linguists have been trying, unsuccessfully, to establish grammatical categories for over 75 years. He mentions three criteria to classify words into grammatical categories in Western languages that fail for Chinese. First, Chinese words cannot be grouped by orthographic or word shape features (generally indicating inflections, e.g., s, ing). Second, Chinese words cannot be grouped reliably according to syntactic function in relation to other words in the sentence, as indicated by the "father writes" and the "hair cut" examples given earlier. Third, the word's inherent meaning does not reliably signal a grammatical category, as observed in connection with the "language game" examples.

In sum, Figs. 5.1, 5.2, 5.3, 5.5 and 5.7 show that all English words contribute to both structure and meaning, but that their *relative* contribution or emphasis differs among lexical categories, with function words emphasizing structure and content words emphasizing meaning. Of particular interest here is that bilinguals view English functors as contributing relatively more to meaning, and content words as contributing relatively more to structure, in comparison to monolingual subjects.

DEVELOPMENTAL IMPLICATIONS OF CHINESE-ENGLISH DIFFERENCES

Our theoretical evaluation of the literature provides evidence for Chinese-English differences that have implications for cognitive and linguistic development in bilingual Chinese-English children. In this section we provide some speculations on such development, based on the past literature. The discussion provides ideas about the cognitive and linguistic background that led up to the performance of the 18-year-olds in our sentence perception experiment.

1. Language Acquisition. The Chinese-English language differences have implications for several aspects of language acquisition. For example, Huang and Hatch (1978) report data on the first 6 months of learning English by a 5-year-old Taiwanese immigrant, reared mostly by his grandmother, who spoke no English. Paul omitted the English copular verb and articles in sentences where they are optional and generally omitted in Chinese (e.g., This [is a] kite; That [is a] baby). Although there can be many reasons for such omissions, Paul's patterns of language acquisition may be partially attributed to his language background. Analogously, Hakuta (this volume) points out that children learning English with Japanese or Korean as their native language, neither of which has an article system, have difficulty with English articles. In contrast, he points out that English-French bilingual children never confuse definite and indefinite articles, as these languages have similar systems.

Bilingual children, such as Paul, may be delayed in other aspects of English syntax, relative to monolingual children. A second aspect is the acquisition of correct word order for sentences, as Chinese (being a 'topic prominent' language) permits far wider syntactic variations than does English. In this respect, an analogous example is the comparison of Italian and English, as Italian also permits more word-order flexibility than does English. Bates and MacWhinney (1976, 1981) suggest that because "Italians apparently listen to massive distortions of SVO order all the time," this "actually delays the acquisition of basic word order in Italian children." Bates, McNew, MacWhinney, Devescovi, & Smith (1982) and MacWhinney, Bates, and Kliegl (1984) show that this difference in permissible word order between the two languages yields interesting experimental data on comprehension of English sentences having ambiguous word-order cues. Bilingual Italian-Americans produced data on word-ordering choices that were intermediate mixtures of the data produced by monolingual Americans (in English sentences) and Italians (in Italian sentences). As Chinese word ordering is more flexible than Italian, we would expect Chinese-American children to take a long time to acquire the basic English word ordering principles, and then, even in grade school, to produce mixture orderings that are not grammatically correct. Indeed, the two students who provided data for our earlier writing analysis, JC and JY, both produced a fair number of sentences whose word order was stylistically unusual, although not quite ungrammatical.

However, bilingualism might yield some trade-offs during acquisition. The bilingual child might benefit from the well-organized semantic system in Chinese, where large word groups are formed in relation to common roots or radicals. Hakuta's chapter in this volume suggests that such benefits could occur. It would be interesting to see data on vocabulary growth in both languages during the first 15 years for Chinese-English bilinguals in comparison (a) to bilinguals in two Indo-European languages (e.g., French-English; German-English) and also (b) to monolingual English speakers. Indeed, the fact that Chinese "content words" represent broad semantic concepts that are used over and over again in the same lexical form, regardless of their grammatical category, may lead to earlier acquisition of those concepts.

2. Reading Skills.   An important aspect of linguistic development is reading, and again, a bilingual background could have both positive and negative implications. As Chinese characters are morphemes, bilinguals may perform lexical access on morpheme-sized units in English sentences in cases where monolinguals may operate on multimorphemic words. Using smaller psychological units could yield slower English reading rates at lower levels of processing. On the other hand, greater global context sensitivity and a tendency to skip over function words that would be optional in Chinese could possibly speed up the English reading rate for bilinguals at higher levels of processing.

If we consider the early stages of learning to read, the differences between an ideographic and phonemic language may play a strong role in acquiring decoding skills. Analogously, Baron and McKillop (1975) classify their *monolingual* American subjects into two groups based on individual differences in decoding skills. The "Chinese" presumably do whole-word decoding and have a "direct path" from the orthography to the semantics of a word. In contrast the "Phonecians" presumably decode letters or syllables into phonological representations before extracting the semantics. Past research suggests that the "Chinese" may progress through the early stages of reading faster and may switch from "controlled" to "automatic" decoding sooner than the "Phonecians." But, when faced with new words, the "Chinese" will lack or be weak in appropriate phonemic decoding skills.

If we consider higher-level linguistic processing during reading, our own research (Aaronson & Ferres, 1984b, 1985; Aaronson & Scarborough, 1976, 1977) suggests that there should be differences between "Chinese" and "Phonecians." When reading for relatively complete and long-term retention of information, as is done when studying for exams, the "Phonecians" should fare better. This is because a phonological representation of the surface structure (a) may yield a more durable mnemonic representation of individual words and (b) may aid in parsing the sentence into memory-span sized phrase units or "chunks," as syntactic and phonological phrases generally coincide in English. On the other hand, when reading for immediate comprehension of gist, as is done when skimming newspapers or novels, the "Chinese" should fare better. A phonological representation here appears to be unnecessary, to slow the reading process, and to interfere with higher level integration that cuts across phrases and sentences. Thus, the bilinguals may do better than the monolinguals under the conditions favorable to "Chinese" individual differences in reading, at both the decoding stages and the higher-level stages of linguistic processing.

3. *Social Communication Skills.* If we consider more general aspects of written and spoken communication that occur as the child matures, it appears that the Chinese depend quite heavily on context, both linguistic and nonlinguistic, to convey the complete meaning underlying individual sentences. If such reliance on context exceeds what is typical for monolingual Americans, it can have both positive and negative results. The bilingual's *production,* particularly spoken, may lead to misperception by a monolingual American listener, as some of the message may be expressed implicitly via context, rather than explicitly. This could lead to social problems during the pre-teen and teenage years. On the other hand, a greater sensitivity to context by the bilingual may lead to better *comprehension* and integration of information in English when he or she communicates with others.

In a more general sense, L. Bloom (1981) stresses the interaction between context, cognition, and language development. She suggests that language development is determined by (a) the "target" language in the child's home and community (in relation to a second language), (b) the child's environmental context (which is one source of the meanings of utterances), (c) the child's social context (which is one source of communicative intentions), and (d) the child's cognition (as utterances are based on knowledge). If we assume that young Chinese-American bilinguals often have Chinese as their "target" language, and are bicultural as well as bilingual, we would expect their social communication skills to differ from those of monolingual Americans. These differences may have both advantages and disadvantages. In our experience teaching at NYU, which is about a mile north of New York City's "Chinatown," we have noticed a few differences in the linguistic and nonlinguistic aspects of social communication in our students. Anecdotally, the Chinese-American bilinguals are often less verbally fluent, and more socially shy, than their more typical "New Yorker" style cohorts. But, their communication appears to be more context-sensitive (both social and verbal context) than their city-wise classmates.

4. Academic Performance.   An important part of children's development is their school performance. As much of this performance is written, language skills can play a major role. As indicated earlier, both JC and JY had quite noticeable writing problems. It appears that this may in part be responsible for lower SAT scores and course grades than would be expected based on their nonlinguistic abilities. An especially difficult academic problem occurred for VT, who had come from mainland China about 5 years prior to his NYU graduation. All of his graduate school applications were rejected because his verbal GRE was about 400 (up from 300 the preceding year). This was in the context of his straight-A, Phi Beta Kappa record, and receipt of $500 for the best all-university honors thesis. Indeed, one would expect academic difficulties to be even more severe in primary and secondary school, where a large amount of the academic performance and of the student's grades are based on the development of writing skills.

However, the fact that Chinese is a more concrete language than English may lead to some positive outcomes in academic work. Based on large numbers of anecdotes, it appears that Chinese-Americans produce an unusually high rate of students who excel in science and engineering, perhaps because they form concrete and meaningful realizations from abstract ideas.

In sum, the differences between the Chinese and English languages can lead to both advantages and disadvantages in the linguistic and cognitive development of Chinese-American bilinguals. These developmental differences are consistent with both the Comparison Hypothesis and the Cognition Hypothesis put forth at the beginning of this paper. Cummins' chapter in this volume provides further information on factors that can lead to advantages or disadvantages for the bilingual's cognitive and linguistic development. These include linguistic and extra-linguistic feedback in the communication context, the nature of the cognitive task demands, and the child's proficiency in each language.

SUMMARY

The comparison of English with a non-Indo-European language revealed interesting information about language-specific differences in cognitive processing that have not been observed when the bilingual's languages are both from the same language family. English writing errors by Chinese-American bilinguals can be attributed to several linguistic attributes, including the paucity of inflections on content words and the optionality of function words in Chinese. Further, Chinese-English bilinguals show differences in handling abstraction that can be attributed to the absence of explicitly marked linguistic structures, such as counterfactuals, generic articles, and entification. These data supported the *Cognition Hypothesis,* that language-specific differences can lead to associated cognitive performance differences between bilinguals and monolinguals in processing the meaning and structure of sentences.

In an experiment on the perception of lexical categories, we found that Chinese-American bilinguals, who were native speakers of both languages, rated the contributions of individual content and function words to the meaning and structure of English sentences in ways that differed from monolingual Americans, and that the trends could be accounted for in terms of semantic and syntactic differences between the two languages. On an *absolute* basis, bilinguals generally rated English words in the various lexical categories as contributing more to both meaning (M) and structure (S) than did monolinguals. On a *relative* basis, bilinguals generally rated English *content* words as contributing more to *structure* (i.e., $S/(M + S)$ scores) than did monolinguals. Also, bilinguals rated English *function* words as contributing relatively more to *meaning* (i.e., $M/(M + S)$ score) than did monolinguals. These data supported the *Comparison Hypothesis*: that bilinguals perceive English words in relation to their past combined linguistic experience in both languages, whereas monolinguals perceive English words in relation to their past experience with the English lexical category system.

Finally, the developmental implications of Chinese-English differences were considered. Language-specific differences could lead to qualitative differences between bilinguals and monolinguals in language acquisition, reading skills, social communication skills, and academic performance. These differences may arise because Chinese differs from most Indo-European languages in ways that cast doubt on the existence of certain linguistic "universals" such as the role of words as basic linguistic units, the existence of a lexical category system that is inherently marked at the word level, and of reliable word ordering cues to sentence structure.

ACKNOWLEDGMENTS

This research was supported in part by PHS Grant MH-16,496 to New York University and by an NYU Research Challenge Grant. We thank Martin Braine, Murray Glanzer, Peter Homel, Michael Palij, Ching-Fan Sheu, and Brain Watts for reading earlier drafts of this paper and for their helpful comments.

REFERENCES

Aaronson, D., & Ferres, S. (1983a). Lexical categories and reading tasks. *Journal of Experimental Psychology: Human Perception & Performance, 9,* 675–699.

Aaronson, D., & Ferres, S. (1983b). A model for coding lexical categories during reading. *Journal of Experimental Psychology: Human Perception & Performance, 9,* 700–725.

Aaronson, D., & Ferres, S. (1984a). A structure and meaning based classification of lexical categories. In S. White & V. Teller (Eds.), *Discourses in reading and linguistics* (pp. 21–57). New York: New York Academy of Sciences, Annals No. 433.

Aaronson, D., & Ferres, S. (1984b). Reading strategies for children and adults: Some empirical evidence. *Journal of Verbal Learning & Verbal Behavior, 23,* 189–220.

Aaronson, D., & Ferres, S. (1985). Reading strategies for children and adults: A quantitative model. *Psychological Review, 93,* 89–112.

Aaronson, D., & Scarborough, H. S. (1976). Performance theories for sentence coding: Some quantitative evidence. *Journal of Experimental Psychology: Human Perception and Performance, 2,* 56–70.

Aaronson, D., & Scarborough, H. S. (1977). Performance theories for sentence coding: Some quantitative models. *Journal of Verbal Learning & Verbal Behavior, 16,* 277–303.

Au, T. K. (1983). Chinese and English counterfactuals: The Sapir-Whorf hypothesis revisited. *Cognition, 15,* 155–187.

Au, T. K. (1984). Counterfactuals: In reply to Alfred Bloom. *Cognition, 17,* 289–302.

Au, T. K. (1985). Language and cognition. In L. L. Loyd & R. L. Schiefelbusch (Eds.), *Language Perspectives II.* Baltimore, MD: University Park Press.

Baron, J., & McKillop, B. J. (1975). Individual differences in speed of phonemic analysis, visual analysis and reading. *Acta Psychologica, 39,* 91–96.

Basic Chinese course in 25 lessons (1981). China: Eastern Normal University Press.

Bates, E., and MacWhinney, B. (1976). *Language and context: Studies in the acquisition of pragmatics.* New York: Academic Press.

Bates, E., & MacWhinney, B. (1981). Second-language acquisition from a functionalist perspective: Pragmatic, semantic, and perceptual strategies. In H. Winitz (Ed.), *Native language and foreign language acquisition, Annals of the New York Academy of Sciences* (Vol. 379, pp. 190–214).

Bates, E., McNew, S., MacWhinney, B., Devescovi, A., & Smith, S. (1982). Functional constraints on sentence processing: A cross-linguistic study. *Cognition, 11,* 245–299.

Bloom, A. (1981). *The linguistic shaping of thought: A study in the impact of language on thinking in China and the west.* Hillsdale, NJ: Lawrence Erlbaum Associates.

Bloom, A. (1984). Caution - The words you use may affect what you say: A response to Terry Kitfong Au's "Chinese and English counterfactuals: The Sapir-Whorf hypothesis revisited." *Cognition, 17,* 275–287.

Bloom, L. (1981). The importance of language for language development: Linguistic determinism in the 1980s. In H. Winitz (Ed.), *Native language and foreign language acquisition, Annals of the New York Academy of Sciences* (Vol. 379, pp. 160–171).

Bond, Z. S., & Gray, J. (1973). Subjective phrase structure: An empirical investigation. *Journal of Psycholinguistic Research, 2,* 259–266.

Brandt, J. J. (1943). *Introduction to spoken Chinese* (American ed.). North Manchester, IN: Heckman Bindery.

Caramazza, A., Grober, E., & Garvey, C. (1977). Comprehension of anaphoric pronouns. *Journal of Verbal Learning and Verbal Behavior, 16,* 601–609.

Chen, Chao-ming. (1982). Analysis of present day Mandarin. *Journal of Chinese Linguistics, 10,* 282–358.

Cheng, R. L. (1978). Teaching in Chinese outside China. In B. Spolsky & L. Cooper (Eds.), *Case studies in bilingual education*. Rowley, MA: Newbury House.

Clark, H. H., & Clark, E. V. (1977). *Psychology and language*. New York: Harcourt Brace Jovanovich.

de Villiers, P. A. (1974). Imagery and theme in recall of connected discourse. *Journal of Experimental Psychology, 103*, 263–268.

Ferres, S. (1981). *A word class encoding model for adults and children in comprehension and recall tasks*. Doctoral dissertation, New York University.

Fincher, B. H. (1978). Bilingualism in contemporary China: The coexistence of oral diversity and written uniformity. In B. Spolsky & R. L. Cooper (Eds.), *Case studies in bilingual education*. Rowley, MA: Newbury House.

Forrest, R. A. D. (1973). *The Chinese language*. London: Faber & Faber.

Foss, D. J., Cirilo, R. K., & Blank, M. A. (1979). Semantic facilitation and lexical access during sentence processing: An investigation of individual differences. *Memory and Cognition, 5*, 346–353.

Gibson, E. J., & Levin, H. (1975). *The psychology of reading*. Cambridge, MA: MIT Press.

Halliday, M. A. K., (1956). Grammatical categories in modern Chinese. *Transactions of the Philological Society*, London, 178–224.

Hatch, E. M. (1978). *Second language acquisition*. Rowley, MA: Newbury House.

Healy, A., & Miller, G. A. (1971). The relative contribution of nouns and verbs to sentence acceptability and comprehensibility. *Psychonomic Science, 24*, 94–96.

Henne, H., Rongen, O. B., & Hansen, L. J. (1977). *A handbook on Chinese language structure*. Oslo, Norway: Universitetsforlaget.

Herdan, G. (1964). *The structuralistic approach to Chinese grammar and vocabulary*. The Hague: Mouton & Co.

Huang, J., & Hatch, E. A. (1978). A chinese child's acquisition of English. In E. M. Hatch (Ed.), *Second language acquisition*. Rowley, MA: Newbury House.

Jeremy, R. J. (1978). Use of coordinate sentences with the conjunction *and* for describing temporal and locative relations between events. *Journal of Psycholinguistic Research, 7*, 135–150.

Karlgren, B. (1962). *Sound and symbol in Chinese*. Hong Kong: Cathay Press.

Kratochvil, P. (1968). *The Chinese language today*. London: Hutchinson University Press.

Kucera, H., & Francis, W. (1967). *Computational analysis of present day American English*. Providence, RI: Brown University Press.

Levelt, W. J. M. (1970). Hierarchical chunking in sentence processing. *Perception and Psychophysics, 8*, 99–103.

Li, C. N., & Thompson, S. A. (1981). *Mandarin Chinese: A functional reference grammar*. Berkeley, CA: University of California Press.

Li, Y. C. (1971). *An investigation of case in Chinese grammar*. South Orange, NJ: Seton Hall University Press.

Liu, I. M., Chaung, C. J., Wang, S. C. (1975). *Frequency count of 40,000 Chinese words*. Taipei, Taiwan: Lucky Books.

Lyons, J. (1979). *Introduction to theoretical linguistics*. London: Cambridge University Press.

MacWhinney, B., Bates, E., & Kliegl, R. (1984). Cue validity and sentence interpretation in English, German and Italian. *Journal of Verbal Learning and Verbal Behavior, 23*, 127–150.

Mathias, J., & Kennedy, T. L. (Eds.) (1980). *Computers, language reform and lexicography in China: A report by the CETA delegation*. Pullman, WA: Washington State University Press.

Miller, G. A., & Johnson-Laird, P. N. (1976). *Language and perception*. Cambridge, MA: Harvard University Press.

Sapir, E. (1921). *Language: An introduction to the study of speech*. NY: Harcourt, Brace & World.

Simon, W. (1937). Has the Chinese language parts of speech? *Transactions of the Philological Society*, London, 99–119.

Spolsky, B., & Cooper, R. L. (1978). *Case studies in bilingual education.* Rowley, MA: Newbury House.

Tewksbury, M. G. (1948). *Speak Chinese.* New Haven, CN: Far Eastern Publications, Yale University.

Venezky, R. (1984). Language, script and reading in China. In J. Y. Mei, *Reading in China.* New York: National Committee on US-China Relations.

6

Acquiring and Processing First and Second Languages: Comments on Hakuta, Cummins, and Aaronson and Ferres

Martin D. S. Braine
New York University

I found all three chapters interesting and often provocative, and almost all my comments are associations to topics discussed, rather than direct comments on the chapters.

My first point is a rather obvious one that is implicit in many discussions. It deals with the question of what the learner's errors are due to, and the relation of this to interference between L-1 and L-2. What I suggest is that an important source of errors occurs when the learner has an idea to express but doesn't have the means to express it; i.e., the learner is trying to say something and lacks some of the rules of the language needed to map the desired meaning into speech. Of course, for this source of error it doesn't matter whether it is first or second language learning, but the available strategies to cope with the situation are not quite the same in the two cases; in particular, the second language learner has more options than the first.

For example, it may be just some morphological exceptions that the learner lacks. Suppose that a learner is at the stage of learning English when the only way he or she knows how to form a past tense is to put a /d/ at the end of a verb. Then if they want to say that somebody went somewhere they are going to have to generate the form *goed;* they have no other way of saying it. Thus, the error is due to the learner's taking the line of least resistance; he or she is expressing the idea in the only way they know how.

Now let me take another example, from my former 24-month-old subject Andrew. His parents want to put Andrew to bed, but he doesn't want to go, and wants them to know that. He has one negation form in his repertory, used for negative requests: it consists of saying *no* followed immediately by a word for whatever it is he doesn't want, all put under one intonation contour. His utterance, *No bed,* expresses his rejection in the only way he knows how.

These examples of errors may be compared with those that Hakuta cites from his subject Uguisu. She wants to say that she made an accidental error and she knows the English word *mistake,* but she doesn't know whether it is a noun or a verb. It turns out that the Japanese word for "mistake" is a verb: you could say *I mistake* in Japanese, although in English you have to say *I made a mistake.* And so Uguisu comes out with things like *not there I mistake; don't give me more because you're mistaking; I've just mistake and I just skipped,* in which the use of *mistake* as a verb is clearly borrowed from Japanese structure.

Now what I'd like to suggest is that when L-1 learners are trying to express an idea, there are only a few things they can do. First, they can use whatever rules they know that are adequate. They will make errors whenever there are little subrules or exceptions that they don't know, as in these morphological cases like *goed* and *singed* and *thoughted* and the like.

A second strategy is to simplify by omissions, as in the many "telegraphic" utterances of young children (Brown & Bellugi, 1964; Brown & Fraser, 1963). in which articles and other small words and morphemes are omitted in children learning English as L-1. Detail is omitted because the learner lacks complete command of rules that would map in the detail (Braine, 1974).

Apart from keeping quiet and not expressing anything, the L-1 is basically limited to these choices. However, the L-2 learner has another possibility, to use the rules of L-1 for L-2. That is, if you don't know how to say your idea in L-2, then say it the way you would say it in L-1 substituting L-2 words for those of L-1. That is where the transfer or interference errors presumably come from. Given the many similarities of form among languages, this strategy will almost always lead to a comprehensible utterance and often to one acceptable to native speakers.

The point is that although L-2 learners make some errors that differ from those of L-1 learners, the errors basically have the same source—having an idea to express with incomplete command of the means for expressing it. The difference between L-1 and L-2 learners comes from the fact that L-2 learners have a resource for coping with this situation that is not available to L-1 learners—using their native language as a temporary template. By the same token, the "inter-ference" errors are not evidence for different *learning* processes in L-1 and L-2 learners; rather, they are evidence that different sentence-production processes are possible.

Nevertheless, there is a way in which the process underlying these "template errors" could bring about the acquisition of wrong rules. If you are earnestly trying to acquire fluency in a second language, one of the things you can do is rehearse and practice the language yourself. You try to talk to yourself silently in the language when you are alone at home, or when you are walking along the street or wherever; you go over conversations and try to work out how you should have said something you made an obvious blunder about; in sum, you try to think in the language and that way you practice the language.

This talking to oneself probably constitutes input to the language acquisition device. Now, this kind of talking to oneself is a kind of rehearsal and we know tat so far as ordinary learning tasks are concerned rehearsal is a relatively powerful aid to learning. I can't think of any theoretical reason why this silent rehearsal would not be input to the language acquisition device. However, a fair amount of what one says to oneself in these circumstances may be generated through the template strategy just discussed and in that case it is certainly going to be a very problematic kind of input. One can really feed oneself some unidiomatic and poorly formed input that way. The result will be the acquisition of some rules for L-2 that are wrong because they are patterned on rules of L-1. Then there will have been an effect on learning, and not just on sentence-production processes.

Now, rehearsal as a metacognitive strategy is a relatively late development in children (Flavell & Wellman, 1977), and the kind of learning strategy discussed is undoubtedly much more likely to occur in adolescents and adults than in younger children. The strategy could therefore be relevant to age differences in acquisition mechanisms for second languages, and to possible age differences in proneness to different kinds of errors. Note, however, that this entire discussion assumes a basic similarity in L-1 and L-2 learning, and in learning as a function of age. Differences are due to the L-2 learner and the older learner having error-prone resources available that the young L-1 learner lacks.

My next point also has to do with age difference in language acquisition. I want to review some interesting but little known data that corroborate and flesh out the details of the correlation that Hakuta argued for in his paper—that there is a high correlation between age of second language acquisition and mastery of the language even after partialing out length of residence in the country where L-2 is spoken.

The data come from Israeli censuses. It is well known that Hebrew is a language that was revived close to the turn of the century by adult speakers for whom it was non-native. By and large, immigrants have been highly motivated to acquire and use Hebrew, and, in any case, they have been subject to considerable social pressure designed to persuade them to acquire it. Israeli censuses have contained questions relating to the languages in everyday use. Figure 6.1 is a summary of some published census data (Bachi, 1956) on ratings of the extent of everyday use of Hebrew as a function of age at the time of immigration, and length of time since immigration.[1]

The curves are not readily interpretable as learning curves. The "length of stay" variable on the abscissa is confounded with cultural differences between various immigrant waves reaching Israel at different times prior to 1948. Also,

---

[1]Figure 6.1 is a plotting of data in Table 8 of Bachi (1956) and is essentially the same as his Fig. 9 with some additional lines added. Data from more recent censuses are also available (State of Israel, 1963, 1966), and although the age variable is tabulated less conveniently for our purposes, these later data indicate that later immigrant groups, predominantly from Asian and African countries, follow the same general age pattern as the earlier immigrants shown in Fig. 6.1.

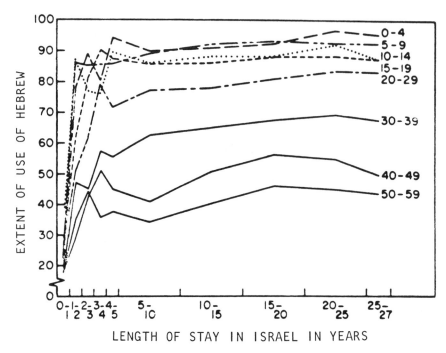

FIGURE 6.1. Extent of use of Hebrew as a function of years since immigration and age at immigration (based on 15,616 Tel Aviv males in 1948—data from Bachi [1956, Table 8]). Note—The ordinate is based on answers to census questions about the languages in everyday use: if respondent said that Hebrew was his only language in everyday use, the response was weighted 100; if he said Hebrew was his primary language in everyday use, the response was weighted 75; if Hebrew was in everyday use, but not as the principal language, the response was weighted 25; responses with no mention of Hebrew as a language in everyday use were weighted zero.

the ordinate, extent of everyday use, is not a measure of competence in the language, although a high rate of everyday use must presumably indicate a comfortable command of the language as a practical vehicle of communication with peers.

A first thing to be noted in these data is the absence of support for a critical period for language acquisition (Lenneberg, 1967), at least for the usual hypothesis according to which the critical period ends at the time of adolescence. If children have special equipment for language learning which they lose at adolescence, how might the change be manifest in these curves? One obvious way would be for the curves for the post-adolescent learners to be lower than those for the pre-adolescents. However, it is obvious that the 15–19 and young adult groups are very similar to the pre-adolescents; any change would be better located at pre- and post-30 than pre- and post-13. Another way a change might be manifest is in the shape of the curves: if the children just soak up the language through the pores of their skin—as the myth goes—whereas the adults have to learn it in unnatural and circuitous ways, then one might expect a difference in curve form. However, it is obvious that all the curves have the same initial rise to practical command of the language, accomplished in the first three or four years after arrival, with little subsequent change in amount of use. In short, these population data provide no support for the hypothesis.

However, there is, obviously, a strong age-trend in these materials, and that strongly confirms Hakuta's argument for a correlation with age. It is conceivable that the lower usage of Hebrew in the 30–39 and older groups reflects a gradual loss of learning ability associated with middle age. Other possible causes of the drop are factors of lesser exposure and reduced motivation and social pressure to learn. Bachi notes that the younger age groups pass through a standardizing process of Hebraization in kindergartens, elementary and working youth schools, the Army, and so forth; i.e., almost everybody young enough (males, especially) went through something like a total immersion procedure. One thing that I take out of these data is that a young adult who goes through total immersion will acquire the language.

Total immersion is a stressful and, for many people, unpleasant procedure. Children who are put into the local school in some foreign country acquire the language, but they are usually pretty miserable for a few months. The older you are the more power you have to refuse this kind of immersion (and if you are old enough such immersion is hard to find even if you seek it). It seems reasonable that it should be these factors rather than differential learning abilities that account for most of the reported age differences in adulthood. But of course there could well be a combination of reduced exposure with reduced learning ability.

After reading Cummins's chapter I was very impressed with the difficulty of knowing what many of the apparently metalinguistic tasks that he describes are really measuring, and I can only applaud his effort to make sense of them. Moreover, I think his distinction between context-embedded and context-reduced tasks is very much along the right lines. The one idea I would add to the distinction is that what context-reduced tasks often demand from the subject is context flexibility (i.e., an understanding that ordinary real-world conversation is not the only possible interpretive context) and an ability to see the appropriate context in which the task is embedded. Thus a "context-reduced" task is often not without context; rather, the context in which it is embedded is not routine, and part of the task for the subject is to construct the appropriate embedding context.

For example, consider *or*-questions. Your spouse or a friend is in the kitchen and calls out "You want tea or coffee or neither?" It would be socially obtuse to take this as a logical task and answer yes, on the grounds that, evidently, you want one or the other. Obviously, you are being asked to choose one of the proffered alternatives. But now suppose some experimenter holds out a fist with a chip hidden in it (e.g., Osherson & Markman, 1975) and says to you "The chip in my hand is blue or it isn't blue—true, false, or can't tell?" It is not socially astute to interpret this like the tea-or-coffee question and thus respond "can't tell" because you can't see the color of the chip (or to guess the color). You should see from subtle details in the form of the question (the most natural form for an *or*-question in this context would presumably be *Is the chip in my hand blue or not?*) and from the nature of the previous questions given in the task that this is not intended as a request to choose a descriptor for an object, and that you should look for some other interpretive context that will make sense of the question. Thus, the problem is not really "context-reduced"; rather, it requires you to use sensitivity to linguistic form and immediate prior context to construct an appropriate non-routine interpretive context.

Reading Aaronson and Ferres's provocative chapter led me to look more carefully than I had at the Bloom-Au controversy (Au, 1983, 1984, 1985; Bloom, 1981, 1984); this controversy and Aaronson and Ferres's discussion and data got me wondering about the Sapir-Whorf hypothesis—to thinking, in particular, that the usual formulation of the hypothesis needs to be changed.

To begin with, I am more inclined than are Aaronson and Ferres to be skeptical about Bloom's claim of an effect of Chinese syntax on Chinese ways of thought. There are issues of replicability of data to be addressed, as Aaronson and Ferres note. Also, because it would no doubt be possible to demonstrate poor comprehension of ideas in the speakers of any language by rendering these ideas verbally in unperspicuous and/or unidiomatic ways, adjudication is needed of Au's claim that some of Bloom's results are due to his choice of how to express the ideas tested in Chinese.

Nevertheless, from Bloom's data and their own, Aaronson and Ferres make an interesting proposal—that there are far-reaching language-specific differences in verbal processing strategies between Chinese and English speakers. "Far-reaching" is my word, not theirs, but I think it is appropriate because they argue that the processing differences affect performances that would ordinarily be thought to extend beyond language per se, e.g., social communication skills and academic performance.

Now, the existence of language-specific comprehension processes and strategies has become well established, with differences found among several languages, e.g., English, Italian, and Turkish, and appearing already at early stages of development (e.g., Bates et al., 1985; Bates, McNew, MacWhinney, Devescovi, & Smith, 1982; Slobin, 1982). It follows, then, that Aaronson and Ferres's proposal is well anchored in previously established fact. The issue that remains to be argued is how far-reaching the effects of the strategies are. I predict that it will take a long time to settle this issue, and that in the interim the arguments that arise will be many, vigorous, and perhaps bitter, with Bloom-Au an initial engagement.

Although I take no stand on the substance of the issue, I think that the way the controversy is shaping up suggests that there may be something wrong in the way the Sapir-Whorf hypothesis has been discussed in recent years. As usually presented, the hypothesis is graduated in degree in only one way: Slobin (1979), for instance, distinguishes a strong form of the hypothesis, in which language structure *determines* thought, from a weak form, in which language merely influences thought. Although that graduation is appropriate, it leaves the distinction between language and thought as an untouched dichotomy, whereas that dichotomy especially needs to be graduated. Indeed, one of the usual points made about the hypothesis is that, in principle, it requires independent assessment of language and thought—in particular, that "thought" be assessed other than through language, in order to be sure that any effect found is an effect of language on thought, not just an effect of language on language or a correlation between language assessments. Of course, this methodological point stems from, and reinforces, the conception of language and thought as a dichotomy. It is obvious, however, that "language" covers a wide range of cognitive phenomena, and that the distinction between "language" and "non-language" tasks is far from all-or-none.

We have long understood that speakers of different languages have acquired different rule systems. We now know that speakers of different languages have acquired different comprehension processes and strategies, in addition to the different rule systems. In the case of written languages, it is obvious that these language-specific processes must include reading as well as comprehension of spoken language, as Aaronson and Ferres's data confirm. One may surmise that they extend to writing processes and strategies. Thus, language-specific cognitive processes extend over a wide range of linguistic performances, and could well extend quite far into that grey area where language and thought are hard to distinguish. It seems to me, therefore, that rather than of a hypothesis we should speak first of all of a Sapir-Whorf *question:* How deeply and into how wide a range of cognitive processes do language-specific processing differences extend? The Sapir-Whorf hypothesis is that the answer to that question is "Quite deeply and quite widely." Of course, the ultimate answer to the Sapir-Whorf question will be determined by research, and will be much more specific than a simple affirmation or denial of the hypothesis.

REFERENCES

Au, T. K. (1983). Chinese and English counterfactuals: The Sapir-Whorf hypothesis revisited. *Cognition, 15,* 155–187.

Au, T. K. (1984). Counterfactuals: In reply to Alfred Bloom. *Cognition, 17,* 289–302.

Au, T. K. (1985). Language and cognition. In L. L. Lloyd & R. L. Schiefelbusch (Eds.), *Language perspectives II.* Baltimore, MD: University Park Press.

Bachi, R. (1956). A statistical analysis of the revival of Hebrew in Israel. *Scripta Hierosolymitana, 3,* 179–247.

Bates, E., MacWhinney, B., Caselli, C., Devescovi, A., Natale, F., & Venza, V. (1985). *A cross-linguistic study of the development of sentence interpretation strategies.* Unpublished manuscript.

Bates, E., McNew, S., MacWhinney, B., Devescovi, A., & Smith, S. (1982). Functional constants on sentence processing: A cross-linguistic study. *Cognition, 11,* 245–299.

Bloom, A. (1981). *The linguistic shaping of thought: A study in the impact of language on thinking in China and the West.* Hillsdale, NJ: Lawrence Erlbaum Associates.

Bloom, A. (1984). Caution—The words you use may affect what you say: A response to Au. *Cognition, 17,* 275–287.

Braine, M. D. S. (1974). Length constraints, reduction rules, and holophrastic processes in children's word combinations. *Journal of Verbal Learning and Verbal Behavior, 13,* 448–456.

Brown, R., & Bellugi, U. (1964). Three processes in the child's acquisition of syntax. In E. H. Lenneberg (Ed.), *New directions in the study of language.* Cambridge, MA: MIT Press.

Brown, R., & Fraser, C. (1963). The acquisition of syntax. In C. N. Cofer & B. Musgrave (Eds.), *Verbal behavior and learning.* New York: McGraw-Hill.

Flavell, J. H., & Wellman, H. M. (1977). Metamemory. In R. V. Kail & J. W. Hagen (Eds.), *Perspectives on the development of memory and cognition.* Hillsdale, NJ: Lawrence Erlbaum Associates.

Lenneberg, E. H. (1967). *Biological foundations of language.* New York: Wiley.

Osherson, D. N., & Markman, E. M. (1975). Language and the ability to evaluate contradictions and tautologies. *Cognition, 3,* 213–226.

Slobin, D. T. (1979). *Psycholinguistics.* Glenview, IL: Scott Foresman.

Slobin, D. T. (1982). Universal and particular in the acquisition of language. In E. Wanner & L. R. Gleitman (Eds.), *Language acquisition: The state of the art.* Cambridge: Cambridge University Press.

State of Israel. (1963). *Languages, literacy, and educational attainment. Part 1, Publication No. 15, 1961 Population and Housing Census.* Jerusalem: Central Bureau of Statistics.

State of Israel. (1966). *Languages, literacy and educational attainment, Part II, Publication No. 29, 1961 Population and Housing Census.* Jerusalem: Central Bureau of Statistics.

III

BILINGUALISM AND COGNITIVE DEVELOPMENT

The Relationship of Bilingualism to Cognitive Development: Historical, Methodological and Theoretical Considerations

Michael Palij[1]
State University of New York at Stony Brook

Peter Homel
New York University

The ability to know and to use two or more languages fluently and appropriately reflects the remarkable functioning of a cognitive system that maintains separation among the languages being used while at the same time allows free and easy interchange among them. The perplexing complexity of bilingual cognitive functioning is belied by the apparent ease of performance that is manifested by the proficient bilingual. Much basic research still remains to be done before we understand how bilingual cognition operates but there are signs that more and more researchers are being attracted to this area. In contrast, within the related area of how children become bilingual and whether bilingualism has any particular effect on cognitive development, there has been much research and discussion though not complete agreement on the findings. In this chapter we examine this research from three perspectives: first, a historical examination of the issues, highlighting the dramatic changes that have occurred in the past 20 years; second, an examination of methodological issues involved and how they relate to the claims that have been made; third, what role theory has played in guiding research and what role it may play in the future.

A HISTORICAL VIEW

The view that is usually presented of bilingualism and its effect on cognitive development or intellectual functioning in many textbooks and reference works

---

[1]Presently affiliated with the Child Psychopharmacology Unit, Department of Psychiatry, New York University Medical Center

on child development is captured in the following quotation from Ausubel, Sullivan, and Ives (1980):

> The weight of the earlier evidence on bilingualism indicates that it is a retarding factor in language development. . . . A bilingual environment apparently has little effect on the acquisition of language but does lead to later confusion in idea-word relationships and in language structure and to less mature use of language. . . . Much of this language retardation reflects a loss of vocabulary in the first language that is not fully compensated for by a corresponding gain in the second language. . . . Thus, bilingual children possess below average vocabularies in both languages and even their combined vocabulary is generally inferior to the vocabulary of their monolingual counterparts. . . .
>
> Although bilingualism does not inhibit the development of nonverbal intelligence . . . it does have an adverse effect on the growth of functional intelligence as measured by verbal tests. . . . Some of this influence can undoubtedly be attributed to language handicap and socioeconomic factors.

Ausubel et al. do qualify these statements somewhat:

> In view of major gaps in our knowledge, however, any conclusions regarding the effects of bilingualism on the development of language and intellectual development can only be accepted on a highly tentative basis. (pp. 370–371)

This bleak view of childhood bilingualism would certainly cause a parent to have great concern about having a bilingual child. What parent would want to burden a child with these avoidable handicaps?

However, the picture with regard to the cognitive effects of bilingualism, especially in childhood, is not as dismal as the preceding account would lead one to believe; indeed, some would claim that the picture is quite bright and optimistic. What does emerge is a far more complicated picture than most would initially assume. A historical review of the research provides us with the broad outline of the picture and some important details.

The earliest studies that examined the relationship of cognitive or intellectual functioning to bilingualism were conducted during the 1920s (Davies & Hughes, 1927; Saer, 1923; Smith, 1923). These studies and others that followed found that bilingual children, with bilingualism defined in various ways, did more poorly in school relative to their monolingual peers, as well as scoring lower on standard measures of verbal or nonverbal intelligence. This pattern of findings continued to be obtained for the next 40 years or so. Major reviews of the research by Darcy (1953), Jensen (1962), and Weinreich (1953) all reported some negative consequence of bilingualism, the main conclusion being that only verbal intelligence was affected and that bilingual children performed as well as monolingual children on tasks involving nonverbal intelligence. Ausubel et al.

and other writers appear to be relying upon these reviews and some of the early research when they discuss bilingualism in childhood.

A turning point was reached, however, in 1962 with the publication of Peal and Lambert's study of bilingual children in Montreal schools. Their original intention for the study was to document how bilingualism negatively affected intellectual performance so that appropriate remedial programs could be developed. In contrast to many previous studies, Peal and Lambert sought to control many factors that could artificially produce differences between bilingual and monolingual children. Subjects in both groups were matched on socioeconomic class, sex, age, and, whenever possible, children from the same school or school system were used. Another novel feature of their study was that Peal and Lambert only used bilingual children who were balanced in their ability to use both languages. Also, their measures of intelligence included tests that were standardized on French-speaking children from Montreal.

On the basis of the previous research it was expected that the bilingual children would be inferior to monolingual children on most measures of verbal intelligence and, perhaps, would be equivalent on measures of nonverbal intelligence. Instead, the bilingual group performed significantly better than the monolingual group on most of the measures (on the remainder there were no differences between the groups). On the measures of verbal intelligence the bilingual children performed significantly *better* than the monolingual children.

A more detailed analysis of the results led Peal and Lambert to conclude that the performance advantages shown by the bilingual children might be the result of greater mental flexibility and a more diversified structure of intellect (Guilford, 1956). In their conclusion they state:

> The picture that emerges of the French-English bilingual in Montreal is that of a youngster whose wider experiences in two cultures have given him advantages that a monolingual does not enjoy. Intellectually his experience with two language systems seems to have left him with a mental flexibility, a superiority in concept formation, and a more diversified set of mental abilities, in the sense that the patterns of abilities developed by bilinguals were more heterogeneous. It is not possible to state whether the more intelligent child became bilingual or whether bilingualism aided his intellectual development, but there is no question about the fact that he is superior intellectually. In contrast, the monolingual appears to have a more unitary structure of intelligence which he must use for all types of intellectual tasks. (p. 20)

And so a trend reverses.

Subsequent studies have tended to replicate and amplify the results of Peal and Lambert. They roughly follow two lines of research: field studies involving large samples of children and experimental studies with small samples. We briefly review examples of both.

A major field study that provided further confirmation for Peal and Lambert's findings and also established the now well known language immersion program of second language acquisition was the St. Lambert experimental school program (Lambert & Tucker, 1972). In this program English monolingual children were enrolled into a 5-year program of bilingual instruction and yearly evaluation, starting with kindergarten and ending with the fourth grade. They were matched with monolingual English-speaking children in a monolingual English curriculum and monolingual French-speaking children in a monolingual French curriculum. Children in the three groups were matched on social class variables and nonverbal intelligence while in kindergarten. (Note: children were entered into the immersion group because their parents had sought a bilingual education for their monolingual children; Lambert and Tucker helped to establish such a program and located the control groups.)

The experimental group (i.e., English monolingual children in the bilingual instruction curriculum) were instructed only in French in kindergarten and the first grade. In the second grade, instruction in English Language Arts was begun and served as the only classroom instruction in English. Instruction in English increased for the experimental group until the fourth grade where half of the classroom time was spent in English. The English and French monolingual controls received all instruction in their native language. The curriculum for the control groups was the standard one used within the school system whereas the experimental group followed the standard French school curriculum when being instructed in French and followed the standard English curriculum when instructed in English.

Testing was conducted yearly to examine the achievement levels and attitudes of the immersion group children and their counterparts. However, because of space limitations, we concentrate on the main results of the immersion program at the end of the fifth year. Testing at the end of the fourth grade revealed the following:

1. The experimental group's level of English proficiency in such areas as word knowledge, language usage, and so forth, was equivalent to that of the English control group and both groups scored above the 80th percentile on national norms. The experimental group also did not differ from the English controls in ability to form word associations, ability to retell or invent short stories in English, and command of rhythm, intonation, enunciation, and overall expression. The children in the experimental group, who were English language natives, did not suffer any impairments in their English language ability as a result of the bilingual immersion program. Indeed, they performed as well as monolingual English children and at a relatively high level on some tests.

2. When compared to the French Control Group the experimental group matched their performance in such areas as vocabulary, listening comprehension, and knowledge of French concepts. The experimental group was somewhat

poorer at oral expression, in rhythm, intonation, and overall expression, when retelling short stories in French. These factors are improved when the child is asked to invent a story and to tell it in French. The experimental group's word associations in French were as rapid, mature, and appropriate as the French control children and they had a comparable degree of comprehension of themes and plots in stories. Although the experimental group was more prone to make errors of production in expressing gender and contraction, overall their ability was quite similar to the French controls. In essence, the originally English native experimental group children were functionally bilingual by the end of the fourth grade.

3. Performance in a nonlanguage subject such as mathematics indicates that the experimental group (which was taught math in French) performed at the same level as the French control group with both groups scoring above the 80th percentile on national norms.

4. On measures of general intelligence the experimental group matched the monolingual control groups. The experimental group also seemed more capable of generating more imaginative and unusual uses for everyday objects, regardless of the language of the test.

It was also noted that the bilingual children could readily transfer a skill learned in one language to usage in the other language. For example, though children were initially taught reading and arithmetic in French, the children were almost immediately able to read and do arithmetic in English when it was introduced. On this point, Lambert and Tucker speculate that a higher level of abstract cognitive processing might exist that allows the transmission of information between languages. This was significant because it showed that cognitive skills did not depend upon the language in which the skill was acquired.

The results of the St. Lambert project have been so dramatic and influential that this type of bilingual curriculum, generally known as a total immersion program, has been implemented in some areas of the United States and Puerto Rico. Though the results from these new programs are often similar to those of the St. Lambert project, not all of them have been successful. McLaughlin (1978) reviews some of these studies and examines how they differ from the St. Lambert Project, both in method and result.

The original finding by Lambert and Peal of some form of cognitive enhancement or flexibility on the part of bilingual children had spurred researchers in Canada and other countries to replicate these findings under controlled experimental conditions. Much of this research has focused on whether bilingual children have greater ability in manipulating language, or metalinguistic awareness, relative to monolingual children.

Ianco-Worrall (1972) reported two experiments on South African monolingual (either English or Afrikaaner) and bilingual (English-Afrikaaner) children in which the children were tested on their awareness of the arbitrary assignment of phonemic labels to objects and whether they were more attuned to the phonemic or semantic dimensions of words. The children ranged in age from 4 to 9 years and each bilingual child was matched with an English monolingual and an Afrikaaner monolingual with respect to intelligence, age, sex, school grade, and social class. In one experiment the children were given a "standard" word followed by two "choice" words: one phonetically related to the standard, the other semantically related to the standard. In the second experiment a variation of a word substitution task initially described by Vygotsky was used to determine the extent to which the children could accept the interchange of names for objects. Ianco-Worrall found that the bilingual children were aware of the arbitrary nature of names at an earlier age than the monolingual control groups and the bilingual children were more attentive to the semantic relationships between words than the monolingual children who focused more on phonemic similarities.

Ben-Zeev (1977), working with children in Israel and the U.S. who were bilingual in Hebrew and English, again found that bilingual children were superior to monolingual children on name substitution for objects (e.g., using the label "macaroni" to refer to the object "cow"). Further, on a verbal transformation task that consisted of the repeated presentation of two nonsense words, bilingual subjects reported more verbal transformations and at an earlier point in the task than the monolingual children (in this case verbal transformation refers to perceived changes in the presented nonsense stimulus, which remains constant). This finding is usually interpreted as indicating ability to rapidly reorganize perceptions. The bilingual children, therefore, were better able to reorganize their perception of the nonsense stimulus, a response that is more similar to older children and adults. On a task involving the description of a matrix of forms varying on two dimensions (e.g., cylinders varying in height and width) and the transposition of the matrix to its mirror image, the bilingual children were also better able to identify the underlying dimensions of the matrix and were better able to describe the process of transforming one form of the matrix to its transpose.

Cummins, in several reports (e.g., Cummins, 1978; Cummins & Mulcahy, 1978) and in his chapter in this volume, has conducted much important research on the question of whether bilingual children actually do have greater metalinguistic awareness than monolingual children. One consequence of this research, however, has been to raise some serious questions as to what one means by metalinguistic awareness and whether it can be adequately defined and measured. The reader is urged to read Cummins' chapter for a review of his work and a statement of his present theoretical position.

The main conclusion drawn from these studies is that the bilingual child appears to be more aware of language functions at an earlier age and has a more analytical approach to the use and comprehension of language.

Several other studies have examined the ways in which bilingual children are superior to monolingual children on various other measures of cognitive performance. Torrance, Wu, Gowan, and Alliotti (1970) were able to administer foreign language versions of the Torrance Test of Creative Thinking to over 1,000 Chinese and Malayan monolingual and bilingual children in the third, fourth, and fifth grades in Singapore. The second language of the bilinguals was English. The children were scored for figural fluency, flexibility, originality, and elaboration. The monolingual children were superior to the bilingual children on figural fluency and flexibility and the bilinguals were superior on figural origi-nality and somewhat better on figural elaboration.

Landry (1974) also used the Torrance Test with a U.S. sample where the bilingual children came from a Foreign Language in the Elementary School (FLES) program. Children were drawn from the first, fourth, and sixth grades (the language that the children were learning in the classroom was not mentioned in the report). The children were given both verbal and figural forms of the tasks involving fluency, flexibility, and originality. He found that the sixth-grade FLES children scored significantly higher on all of the tasks than the mono-lingual children whereas the fourth-grade FLES children only indicated a nonsig-nificant trend in the same direction. No differences were obtained between the FLES children and the monolingual children in the first grade. The FLES experi-ence appears to provide some form of cognitive enrichment as measured by the Torrance Test of Creative Thinking.

Cummins and Gulutsan (1974) present the results of an experiment that tested for differences between bilinguals and monolinguals on aspects of memory, reasoning, and divergent thinking. They found that bilinguals demonstrated greater verbal ability, performed better on measures of concept formation, and scored higher on measures of verbal originality. The only difference found between the groups in performance on memory tasks was that the monolinguals were better able to recall abstract words than bilinguals. In sum, these studies all make the point that bilingualism has some sort of enhancing effect on cognitive development.

How is it then that it is still commonly believed that bilingualism has only negative effects on cognitive development? There are probably several reasons. First, there is always a lag between the publication of research in journals and its appearance in secondary sources such as textbooks. Although the work of Peal and Lambert and the results of the St. Lambert project have been available for quite a while, this research may be seen as more relevant to educational psychol-ogy, and the implications for developmental psychology may take longer to be drawn. Second, although an important topic, research on childhood bilingualism and biculturalism has never been a major component in mainstream American psychology. As has been discussed elsewhere in this volume (Chapter 2) the culture of the United States has had an ambivalent attitude toward the mainte-nance of languages of minority groups. Since the culture undervalues bi-lingualism in general it is not surprising that specific disciplines undervalue the study of such topics. However, as evidence accumulates on the specific effects of bilingualism a more balanced portrayal of it is bound to appear.

METHODOLOGICAL CONSIDERATIONS

An important factor accounting for the differences in the results between the earlier studies and the results of Lambert and Peal (1962) and later researchers is the quality of the methodology used. In many of the early studies, variables other than bilingualism can be identified that can account for the inferior performance of bilinguals. For example, Saer (1923) had collected information about the socioeconomic status of the children's family, the language used at home, and the age of the children but there was no matching of monolingual and bilingual children on these variables. In some other studies the determination of whether a child was bilingual or not was based upon either the nationality of the parent (Pintner & Keller, 1922) or the surname of the child (Pintner, 1932). This is in marked contrast to the methods of Peal and Lambert; they had attempted to control for a number of background variables as well as language proficiency.

It is as easy to forestall discussion of methodology in this area as it is in any content area in psychology: though research methods form the skeleton for every study, it is the issue being discussed that is the meat. Yet, when one realizes that the major change in our understanding of the relationship of bilingualism to cognitive development hinged on the usage of rigorous methods, one must stop and ask how methodology, apart from theoretical insight into the problem under study, will be able to further our understanding. Such an evaluation of our current methodological tools might allow us to decide whether we can answer a question such as "Is there a casual link between bilingualism and cognitive development?" If it is answerable, what sort of methodology will have to be used?

First of all, it must be noted that a true experiment can never be conducted to determine what sort of relationship exists between bilingualism and cognitive development. A *true* experiment, in the traditional sense (e.g., Fisher, 1935), is defined by the high degree of control a researcher has in defining the experimental conditions and eliminating unwanted, confounding factors. But the most important component of this type of study is the random assignment of subjects to conditions. If we were to conduct this sort of experiment, the mode of language acquisition would be defined as an independent variable; various background variables would be manipulated as control variables, and performance on measures of cognitive processing would be the dependent variables. Obviously, children could never be randomly assigned to different language learning situations (such as single-language conditions, separate bilingual, intermixed bilingual, etc.) nor could an experimenter manipulate such important variables as the socioeconomic level of the family, the degree of exposure to the different languages, intelligence of the parents, cultural support for language usage in the community, and so on.

If we cannot use mode of language acquisition as an independent variable might we not simply equate subjects on major background variables, attempt to identify subjects with homogeneous language-learning backgrounds, and then run them through an experimental task? The problem here is whether we can identify the crucial background variables that need to be controlled. Even if we can identify them, what method of control should be used? Matching the subjects may not always be possible, and statistical adjustment, which may be made on a legitimate mathematical basis, may not always make either ecological or theoretical sense. This type of cross-sectional design may allow us to identify sources of differences between monolinguals and bilinguals on various cognitive tasks but one may not be able to explain why the differences exist.

The traditional type of experimental design that most psychologists use is therefore inadequate in assessing the relationship of bilingualism to cognitive development. The small sample studies of researchers like Ianco-Worrall (1972), Ben-Zeev (1977) and others provide only a snapshot of the bilingual child's development. Cross-sectional experiments of this sort are useful when they are conducted to test specific predictions, such as replicating the finding of greater cognitive flexibility or metalinguistic awareness, but in this situation the value of such studies is based on their relationship to other studies that have taken a longitudinal approach. In sum, cross-sectional experiments can provide valuable descriptions of processes operating at a single point in time as well as establishing differences between groups, but they cannot tell us how those processes or differences developed.

Though true experiments are not possible in this area, we can still test hypotheses about the relationship of bilingualism to cognitive development through the use of longitudinal quasi-experiments such as the St. Lambert project. Systematic study of bilingual and monolingual children over long periods of time will provide important data about both groups, but differences between the two groups can never be completely accounted for because, obviously, not all variables can be controlled. For example, in the St. Lambert project differences between the experimental and control groups were minimized as much as possible, but there is no guarantee that some unknown but influential confounding variable did not cause the differences to emerge between the groups.

A researcher may attempt to statistically control for the effects of background variables through the analysis of covariance or multiple regression analysis, but a researcher can never be sure that all of the relevant variables have been included in the analysis. Nor is there any guarantee that results from such analyses have much external validity or generalizability since the statistical control of background variables may produce results that are mathematically correct but ecologically irrelevant (e.g., bilinguals may outperform monolinguals on certain tasks after socioeconomic status is factored out but in real life we cannot remove the effects of SES).

The use of more sophisticated mathematical procedures such as path analysis (Li, 1975), so-called causal analysis (Heise, 1975), and structural equation modeling (Bentler, 1980; Joreskog & Sorbom, 1979) will not provide a complete solution. In these methods specific models are postulated for a set of data. Within these models relationships among variables are specified and then statistical tests are conducted to determine whether the models agree with or fit the data. When the model indicates a lack of fit with the data, a researcher can use this result to eliminate the model from further consideration. Because a model can represent a set of hypotheses or a theory, the rejection of the model is tantamount to the rejection of a particular theory. But obtaining a model that fits the data adequately does not serve as confirmation of the underlying theory for the model (remember, you can only reject the null hypothesis; inability to reject it does not mean it is true). In general, structural equation modeling will not be able to tell a researcher what is the true set of relationships among variables but gives one the option of "fitting various models with different numbers of parameters and of deciding when to stop fitting" (p. 48, Joreskog, 1979). Enough data and theoretical insight into relationships among factors may eventually give rise to models that mirror reality more accurately, but much groundwork needs to be laid before this is realized.

No single type of research design, either true experiment or quasi-experimental longitudinal study, will provide us with information about the link between bilingualism and cognitive development. However, a combination of the two will help to establish it: longitudinal designs will provide information about the general nature of the relationship, such as the beneficial effects reported by Lambert and others, and true experiments will allow the testing of specific hypotheses that will provide necessary detail on the relationship.

One could argue that as more studies of both types are produced, the greater the evidence for a particular model or theory relating bilingualism to cognitive development. This argument would be misleading. Just as studies prior to Peal and Lambert seemed to lead to an overwhelming conclusion (which appears to be false) it is possible that current and future studies may seem to lead to an equally overwhelming but false conclusion. The problem in this case is not with the methodological rigor of the research but with how research issues are defined, which in turn directs attention toward one set of variables and away from other variables. An example of such a problem can be seen in how some researchers have reacted to the finding of positive cognitive effects from bilingualism.

For methodological reasons, MacNab (1979) has taken issue with the results of the Peal and Lambert study and others that purport to show a cognitive enhancement effect. Basically, MacNab has argued that the quasi-experimental or associational methodology used in some of these studies does not allow one to determine the direction of the casual arrow (i.e., does bilingualism improve cognition by increasing certain functions or do brighter people become bilingual). Other factors, such as learning a second language later in life, which would prevent "balance" in both languages and self-selection of subjects in some of the studies, could also compromise the studies. MacNab does not feel that bilingualism is necessarily a bad thing, rather he takes issue with the contention that there is unambiguous evidence for positive consequences from bilingualism.

From the discussion of methodology earlier in this section the reader should be able to appreciate two points: (a) MacNab's criticisms have some validity given the types of designs used and (b) the type of evidence that MacNab seems to be asking for before he is convinced that bilingualism has some effect on cognition is almost impossible to obtain at this time. On the latter point, a true experiment might convince a researcher like MacNab, but for obvious reasons, such a thing cannot be done. Ultimately, the convergence of results from different rigorous studies with solid theoretical modeling will provide the basis for elucidating the relationship between cognitive functioning and bilingualism.

However, the reader should be aware that this type of argument, of whether bilingualism has beneficial or detrimental effects, causes one to focus on a logically secondary issue. The primary issue is how the cognitive system accommodates the usage of two or more languages. It could be that a bilingual cognitive system has to be involved in types of processing that a monolingual never has to engage in, such as translation between languages. How this translation process operates, along with its costs and benefits, is of greater practical and theoretical interest than whether there is some ambiguous cognitive benefit. Indeed, it is only by examining the costs and benefits of the specific processes needed for bilingual cognition that we can make any statement about the "good" or "bad" effects of bilingualism. In all likelihood there will probably be no clearcut evidence for overwhelming positive or negative consequences; instead, we may see a subtle interplay between the costs and benefits for the processes involved. Such a concern is lost if one gets mired down in a debate about whether bilingualism is good or bad.

It must also be acknowledged that the argument about the merits of bilingualism, its cognitive benefits and costs, occurs within a social context that is not neutral in its view on the desirability of having a bilingual populace (see the chapter by Homel and Palij in this volume on bilingualism and social policy for a greater discussion of this issue). In those communities where bilingualism is both desired and viewed as being necessary, bilingualism will be fostered and maintained regardless of the costs. Similarly, in those communities where bilingualism is denigrated and unwanted, bilingualism will be stifled regardless of any benefit it may provide. Researchers should be sensitive to whether the questions they are asking are truly fundamental to the phenomenon they are studying, or are motivated solely by the socio-political views of their community.

THEORETICAL ASPECTS

The traditional focus on the relationship of bilingualism to cognitive functioning has been motivated by empirical findings and not by theoretical considerations. Several factors seem to have been operating to cause this. One reason for this has been the context in which the research has been conducted. Many of the studies come from applied areas such as educational or clinical psychology that had to confront the reality of having to deal with bilingual children who were not performing at the same levels as monolingual children. Unfortunately, the foreign language that the child spoke or the ethnic background of the child was perceived as being the source of the difficulty instead of other factors such as socioeconomic status of the child's family. Experimental psychology was ill-prepared to address the possible connection between bilingualism and cognition because it simply was not prepared to do so until relatively recently. Again, some history may clarify this point.

The study of language functioning and cognitive processing as we know it today is the result of several factors that appeared in the 1950s. Among the most important of these was the application of information theory, both its mathematics and theoretical framework, to problems in psychology, and the use of computers and programming as a means of studying human cognition. The predominant influence in experimental psychology prior to this time, as well as for some time to come, had been behaviorism, in variant forms, with an accompanying philosophical framework based on logical positivism. With the desire to model the psychological sciences after the physical sciences, a rigorous implementation of strict empiricism forced many researchers to focus on behavior and to ignore or downplay unobservable cognitive processes. There were some exceptions, such as the gestalt psychologists, who felt this was an unnaturally restrictive view of the mind, as well as a mistaken understanding of how the physical sciences developed (which, they argued, allowed for many unobservables), but they tended to be in the minority. Consequently, instead of language acquisition we had verbal learning, instead of language processing we had verbal behavior, and instead of transformation grammars we had verbal conditioning.

With the work of Chomsky in linguistics, Newell and Simon in human problem solving, and others like George Miller, Ulric Neisser, and so forth, an alternative framework was slowly established that allowed a fuller consideration of more theoretical issues in human cognition. This framework provided a rigorous means for stating and testing hypotheses about unobservable cognitive processes that showed them to be neither metaphysical nor supernatural. But, though this framework of cognitive psychology is apparent to us today, its influence in other areas of psychology was slow to develop. As shown in the earlier section on historical considerations, it is the bilingualism research of the 1970s that begins to ask questions emanating from a contemporary framework of cognitive psychology. Recall that Lambert and Peal were not concerned with testing hypotheses about the negative cognitive consequences of bilingualism: rather they wanted to get a clear description of what these negative consequences were so that a program of remediation could be developed. And in the case of the St. Lambert project, the original motivation was to establish an educational curriculum that would produce bilingual children, not to test any particular theory of second language acquisition. However, because of the results from these studies, other researchers went on to replicate the results and to test hypotheses based upon cognitive theory.

In sum, the absence of a full theoretical treatment of the relationship of bilingualism to cognitive processing can be attributed, in part, to the late development of appropriate cognitive theories to researchers in the area.

A second reason is that the measures often employed, such as standardized intelligence tests, do not tell us about the specific cognitive processes involved in performance on the tests. For example, the extraction of a verbal factor from a series of tests, which on their face require the processing of linguistic information, does not tell us what forms that processing takes. All that it can tell us is that a common process might be underlying the responses made to questions on the tests. Indeed, the use of such factors obscures the very real differences in strategies that people might employ. The algorithmic specification of processes, the explicit statement of cognitive components and related processes, is a recent innovation derived from the application of information processing theory to human cognition. Although such an approach is mechanistic and computationally oriented it has the benefit of identifying specific mechanisms that hopefully can be manipulated in experiments. Instead of hypothesizing a generalized verbal factor we can now inquire about how a person processes linguistic information and how the processing varies as a function of the type of linguistic information.

A third reason for the delay in the development of an adequate theoretical framework for bilingual cognition is culturally based: There is a popular conception that the U.S. is primarily a culturally homogeneous, English-speaking nation and that foreign languages and ethnic identities fall by the wayside as each individual is transformed into a typical English-speaking "American." This is exemplified by the English-first groups, which want to pass an amendment to the constitution mandating that English be recognized as the official language of the U.S. (the U.S. does not have a legally recognized official language, unlike Canada, which has a legally mandated policy of bilingualism). As noted elsewhere in this volume, the U.S. officially views bilingualism as a transitional phase in the lives of people living in the U.S. and thus bilingualism is undervalued. Research into such a marginal area is not well supported or encouraged. Because of such a context both research and theory building are unlikely to develop to any great extent. It is expected that significant progress on issues relating bilingualism to cognitive development and processing will be made in countries like Canada where there is not only academic support for research into such issues but cultural approval of such activities.

With respect to present-day theory, Segalowitz (1981) outlines some of the frameworks that have been developed in studying bilingual development: Taylor's (1974) network model, which is based on the Norman and Rumelhart (1975) model of semantic memory; Slobin's (1973) theory of language acquisition in which children acquire strategies which orient them to salient cues in language acquisition contexts; and Brown's (1973) work on cognitive factors in monolingual language acquisition. The defining feature of a theory of bilingual development is that it takes as its starting point not the experience of monolingual development but the special circumstances associated with the bilingual experience. A unique aspect of bilingual cognitive development that has no counterpart in monolingual experience is language interaction in the cognitive system and we focus on that in this section.

What is remarkable about bilingual cognition is the ability to maintain language separation while allowing ready intermixing of the languages. Various schemes have been developed to account for this ability but none seem to have been particularly persuasive. The best known of these schemes is the compound-coordinate distinction, which was originally developed by Weinreich (1953) and elaborated on by Ervin and Osgood (1954). A compound bilingual was one who learned both languages in the same environment from birth. The experience was supposed to form a single system for the two languages. Originally, this formulation was in terms of verbal mediation theory but was later discarded in favor of the notion of a single interdependent memory store for both languages. For the compound bilingual the two languages in the cognitive system should have relatively easy and frequent interaction with each other (though it has never been clear whether the interaction takes place only at one level of language representation, such as the semantic level, or whether it takes place at all levels, e.g., phonemic, graphemic, syntactic, etc.). The coordinate bilingual is one who learned one language from birth and learned the second language later in life in contexts different from those of the first language. This separation in learning contexts would have caused the separation of languages in the cognitive system, indicating that very little interaction occurs between the two languages; that is, each language would have its own independent storage area in memory.

Support for this compound-coordinate distinction has been inconsistent, and some researchers dismiss it as being irrelevant to understanding how bilingualism affects cognition. Recent research indicates that bilingual cognition may in fact have features of both, that is, language intermixture and separation, but in different areas of the cognitive system. Studies using the lexical decision paradigm have produced some very interesting data in this regard. Palij (1980) has shown that French-English bilinguals produce a semantic facilitation effect on a bilingual version of the lexical decision task that is independent of the subject's learning history (i.e., compound and coordinate bilinguals both provided substantial facilitation effects). The semantic facilitation effect, the faster recognition of a second word after first seeing a semantically related word (e.g., faster recognition time to *doctor* after just seeing *nurse*), in the bilingual situation (i.e., first seeing the translation of *doctor* and then seeing the English word *doctor*) indicates that the languages share a common semantic store. Meaning for words and other concepts seem to be represented in an abstract form across languages and related concepts as "closer together" in semantic memory regardless of the language of origin. This finding dovetails with those reported earlier by Lambert and Tucker in the transfer of skills learned in one language to the other language of the bilinguals.

Other research (Scarborough, Gerard, & Cortese, 1984) indicates that one level at which languages are separated is at the sensory representation level (by sensory level representation we follow the usage developed by Nelson, 1979, where the visual and phonemic mental representation of words constitutes the sensory level). Using a lexical decision task, but without varying semantic relatedness, Scarborough has shown that repetition effects occur more readily within languages than they do between languages. Repetition effects refer to faster recognition times for words that are presented several times during the course of the experiment. Repetitions that are close together (e.g., the repetition occurring immediately or after the presentation of a single intervening different word) produce faster reaction times than repetitions with greater separation (more words between repetitions). In the bilingual context this finding suggests that the sensory features of languages are organized on the basis of featural similarity. Since words within a language are more similar to each other, because of common rules of phonetics and orthography, it is not surprising that there is reduced language interaction at the sensory level.

Yet another level of language interaction that is particularly interesting is that of syntactic interaction. At this level there are several questions: Do the rules of syntax remain separate for the two languages? Does the syntax of one language have some effect on the productions of the other language? For languages with radically different underlying syntactic systems (e.g., Chinese and English) how do productions in one language map onto productions in the other language (how does translation occur)?

Research on the effect of one syntax upon another in cognition comes from several sources. Bates and MacWhinney (1981) examined how the surface role of the sentence subject is differentially determined in English, Italian, and German. For example, it was found that Italians primarily used animacy as a cue in interpreting simple sentences whereas Americans (English) primarily relied upon the ordering of the words in the sentence. This type of strategy clearly differentiates the two groups. This type of information can be used to determine whether, say, an Italian-American bilingual utilizes an Italian interpretation strategy while functioning in English, which Bates and MacWhinney go on to demonstrate.

Additional examples of such interactions are provided in other chapters of this book. Hakuta (this volume) deals with a variety of issues related to syntactic interaction. Aaronson and Ferres (this volume) examine the related issues with regard to the interaction of Chinese and English.

The importance of these studies is that they focus on the specific features of languages and how the cognitive system adapts to these features. In the bilingual child not only does the cognitive system have to adapt to each of the languages that the child knows, but it must also accommodate the joint functioning of the two languages. The interaction of the two languages may be specific to the languages under consideration. That is, the interactions found in the Chinese-English bilingual may not be the same as those found in the French-English bilingual. The situation is obviously more complicated when dealing with tri-linguals and multilinguals. Interactions among the languages in these individuals may be simple extensions of the two-way interactions seen in bilinguals or may represent higher order interactions among all of the languages.

Clearly, these concerns go far beyond the simple question of whether bilingualism has beneficial or negative cognitive consequences. It is perhaps more reasonable to assume that bilingualism will have both some negative consequences and some positive consequences; the determination of what is negative and positive being conditioned by the specific variables being studied and, perhaps, the age of the child being tested.

CONCLUSIONS

What can we conclude about the relationship between bilingualism and cognitive development? This much seems to be clear: Bilingualism does not seem to have any major detrimental cognitive consequences in and of itself. There is evidence for the assertion that bilingualism may have some beneficial cognitive consequences in the form of enhanced language awareness and greater flexibility in its usage. Nonetheless, the magnitude of such benefits should not be overemphasized until we have more detailed information on its nature. It is inarguable that bilingualism has some sort of influence on the organization of information in the cognitive system and how that information is processed, but much more research is needed to elaborate on what this influence is like. Should we think of language as something that categorizes cognitive functioning (i.e., separates storage areas, processes) and requires unique processing (e.g., translation processes) or have we made too much of language as a conceptual entity, only to find that knowledge of more than one language makes no special demands on the cognitive system? That being a bilingual makes cognitive demands that are similar to, though not identical to, knowing and being able to use mathematics or music? And when was the last time you heard someone discussing the cognitive costs and benefits of knowing those subjects?

ACKNOWLEDGMENT

We would like to thank Doris Aaronson for reading and commenting on earlier drafts of this chapter.

REFERENCES

Ausubel, D. P., Sullivan, E. V., & Ives S. W. (1980). *Theory and problems of child development* (3rd ed.). New York: Grune & Stratton.

Bates, E., & MacWhinney, B. (1981). Second-language acquisition from a functionalist perspective: Pragmatic, semantic, and perceptual strategies. In H. Winitz (Ed.), *Native language and foreign language acquisition, Annals of the New York Academy of Sciences* (Vol. 379, pp. 190–214).

Ben-Zeev, S. (1977). The influence of bilingualism on cognitive strategy and cognitive development. *Child Development, 48,* 1009–1018.

Bentler, P. M. (1980). Multivariate analysis with latent variables: Causal modelling. *Annual Review of Psychology, 31,* 419–456.

Brown, R. (1973). *A first language: The early stages.* Cambridge, MA: Harvard University Press.

Cummins, J. (1978). Bilingualism and the development of metalinguistic awareness. *Journal of Cross-Cultural Psychology, 9,* 131–149.

Cummins, J., & Gulutsan, M. (1974). Some effect of bilingualism on cognitive functioning. In S. T. Carey (Ed.), *Bilingualism, biculturalism, and education.* Proceedings of the conference at College Universitaire Saint-Jean, The University of Alberta, Canada.

Cummins, J., & Mulcahy, R. (1978). Orientation to language in Ukrainian-English bilingual children. *Child Development, 49,* 1239–1242.

Darcy, N. T. (1953). A review of the literature on the effects of bilingualism upon the measurement of intelligence. *Journal of Genetic Psychology, 82,* 21–57.

Davies, M., & Hughes, A. G. (1927). An investigation into the comparative intelligence and attainments of Jewish and non-Jewish school children. *British Journal of Psychology, 18,* 134–146.

Ervin, S. M., & Osgood, C. E. (1954). Second language learning and bilingualism. *Journal of Abnormal and Social Psychology, 49,* 139–146.

Fisher, R. A. (1935). *The design of experiments* (3rd ed.) Edinburgh: Oliver & Boyd.

Guilford, J. P. (1956). The structure of intellect. *Psychological Bulletin, 53,* 267–293.

Heise, D. R. (1975). *Causal analysis.* New York: John Wiley.

Ianco-Worrall, A. D. (1972). Bilingualism and cognitive development. *Child Development, 43,* 1390–1400.

Jensen, A. R. (1962). The effects of childhood bilingualism. *Elementary Education, 39,* 132–143, 358–366.

Joreskog, K. G. (1979). Analyzing psychological data by structural analysis of covariance matrices. In K. G. Joreskog & D. Sorbom (Eds.), *Advances in factor analysis and structural equation models.* Cambridge, MA: Abt Books.

Joreskog, K. G., & Sorbom D. (1979). *Advances in factor analysis and structural equation models.* Cambridge, MA: Abt Books.

Lambert, W. E., & Tucker, G. R. (1972). *Bilingual education of children: The St. Lambert experiment.* Rowley, MA: Newbury House.

Landry, R. G. (1974). A comparison of 2nd-language learners and monolinguals on divergent thinking tasks at the elementary school level. *Modern Language Journal, 58,* 10–15.

Li, C. C. (1975). *Path analysis—A primer.* Pacific Grove, CA: Boxwood Press.

MacNab, G. L. (1979). Cognition and bilingualism: A reanalysis of studies. *Linguistics, 17,* 213–255.

McLaughlin, B. (1978). *Second-language acquisition in childhood.* Hillsdale, NJ: Lawrence Erlbaum Associates.

Nelson, D. L. (1979). Remembering pictures and words: Appearance, significance, and name. In L. S. Cermak & F. I. M. Craik (Eds.) *Levels of processing in human memory* (pp. 45–76). Hillsdale, NJ: Lawrence Erlbaum Associates.

Norman, D., & Rumelhart, D. (1975). *Explorations in cognition*. San Francisco: W. H. Freeman.

Palij, M. (1980). *Semantic facilitation on a bilingual lexical decision task*. Stony Brook: State University of New York. (ERIC Document Reproduction Service No. ED 192 611)

Peal, E., & Lambert, W. E. (1962). The relation of bilingualism to intelligence. *Psychological Monographs, 76*(27, Whole No. 546).

Pinter, R. (1932). The influence of language background in intelligence tests. *Journal of Social Psychology, 3*, 235–240.

Pinter, R., & Keller, R. (1922). Intelligence tests of foreign children. *Journal of Educational Psychology, 13*, 214–222.

Saer, D. J. (1923). The effects of bilingualism on intelligence. *British Journal of Psychology, 14*, 25–38.

Scarborough, D. L., Gerard, L., & Cortese, C. (1984). Independence of lexical access in bilingual word recognition. *Journal of Verbal Learning and Verbal Behavior, 23*, 84–99.

Segalowitz, N. S. (1981). Issues in the cross-cultural study of bilingual development. In H. C. Triandis & A. Heron (Eds.), *Handbook of cross-cultural psychology: Vol. 4, Developmental psychology* (pp. 55–92). Boston: Allyn & Bacon.

Slobin, D. (1973). Cognitive prerequisites for the development of grammar. In C. A. Fergueson & D. Slobin (Eds.), *Studies of child language development* (pp. 175–208). New York: Holt, Rinehart & Winston.

Smith, F. (1923). Bilingualism and mental development. *British Journal of Psychology, 13*, 270–282.

Taylor, M. (1974). Speculations on bilingualism and the cognitive network. *Working Papers in Bilingualism, 2*, 68–124.

Torrance, E., Wu, J.M., Gowan, J.C., & Alliotti, N.C. (1970). Creative functioning of monolingual and bilingual children in Singapore. *Journal of Educational Psychology, 61*, 72–75.

Weinreich, U. (1953). *Languages in contact*. New York: Linguistic Circle of New York.

Bilingualism, Cognitive Function, and Language Minority Group Membership

Edward De Avila
Linguametrics Group, San Raphael, CA

INTRODUCTION

The study of childhood bilingualism may be described as having both theoretical and applied importance. With respect to theoretical interests, researchers have studied the relationship between bilingualism and various cognitive processes such as intellectual development and cognitive style. On the applied side, researchers have used results from theoretical studies to design and test hypotheses regarding the effectiveness of different treatment approaches such as those found in bilingual education. The purpose of this chapter is to discuss a number of issues related to both theoretical and applied interests in the intellectual and social functioning of bilingual children in school. The chapter is presented in two major sections. In the first, we make a few introductory comments regarding the study of bilingual students. In the second section, we review the results of a number of studies conducted at the Center for Educational Studies (CERAS) at Stanford University over the past 5 years that have addressed several important theoretical and applied questions within the context of an educational program designed to accommodate the linguistic and educational heterogeneity of ethnolinguistic minority students.

BACKGROUND OF STUDIES

A substantial number of sources have documented the poor academic performance of language minority students in the United States. Similarly, a good number of researchers have attempted to explain this poor performance. Of particular interest to the present discussion is the widespread belief that somehow language minority students are at an academic disadvantage by virtue of intellectual, verbal, motivational, and cognitive style-differences that have been equated with bilingualism. Unfortunately, studies offered in support of this contention have tended to confound both poverty and ethnolinguistic group membership with linguistic proficiency. De Avila and Duncan (1980) reviewed over 100 studies on the effects of bilingualism conducted in the United States over the past 50 years and found that in only a few cases (four) was the actual extent of "bilingualism" assessed. With rare exception, subjects were grouped on the basis of ethnicity, assuming language proficiency.

A concrete example of this confusion is found in a recent article where Mestre, Gerace, and Lochhead (1982) found that even though the bilinguals (i.e., balanced) were . . . nearly equivalent in both Spanish and English, the level of proficiency in either language for the bilingual group was substantially below the level of the monolingual group in English. In other words, to the extent bilingualism means proficiency in two languages, this group of "Hispanic bilinguals" was not bilingual. The review of problems associated with the definition and bilingualism by De Avila and Duncan (1980) cites numerous examples of this type in a variety of research contexts. In practical terms, this shows that within the United States it is impossible to discuss the effects of bilingualism without consideration of language minority group membership.

As further example of the confounding of group membership with linguistic characteristics, one finds the following logic. Mexican American students are found to be more "field dependent" than Anglo counterparts (Buriel, 1975; Ramirez & Price Williams, 1974; Sanders, Scholz, & Kagan, 1976). To the extent Mexican American students are assumed to be bilingual, obtained cognitive style differences are equated with linguistic differences. Thus, bilinguals come to be viewed as field dependent. In a review of the literature on cognitive style, De Avila and Duncan (1980) concluded "virtually no studies involving Spanish language background children have controlled for language proficiency in either Spanish or English or for intellectual development. Given the failure to control for these potentially important variables, any differences with respect to groups must remain equivocal."

Using an approach based on the earlier work of De Avila, Havassy and Pascual-Leone (1976), Duncan (1979), Duncan and De Avila (1980), De Avila, Duncan, and Ulibarri (1982) found that when differences in linguistic proficiency were controlled through assessment in both languages, differences in cognitive style were, to a large extent, test-specific with only fully proficient bilingual students demonstrating consistent differences (higher levels of cognitive development on both Witkin and Piaget-type tasks). These results replicate a number of similar studies conducted over the past 15 years which have shown that when linguistic and test demand characteristics are controlled, many of the reported ethnolinguistic group differences in cognitive functioning fail to emerge (see De Avila & Duncan, 1980, for a review).

Finally, most of the ethnolinguistic group comparison studies have been motivated by an attempt to understand the impact of group variation on school performance. Findings of between-group differences on various cognitive tasks such as the Children's Embedded Figures Task (Witkin & Goodenough, 1977) are taken to explain differences in academic achievement (Chan, 1983). In an extensive 3-year cross-cultural study involving over 1,200 students from six different ethnolinguistic backgrounds, De Avila, Duncan, and Ulibarri (1982) found that cognitive style differences contributed less than 10% to the total variance in predicting the school performance of language minority students. On the other hand, linguistic variation accounted for as much as 70% of the total variance. Cognitive style and intellectual development variables accounted for significant proportions of the variance in predicting school performance only for mainstream Anglo students.

As a result of our own studies and review of various approaches to the study of the relationship of school achievement, and such factors as bilingualism or linguistic proficiency, intellectual development, and cognitive style, we have come to the conclusion that researchers would do well to consider the issue of treatment and environmental circumstances before attributing differences in school performance to either "bilingualism" or "cognitive style" variation. In this connection, the underlying theory that drives our design of programs could be considered. Finally, it can be argued that understanding of the effects of bilingualism on cognitive style (or vice versa) cannot be achieved without the study of the contexts and processes by which it develops. On this last point, De Avila and Duncan (1979) make the argument that cognitive style and bilingualism develop in a fashion that is indistinguishable from that of intelligence.

The major policy focus for bilingual education in the United States since the passage of the 1968 Bilingual Education Act (Title VII, ESEA) has been one of compensatory assistance. The view held by most educators has been that the difficulties faced by language minority students result from lower intellectual levels of development assumed to be associated with bilingualism, cognitive style differences, motivational deficiencies and a host of factors referred to under the rubric of SES (see Rosenthal, Milne, Ginsburg, & Baker, 1981). By means of increased resources associated with the remediation of English language deficiencies (ESL), it is expected that children will gain English language skills sufficient to full participation in English-only classrooms. This perspective has been coupled with an increased recognition of the demands for equity in educational opportunity (Lau v. Nichols, 1974). Similarly, increasing and shifting demographic patterns within the US population have forced a consideration of the increasing numbers of children who come from homes where English is not the primary language. As a result, American educators have become increasingly aware of the special demands placed on the schools by ethnically and linguistically heterogeneous students.

Unfortunately, however, recent reviews of the content of bilingual programs suggest an even greater emphasis on programs that foster a dependence on predetermined approaches to problem solving than is found in regular classrooms (Aries, 1982; Laosa, 1977; Nieves-Squires, 1980). Clark and Peterson (1976) report that teachers use extremely simple logic in their interactions with students. This simplified logic is particularly evident in bilingual classrooms in the "modified speech" patterns used by English-speaking teachers when interacting with students of "limited English proficiency" (Takahashi, 1982). Not surprisingly, one finds that current classroom practices focus on the rote learning of facts to the exclusion of more complex forms of information processing. Taba (1966) argues that the main reason for the low status of "thinking" in American classrooms in general and in bilingual classrooms in particular derives from the belief that thinking is predicated on learning a body of factual knowledge—i.e., one must know content before one can think. With respect to language minority students, English language proficiency becomes an additional prerequisite to thinking. The observation that teachers face a difficult task is underscored by the experience of any practitioner who has worked in classrooms, continually confronted with complex classroom management problems that tend to subordinate thinking to content. Thinking is difficult to foster in any classroom, let alone in a linguistically heterogeneous bilingual (or even multilingual) environment.

Organizational sociologists (Cohen, Deal, Meyer, & Scott, 1979; Intili, 1977; Perrow, 1967) point out that difficult tasks require complex support systems. To organizational sociologists and psychologists alike, the "teaching" of thinking is a much more complex operation than is normally found in the traditional classroom. This is particularly the case where teachers have little understanding regarding the nature of the learning process and have been encouraged to treat all content as the same (Berliner & Rosenshine, 1976; De Avila & Cohen, 1983), as if it were acquired by the same process. Moreover, many approaches to the teaching of content encourage routine at the expense of the more complex processes required for concept formation. Shavelson and Sern (1981) have analyzed a good deal of teacher behavior as a strong adherence to routine. According to De Avila and Cohen (1983), more individually relevant materials, more staff, and most important, more interaction among participants are required to adequately implement the processes underlying concept formation (see Bourne, 1966). Thus, fostering the development of "thinking skills" would require, according to these writers, more complete interdependent staff arrangement. Most teachers (let alone aides) have not been trained for these more complex arrangements and most administrators whose training was based on the theory of "cultural deprivation" (see Riessman, 1962) are not accustomed to them.

From a psychological point of view it appears that the curriculum in most classrooms requires recall skills for factual information and little else. The disadvantage of this approach, for all children, is that it limits the commitment to individual growth and self-development espoused in the goals of "good teaching" (Intili & Flood, 1976) and actively discriminates against those language minority students who do not share in the content referent embodied in the curriculum (De Avila & Havassy, 1975). In this way, language minority students, to the extent they are seen as "bilingual," are denied access to programs that go beyond paired associate or rote learning (see De Avila & Cohen, 1983).

SAMPLE

The classrooms selected for this research were part of a larger group receiving bilingual instruction under a grant from the U.S. Office of Education (Title VII). The Title VII program provided remedial services in both English and Spanish with an emphasis on the basic skills. Children participating in the program (FO/D) were approximately 253 second-, third-, and fourth-grade students drawn from a population of students living in suburban and metropolitan areas surrounding San Jose, California. A total of nine classrooms from nine different schools were involved. More detailed descriptions of the sample can be found in the various publications and reports resulting from the program. For the present, note that the students making up the sample were predominantly from lower middle-class Mexican-American backgrounds. Although there were several Black and Asian American students, the group as a whole was widely heterogeneous with respect to linguistics proficiency in both English and Spanish.

In addition to the students who participated in the FO/D program, 300 other students who were part of the bilingual program were used to constitute a comparison group. Note that the term *comparison group* has been used as opposed to *control group* because this was a field study and not an experiment in the traditional sense. For example, students were not randomly assigned to treatment and control groups. See Wilson, De Avila, and Intili (1982) for a more detailed discussion on this issue as it relates to the present study. The comparison group was quite similar to the study in all other respects save exposure to the science and math activities described as follows.

DESCRIPTION OF TREATMENT APPROACH (FINDING OUT/DESCUBRIMIENTO)

The specific classroom or treatment activities were taken from a bilingual science and math program entitled Finding Out/ Describrumiento (De Avila & Duncan, 1979–1982). FO/D is designed for use with small groups and is made up of approximately 150 activities that require measuring, counting, estimating, grouping, hypothesizing, analyzing, and reporting results. Basic skills are presented in the context of activities. For example, there are numerous situations in which students are asked to make estimations and then to check the accuracy of their estimations through subtracting estimated values from obtained values. The activities require cognitive operations found in problem-solving tasks used in cognitive psychology research (see Sternberg, 1981; Valett, 1978). Individual activities are organized and presented in much the same way as in a laboratory concept-formation or learning set experiment. Thus, there are a great number of trials or activities requiring the use of the same concept while the irrelevant aspects or dimensions are varied. In this way, for example, students are exposed to various aspects of the concept of number in at least 12 different activities, each presented in slightly different configurations while the "principle of solution" is held constant (see Hunt, 1961).

Students were required to work in small groups to increase verbal interaction. By presenting all material in both languages, an attempt was made to make the concepts underlying each task invariant with respect to language. Students were free to interact in whatever language or combination of languages was needed in order to facilitate communication. Linguistic differences were viewed as one more way in which concepts could be repeated without changing the underlying concept (i.e., principle of invariance). All students were asked to complete each activity and a corresponding worksheet (also provided in both languages). Students worked in small groups where they were free to interact or discuss each activity, as well as to assist one another in filling out the worksheets. Student flow was managed by the teacher who also facilitated understanding of the task instructions, which were provided in cartoon format with text in both English and Spanish. The child could thereby use the multiple resources provided by the pictograph, text, teachers, or peers.

OUTCOME MEASURES

Student progress and behavior were assessed at different points during the 14 weeks required to cover all of the activities. A variety of commercially and specially developed instruments were used. Taken as a whole, the data collected were based on both direct and indirect assessment methods including (1) paper and pencil tests, (2) classroom observations, (3) daily performance on worksheet assignment. Results are reported in three sections.

I. Paper-and-Pencil Outcome Measures

Three paper-and-pencil measures were administered on a pre/post basis to assess learning outcomes. Their content and administration are described as follows.

Intellectual Development

The Cartoon Conservation Scales (De Avila & Pulos, 1978; Fleming & De Avila, 1980) are a collection of Piagetian-inspired tasks that are group administered by means of a cartoon booklet. In all, there are 32 items that fall into the eight subscales including (a) number, (b) length, (c) substance, (d) distance, (e) horizontality, (f) egocentricity, (g) volume, and (h) probability. The concepts embodied in the CCS more closely resemble various definitions of thinking skills than any other of the measures in the test battery. However, insofar as the concepts underlying the CCS are not directly covered as part of the activities, they should be viewed as measures of the extent to which concepts covered in the activities "generalized" to broader mental processes. See Bruner, Oliver, and Greenfield (1966) for a more general discussion between conservation tasks and "thinking skills."

Academic Achievement

The Comprehensive Test of Basic Skills (CTBS) is a nationally norm-referenced test of school achievement. It is made up of two sections, math and reading. For the present purposes, let us bear in mind that the math section is broken down into three subscales: computation, concepts, and applications. The items that make up these subscales differ from one another not only in content but in the methods used to teach them. See De Avila and Cohen (1983) for a more detailed analysis of these differences. For example, math computation is routinely taught through memorization, rote, or paired associate learning. On the other hand, math concepts items more closely resemble concepts found in the literature on concept formation (see Bourne, 1966). It was expected that the FO/D experience would have a stronger impact on Math Applications than on subscales requiring less in the way of "thinking skills," i.e., math computation.

Science–Math

The MINI test was designed as a content-referenced multiple choice test of the vocabulary and concepts covered in the activities (see Hansen, 1980, for a description of its development and psychometric properties). It was presented in both pictorial and written formats in an attempt to reduce the effects of reading skills. The test was administered in either English or Spanish versions depending on the proficiency of the student. Scores are reported as the total number of items correctly answered divided by the number attempted. In all, there were 55 items.

II. Observational/Process Measures

Data on classroom behaviors were collected through the use of three different observational instruments that focused on (a) the teacher and aide, (b) the student, and (c) the classroom as a whole. Each is briefly described as follows.

Teacher-Aide Behaviors

Periodic classroom observations were made through the use of an observation system designed to assess the frequency of the following behaviors:

1. Asking and/or responding to student questions
2. Facilitating performance on the activities (showing students how to complete the activity
3. Providing feedback as to the correctness of worksheet and/or activities
4. Disciplining unacceptable behavior or providing management directions
5. Providing direct instruction (see Berliner and Rosenshine, 1976)

Student Behaviors

Student behaviors were observed periodically throughout the 14 weeks the study was in operation. Because of the difficulty and expense of obtaining these data, observations were made on only a subsample of students ($N = 106$). The subsample of "target" students was drawn on the basis of "relative language proficiency" according to the partitions reported in De Avila and Duncan (1983). In this way, the subsample was composed of students who were proficient monolinguals in English or Spanish, fully proficient bilinguals, partially proficient in one or the other language, somewhat limited in both, or totally limited in both. See De Avila, Cohen, and Intili (1981, 1982) for a more detailed discussion of the procedures. In all verbal interactions, the extent of both English and Spanish usage was recorded. The specific behaviors observed are listed as follows:

1. Task-related talk
2. Requests for assistance
3. Offers of assistance
4. non-task-related talk
5. Talk to teacher as opposed to other
6. Cleaning up
7. Working alone as opposed to working in either small or large groups
8. Observing others working
9. Waiting for directions from an adult
10. Task related transition versus "wandering"

Stated briefly, the purpose of the target child observation was to provide qualitative information as to the language, specific socially defined learning behaviors, task-related interactions, and levels of engagement. The collection of these data enabled us to link classroom social behavior to learning outcome as a function of student linguistic characteristics. A more detailed discussion of the relative reliability and validity of the observational measures may be found in Cohen and Intili (1981, 1982).

Whole-Class Behaviors

To describe the organizational features of the classroom, a process measure of grouping practices was employed. Weekly observation was made of each class as to size of groups, nature of activity, and interaction. Whole-class observation was also used as a check for the individual target student and teacher observations. For a more detailed description of the procedure and its agreement with individual observations see Cohen and Intili (1982).

III. Performance Measures

In addition to the data provided by paper-and-pencil and observational measures, data were also collected on the linguistic proficiencies of all participating students in both English and Spanish. Performance data on worksheets was also collected for target students.

Language Proficiency

Proficiency in both English and Spanish was assessed in the beginning of the study and its completion by means of the Language Assessment Scales (De Avila and Duncan, 1981-1982), Form A-Level I. See De Avila and Duncan (1983) for a detailed discussion of the psychometric properties of the test. The LAS is made up of the following subscales:

1. Phonemes
2. Minimal pairs
3. Vocabulary
4. Sentence comprehension
5. Production (story retelling)

Scores of the combined subtests are summed to provide a composite weighted score which represents the student's level of oral linguistic proficiency: Score values range from "*no proficiency*" to "*fully proficient.*" The scores on the story retelling section of the test are the only subjective ratings; therefore, this section was blind-scored by non-project staff. Scoring for all of the other project developed measures was conducted by project staff. Scoring of the CTBS was by the publisher.

Student Worksheets

Worksheets were collected for each. They were scored for:

1. Total number completed
2. Accuracy of computations and/or descriptions

3. Use and quality of written language
4. Use and completeness of drawings
5. Complexity of reasoning and use of inference

Worksheets were available to students in both Spanish and English versions. The interrater reliabilities for the coding categories used to score worksheet performance are reported in Cohen and Intili (1982).

RESULTS

The results were generated in several separate series of analyses. In the first series the general question of outcomes was addressed. In the second series an attempt was made to examine the results of the first series of analyses; outcomes, student characteristics, and classroom behaviors were examined in conjunction with classroom processes and instructional methods. Thus, the first series was directed at examining outcomes, whereas the second was aimed at examining underlying processes. The analyses of outcomes were based on the entire sample, whereas the analyses of process (observational) data were based on the target student subgroups.

Series I: Outcomes

Pre-Post Gains

Treatment effects were examined by time, condition, school, sex, and age for each set of dependent variables. Consistent statistically significant test gains were found on pre-post comparisons for all major variables (i.e., CTBS, MINI, LAS, etc.). Gains interacted with treatment and school variations. School variation, however, was associated with level of implementation (see Anthony et al., 1981). That is, although the FO/D period was intended to be 1 hour per day, some teachers allocated less time. Treatment was significantly related to five of the eight outcome measures. Examination of sex differences revealed that there were no meaningful differences between boys and girls as to either initial (pretest) base rates or gains over time.

Age differences were also examined. In this series of analyses significant age effects were found, suggesting that the program was least "effective" for a subgroup of older students. Examination of language data indicated that this group was made up of 14 monolingual Spanish speakers. Although there were other Spanish monolinguals in the sample, these 14 students tended to be substantially older than other students, in some cases by as much as 2 to 3 years. In subsequent analyses, it was found that these students were recent immigrants and tended to be of "low status" in the classroom (see Cohen & Intili, 1982). They also had fewer verbal interactions with either peers or adults. The general importance of "talking and working together" is addressed later.

Comparisons with Norms and Post Hoc Groups

In a second phase of this series of analyses, the performance of participating students was compared to publisher norms and to post hoc comparison groups. Due to a number of problems beyond our control, these comparisons were available for CTBS scores only. Consistent significant gains were found for both FO/D and comparison groups that slightly favored the FO/D group. In a second set of comparisons, expected gains in the academic content areas (i.e., reading and math) were calculated by obtaining the difference between publisher raw-score norms equivalent to the 50th percentile for fall and spring test administration. The differences between these two raw scores were then treated as "expected gain" scores and compared to pre/post gains scores obtained by FO/D and comparison students.

Results for the comparison group revealed that actual gains did not always match the Title VII program expectations. In several instances, as predicted from our initial content analyses of the CTBS subscales, comparison students fell further behind publisher norms or subscales requiring conceptual problem solving even though they improved in an absolute sense. When relative gains of the comparison students were compared to gains experienced by the FO/D group, significant differences were found in favor of the FO/D group on the predicted CTBS subscales, math application, and concepts. Thus, although the comparison group was making substantial gains in math computation, a skill usually taught through rote methods, students were actually falling further behind the norms in the more conceptual skill areas.

Student Characteristics

In an attempt to determine the extent of improvement as a function of student characteristics, prior to the implementation of FO/D, a subgroup of "problem" students (see Rosenholtz, 1981) were identified ($N = 60$) from the 106 target students in the following way. During the pre-test period, each teacher was asked to identify 6 to 8 students who they felt would be likely to experience difficulty in mastering the basic school curriculum and/or the science/math concepts embodied in the CO/D activities. By this procedure we were able to identify a group of students for whom the teacher held lower expectations. Comparisons between low-expectation and remaining FO/D students showed low-expectation students to perform consistently lower at both pre- and post-test administrations. Nevertheless, the absolute gains for the two groups were virtually identical. In other words, even though the "problem" group" scored lower at both points in time, their rate of improvement was indistinguishable from the rest of the group despite the lower expectations.

In a second attempt to examine gains as a function of student characteristics, a subgroup was formed on the basis of intellectual development. For this purpose the CCS provided a means for identifying potentially "gifted" students. An arbitrary criterion score of 28 points out of a possible 32 was used to generate a group of 40 students. Pre/post analyses on the outcome measures were then run. Results revealed significantly greater gains across time for gifted students on most of the measures where comparisons were possible. The only exception to this finding was on the CTBS math computation subscale where improvement was substantially the same as for the rest of the sample. Of particular significance were the gains in reading (vocabulary and comprehension) and math (concepts and applications).

In a final attempt to examine program effects as a function of student characteristics, data were also examined on the basis of linguistic considerations. This question was examined in two ways. In the first, the total sample was subdivided into two groups on the basis of oral English language proficiency scores (LAS). The resultant two groups were defined as "limited English proficient" (LEP) and "fluent English proficient" (FEP). A comparison of the relative pre/post gains for the two groups revealed significant improvement for both groups on most outcome measures. Further analyses revealed slightly stronger gains for the FEP group on the more traditional measures of school achievement, which included reading and math total scores and several subscales. On the other hand, LEP students showed slightly stronger gains in the CCS, LAS, and MINI test.

The fact that the CTBS was administered only in English would account for the slightly stronger gains on the part of the fluent English speakers. Nevertheless, LEP students did show significant improvement on the CTBS. This improvement was simply not quite as great as that of the fluent speakers. Furthermore, the importance of the linguistic factor is revealed by the fact that on the tests that students were able to take in either language, gains were stronger for the LEP group. Finally, the failure to find gains on the LAS for the FEP was certainly attributable to a ceiling effect and to the arbitrary definition of groups.

The analyses of data by LEP and FEP subgroups were conducted without consideration of home language proficiency. To gain insight into the nature of the interaction of the two languages, students were regrouped according to "relative linguistic proficiency." Using LAS scores, five linguistic subgroups were generated. They included:

1. English monolinguals
2. Spanish monolinguals
3. Limited speakers of both
4. Minimal speakers of both
5. Bilinguals (i.e., fully proficient in both)

Analyses of program effects by linguistic group showed that the proficient bilingual speakers exhibited the strongest and most consistent gains. Bilinguals were followed by limited bilinguals (Group 3) and Spanish monolinguals (Group 2) who were followed by minimal speakers (Group 4) and English monolinguals (Group 1). Note that even though there were between-group variations, all groups showed significant improvement on all the measures except on the LAS, which was due to an artifact of group definition (ceiling effects).

Series II: Process Analyses

In an attempt to examine the relationship of "process" variables to learning outcomes, a number of analyses were conducted using "observational data" in conjunction with the outcome measures just described. Two sets of analyses are of particular importance. In both instances, data were based on the target students. In the first set, Uyemura-Stevenson (1982) examined the relationship of student-student consultation to academic performance. In the second set, De Avila and Cohen (1983) compared teacher behavior in regular math classrooms with behavior observed during the FO/D class period, and then tied "method of instruction" to specific learning outcomes.

Uyemura-Stevenson (1982) examined three specific questions derived from sociological and psychological principles. In the first, the effect of student-student consultation was examined. Student-student consultation was defined as "task-related talk between students or other means of exchanging information about the task (i.e., modeling or demonstration)" (p. 20). Student consultation was operationalized on the basis of the observed behaviors coded on the "target student observation form" just described. Specific behaviors coded included task-related talk, requests for assistance from another student, offers of assistance, and working together without verbal interaction. Examination of the correlations between "talking and working together" and the outcome measures just described revealed significant relationships between student-student consultation and math conceptualization as measured on the student worksheet and total math scores as measured on the CTBS. In fact, it was found that "consulting with fellow students was a more powerful predictor of learning outcomes than consulting with teachers" (p. 44).

In addition, Uyemura-Stevenson found that student interaction facilitated performance on other academic behaviors such as the student's level of accuracy and use of written language (as opposed to drawing pictures) to describe the procedures and results of the activities. Thus, Uyemura-Stevenson found that the extent of student interaction seemed to be related to the improvement of a fairly broad range of behaviors. Note that the student data on which these analyses were conducted were based on a linguistically heterogeneous sample of students including monolinguals, proficient bilinguals, and children who had little proficiency in either standard Spanish or English. One interpretation of these findings suggests that the linguistic variability of the sample may have actually contributed to gains in conceptual areas.

In a second set of analyses Uyemura-Stevenson examined the extent to which consultation was more effective for students who exhibited "low academic and problem solving skills" and for those with higher skills in these areas. This question was similar to that addressed by De Avila, Cohen, and Intili (1981), and by Rosenholtz (1981). Rosenholtz found that students who were seen by the teachers as having a low probability for success showed about the same improvement as other students although at lower absolute levels.

To test the notion of a differential effect, regressions were conducted for students divided at the median on prior academic or "cognitive resources." With concrete tasks such as filling out the worksheets, analyses showed that student consultation was more important for students with fewer academic resources (i.e., lower prior academic achievement) than for students who had experienced less difficulty. On the other hand, results showed that student consultation was more effective for high achievers on more conceptual material.

Uyemura-Stevenson points out, however, that there was an important relationship between "status" and student interaction that would have an impact on the extent of consultation between high- and low-status children. In a related study on these data, Cohen and Anthony (1982) found that "high status" students were more likely to be found "talking and working together" than children of lower status characteristics. It appears that social status affects student interaction and that student interaction in turn affects learning outcomes. If status characteristics include teachers and peer perception of the child's ability to "speak English" then it would also seem clear that the problem of language difference faced by these students is exacerbated by a "social distance" that denies them access to verbal interaction.

In a third set of analyses, Uyemura-Stevenson tested the proposition that combined teacher and student consultation would have an "interactive effect" that would lead to "better quality learning outcomes than would be expected from adding the effects of each type of consultation." When this proposition was tested, regression analyses failed to reveal any statistically significant "interaction effects" between teacher and student consultation; student-student consultation remained the most significant predictor of worksheet performance. According to Uyemura-Stevenson, the results of this set of analyses suggests that talking and working together seem to have two specific functions: (a) regardless of linguistic "deficiencies," it allows students to use one another as resources, and (b) it promotes interaction, which in turn facilitates conceptual learning, particularly when the teacher is a scarce resource and unable to provide the type of "immediate feedback" widely advocated by such writers as Berliner and Rosenshine (1976).

De Avila and Cohen (1983) conducted secondary analyses of the data just described in which the relative effectiveness of "direct" and "indirect" instruction techniques were compared. In this series of analyses, De Avila and Cohen (1983) observed teacher and student behaviors in two settings and were able to link these behaviors to specific predicted academic outcomes.

The data consisted of observations made during FO/D and regular math periods. Original data collected by Rosenholtz (1981) had shown that the math classes and FO/D classes were two very different types of environments. Math classes were typified by "direct instruction," with teacher and aide providing direct supervision over two or three "ability groups." In sharp contrast to the FO/D period, there was very little in the way of "student-student consultation" or verbal interaction between students. Rosenholtz's data also showed that engagement was higher under complexity.

As predicted, observed rate of "direct instruction" was related to gains on CTBS Math Computation, whereas rates of "talking and working together" were associated with gains in CTBS Math Applications. Their findings lead De Avila and Cohen (1983) to conclude that there are interrelationships between the nature of learning, type of classroom organization, and method of instruction that must be taken into account. Whole-class instruction seems to be perfectly adequate for tasks requiring memorization of facts and figures. Conceptual learning, on the other hand, seems to imply a more complex classroom organization. In other words, given the complexity of the situation brought on by the diversity of student population and by the nature of the task, the teacher has little choice but to "delegate authority" (see Cohen & Intili, 1982) when educational objectives require conceptual learning.

Nieves-Squires (1980) examined academic and linguistic gain as a function of relative linguistic proficiency and interaction. Results of this series of analyses revealed that, with slight variation, interaction covaried with academic and linguistic gain as a function of linguistic subgroup. Bilinguals were found to have had more total interaction than any other group with the exception of Spanish monolinguals. The verbal interaction of Spanish monolinguals, however, was restricted to itself. Moreover, gains tended to be less consistent than for Bilinguals. Lowest levels of interaction were found for the Limited group with the other groups falling intermediate to the extremes.

CONCLUDING REMARKS

A number of issues of theoretical and applied interest have just been discussed. On the theoretical side we have reviewed research on the relationship between bilingualism and intellectual functioning. On the applied side we have considered a number of psychosocial issues as contributors to the school success of language minority students. Ostensibly, the first issue addresses the question of cognition and bilingualism, whereas the second addresses the question of appropriate treatment for bilinguals. De Avila (1982) has recently suggested that the school behavior of language minority students could be understood as a function of three interacting factors, including (a) intelligence/style, (b) interest/motivation and (c) opportunity/access. In the following concluding remarks, rather than simply restating the results, we discuss our results within the framework provided by these three factors.

Consider the question of the interaction of intelligence, cognitive style, and bilingualism as contributors to language minority performance on academic subject matter. For many, poor academic performance is attributable to, if not caused by, bilingualism. This conclusion seems faulty on three grounds.

First, in the review of various literatures, it was found that conflicting results are the result of a failure to distinguish between ethnolinguistic group membership and relative linguistic proficiency. That is, the failure to control for the absolute language proficiency of comparison groups has resulted in a confounding of language with intellectual development and cognitive style.

Second, in past research where language proficiency differences have been controlled, few if any meaningful differences in intellectual development or cognitive style have been found that could be attributed to bilingualism. In this connection Saarni (1973), using Piaget-inspired tasks similar to those used in the present research, found that differences in cognitive style between boys and girls did not predict to differences in intellectual functioning. Similar to our own work, Hyde (1981) reviewed the literature on sex differences in mathematical reasoning, conducted a meta-analysis of the results, and concluded that reported sex differences, although statistically significant, tended not to account for meaningful proportions of the total variance. Finally, we have found linguistic proficiency among language minority students to be a far stronger predictor of academic performance than either cognitive style or intellectual development. However, linguistic proficiency in English, although necessary, does not seem to be a sufficient condition.

Third, we find that comparisons between the total group of FO/D students and norms on the CCS collected over the past 15 years ($N = 6,000$) failed to reveal any statistically significant differences. With respect to intellectual development as measured by Piagetian tasks, this group of students was no different from any other group of students. On the other hand, however, the group was substantially behind their mainstream counterparts in level of academic performance. Although they seem to possess necessary levels of intellectual development, intellectual development per se, like linguistic proficiency, is not sufficient for school achievement.

Our conclusion on the question of the relationship between bilingualism and cognitive style or intellectual functions is threefold: (a) To the extent that differences in academic performance exist between language minority students, they cannot be attributed to the groups presumed bilingual; (b) Students, to the extent they are proficient bilinguals, experience a wide range of cognitive and social advantages over other students; (c) Although linguistic proficiency and intellectual development are necessary for the success of language minority students (and other children), they are not sufficient given traditional classroom practices and organization.

The second major factor in our framework deals with the issue of motivation and interest whereby the literature on differences between language minority and majority populations suffers from the same problems as the literature on intellectual and cognitive style differences. Although this chapter did not cover the issue of motivation in any direct sense, a few comments are in order. A number of recent writers have found student engagement to be a strong predictor of success in academic subject areas and have reported engagement rates on academic tasks to be as low as 10% of allocated time. Based on the finding that individualized seatwork tends to produce low levels of student engagement, Berliner and Rosenshine (1976) have concluded that the best way to remediate poor academic performance is by means of the method of "direct instruction." The major thrust of this methodological approach is to improve academic performance by increasing "time on task" through direct teacher supervision and whole-class instruction. However, student engagement can be viewed as an index of interest and motivation to complete academic tasks. In this connection, Rosenholtz (1981) showed that direct instruction did not always maximize time on task, especially when it occurred in complex (multiple groups and materials) classroom organizational structures such as required by FO/D. Rosenholtz found that peer task talk was related to engagement in both math and FO/D classes. However, task engagement was correlated with direct instruction only in the math class and was uncorrelated in the FO/D period where there were multiple groups and activities in simultaneous operation. In general, it was found that the level of engagement during the FO/D period was in excess of 80%. What can be concluded from these data is that students are internally motivated to complete tasks that they find interesting. We further speculate that part of the interest is derived from the peer interaction required to complete the tasks and not from the direct supervision of the teacher. Finally, it appears that different educational objectives require different instructional methods, which, in turn, imply different classroom organizations.

The third factor in the facilitation of academic success deals with the issues of opportunity and access. Opportunity and access may be discussed at several levels including social, curricular and interpersonal. The concept of educational equity that motivates the social justification of the development and funding of categorical programs such as Title VII Bilingual Education, is based on the notion of "equal opportunity regardless of sex, religion, race or national origin." Although the avowed purpose of compensatory education programs has been to provide equal opportunity through remedial programs, it is doubtful that much of the social science research base underlying the design of many programs actually provides equal access to education and intellectual development on a broader scale. Opportunity implies access but it does not guarantee it. For example, the belief that English language and basic skill deficiencies preclude thinking and scientific reasoning has led to programs for the language minorities that, by default, emphasize rote skills at the expense of higher order intellectual processes. Thus, although students are provided with the opportunity for success by placement in special classes, presumed deficiencies, ironically, preclude access.

The social sciences have identified a wide variety of student characteristics thought to contribute to academic success. What we have found is that the wholesale application of many of these findings is fraught with danger. Of particular importance to this discussion is the relation between social status variables operating both within and without the school setting and the extent to which differences (often more presumed than real) on these variables lead to differences in the design of programs which, in turn, preempt particular important process in learning. The case of student interaction is a prime example. What the previous findings have illustrated is that student interaction is a significant contributor to the learning process, particularly as related to concept formation. Interaction within the classroom, however, is to some extent modified by social status factors. To the extent that English language proficiency operates like other academic status variables, such as reading, it can be expected from these data that students with limited proficiency will exhibit lower levels of interaction with English-speaking classmates. Finally, what these data have shown is that under classroom organizational conditions where language minority students are provided with access to multiple resources, including home language, peer consultation, observation, manipulation, and so on, they will acquire concepts as readily as mainstream students and, at the same time, acquire English language proficiency and basic skills. In fact, what the data show is that the ''bilinguals'' are at a head start in this regard.

REFERENCES

Anthony, B., Cohen, E. G., Hanson, S. G., Intili, J. K., Mata, S., Parchment, C., Stevenson, B., & Stone, N. (1981, April). *The measurement of implementation: A problem of conceptualization.* Paper presented at the Annual Meeting of the American Educational Research Association, Session 40.11.

Aries, B. (1982, March). *Contextual variation and the implementation of the bilingual curriculum.* Paper presented at the Annual Meeting of the American Educational Research Association, New York.

Berliner, D., & Rosenshine, B. (1976). The acquisition of knowledge in the classroom. in R. C. Anderson, R. J. Spiro, & W. E. Montague (Eds.), *Schooling and the education process* (pp. 375–398). Hillsdale, NJ: Lawrence Erlbaum Associates.

Bourne, L. E. (1966). *Human conceptual learning.* Boston: Allyn & Bacon.

Bruner, J. S., Olver, R. R., & Greenfield, P. M. (1966). *Studies in cognitive growth: A collaboration of the Center for Cognitive Studies.* New York: Wiley.

Buriel, J. W. (1975). Cognitive styles among three generations of Mexican-American children. *Journal of Cross-Cultural Psychology, 6,* 417–439.

Chan, K. S. (1983). Limited English speaking, handicapped, and poor: Triple threat in childhood. In M. Chu-Chang (Ed.), *Asian and Pacific American perspectives in bilingual education: Comparative research.* New York: Teachers College Press.

Clark, G. M., & Peterson, P. L. (1976, April). *Teacher-stimulated recall of interactive decisions.* Paper presented at the Annual Meeting of the American Educational Research Association, San Francisco, CA.

Cohen, E. G., & Anthony, B. A. (1982, March). *Expectation states theory and classroom learning.* Paper presented at the Annual Meeting of the American Educational Research Association, New York.

Cohen, E. G., Deal, T. E., Meyer, J. W., & Scott, W. R. (1976). *Organization and instruction in elementary schools.* (Technical Report No. 50). Stanford, Ca: Stanford Center for Research and Development in Teaching.

Cohen, E. G., & Intili, J. K. (1981). *Interdependence and management of bilingual classrooms* (Final Report to NIE). Stanford, CA: Stanford University, School of Education.

Cohen, E. G., & Intili, J. K. (1982). *Interdependence and management of bilingual classrooms* (Final Report to NIE). Stanford, CA: Stanford University, School of Education.

De Avila, E. A. (1982). Keynote address at the Council for Exceptional Children's National Conference on Training Workshops on the Exceptional Bilingual Child, Oct. 31–Nov. 2, Phoenix, Arizona.

De Avila, E. A., Cohen, E. G., & Intili, J. K. (1981). *Multi-cultural improvement of cognitive abilities* (Final Report). Department of Education, State of California, Sacramento, CA.

De Avila, E. A., Cohen, E. G., & Intili, J. K. (1982). Improving cognition: A multi-cultural approach. In S. S. Seidner (Ed.), *Issues of language assessment: foundations and research.* Illinois State Board of Education, Springfield, IL.

De Avila, E. A., & Cohen, E. G. (1983). *Indirect instruction and conceptual learning.* In preparation.

De Avila, E. A., & Duncan, S. E. (1978). *Language Assessment Scales (LAS®).* Corte Madera, CA: Linguametrics Group.

De Avila, E. A., & Duncan, S. E. (1979, winter). Bilingualism and the Metaset. *NABE Journal, 3*(2), 1–20.

De Avila, E. A., & Duncan, S. E. (1980). Definition and measurement of bilingual students. In *Bilingual program, policy, and assessment issues.* California State Department of Education, Sacramento, CA.

De Avila, E. A., & Duncan, S. E. (1979–1982). *Finding Out/Descubrimiento.* San Rafael, CA: Linguametrics Group.

De Avila, E. A., & Duncan, S. E. (1981–1982). *A convergent approach to oral language assessment: Theoretical and technical specifications on the Language Assessment Scales (LAS®), Form A.* San Rafael, CA: Linguametrics Group.

De Avila, E. A., & Duncan, S. E. (1983). *The language minority child: A psychological, linguistic, and educational analysis.* San Rafael, CA: Linguametrics Group.

De Avila, E. A., Duncan, S. E., & Ulibarri, D. M. (1982). Cognitive development. In E. E. Garcia (Ed.), *The Mexican American child: Language, cognition and social development.* Tempe, AZ: Center for Bilingual/Bicultural Education.

De Avila, E. A., & Havassy, B. E. (1975). Piagetian alternative to IQ: Mexican American study. In N. Hobbas (Ed.), *Issues in the classification of exceptional children.* San Francisco, CA: Jossey Bass.

De Avila, E. A., Havassy, B. E., & Pascual-Leone, J. (1976). *Mexican-American school children: A neo-Piagetian analysis.* Washington, DC: Georgetown University Press.

De Avila, E. A., & Pulos, S. M. (1978). Developmental assessment by pictorially presented piagetian material: The Cartoon Conservation Scales (CCS®). In G. I. Lubin, M. K. Poulsen, J. F. Magary, & M. Soto-McAlister (Eds.), *Piagetian theory and its implications for the helping professions* (pp. 124–139). Los Angeles, CA: University of Southern California.

Duncan, S. E. (1979). *Child bilingualism and cognitive functioning: A study of four Hispanic groups.* Unpublished doctoral dissertation, Union Graduate School.

Fleming, J. S., & De Avila, E. A. (1980). Scalogram and factor analyses of two tests of cognitive development. *Multivariate Behavioral Research, 15,* 73–93.

Hansen, S. (1980). *Psychometric properties of the MICA mini-test.* Unpublished manuscript, Stanford University.

Hunt, J. M. (1961). *Intelligence and experience.* New York: Ronald Press.

Hyde, J. (1981). How large are cognitive gender differences? *American Psychologist, 36* (8), 892–901.

Intili, J. K. (1977). *Structural conditions in the school that facilitate reflective decision making.* Unpublished doctoral dissertation, School of Education, Stanford University.

Intili, J. K., & Flood, J. E. (1976, April). *The effect of selected student characteristics on differentiation on instruction in reading.* Paper presented at the Annual Meeting of the American Educational Research Association, San Francisco, CA.

Laosa, L. M. (1977). Cognitive styles and learning strategies research: Some of the areas in which psychology can contribute to personalized instruction in multicultural education. *Journal of Teachers Education, 28*(3), 26–30.

Lau v. Nichols (1974). No. 72–6520 (414 U.S. at 566, 1974).

Mestre, J. P., Gerace, W. J., & Lochhead, J. (1982). The interdependence of language and translational math skills among bilingual Hispanic engineering students. *Journal of Research in Science Teaching, 19* (5), 399–410.

Nieves-Squires, S. (1980). *Bilingual instructional features planning study.* Cambridge, MA: ABT Associates.

Perrow, C. (1967). A framework for the comparative analysis of organizations. *American Sociological Review, 32,* 194–208.

Ramirez III, M., & Price-Williams, D. R. (1974). Cognitive styles of children of three ethnic groups in the United States. *Journal of Cross-Cultural Psychology, 5,* 212–219.

Riessman, F. (1962). *The culturally deprived child.* New York: Harper & Row.

Rosenholtz, S. (1981). *Effects of task arrangements and management systems of task engagement of low achievement students.* Unpublished doctoral dissertation, Stanford University.

Rosenthal, A. S., Milne, A., Ginsburg, A., & Baker, K. (1981). *A comparison of the effects of language background and socioeconomic status on achievement among elementary school students.* Washington, DC: AUI Policy Research, Office of Planning and Budget, Department of Education.

Saarni, C. I. (1973). Piagetian operations and field independence as factors in children's problem-solving performance. *Child Development, 44,* 338–345.

Sanders, M., Scholz, J. P., & Kagan, S. (1976). Three social motives and field-independence-dependence in Anglo American and Mexican American children. *Journal of Cross-Cultural Psychology, 7*(4), 451–462.

Shavelson, R. J., & Stern, P. (1981). Research on teachers' pedagogical thoughts, judgments, decisions, and behavior. *Review of Educational Research, 51,* 455–498.

Sternberg, R. J. (1981). Testing and cognitive psychology. *American Psychologist, 36* (10), 1181–1189.

Taba, H. (1966). *Teaching strategies and cognitive functioning in elementary school children.* U.S.D.E. Cooperative Research Project No. 2404. San Francisco State College.

Takahashi, Y. (1982). *The effects of modified input and interaction patterns on language acquisition.* Unpublished manuscript, Stanford University.

Uyemura-Stevenson, B. (1982). *An analysis of the relationship of student-student consultation to academic performance in differentiated classroom settings.* Unpublished doctoral dissertation, Stanford University.

Valett, R. E. (1978). *Developing cognitive abilities: Teaching children to think.* St. Louis: C. V. Mosby.

Wilson, B., De Avila, E. A., & Intili, J. K. (1982, March). *Improving cognitive, linguistic and academic skills in bilingual classrooms.* Paper presented at the Annual Meeting of the American Educational Research Association, New York.

Witkin, H. A., & Goodenough, D. R. (1977). *Field dependence revisited* (ETS RB 77–16). Princeton, NJ: Educational Testing Service.

Bilingualism: Cognitive and Social Aspects

Joseph Glick
City University of New York, Graduate Center

It is, perhaps, every social scientist's dream to do research of such vital importance that it can show up in an enlightened social policy. Indeed, the hope is that information found out in the laboratory (either nature's or the university's) will prove to be of direct relevance to the various social ills and social problems that surround us. By doing more advanced and sophisticated research we hope to replace benighted policies with enlightened ones. We would like to believe that we are able to build a society based on refined knowledge.

Perhaps this dream is destined to remain a dream. We may have to come to understand that it is entirely possible that research design and experimental thinking are not well adapted to the realities of social action. Nor may the world of social realities be amenable to being researched in the way we might wish it to be.

The difficulties of doing socially relevant research derive directly from the fact of its social relevance. Social facts do not operate like variables in research designs. While the condition for a research design is that a variable is isolatable for study, it is most often the case that the social world offers us ''bundles'' of factors that are intertwined.

In the following I identify some of the problems involved in the extension of standard research methods, particularly as they bear on issues of bilingualism.

SOME COMMENTS ON BILINGUALISM

Considered from a theoretical and experimental (research design) point of view it seems quite reasonable that the basic arguments adduced by Palij and Homel

171

(this volume) and De Avila (this volume) to show the non-negative and possibly positive impact of bilingualism on various cognitive functions are correct, or, are at least, not necessarily wrong. I can think of no strong cognitive developmental theory that would seriously argue against bilingualism on theoretical grounds.

Piaget (1967), for example, would treat bilingualism in much the same way that he would treat the relationship between one language and cognition. The important variance exists at the level of the cognitive structures that are available and not in the code that is used to represent them or access them. The general Piagetian position might be represented as asserting that language changes follow on rather than lead changes in cognitive organization. Primary emphasis is placed on the availability of the concept in the individual's repertoire.

The concept itself comes from a variety of types of structuring activities within the organism and is not simply an appropriation of an existing linguistically encoded social meaning. Within this theoretical position bilingualism would not be bad; it would be merely irrelevant to issues of cognitive growth.

In a vein similar to Piaget's, some of the work on human information processing (laboratory variety) would also suggest the primacy of the availability of concepts in considering issues of language, bi-language, and cognition (Conrad, 1964; Siegler, 1983). Much of the information processing work suggests that the surface form of statement of a proposition (e.g., the particular syntax or the particular words used to express it) quickly disappears as processing proceeds to deeper levels for longer term storage. Longer term encoding is in terms of the idea expressed (semantic or conceptual level).

Because it may be well argued that different languages express the same basic semantic notions but use different lexical and syntactic means to do so, we might not expect any losses of function attendant on bilingualism.

We could reasonably expect language interference if there are aspects of language that define semantic domains in a radically different way. Any negative effects would exist only within mismatched semantic domains and not at the level of global language differences per se.

Vygotsky (1962, 1978), who emphasizes cultural mediational systems as being of importance to cognitive growth and performance, would emphasize the existence of an external mediator more than would Piaget. The Vygotskian position would be inclined to stress the potentially favorable effects of bilingualism, but only under conditions where the availability of multiple mediators is not confusing (e.g., where the mediators map the same semantic and conceptual contrasts). Indeed, some of the cross-cultural work of Luria and Vygotsky among Georgian peasants might suggest that the presence of more than one coding system for a given concept could greatly advance the abstractness of conceptual organization (Luria, 1971).

To the extent that mediation is important, having multiple mediators may allow concepts to be detached from single mediators and, hence, allow for a distinction to be made between word and thing (see also Werner & Kaplan, 1984, for similar arguments).

The discussion of issues of bilingualism in terms of the availability of multiple concept-to-mediator matches suggests another angle of approach to the issues involved in bilingualism. There is a body of work that views the importance of multiple coding of information as is implicated, for example, in the ability to write and read. Writing and reading involve a bilingualism-like multiple coding situation. Linguistic information exists in both an aural and a written code. Arguments have been made, and some evidence adduced for the cognitive advances that follow on having this multiple coding available (Luria, 1982).

However, some of the recent work of Scribner and Cole (1981) on literacy in Africa suggests that the issue must be considered in terms of specific mapping between speaking-writing and cognitive performance. This recent work has argued for a specificity of analysis that takes the question well beyond issues of whether it is better (or not) to be able to read and write. The more basic question is the relationship between a task demand and the implied ability, and as well, on the manner in which literacy has been achieved. There are some forms of literacy where reading is not treated as a transparent cognitive tool for reading anything. Rather it is a branch of sacred activity accessing scriptural truths (for example, as might be contained in the Koran or any other sacred text).

In sum, from the point of view of many dominant developmental theories (which are not necessarily right, only dominant) there seems to be no overwhelming indictment of bilingualism. If the field was called on to give its collective wisdom on this matter, it would probably come forth with a resounding "can't hurt, maybe it could help."

However, most developmental theorists would ask, at a minimum, that the research questions posed in investigating bilingualism must be posed with great specificity. The issue would not be the big issue of whether having more than one language is good or bad. Rather, the question would come down to an analysis of the specifics of language structure and language use.

We would study the issues in highly specific domains with precisely diagnostic tests to examine specific predictions that might be derived from areas of language match and mismatch. And, as with the discussion of the theoretical similarities of bilingualism to reading and writing (multiple mediation), the developmental psychologist would likely want to extend the study of bilingualism beyond its current boundaries.

However heartening this tour of developmental theories might be to advocates of bilingual education, it is largely irrelevant. In the remainder of this section I try to carve out the dimensions of the irrelevance of developmental theories to the issues involved in bilingualism and show other directions for where important studies are needed.

THE SOCIAL NATURE OF BILINGUALISM

Let me start with a simple popular cultural observation. Noone talks about "bilingualism" when talking about the upper classes of society. Bilingualism seems to be a poor man's (woman's, child's) affliction. No one seems to have been worrying about confusing everything when it was deemed desirable to have "foreign language requirements" an enforceable part of the high school curriculum. Indeed, as colleges have returned to a more basic "core curriculum" so too have foreign languages come to be seen as an essential part of a rounded and basic education. And, indeed, there is not a right-thinking graduate student who has not rebelled at the idea of having to pass a language examination in order to get a Ph.D in some non-linguistic and non-foreign field.

For the adult or near adult having proficiency in more than one language is a sign of status: being "international," being non-parochial, being a part of the wider world. The problem of bilingualism, when thought about in an adult context, is a problem only where there is an unassimilated or culturally separate ethnic group living within a dominant culture. The problem of adult bilingualism is clearly a political problem. What is phrased as a linguistic phenomenon is, in fact, a political phenomenon (Homel & Palij, this volume).

I have been doing political research for the last several years. Issues of bilingual, bicultural policies inevitably arise within the political context and they clearly signal a massive resentment of culturally different groups by the cultural majority. We have all heard it. "Why do they want to be taught in their own language . . . when my parents came here they learned to assimilate and become Americans." "They want to stay different . . . that really means that they don't want to be a part of us." "Why should my tax dollars pay for a group of people that do not want to become American."

In short, none of the discussions of bilingualism in the popular culture or the political context have anything to do with deep issues of cognition. They deal with issues of cultural assimilation and multicultural acceptance. The bilingualism debate is a debate about cultural belonging and the nonunderstandable rejection of the mainstream culture by people who insult us by not becoming like us. For many, thinking about bilingualism is really thinking about whether a different people is willing to pay its dues by learning to become "like us."

This situation makes the discussion of bilingualism in cognitive terms extremely difficult. We are dealing with a variable that has an enormously powerful social-cultural meaning. The loadedness of the issue of linguistic assimilation is of clearly dominant power when bilingualism is the topic.

It appears to me that the cultural significance of bilingualism and biculturalism in political and social terms is of overwhelming importance in assessing the research literature on bilingualism. The issue is unlikely to be simply cognitive.

On this point I take some small exceptions to the analysis of the situation as presented by Palij and Homel (this volume). While they acknowledge the cultural dimension and the difficulties of doing a "true experiment" they seem to focus more on such issues as whether the languages are of equal strength when children are assessed, and whether children who are bilingual do better or worse on IQ and other achievement tests. To be sure, these are critically important issues when bilingualism is treated as an experimental or quasi-experimental variable and the desire is to adduce evidence in support of or against bilingual education programs by measuring this variable and its impact correctly.

My point is that bilingualism is precisely *not* an experimental variable, not because it cannot be randomly assigned to populations and the like. It cannot be a variable even in covariate designs because bilingualism is a coded expression of a multiplicity of experimental variables that are packaged together in such a way that the isolation and precise measurement of a variable is impossible.

I might add that dependent variables, such as IQ or achievement, are part of the same package. IQ is measured by means of some group's ideas of what intelligence is all about. Achievement is an even more institutionalized version of what progress means. Of course, a sub-group living within a main cultural group will, in reality, be held accountable to the expectations of the majority. Surely, however, this is not a cognitive-developmental issue. It is in fact a social issue having more to do with accountability practices within a society than with development or intelligence.

It is quite likely that the positive results of Lambert and his coworkers in Quebec have as much to do with the officially bilingual policy of the government of the Province of Quebec as they have to do with the experimental nicety that the language proficiency variable was equated prior to testing. Similarly, it is not surprising that De Avila's program required the presence of a massive support system for bilingual bicultural Spanish-English bilinguals in California. In the United States the continued maintenance of Spanish-speaking communities is not culturally accepted. To support Spanish-English bilingualism programs is to swim upstream in the face of formidable obstacles of a social-cultural variety. Indeed, people need a great deal of support to swim upstream.

There is too great a tendency for social scientists to simply extend and assimilate the values of social science when dealing with social problems. The laboratory-izing of social problems is of questionable value even when applied in optimum conditions (the laboratory). As we extend social science thinking to social domains, the extension of the isolation of variables and assessment of their isolated impacts comes to be of even more questionable value. To be sure, knowledge of precisely measured and controlled variables is important. Equally, this way of thinking introduces highly artificial frameworks for discussion.

Let me cycle back on this point and try to develop it a bit more. Let us say that it *is* the case that the cognitive performance of bilinguals is much better when the languages are of close to equal strength. Now let us consider how this might be achieved in the real world. In order to achieve the condition of equal strength it seems reasonable to assume that the languages must be given equal status. The equal status argument applies no matter what version of language acquisition theory we might be using.

For a nativist who equips the child with a variety of pretuned language or concept acquisition devices there is still the necessity for language-specific inputs so that universal rules may be extracted from each language that is being acquired. This requires some rough equation of amount of contact with the languages to be acquired. If a culture gives roughly equal status to two languages, it stands to reason that contact with the languages would be roughly equated and that therefore the various acquisition devices can be applied to yield an "equation" on the strength of language variable.

For the more learning theory oriented, the same arguments apply, except now they are applied to the equality of stress on teaching of the various languages. This again bears on issues of the cultural status accorded to the various languages involved. A low-status language might not receive the same teaching stress as the high-status language.

There are even some variants of the learning theory view that will stress, with the nativists, the importance of mere contact as a controlling variable in determining the strength *and depth* of language acquisition. For example, Reber and his associates (see, for example, Reber & Glick, 1979, for a summary) have been studying people's ability to extract deep structure rules from artificial languages. They have found that people are more likely to extract rules under "incidental learning" conditions (where they are merely exposed to input) than they are under "intentional conditions" where specific rules are sought (or taught).

In recent years both nativists and learning theorists are beginning to agree that language acquisition occurs with greater completeness earlier than we had before imagined. As we find new ways of testing children's linguistic abilities, the almost inevitable finding is that the important evidences of linguistic structure are visible at earlier and earlier ages. If we take this trend seriously then it becomes less and less tenable to argue for mono-linguistic training for a long period so that a language can be established before another one is added. It seems more and more reasonable to assume that language acquisition by the time that children have achieved school age is sufficiently advanced so that we cannot imagine that the child is deprived of learning any language well by being forced to learn too many languages.

These arguments would suggest that the real issues in bilingualism are neither developmental nor cognitive. Rather, the main issue is an argument about the respectable status of a subcultural language.

Rather than being a neat academic point, this is a point that has profound implications for social policy. If we think only of language strength as being equal or not, we may believe that all we need to do is train the languages up to positions of near equality and our educational problems are solved.

But the problems are deeper. I believe that much of what is underlying the measured changes in "cognition," which seems to be the topic of the research literature, is really an issue of "performance" under friendly or unfriendly conditions.

It has become almost a truism of developmental research that it most often turns out to be the case that measured abilities are highly impacted on by both variations in task demands and by the level of communication that is established between child and experimenter. The level of communication will indeed be determined by linguistic variables, but it is also determined by social-cultural variables that serve to enable or disable efforts at establishing shared meanings between child and experimenter.

In cases where shared meanings are established, measured performance is inevitably better. We delude ourselves by thinking that this merely reflects cognitive advances or cognitive deficits on the part of the child. The psychological test and the experimental situation is a transaction between two parties who either establish grounds for communication or do not. If they do not, performance suffers. This has been classically exemplified by the work of Zigler and Butterfield (1968) who have been able to produce instant 10-point gains in measured IQ of culturally "disadvantaged" populations simply by varying the level of communication between tester and child.

If these rather general and, by now, banal points are accepted, there is a clear and non-banal conclusion. Research paradigms that focus on the child's performance or lack of it miss the boat in important ways. If it is accepted that social conditions of communication are of great importance in allowing children to display their competencies, then we probably should not focus on the children and their performance in order to address social issues. Their performance is variable depending on the way that they are treated. The way the child is treated in the school and in the experimental situation itself depends on more general cultural attitudes of teachers and experimenters.

Similarly, if we accept the point that the very notion of achievement is culturally defined, we may want to refocus from issues of children and their achievement to issues of the cultural definition of achievement. Is there one standard or not?

Some developmental theorists would argue for a single standard, others would disagree. My point here is that this sort of issue should be the focus of our concern. It is the sort of issue that is more about problems within intellectual disciplines than about children and their abilities or lack of them.

There is some sense to the argument that focusing on an issue such as bilingualism, and measuring it as we do in terms of the performances of children on various cognitive and educational indicators, shifts the debate from where it should belong—on the structure of society and its policies toward a multicultural population—to the victims of the situation—the minority groups and their linguistic or bi-linguistic abilities. In this way we are in danger of blinding ourselves to real problems in need of profound solutions. There is a danger in focusing on "abilities" rather than political and cultural "rights."

The debate over bilingualism is an important social debate. Because it is so important we must clearly think through the intended and unintended consequences of joining that debate with our focus on the cognitive status of the bilingual.

The debate over social policy will not be won by pointing toward linguistic or cognitive data. The more fundamental issues have to do with social attitudes and social policies themselves.

To the extent that bilingual education serves to legitimize a subcultural group then I am all for it. So too, probably, are cognitive developmental theories.

However, as I have seen in my political research, bilingual and bicultural programs are creating a backlash. Dominant culture members have become resentful. They are not swayed by our prettiest and most pristine data. They are, instead, angry at peoples who wish to maintain their identity, and the public costs involved.

In the current political climate there is a hardening of class and cultural divisions. The political ideal of a melting pot America is directly challenged by cultural separateness. As the non-military sector of the federal budget decreases, we are becoming less and less prone to invest scarce dollars in maintaining subcultural identity and securing subcultural advancement no matter how compelling the data might be.

I fear that the research data and developmental theory may align on the side of bilingual-bicultural education but that the social-structural issues perhaps align on the side of the cultural assimilationists.

It may well be argued that even the data brought forward to support bilingual programs use evidence structures (e.g., focusing on kids and their performance as the major data source; using culturally dominant notions of intelligence and achievement as the dependent variables), which ultimately imply the assimilationist position.

The cause implicit in the organization of this volume might indeed be better served by a refocusing of attention on issues involved in building a multicultural society. We might turn our attention to the issues of standards that are used to evaluate subcultural kids in our schools and our experiments, and examine if these standards are cognitive-developmental in some universal way or are themselves reflect-dominant culture values "pretending to be" universal. We might even shift focus from issues of "meeting standards" to issues of civil rights.

We invite difficult and soul-wearying questions by this examination, but it is one that must, at some point, be done. I fear that the attempt to argue the issues out, as if they were issues relating solely to whether kids are smarter or dumber with one language or two, leaves some of the major underlying issues untouched.

REFERENCES

Conrad, R. (1964). Accoustic confusions in immediate memory. *British Journal of Psychology. 55,* 75–84.

Luria, A. R. (1971). Toward the problem of the historical nature of psychological processes. *International Journal of Psychology, 6,* 259–272.

Luria, A. R. (1982). *Language and cognition.* Ed., J. V. Wertsch. New York: Wiley.

Piaget, J. (1967). *Six psychological studies.* New York: Vintage.

Reber, A., & Glick, J. (1979, June). *Implicit learning and stage theory.* Paper read at the ISSBD conference, Lund, Sweden.

Scribner, S., & Cole, M. (1981). *The consequences of literacy.* Cambridge, MA: Harvard University Press.

Siegler, R. S. (1983). Information processing approaches to development. *Handbook of developmental psychology.* New York: Wiley.

Vygotsky, L. S. (1962). *Thought and language.* Cambridge, MA: MIT Press.

Vygotsky, L. S. (1978). *Mind in society: The development of higher psychological processes.* Ed., M. Cole, V. John-Steiner, S. Scribner, & E. Souberman. Cambridge, MA.: Harvard University Press.

Werner, H., & Kaplan, B. (1984). *Symbol formation: An organismic-developmental approach to the psychology of language.* Hillsdale, NJ: Lawrence Erlbaum Associates.

Zigler, E., & Butterfield, E. C. (1968). Motivational aspects of changes in IQ test performance of culturally deprived nursery school children. *Child Development, 39,* 1–14.

IV

BILINGUALISM AND SOCIAL DEVELOPMENT

Social Psychological Barriers to Effective Childhood Bilingualism

Donald M. Taylor
McGill University

The study of bilingualism, or more generally second language learning, has come a long way. That a number of serious controversies over the implications of bilingualism dominate the literature does not belie this assertion, for much pioneering groundwork is needed before different points of view surface and crystalize into important, recognizable issues. My own concern is with what I believe to be an understudied aspect of second language learning and effective bilingualism, that of social variables in general, and the intergroup context within which language learning takes place in particular.

This focus of concern is viewed as a natural outgrowth of the progression in the understanding of second language processes. The initial interest was on abilities and aptitudes (Carroll, 1958, 1974; Carroll & Sapon, 1959) involving such variables as phonetic coding, grammatical sensitivity, memory, inductive learning, and, of course, the role of first language proficiency in second language learning.

Attention then shifted to attitudinal/motivational variables prompted by the initial and continuing work of Lambert, Gardner, and their associates (Gardner, 1981; Gardner & Lambert, 1972). Included in this constellation of variables are attitudes toward the group speaking the second language, toward the language itself, and toward the instructional process. The motivational component includes the implications of instrumental, as opposed to integrative, reasons for learning a second language. Concomitant with the development of interest in these variables came questions about the cognitive and personality implications of bilingualism.

It would seem a natural extention to focus attention on the larger social context of intergroup relations and appreciate the role it may play for children enrolled in, and coping with, various forms of bilingual programs. The attitudes and motivations of the second language learner have, to date, tended to be viewed as individually based orientations which affect that particular individual's success at learning the target language. The concern here is with the set of shared perspectives that arise in a group when it finds itself in a particular power relationship and history of conflict or accommodation with other groups. Specifically, it must be recognized that one's language plays a central role for self-definition in terms of group identity. As such, the group one is identified with and relations between one's own group and other groups in the social environment provide the crucial context in which learning a language operates. And the intergroup context does have a direct and dramatic impact on the classroom environment. It is no coincidence, for example, that Anglophone children in Quebec are exposed to French instruction as early as kindergarten, whereas there is an explicit regulation against the teaching of English in French schools until Grade 4, and even then it is not required. Such nonreciprocal practices may seem irrational until account is taken of the intergroup context of Francophones and Anglophones in Canada.

The whole question of bilingualism raises fundamental questions about its implications. Do children learn the second language successfully? Is the home language reinforced and kept vibrant? Does using the mother tongue as the language of instruction facilitate the transition into learning through the dominant language? Are there hidden costs to bilingualism in terms of personal, social, and intellectual development? It is clear that the answer to each of these questions is "It depends." Under the scrutiny of objective analysis, certain bilingual programs seem highly successful, others much less so. The present perspective argues that certain key features of the intergroup context in a community may serve as barriers to effective childhood bilingualism and that our awareness of these key features may allow for program adjustments in order to maximize the experience for our children.

MULTILINGUAL IDEOLOGIES

Children do not acquire language in a vacuum. By their very exposure to a particular language or languages they are reflecting and in some ways creating or altering a social reality. It comes as no surprise that in Quebec Anglophone children participate in programs to learn French and their Francophone counterparts focus on learning English, or that in Wales, where English has come to dominate, the concern is with maintaining Welsh, and that in the southeast and southwest U.S.A. Spanish and English are often the languages at issue. All communities that concern themselves with childhood bilingualism have one thing in common: linguistic and cultural diversity. There are at least two, and often more, language subcommunities that must share the social environment.

How this sharing is to take place becomes the central issue. Everyone has at least a vague idea of how diverse groups in a community should relate to one another in general, and how they personally should relate to their own group and other groups in particular. No two groups (or individuals for that matter) will have the same idea, ideology, or aim in mind. The orientation to cultural diversity held by educators, planners, teachers, and parents of the groups directly and indirectly affected by a bilingual program will have a profound impact on the final product to which the child is exposed. Berry (1975, 1983), building on earlier sociological notions, has identified four orientations people may adopt to cope with diversity: assimilation, integration, separation, and deculturation.

The *assimilation* view is that diversity is harmful, creating and maintaining group barriers, fragmenting society at the very least, ultimately setting up conditions for prejudice and discrimination. The solution is to believe that diversity in general, and different languages in particular, must be eradicated and replaced with homogeneous cultural and linguistic standards and use. Of course, the implied assumption is that less powerful groups will accommodate to the language norms of the dominant group. The traditional "melting pot" description of the United States as having a singular "American" culture and language is consistent with an assimilation orientation.

This assimilation model can be contrasted with one emphasizing *integration*. Cultural groups would be encouraged to retain their heritage language and thereby their identity. This cultural status and security would provide the environment necessary for cooperative intergroup relations. Canada's official multicultural policy represents such an orientation.

A *separation* ideology also emphasizes the need to retain language but believes all interaction between one's own group and other groups should be suspended. Extremes of the Black nationalist or Quebec separation movement are prime examples of such an ideology.

Finally, a *deculturation* ideology may prevail. Berry (1983) and others describe this as one where the person feels a lack of identity with any group, as might arise when an immigrant attempts to shed all traces of his or her heritage language and culture. The result may be the loss of this identity with no real feeling of identity for the host culture to replace it; clearly an undesirable condition involving feelings of anomie and marginality. A different, more optimistic form of deculturation may arise when a person emphasizes individual characteristics for human relations, feeling that interaction with others on the basis of their cultural identity strips them of their individuality.

These four broad ideologies, and the various alternatives within each category, set the stage for the intergroup context within which language is acquired. The four ideologies about diversity are distinguished on the basis of two fundamental attitudes; first, the desire to maintain or not maintain one's culture and language and, second, the desire for positive or negative relations with other groups. Answers to these two fundamental attitudes combine to produce the four ideologies.

TABLE 10.1
Conceptual Analysis of Ideology

	Own language and culture should be maintained?	
	YES	NO
Positive relations with other groups? **YES**	Integration	Assimilation
NO	Separation	Deculturation

Note: Adapted from Berry, Kalin, & Taylor, 1977.

The predominant ideology in a particular ethnolinguistic community will have a profound effect on how bilingualism is viewed by that community. A detailed examination of the deculturation, separation, assimilation, and integration alternatives depicted in Table 10.1 provides some appreciation for the potential barriers to effective bilingualism. Each of the four ideologies presents its own unique problems for effective bilingualism; however, one of the predominant themes that will emerge is the important role played by threats to ethnic identity.

DECULTURATION IDEOLOGY

This orientation, with its emphasis on the lack of identity with any cultural or linguistic collectivity, would at first seem to be irrelevant to the present discussion. Upon closer examination, however, an understanding of the particular deculturation ideology that is prevalent can shed light on the context of bilingual programs. Earlier, two forms of deculturation were noted. In the first case people feel alienated from all potential cultural identities. In this circumstance a bilingual program that offers formal recognition of a person's heritage through offering instruction to children in the mother tongue may be an important positive force in providing the basis for a secure identity. It may help alleviate the feelings of marginality and alienation associated with this form of deculturation.

The second form of deculturation arises when people feel that it is inappropriate to interact with another on the basis of their cultural grouping, preferring, instead, to focus on their individual characteristics. Such an orientation ignores reality. If one's ethnic group is to be ignored, then the national cultural norm is taken as the operating standard. For even interactions on an individual level require a shared language, set of assumptions, and norms to allow for communication to be meaningful. So, by default, an individualistically based deculturation ideology ultimately becomes one of assimilation, an ideology whose implications for bilingualism is addressed later.

SEPARATION IDEOLOGY

Widespread bilingualism will be rejected with a separationist ideology. Any overture at learning the language of the other group would indicate an accommodating attitude totally inconsistent with the separationist ideology. It is precisely this ideology that helps explain current bilingual efforts in Quebec. The majority of English-speaking children attend an immersion form of bilingual program and the success of this program is visible to everyone. And yet French-speaking children, who might certainly benefit from a knowledge of English in the North American context, are exposed to very little opportunity to learn English in school. This apparent irrationality becomes comprehensible when account is taken of the prevalent ideology in the French-speaking community: one that is separationist not necessarily in a political sense, but in the sense of a disengagement from direct competition with the historically privileged English community.

The specific barrier to bilingualism in this case is ethnic identity, a deeply felt personal need that is potentially threatened when there is interaction with members of another group. It has been difficult to appreciate how the learning of another language might be threatening. The ability to speak a second language has usually been judged desirable. Debates about the mental confusion associated with bilingualism notwithstanding, the overwhelming scientific conclusion (Ben-Zeev, 1977; Genesee, 1981; Peal & Lambert, 1962) and the popular belief has been that knowing another language is an achievement. Whether it is learning Latin at school, or the admiration we feel for those who are bi- or multilingual, the acquisition of another language is seen as additive—as adding a skill to the person's existing repertoire. Until recently this notion has gone unchallenged because most bilingual programs have been initiated by families representing the dominant group, White Americans or Anglo Canadians, groups whose ethnic identity is secure.

When the implications for minority groups are considered, however, there arise important instances of what Lambert (1974) has labeled ''subtractive'' bilingualism. That is, a situation where any positive consequences of learning a second language are far outweighed by the negative consequences in other, more important domains of the person's life. The particular loss in question is to one's ethnic or, more broadly, group identity. If learning in the second language contributes to the demise in knowledge and use of the heritage language, the results can be devastating.

It is important to note that the key issue that distinguishes an additive from a subtractive language experience is power in the intergroup context. Members of a powerful group who are secure in their position will experience no negative consequences to learning the language of another group. It is where, for whatever reason, a group has less power that ethnic identity and group survival become an issue.

The formal idea that fear for one's ethnic identity is perhaps a barrier to second language learning was advanced initially by Taylor and Simard (1975). As early as 1963, however (Lambert, Gardner, Barik, & Tunstall, 1963) there was evidence to suggest that as people begin to master a second language, they may develop feelings of ethnic anomie. It has also been noted, in the context of Quebec, that French Canadian parents whose children are educated in English language schools show patterns of ethnic identity different from those parents whose children attend the normal French schools (Frasure-Smith, Lambert, & Taylor, 1975). French Canadian parents whose children attend a French school display close allegiance to a monolingual French-speaking reference group. French Canadian parents of children in the English school appear divided in their ethnic identity between monolingual French Canadians on the one hand, and bilingual French and English Canadians on the other. Such a shift in identity associated with exposure to English could have serious negative consequences for a group which feels that survival of the French language in North America is threatened. Specifically, it is possible that with further exposure to the English language the French language and culture might eventually be eradicated.

Direct evidence for the motivational importance of ethnic identity comes from a study by Taylor, Meynard, and Rheault (1977). Two of the more well established "additive" motivations associated with learning a second language are instrumental and integrative. Instrumentally motivated persons learn a second language mainly for its practical value, as in qualifying for a better job; an integrative motive reflects a personal interest in the people and their culture and involves learning a second language in order to learn more about another group, meet more and varied people within that group and to be able to think and behave like its members. Although both motivational orientations have proved essential for success, an integrative motivation has been found to be the orientation that best sustains the long-term dedication needed for second language learning. The purpose of the Taylor et al. (1977) study was to establish whether threat to ethnic identity forms a separate motivational cluster, distinct from the already established instrumental and integrative motives, and whether such a motivational cluster might pose a barrier to second language learning. To this end a sample of 246 Francophone junior college students were asked to make ratings on 11 motivation questions. The ratings were then factor analyzed in order to determine the structure of motivation for learning a second language. The results of this analysis are presented in Table 10.2, which describes the particular items as well as the motivation structure.

From Table 10.2 it is clear that threat to ethnic identity (Factor III) is a motivation related to bilingualism, which is conceptually distinct from the traditional instrumental (Factor I) and integration (Factor II) motivations. Having established threat to ethnic identity as a distinct motivational cluster, the crucial question remains: How does it affect second language learning? In order to address this question the Francophone students made a subjective rating of their

TABLE 10.2
Partial Results of Factor Analysis of Motivation for
Second
Language Learning

Consequences of Learning English	Factors		
	I	II	III
Earn more money	77	02	−04
Get a better job	82	04	−12
Improved control on economy	74	18	−06
To better fight Americanization	40	57	−03
Openness toward other cultures	08	68	−46
Interact more with English people	08	69	−41
Loss of cultural identity	−02	−04	71
Increased chance of assimilation	−05	08	63
Increased anonymity	−00	−10	79
Great effort for little return	−07	−15	73
Only material gains at great cost	11	−20	76

Note: Adapted from Taylor, Meynard, & Rheault, 1977.

ability to function in English. A multiple regression analysis was then performed to determine which factors best predicted ability in English. The predictor variables used for the analysis included threat to identity, integrative motivation, instrumental motivation, personal contact with Anglophones, and contact via the mass media, to name a few. The analysis yielded a multiple regression of .59 and the only two variables to make a significant contribution to the regression were (a) personal contact with Anglophones and (b) threat to ethnic identity.

The results reveal that those with more contact with English speakers are themselves better speakers of English, and those who do not feel their own ethnic identity to be threatened are more competent speakers of English. That contact is important comes as no surprise. But the role of threat to ethnic identity is striking. If this variable had played even a minor role, it would argue for it being considered carefully in the context of bilingualism; for it to override other well established factors associated with bilingualism makes it an issue that must not be avoided.

Which groups are likely to encounter this powerful barrier to effective bilingualism? First, as we have noted, minority groups who feel their own language and way of life threatened by bilingualism would be expected to avoid or even sabotage all bilingual programs involving the dominant language. Such groups may not only feel directly threatened, in which case bilingual programs may be rejected outright, but also indirectly where the motives of the dominant group are ambiguous. Take the case of a bilingual program where members of a minority group receive some instruction in their heritage language. The ideology underlying the program may be assimilationist—that is, teaching in the heritage language is viewed as an effective vehicle for minority students to ultimately make a successful transition into English instruction. But what if the minority group interprets the ideology as one of separation. That is, minority groups may believe that instruction in the heritage language is being used by the dominant or mainstream group not as a way of facilitating transition into the mainstream, but to ostracize the minority group. What better way than to have them work in a language that clearly marks them as different, and at the same time robs them of the opportunity to develop native-like skills in the dominant language.

A separationist ideology may seem somewhat extreme. However, cultural security, or in this case insecurity, can be a harsh reality. For example, certain groups face the reality of little potential for growth in numbers either because of a stringent set of immigration practices or because political realities make it impossible. The Francophone population in Canada sees little chance for itself growing significantly in numbers in the context of an English-dominated North America. Recent language legislation within Quebec has led Anglophones to believe that the very existence of an English-speaking community is threatened. Various native groups in both Canada and the United States cannot look forward to significant growth in terms of numbers. This is not to suggest that a separationist ideology is or will be adopted by all of these groups but only to suggest that their relative position make the issue of cultural identity a very salient issue.

In summary, threats to ethnic identity can lead to a separationist ideology and under such circumstances, real or imagined bilingual programs will encounter serious barriers.

ASSIMILATION IDEOLOGY

An assimilation ideology has the appeal of producing standardization, similarity, and conformity—essential ingredients for a shared understanding of the environment and thereby the potential for effective communication. Until recently the predominant sociological prospective (see Glazer & Moynihan, 1963; Gordon, 1964; Park, 1950) was that cultural assimilation would prevail, and that ultimately a cultural consensus would be attained through the absorption of minority groups into the majority or the mingling of all to form a new, emergent homogeneous society. Of course, in a homogeneous linguistic environment the concept of bilingualism is irrelevant. However, the cost of assimilation is the fundamental psychological need individuals have for a primary, distinctive social identity with groups who share a perspective on the environment and who provide a sense of continuity, social reality, and anchor points for the individual.

Despite this heavy cost, assimilation, as a blueprint for harmonious relations, cannot be summarily dismissed. There is, after all, a well-established body of psychological literature to support the notion that similarity is related to attraction (Byrne, 1969). Highlighting cultural differences, especially on a dimension as salient as language, would then apparently only serve to lessen the chances for mutual attraction. Direct evidence for the implications of the similarity/attraction model in the context of ethnolinguistic groups is provided by Simard (1981). In her study of French-speaking and English-speaking Montrealers forming friendships, she found that for a person of the other group to be a potential friend, that person had to be more similar on other dimensions than a member of the same group. In short, assimilation results in the eradication of certain differences, which at least ensures that entire groups are not eliminated as potential targets for desirable forms of human interaction.

The similarity/attraction model notwithstanding, there is a growing recognition that at both the individual and collective level, similarity may not always be associated with attraction. One of the fundamental propositions of social identity theory, a recent theory of intergroup relations proposed by Tajfel and Turner (1979), is that groups strive for distinctiveness along positively valued dimensions. The implication of their position is that individuals need a primary social identity that is distinctive. When a rival group becomes too similar, group distinctiveness can be threatened and actually lead to heightened conflict. There is already some experimental and field research that supports this contention in intergroup contexts (Brown, 1978; Turner, 1978). It is also interesting to note, at the individual level, that deindividuation, the ultimate in similarity where all individuals become virtually anonymous, has been described as a potentially negative psychological state, one which robs the person of his or her individuality (Dipboye, 1977). In summary, the psychological literature does provide some basis for suggesting that the lack of primary social identity may be a significant cost of assimilation.

Beyond this there is indirect evidence supporting the importance of primary social identity from recent research on multiculturalism. For example, Canada's multicultural policy supports the maintenance of ethnic identity for all Canadian groups. The assumption underlying the policy is that confidence in one's own ethnic identity creates a climate of tolerance and respect for others. A large-scale Canada wide investigation of multiculturalism was conducted by Berry, Kalin, and Taylor (1977). It was found that a secure cultural identity was associated with positive attitudes toward immigrants, toward the policy of multiculturalism, and toward a number of specific Canadian ethnic groups. These results were partially corroborated in a study with a more restricted sample by Taylor, McKirnan, Christian, and Lamarche (1979).

In summary, an assimilationist ideology leaves no room for bilingualism. Instead, the aim would be to eradicate any programs designed to promote linguistic diversity. The appeal of such an ideology is in the notion that communication will be facilitated where everyone uses the same linguistic system. So opponents of bilingual programs are not merely prejudiced individuals who wish to subjugate minority groups—many are sincere individuals who believe that only a vigorous assimilation policy can provide ethnolinguistic minorities with a fair chance at full participation in society. What becomes lost in the process is the primary need for social identity. Indeed, it is no accident that the decade of the seventies has been characterized by an unparalleled revival in ethnic identity. In Canada the emergence of multiculturalism, the militancy of native peoples, and the rise of French Canadian nationalism are prime examples, and in each case language has been a fundamental issue. The United States has witnessed a decade of aggressive demands for civil rights, the emergence of a coherent Hispanic community and a generalized awareness of ethnolinguistic identity. It appears that the simplistic logic of an assimilationist ideology cannot meet more fundamental needs.

INTEGRATION IDEOLOGY

It was necessary to discuss the essential components of an integrationist ideology in the context of assimilation. The need individuals have for a primary social identity is recognized in an integrationist ideology and yet the aim is good relations with other groups. Such an ideology is, of course, entirely consistent with the concept of bilingualism and it is in precisely such an ideological context that we would expect such programs to flourish.

At this stage, then, we shift attention from the ideologies that serve as barriers to effective bilingualism, to the social psychological conditions that can maximize the experience of learning another language. Atlhough it would seem that an integrationist orientation would provide the climate most conductive to bilingualism, achieving the delicate balance between the maintenance of good intergroup relations while retaining primary social identity through language is problematic. If each group in the community guards its own culture and language, any sense of a larger community is lost to the proliferation of separate subcommunities even if there are good relations between groups.

How can the "communality" feature of assimilation be achieved while retaining the "primary social identity" component of integration? Perhaps the answer lies in the fact that when ethnolinguistic groups occupy the same social environment, it is reasonable to assume that they share overriding values and goals (see Lambert & Taylor, 1983; Taylor, 1981). By sharing the same environment, groups come to share important attributes derived from common political, social, educational, and religious institutions. To cite one example, Isajiw (1977) has discussed the notion of "technological culture," arguing that such a culture involves a set of values that is shared by virtually all ethnic groups comprising the Canadian mosaic. The various ethnic identities of groups making up the larger community, then, represent layers that build upon a shared set of broader social values. In terms of language, the need would be for some agreed-upon set of linguistic norms that permit interaction among all members of a community. Beyond this each group might be encouraged to make vibrant use of its own language where it differs from the shared code. Those whose native language coincides with the norm would be encouraged to add a language to their repertoire. This would permit interaction with a key minority group in the community through a language other than that designated by the shared norm.

The fundamental question to be addressed in this context is, What is the broadly based shared linguistic norm and who should define it? The answer to the question is that usually the shared linguistic norm is precisely what the most powerful group in the community decides should be the norm. The problem is that what appears as a shared linguistic norm is really one that has been imposed upon less powerful groups. To be neglected in the process of articulating shared norms will leave less powerful groups only partially committed to such norms. In order for a linguistic norm or standard to become truly shared it requires that members of all groups participate in the process of defining that norm. Naturally, larger, more powerful and historically precedent groups will have a greater impact on the definition process. So, English will no doubt emerge as the communal language in the United States, and English, French, or both will represent the shared norm in different regions of Canada. Nevertheless, the particular form of the language and the range of code variations accepted as normative may be broadened through the participation of other groups. Community language norms defined in this fashion should lead all groups to a greater commitment to the realization of these language norms and affect the motivation of students to achieve proficiency in them.

Beyond the shared language norms, ethnolinguistic groups can be encouraged to define their own unique language needs, be it to keep the mother tongue vibrant, recover a language nearly lost, or broaden social contacts. Encouragement cannot be limited to lip service but must take the form of an equitable distribution of community resources, financial and otherwise. Viewed from this perspective, bilingualism in a multilingual community is an issue for everyone. No one group is singled out for special treatment that can make them feel privileged on the one hand or stigmatized on the other. With everyone clear on the shared linguistic aims, programs can then be designed to meet those aims while at the same time attempting to meet the unique linguistic needs of each group.

For example, an ethnolinguistic minority may well require a bilingual program with a dual function to support the minority language while at the same time developing competence in the shared language norms. Children whose native language is largely coincident with the norm may focus on the language of the minority, thereby ''adding'' a linguistic skill while at the same time providing the minority language with increased status.

The key to successful implementation of bilingual programs is the underlying multicultural ideology represented in parents and educators, which will be communicated, however indirectly, to the children. The four major orientations are the result of simultaneously considering two fundamental motivations: the desire to foster good intergroup relations and the desire to retain one's ethnic identity. The significance of having a climate of good intergroup relations has long been recognized and needs only to be underscored in the present context. The importance of creating or maintaining a secure ethnolinguistic identity emerges as a central issue that is only beginning to be appreciated. Threats to ethnic identity arose in the context of a deculturation ideology only indirectly but were central to the assimilation, integration, and separatism ideologies. The process of identity is as yet not well enough understood to allow a confident appreciation of its role in successful bilingual programs. It is in this uncertain context that a tentative suggestion is made about the multicultural ideology, which offers the best chance for ensuring the success of bilingualism. Specifically, an integrationist orientation building on a shared perspective in which all concerned have contributed to that perspective may eliminate many of the intergroup barriers to effective childhood bilingualism.

ACKNOWLEDGMENT

I wish to thank M. P. Walker for comments made on an earlier draft of the paper.

REFERENCES

Ben-Zeev, S. (1977). The influence of bilingualism on cognitive development and cognitive strategy. *Child Development,* 1009–18.

Berry, J. W. (1975). Amerindian attitudes toward assimilation: Multicultural policy and reality in Canada. *Journal of Institute of Social Research, 1,* 47–58.

Berry, J. W. (1983). Acculturation: A comparative analysis of alternative forms. In R. J. Samuda & S. L. Woods (Eds.), *Perspectives in Immigrant and Minority Education.* (pp. 65–78). Lanham, Maryland. University Press of America.

Berry, J. W., Kalin, R., & Taylor, D. M. (1977). *Multiculturalism and ethnic attitudes in Canada.* Ottawa: Minister of Supply and Services.

Brown, R. J. (1978). Divided we fall: An analysis of relations between sections of a factory workforce. In H. Tajfel (Ed.), *Differentiation between social groups: Studies in the social psychology of intergroup relations* (pp. 395–429). London: Academic Press.

Byrne, D. (1969). Attitudes and attraction. In L. Berkowitz (Ed.), *Advances in experimental social psychology (Vol. 4)* (pp. 35–89). New York: Academic Press.

Carroll, J. B. (1958). A factor analysis of two foreign language aptitude batteries. *Journal of General Psychology, 59,* 3–19.

Carroll, J. B. (1974). Aptitude in second language learning. *Proceedings of the Fifth Symposium of the Canadian Association of Applied Linguistics,* 8–23.

Carroll, J. B., & Sapon, S. M. (1959). *Modern language aptitude test, Form A.* New York: Psychological Corporation.

Dipboye, R. L. (1977). Alternative approaches to deindividuation. *Psychological Bulletin, 84,* 1057–1075.

Frasure-Smith, N., Lambert, W. E., & Taylor, D. M. (1975). Choosing the language of instruction for one's children: A Quebec study. *Journal of Cross-Cultural Psychology, 6,* 131–155.

Gardner, R. C. (1981). Second language learning. In R. C. Gardner & R. Kalin (Eds.), A Canadian social psychology of ethnic relations (pp. 92–113). Toronto: Methuen.

Gardner, R. C., & Lambert, W. E. (1972). *Attitudes and motivation in second-language learning.* Rowley, MA.: Newburv House.

Genesee, F. (1981). Cognitive and Social Consequences of Bilingualism. In R. C. Gardner & R. Kalin (Eds.), *A Canadian social psychology of ethnic relations.* (pp. 114–131). Toronto: Methuen.

Glazer, N., & Moynihan, D. P. (1963). *Beyond the melting pot.* Cambridge, MA: MIT Press.

Gordon, M. M. (1964). *Assimilation in American life.* New York: Oxford University Press.

Isajiw, W. W. (1977). Olga in wonderland: Ethnicity in technological society. *Canadian Ethnic Studies, 9,* 77–85.

Lambert, W. E. (1974). Culture and language as factors in learning and education. In F. E. Aboud & R. D. Meade (Eds.) Cultural factors in Learning and Education (pp. 91–122). Bellingham: Western Washington State College.

Lambert, W. E., Gardner, R. C., Barik, H. C., & Tunstall, K. (1963). Attitudinal and cognitive aspects of intensive study of a second language. *Journal of Abnormal and Social Psychology, 66,* 358–68.

Lambert, W. E., & Taylor, D. M. (1983). Language in the education of ethnic minority immigrants: Issues, problems and methods. In R. J. Samuda & S. L. Woods (Eds.), *Perspectives in immigrant and minority education* (pp. 267–280). Lanham, Maryland: University Press of America.

Park, R. E. (1950). *Race and Culture.* Glencoe: Free Press.

Peal, E., & Lambert, W. E. (1962). The relation of bilingualism to intelligence. *Psychological Monographs, 76,* 1–23.

Simard, L. M. (1981). Cross-cultural interaction: Potential invisible barriers. *Journal of Social Psychology, 113,* 171–192.

Tajfel, H., & Turner, J. C. (1979). An integrative theory of intergroup conflict. In W. Austin & S. Worchel (Eds.), *The social psychology of intergroup relations* (pp. 33–48). Monterey: Brooks/Cole.

Taylor, D. M. (1981). Stereotypes and Intergroup Relations. In R. C. Gardner & R. Kalin (Eds.), *A Candian social psychology of ethnic relations* (pp. 151–171). Toronto: Methuen.

Taylor, D. M., Meynard, R., & Rheault, E. (1977). Threat to ethnic identity and second language learning. In H. Giles (Ed.), *Language, ethnicity and intergroup relations* (pp. 99–116). London & New York: Academic Press.

Taylor, D. M., McKirnan, D. J., Christian, J., & Lamarche, L. (1979). Cultural insecurity and attitudes toward multiculturalism and ethnic groups in Canada. *Canadian Ethnic Studies, 16,* 19–30.

Taylor, D. M., & Simard, L. M. (1975). Social interaction in a bilingual setting. *Canadian Psychological Review, 16,* 230–254.

Turner, J. C. (1978). Social comparison, similarity and ingroup favouritism. In H. Tajfel (Ed.), *Differentiation between social groups: Studies in the social psychology of intergroup relations* (pp. 235–250). London: Academic Press.

The Effects of Bilingual and Bicultural Experiences on Children's Attitudes and Social Perspectives

W. E. Lambert
McGill University

Attitudes are related to second language learning and bilingualism in various ways. What little we know about this relationship thus far comes from both commonsense observations and behavioral research, and usually common sense and research are mutually supportive. For instance, it makes good sense to expect that a favorable attitude toward another ethnolinguistic group should affect positively one's acquisition of that group's language, and research findings generally support this expectation (see Clément, Gardner, & Smythe, 1977; Gardner, 1982; Gardner & Lambert, 1972; Gardner & Smythe, 1975). What goes beyond common sense are the details of how attitudes affect motivation-to-learn and how it in turn affects the language acquisition process. To understand these important complexities we have to rely on elaborate research, and thus research, more than common sense, produces instructive, often unexpected information. On the other hand, common sense, more than research, gives a direction and purpose to research. For instance, it reminds us that people sometimes master an ''enemy's'' language, an example where the attitudes involved are anything but friendly and open. Research has to explain the complexities of both extremes, that is, explain how attitudes and motivation-to-learn sometimes function quite independently of one another and other times quite interdependently (see Gardner, 1981; Gardner, Glicksman, & Smythe, 1978). It is also true that research can stimulate common sense. For instance, in reviewing various earlier research findings, Genesee, Rogers, and Holobow (1982) were led to a new set of questions about attitudes and language learning. They realized that a learner's motivation might be only one determiner of rate and level of achievement in learning a new language; the learner's expectations of receiving or not receiving motivational support from the other group could be a separate and equally important predictor of success in second language learning. And that's what they found when they put this new composite idea to test.

This preoccupation with attitudes is much more than an academic issue. There are socially important decisions to be made that require reliable information about attitudes, for example, decisions about bilingual education programs or programs to integrate or assimilate immigrants. We need to know how attitudes function both as determiners or predictors of the rate of second or foreign language achievement—attitudes as "input" factors—as well as the effects bilingual skill development might have on attitudes toward outgroups—attitude change as an "outcome" effect. In other words, to be helpful to decision makers, researchers need to determine (a) if (and how) hostile, suspicious attitudes toward another ethnolinguistic group hamper the acquisition of that group's language, and (b) if (and how) successful acquisition of another group's language promotes more friendly, open attitudes toward that group or more generally toward ethnically different peoples. Because researchers and educators have drawn attention to the issues underlying such questions, important changes in values seem to be taking place. For instance, it is now recognized that outlawing a language—as when an immigrant child's home language (the language used for the basic development of conceptual thinking from infancy on) is prohibited as a mode of expression in school settings—is nothing less than a subtle form of tyranny. The psychological consequences can be enormous for the linguistic group involved because attitudes toward own group, toward self, and toward society are seriously affected in such instances. Today oppressive policies of this sort seem to be giving way to more democratic ones wherein people are aloud to speak and let speak, and where more than one form of speaking becomes socially acceptable and correct. The inter-ethnic group attitudes in these cases are automatically made more friendly, permissive, and open, and as a consequence the societies involved are made much more interesting.

For those interested in exploring further the role of attitudes in language learning, there is an established research base they can build on. The need for a social psychology of language learning became apparent to several of us in the 1950s and 1960s. At that time, O. H. Mowrer (1950) began to study the emotional attachments that develop between talking birds and their trainers, and the effects such attachments had on the birds' skill at talk development. If attitudes affect bird talk, we argued, there was much to expect from attitudes and human talk. In this atmosphere, Susan Ervin (1954) started her work on the role of emotions and attitudes in children's language development, and Robert Gardner and I began to look at bilingual skill development from the same perspective (see Gardner & Lambert, 1959, 1972; Lambert, Gardner, Barik, & Tunstall, 1963). The Gardner-Lambert studies, exploratory and factor analytic as they were, convinced us that prejudiced attitudes and stereotypes about the other ethnolinguistic group—quite independent of language learning abilities or verbal intelligence—can upset and disturb the motivation needed to learn the other group's language, just as open, inquisitive, and friendly attitudes can enhance and enliven the language learning process. We also saw that parental attitudes, positive or negative, are picked up by children, so that pupils bring a family complex of attitudes to the language class with them. Gardner and Smythe (1975) have gone further into these aspects of attitudes and have found that persistence in language study and eagerness to interact in language classes also hinge on the attitudes and motivations pupils bring to school (see Gardner, 1981).

These research studies were just a start and there is much more to be studied in this domain. For instance, Genesee and Hamayan (1980), working with Grade 1 Anglo-Canadian pupils, did not find any neat, simple relationship between attitudes and second language achievement, indicating that we need to explore a broader age range. More recently, Clément et al. (1977) and Taylor, Meynard, and Rheault (1977) have extended the research domain by focusing on the attitudes of members of an ethnolinguistic minority group when faced with learning a dominant group's language. For example, Taylor et al. (1977) find that the learning of English can pose a threat to personal and cultural identity for French Canadian university students and that this threat can hamper the progress made in learning that language. The socially significant fact is that threats of this sort can lead to suspicion and distrust. Other studies have shown that parents' suspicions and prejudices about outgroups or about own group can determine the academic route their children will follow and also the language identity their children will develop. Thus, French Canadian parents who see little value in being French in the North American scene are prone to route their children into an entirely Anglo educational system, whereas those who have hope in the French fact in Canada and pride in being French keep their children in French academic settings without hesitation and create for them a comfortable French social environment (Frasure-Smith, Lambert, & Taylor, 1975).

On the outcome or effect side, there are also some basic studies for researchers to build on. Common sense would suggest that as skill with the other language evolves, attitudes toward the other ethnolinguistic group should become less suspicious and hostile because the learners are breaking through the language barrier and reducing the foreignness of the other language group with the help of a teacher from that group. As ignorance of the other group dissipates, attitudes should become less suspicious and possibly more compassionate, but one must be cautious in predicting because value contrasts and clashes can surface as knowledge about the other group grows, and these contrasts can generate a new form of suspicion. Richard Tucker and I studied the attitudes of Anglophone Canadian youngsters as they moved through 4 or 5 years of immersion-in-French schooling; these pupils were compared with "control" pupils who had had conventional English language schooling only (Lambert & Tucker, 1972). As of the start of the experience (i.e., at the kindergarten year) the attitudes toward French Canadians were basically identical for the parents of the immersion and control groups. By Grade 5, however, the immersion pupils relative to the controls "liked" French people more; were much more prone to say that they would be "just as happy" had they been born into a French family; and were much more likely to see themselves as becoming both English and French Canadian in makeup. Apparently, much of the foreignness of the other group was dispelled for the immersion pupils and they began to appreciate both the distinctive and the shared characteristics of the other ethnolinguistic group. But other follow-up studies of immersion pupils, using different probing techniques and different age levels, sometimes replicated and sometimes did not replicate these favorable attitude outcomes, although in no case were the immersion children less favorable to the other group than the controls. It is, of course, our responsibility as researchers to explain cases that work out as expected as well as those that don't.

My purpose here is to review and analyze a subset of research studies that have dealt with attitudes of the type just described in order to highlight both the social importance of attitudes in language learning and bilingualism as well as the difficulty researchers have in capturing and examining them. The review focuses on data from English-speaking pupils and students in immersion programs, like the one just referred to, because these programs provide us with a quasi-experimental format wherein a relatively clear picture of the attitudes of pupils and their parents at the kindergarten level is available, and where some of these youngsters (those in the "experimental" groups) are schooled mainly through a foreign or second language (French) while others (those in the "control" groups) follow conventional English-language educational programs. I will select examples of attitude change (positive or negative) and of no change, as well as changes in social perspectives at various points from the early school grades up through high school. This review then deals mainly with "outcome effects," that is, the effects of developing high-level skills in another group's language on students' attitudes and social perspectives. Throughout, comparisons will be made of pupils who have become functionally bilingual through immersion programs in school or equivalent real-life experiences (the "experimental" groups) and those who have not had such experiences (the "control" or "comparison" groups). In most cases, the attitudes of the pupils as of Grade 1 or of their parents were measured and found to be essentially alike on relevant dimensions. In cases where we have no Grade 1 baseline attitude data, we assume that the family attitudes were essentially the same.

ATTITUDES AND THEIR MEASUREMENT

What do we mean by "attitudes" and how do we go about measuring them? The concept "attitude" is a creation of philosophers and psychologists who tried to explain and describe certain consistencies in their own and other people's thoughts, feelings, and reactions. Attitudes characterize biological systems not physical systems, and so, unlike atoms and physical structures, they are pre-sumed to be highly variable from person to person and from one time to another for any person. The fun comes in trying to capture and measure attitudes relia-bly—a much more demanding task than most measurement problems in the physical or purely biological sciences. The following definition (Lambert & Lambert, 1973) is typical of what psychologists mean by an attitude:

> An attitude is an organized and consistent manner of thinking, feeling and reacting to people, groups, social issues or, more generally, to any event in the environ-ment. The essential components of attitudes are thoughts and beliefs, feelings or emotions, and tendencies to react. We can say that an attitude is formed when these components are so inter-related that specific feelings and reaction tendencies be-come consistently associated with the attitude object. Our attitudes develop in the course of coping with and adjusting to our social environments. Once attitudes are developed, they lend regularity to our modes of reacting and facilitate social adjustment. In the early stages of attitude development, the components can be modified by new experiences. Later, however, their organization may become inflexible and stereotyped, usually because we have been encouraged over long periods of time to react in standard ways to particular events or groups. As an attitude becomes firmly set, we become too ready to categorize people or events according to emotionally toned patterns of thoughts so that we fail to recognize individuality or uniqueness. Fixed or stereotyped attitudes reduce the potential richness of our environments and constrict our reactions. (p. 42)

We will refer to three major components: the *stereotype,* the *feeling,* and the *reaction tendency* components of attitudes. Complexity enters because the com-ponents appear to develop in different fashions and at different rates, and, al-though always integrated, they come together in unexpected combinations. Thus one's thoughts and stereotypes about another group or event may be positive or negative whereas the feelings and reaction tendencies toward that group or event may or may not be predictably aligned. Accordingly, attitudes sometimes cover love-hate relationships, where one's stereotypes are unfavorable toward a social group, but one is nonetheless attracted to representatives of that group, or vice versa. It is also true that social constraints can force people to react to a group in one way while their feelings and stereotypes work in different emotional direc-tions.

In the research to be described, typical measurement methods are used and these reflect mainly one component or another. For instance, the stereotype component is measured through rating scales, e.g., respondents are asked to give their personal estimates, by ratings on scales, of how friendly . . . unfriendly, nice . . . bad, dependable . . . undependable, and so forth, members of a par-ticular group seem to them to be. The feeling and reaction components are measured through direct questions—e.g., how respondents would feel (or react) if they had to interact with members of another group in particular ways. The feeling and reaction components are also measured through various scaling procedures—e.g., respondents are asked to estimate how similar or different members of another group seem when compared to own-group members or to one's self.

The Stereotype Component of Attitudes

Since 1967, we have collected data from numerous samples of English-speaking Canadian (EC) children who were in French immersion programs in Montreal public schools, and from EC "controls" those in conventional English language school programs that provided only 30 to 60 minutes per day of French taught as a second language (FSL). For most samples, parents' attitudes toward French-speaking Canadians (FCs) and the FC culture were assessed through questionnaires and interviews as of the time their children entered kindergarten or Grade 1. Typically, the parents of the experimental and control children have very similar attitudes toward FCs, attitudes that usually reflect little personal experience with or knowledge about the FC people and culture. Rather than being hostile, the attitude reflects more feelings of stranger-to-stranger, colored with some suspicion (see Lambert & Tucker, 1972).

The "immersion" experience is based on the interaction of 30 to 32 EC pupils who have no prior knowledge of French and a teacher who, from the first encounter, speaks only French to them. The teacher, usually a woman, would be either from Europe or from French Canada, and if not actually monolingual in French, would play as though she knew no English at all. French is the sole medium of instruction from the first day on through the first 2 or 3 years of school; English is progressively introduced, by separate teachers, as a second medium of instruction from Grade 3 on, reaching a 50-50 French-English curriculum by Grade 6. The outcomes of the immersion experience on cognitive development, English and French language progress, and content subject achievement are remarkable. They have been described thoroughly elsewhere (see Genesee, 1978; Lambert & Tucker, 1972; Swain, 1974).

Information on attitudes and attitude changes related to the immersion experience is based largely on parent and pupil ratings on 7-point scales such as intelligent . . . stupid; strong . . . weak; friendly . . . unfriendly; affectionate . . . unaffectionate; industrious . . . lazy; kind . . . mean; happy . . . sad; humble . . . proud; self-confident . . . not; good looking . . . ugly; pleasant . . . unpleasant; calm . . . emotional; talkative . . . non. Terms vary according to the respondent's age; ratings are made with regard to various reference groups, e.g.: English Canadians, French Canadians, European French people, as well as self-ratings, e.g., Me, Myself.

Political and Academic Background Events

The attitudes we discuss here were measured in a highly emotionally charged time period for Quebec, starting in June of 1968. In this period many political changes took place, all focused on progressively stronger demands on the part of

Francophone Canadians in Quebec for language rights and political sovereignty. The roots of Quebec demands for political independence are deep (see Guindon, 1971), but an effective separatist political movement was started only in the 1960s. At the social-psychological level, researchers in the late 1950s were documenting a striking tendency among FCs in Quebec to denigrate their own ethnicity, portraying French-speaking Canadians as less likely to succeed, less socially attractive, and generally inferior to Anglophone Canadians (see Lambert, 1967). This colonial outlook with its stereotyped self views—similar in many respects to the traditional views black Americans have had of them-selves—was evident in the thinking of pre-adolescent FCs (see Lambert, Frankel, & Tucker, 1966), suggesting that a defeatist outlook had a disturbingly early base among FCs. It is likely that these sentiments of inferiority, touching even the youth of the FC society, was one factor prompting separatists to forcefully and openly argue for a separate, French Canadian state, one comfortably inde-pendent of the rest of Canada. Canadian separatists had powerful American models to draw on, especially the Civil Rights and Black Power examples of the 1960s.

In June of 1968, we began our surveys of the attitudes of Anglo-Canadian elementary school pupils toward FC people and FC culture. By this time, the political movement for FC control over their own affairs ("maîtres chez-nous"), starting with language legislation favoring the use of French over English, was clearly evident in a series of events.

1. 1969: The St. Leonard Demonstrations. St. Leonard, a mainly Italian-Cana-dian region of Montreal, demonstrated against new legislation that forced some Italian-Canadian children into French language schools. Nearly all immigrant groups, when given a choice, had overwhelmingly chosen English language schooling.

2. 1970: The F.L.Q. Crisis. A radical underground group known as Le Front pour la Liberation du Québec gained attention and provoked a War Measures Act reaction from the fedral government in Ottawa when the FLQ kidnapped a Quebec politician (and later murdered him), as well as a British diplomat, later found and released by federal police.

3. 1974: Education Bill 22. The Liberal Party of Quebec put into law a bill that restricted free choice of schooling, especially limiting FC children's access to English language schools; the bill also started a French-as-the-language-of-work movement.

4. 1976: The Parti Quebecois Victory. In a surprise victory, the Liberal Party of Quebec was replaced by a new party openly working for independence, sou-veraineté and separation of the "State of Quebec" from Canada.

5. 1977: Education Bill 101. A no-compromise bill was passed that made French the only official language of Quebec, French the only language of work, and French the language of schooling for everyone except the children of those ECs who themselves had attended English language schools in Quebec. Thus, all immigrants and Anglophones from other parts of Canada were (and are) required

to attend French language schools. The Parti Québecois was reelected for another term in the early 1980s.

Just as these political events could easily color the attitudes of children, whether EC or FC, so too could certain events that transpired in the English language schools that introduced immersion programs. From the start of the immersion experiment in the 1965–66 academic year, the public schools involved (all part of the city's Protestant School System) had to find French-speaking teachers who were Protestants. Consequently they chose recent immigrants from Europe (France, Belgium or Switzerland) or actual residents of these countries who were of the Protestant faith. It was not until 1969–70 that the Protestant requirement was relaxed so that equal numbers of French Canadian teachers could be introduced into the growing number of immersion classes in Montreal. Thus there was a strong European French character to the early years of immersion; aside from the teachers, the educational model was a no-nonsense, highly structured, lycée-type program of instruction. These features may well have strengthened the immersion teaching, but it may also have created invidious comparisons between European French and Canadian French languages and cultures.

Furthermore, in the academic year 1968–69, it was decided to introudce FC youngsters, in small numbers, into the French immersion classes so as to approximate even closer a total French learning environment for the Anglophone pupils. The trouble was that the FC pupils had to be Protestant (meaning non-Catholic) because of the religious division of Montreal schools at that time. The trouble with that was that the FC Protestant youngsters happened to come in large part from lower socioeconomic home and community backgrounds than the Anglophones in those schools. Differences in social class of this sort make substantial differences not only in measured IQ and scholastic attainment, but also, it turns out, in type and magnitude of discipline problems. It became apparent immediately to teachers, principals, and pupils alike that the FC Protestant pupils, as a subgroup, were clearly poorer students in all content matters, French included, and very undisciplined. After a 2-year trial period, the introduction of FC Protestant pupils into immersion classes stopped, but it is very likely that while in the classes, they left a strong negative impression on the EC pupils.

Stereotypes of Anglophone Immersion Pupils, 1966–1978. By June of 1968, the first immersion class in the Montreal program (the ''Pilot'' class, according to Lambert & Tucker, 1972) had reached Grade 2, and their ratings of French people were unambiguously favorable, significantly more favorable than the EC controls, and constituting what we refer to as a clear ''immersion effect.'' They also, relative to the EC controls, presented a more balanced perspective of FC people, rating them higher on such scales as good, smart, friendly, and nice, and lower on scales like short, small and fat. We will refer to this as a ''balance effect,'' indicating that the immersion children rated FCs at or above the neutral point of the scales, thereby bringing their perspectives of FCs more in balance with their views of their own group, the ECs. In this case, they did not achieve the balance by downgrading their own group in any way. Rather, compared to the EC controls, they elevated their perceptions of FCs. Furthermore, their self-views (their ratings of "me") were in every way as favorable and wholesome as were those of the EC controls; both groups saw themselves as friendly, nice, big, tall, smart, and good. This favorable self-view, incidentally, holds for all immersion groups examined to date, regardless of the age level (see Lambert & Tucker, 1972).

By the end of Grades 3 and 4 (June 1969 and 1970), the attitude pattern had changed. At that time, the group "French people from France" was included in the comparison, and for the 1969 and 1970 periods, there was no immersion effect (i.e., no difference in ratings between immersion and EC control pupils), and thus no balance effect for their ratings of FCs or of European French people. All ratings fell around and slightly below the neutral point (scale position 4), meaning that all Anglophone groups viewed FCs as slightly dumb, bad, unkind and mean. The trend was somewhat less negative toward European French people, but not significantly so.

In contrast, for pupils in the "Follow-up" class who finished Grade 2 in June 1969, there were strong immersion and balance effects in their ratings of European French people, but not of FCs, who were viewed negatively, particularly on the good-bad, and intelligent-dumb scales. Pupils reaching Grade 2 the following year (June, 1970) presented the same picture—a strong immersion and balance effect for European French people, but not for FCs. In both cases, the self-views of immersion pupils were as favorable and wholesome as were the self-views of the EC controls.

A Second Attitude Survey: Grades 4, 5, and 6.   To avoid overtesting the same pupils, we switched to new groups of immersion and EC control pupils who had finished Grades 4, 5, and 6 in June of 1976 or 1977 (see Cziko, Holobow, & Lambert, March, 1977; Cziko, Holobow, Lambert & Tucker, December, 1977). The results in 1976–77, some 5 years later, were essentially the same as those found in 1970–71 with younger children; that is, for pupils in Grade 4 as of 1976–77, there was no immersion effect for their ratings of FCs (all groups rated FCs around the neutral point (4) on the evaluative scales), and no balance effect because their ratings of their own group fell between scale points 5 and 6, on the average. However, with regard to European French people, there was both an immersion and a balance effect; that is, the immersion pupils saw European French people as significantly more affectionate, kind, and self confident than did the EC controls. Thus the immersion pupils had views of European French people that were relatively close to the views they had of their own group.

The Grades 5 and 6 pupils in the 1976–77 testing, however, showed a very strong immersion and balance effect in their ratings of European French people *and* of French Canadians as well. Here there were clear signs of more favorable attitudes toward French people in general among the immersion pupils. However, it was not that the immersion pupils at grades 5 and 6 were so favorable (their ratings also fell at or slightly above the neutral point), but that the EC control pupils had very negative stereotypes of French people, particularly of FCs. Thus in these cases it appears that the immersion experience had protected students from the strong anti-French sentiments that characterized the EC controls.

A Third Attitude Survey: Grade 7.   In June of 1976, three new groups of Grade 7 students were surveyed in the standard manner, using the same scales. One group comprised those who had been in a French immersion program from kindergarten through Grade 6; a second group had FSL instruction until Grade 7 at which time they followed a 1-year French immersion program; and the third was an EC control group who had FSL instruction only from Grade 1 on (see Cziko, Holobow, & Lambert, April 1977). Here there was no evidence of an immersion or balance effect, since all three Anglophone groups, immersion or not, gave generally similar ratings for both FC and European French people. In this case it is not that the immersion pupils were more negative than usual in their views (their ratings fell at or slightly above the neutral point, on the average), but that the EC controls at the Grade 7 level had views of French people that were less negative than those seen at the Grade 4–6 levels with other EC controls. It is thus possible that the FSL experience has a similar ultimate effect of ameliorating Anglophone students' views of French people, but that it just takes much more time, finally showing itself at the high school level. This does not mean that what appears to have been a more immediate ameliorative effect attributable to immersion had pushed the pupils' ratings to the upper limits of the scales. Instead, the views of French people that Anglophone students arrive at, either early or late, are neutral or at best only slightly favorable. This essentially neutral perspective of French people among the older children stands in sharp contrast to the much more favorable view they have of their own group.

A Fourth Attitude Survey: Grade 7 and 11 Students.   In June of 1974 a similar survey was conducted in a totally different school system with Grades 7 and 11 students. The students had followed a different type of immersion program—a 1-year immersion in French at Grade 7 after 6 years of conventional English language program with an FSL component from Grade 1 on (see Genesee, Morin, & Allister, 1974a, 1974b). As for the other surveys, comparisons were made at Grades 7 and 11 with EC controls who had not had the 1-year total immersion experience. In this case, a clear immersion effect was found at the Grade 7 level, i.e., immersion pupils displayed more favorable attitudes to both FCs and European French people than did the EC controls. Again, the differences were due mainly to less favorable views on the part of the EC controls; the immersion groups again restricted their ratings of French people to the 4–5 scale range. At the Grade 11 level, however, there were no signs of an immersion or balance effect because the Grade 11 EC controls displayed essentially the same views of French people as did the early immersion and the Grade 7, 1-year immersion students.

CONCLUSIONS ABOUT IMMERSION PROGRAMS' EFFECTS ON STEREOTYPES

There are several general conclusions that can be safely drawn from this series of attitude surveys, and although we are fortunate to be dealing with longitudinal data, we nonetheless view these conclusions as tentative, requiring further verification through replications in similar and different settings.

1. First, we are dealing here with surveys, i.e., group-administered, checklist, essentially superficial measures of pupils' stereotypes, not in-depth, personalized probes. Their saving feature is their reliability and their procedural clarity. Furthermore, they are surveys of the attitudes of EC school children toward French people conducted in the intensely emotional political climate of Quebec in the 1960s and 1970s when French-English relations were colored by mutual suspicion, distrust, and fear. A baptism under fire of this sort may well have been the best possible period for testing our main ideas. One consistent finding is that children with immersion experience attained and maintained an average evaluative rating of French people in the 4- to 5-point range on 7-point scales, reflecting a neutral to slightly positive stereotype of French people. Why didn't immersion-in-French push attitudes to a higher level? For one thing, getting to know another group through learning their language and culture might not generate extreme affection if the group in question slowly emerges as being essentially at odds with one's own basic values and points of view. Like marriages that lead to divorce in one out of two or three cases in the Western world, getting to know other people well is often an eye-opener! Furthermore, in this instance, the other group in question is one that has shared democratically a common land with your own group for generations and has suddenly expressed a desire to separate by forming an autonomous French Canadian state. Thus, maintaining ratings in the 4–5 range may be all one should expect from those who are being distanced by that sought-for separation.

2. Second, the results show that children in immersion classes generally have either more favorable or less negative views of FCs and European French people than do children who were not in immersion programs. Even in the cases where the immersion and control children's views do not differ, there are no instances where the immersion pupils express less favorable views than the controls. Thus, immersion is more likely to foster more favorable attitude profiles toward the

group whose language is being learned than is the case for children without immersion experience.

3. In no case does immersion affect negatively the children's views of their own ethnolinguistic group (views of "English-speaking Canadians") or their self-views (views of "me").

4. The immersion effect is most likely to emerge at the start of the immersion experience, either at the Grade 1 level of early immersion programs or at the Grade 7 level for late, 1-year immersion. This is understandable if one realizes that the immersion pupils have virtually no social contact with French-speaking people other than that of their teacher. Thus, there is no social support to maintain personalized, favorable attitudes towards French people except for the contact pupils have with their French-speaking teacher.

5. The immersion experience, therefore, does not amplify highly favorable stereotypes of the group whose language is being learned so much as it protects students from the highly charged, usually uninformed, perspectives of the other group that are more likely to run unchecked through the minds of children in the control groups. In several instances we saw how the immersion children, even in the political peak periods, were less sour, hostile and negative in their views of the other group than were the non-immersion control children.

6. Another possible explanation for the occasional lack of an immersion effect in our comparisons, especially those at the high school level, is the fact that all the EC controls had a 30–40 minute period of FSL instruction throughout their schooling. The FSL component is expertly and sympathetically taught, usually by native-speakers of French, and thus FSL may simply require more time to lift the control children's attitudes up to the levels attained by the immersion children at earlier grade levels.

7. More often than not, the children's attitude profiles showed a more favorable view of French people from France than of French Canadians. This may be due in part to the public image of France that has been projected historically. It is also possible that Canadians, English and French, have inherited a colonial mentality about the old countries (England and France) as being preferred, more civilized nations. We also believe, however, that other factors were very likely involved in the more favorable ratings given European French people: a tendency to hire more European-born than Canadian-born French teachers, and an unhappy administrative plan to integrate small numbers of French-speaking Protestant children into the immersion classes. The trouble was that the children brought in were disadvantaged in terms of socioeconomic home backgrounds, making them appear comparatively dumb academically and unmanageable from a discipline point of view. Until they were taken out of the immersion classes, their presence appeared to work against the development of favorable stereotypes of French-speaking Canadians because this decidedly unrepresentative sample of FCs was clearly seen as "dumb" and "not nice."

In summary, the stereotype component of attitudes is seen in full operation in the surveys described here, and the ups and downs of the children's views of the other group seem to reflect sensitively the political background, the administrative policies attempted by school principals, and, most important, the generally favorable effects on stereotypes which are attributable to the immersion experience, but which are not pronounced in magnitude nor durable beyond the first 2 years of the start of such programs.

THE FEELINGS AND REACTION-TENDENCY
COMPONENTS OF ATTITUDES

Quite different probing procedures were used to get at students' feelings for (or against) French-speaking people and their willingness or readiness to interact with them.

The Use of Direct Questioning.   A procedure we found very informative was to ask direct questions about feelings and psychological reactions, for example: Having learned French and about French people for sometime, do you feel closer to French people now then you once did? Do you feel you like them more now? Would you like to get to know more about them and their language? The first two classes of immersion pupils were asked such questions as they finished Grade 5 (the Pilot class) or Grade 4 (the Follow-up class) in June of 1971 (Lambert & Tucker, 1972). These happen to be the same pupils just referred to whose stereotypes of French-speaking people were no different from the controls as of the 1970 and 1971 surveys (see also Lambert, Tucker, & d'Anglejan, 1973). What is interesting is that their feelings about French-speaking people are clearly more favorable than those of the controls, especially so for those in Grade 5. (See chapter 9 of Lambert & Tucker, 1972.) Thus, to the question: "Since you have started learning about French-speaking people at school, do you like French Canadian people (also, European French people) more now?" the Grade 5 immersion pupils said they liked French Canadians more now than they did at the start of schooling, much more so than did the Grade 5 control pupils. (Mentioned here are statistically significant differences.) Similarly, when asked "Suppose you happened to be born into a French Canadian family, would you be just as happy?" the Grade 5 immersion pupils were again much more likely to say that they would be "just as happy." Both Grades 4 and 5 children showed more favorable reactions when asked: "Do you think, in the course of your studying French, that you have become less English Canadian in your thoughts and feelings, or do you see yourself now being both English and French Canadian, or as more English Canadian?" In this instance immersion pupils at both grade levels were decidedly more likely to think of themselves as becoming both

English and French Canadian in makeup. When asked if they felt too much emphasis was placed on French in school so that they might like now to go to an "all-English" school, again the immersion pupils at both grade levels differed significantly from the controls in rejecting an all-English alternative. Then, when asked if they would like to continue learning French, the immersion pupils were much more prone to continue than are the controls, as the recent theorizing of Gardner (1981, 1982) would predict. (The details are in Lambert & Tucker, 1972, p. 192ff.)

Direct Questioning as of High School Leaving. The same groups (Pilot, Follow-up, and English Control) were surveyed again as they finished high school. They were asked to think back on their schooling and the part language learning had played in it. They were also asked attitude-related questions, for instance, questions about their willingness to integrate with, develop friendships with, work in French settings with, or continue studies in French schools with French-speaking people. Responses were treated statistically in instances where direct group comparisons could be made, and less formally in instances where extended statements were made. Parents of students in each group were also surveyed. (The details are available in Cziko, Lambert, Sidoti, & Tucker, 1980; and in Wolfe & Lambert, 1979). The following conclusions were drawn from these analyses.

1. There was a very clear expression of appreciation for the immersion experience on the part of the immersion students as well as their parents, the majority of whom said they would choose the immersion option again if they had to do it all over. The general satisfaction on the part of immersion parents stood in sharp contrast to the control parents who directed harsh criticism at the school system for having failed them and their children by not teaching them French. Control parents were also more likely to send their children to private schools in the high school years, perhaps as an assurance for their children's future.

2. In general, immersion students expressed a feeling of well-being, self-assurance, and satisfaction with their level of attainment in French, which showed itself in various ways: (a) the immersion students had already had more part-time and summer experiences working in French; (b) they felt much more capable of working in French or (c) studying in French at the college or university level; and (d) they were more eager to study other languages, as though the taste of success with learning French and the realization that one can master a foreign language stimulated a more general interest in learning other languages.

3. They also as a group showed a more positive attitude toward French-speaking Canadians and a greater willingness to make contacts with French-speaking people with whom they used French in communication.

4. A larger proportion of the immersion than the control students also expressed a desire to stay in Quebec (even though a majority of both groups thought in terms of leaving the province in the following few years).

5. A much larger proportion of immersion students also felt that they could, given more occasions to use the language, become fully bilingual. These feelings were shared as well by the respective groups of parents. The contrast is highlighted by the delight of two students who said they had been highly complimented when taken to be native speakers of French. The control students, on the other hand, gave the impression that they had little hope of really mastering French or that it was too late to expect that degree of competence.

6. Both the immersion students and their parents were more inclined than the controls to see the merits of extended forms of immersion, e.g., submerging themselves with French students in French-language schools. Submersion in a totally French school was not seen as a radical step or one that might adversely affect one's identity or native language competence. Rather, it was seen more as a natural and obvious extension of early immersion by a substantial number of immersion students and their parents.

7. Overall then, the early immersion experience has a strong impact: it develops high degrees of skill in the French language; it helps develop confidence that one can work, study, and live in a French environment as well as in an English one; it convinces most graduates that they could, given simple opportunities to use French, become fully bilingual; and it generates a willingness and desire to meet and integrate with French-speaking Canadians.

At the same time, our analysis brought to light various hurdles that these well-prepared and motivated young people faced when they tried to penetrate the French world around them in Quebec. Some of these hurdles were very likely rooted in the English-speaking society itself, which provided few examples of ways to make contact with French-speaking people; other hurdles were just as likely rooted in the French-speaking society of Quebec, which also provides few models of how one might encourage and follow up on gestures of appreciation and interest (like learning the French language well) coming from English-speaking Canadians. Furthermore, ECs graduating from secondary school in Quebec in the late seventies were entering a society that was divided and polarized along ethnic and linguistic lines to a degree their parents or grandparents never experienced. The main point is that it may well be because of their immersion experiences that this subgroup of EC students can see into the societal problems they have inherited. Frustrated as they are, they may be the best agents to make substantive changes in the society of the future. They show signs of genuine bewilderment as to why society makes it so difficult for them to learn the other group's language or make social contacts with members of the other group.

As a consequence, perhaps the most important conclusion to be drawn from this investigation of graduates of immersion programs is that the upcoming generation may have fresh ideas about the problems of social segregation and cleavage within the society. The beginnings of a solution are apparent in what the immersion students seemed to ask of the society—an opportunity to put their

competence in the other language to meaningful use. Attaining functional bilingual skill in French had apparently provided them with feelings of competence
in a new language and culture, and a willingness to be bicultural citizens, even
though the parent-run society they lived in frustrated their attempts to actualize
their potential. In contrast, the EC control children felt much less competent and
less ready to be bicultural, and our guess is that their less favorable feelings
toward the other group derive at least in part from a lack of opportunity to
become bilingual and bicultural.

The Use of Multidimensional Scaling.   There is a relatively recent revival of
interest in psycho-physical scaling procedures that tap the feeling component of
attitudes indirectly by asking respondents to gauge how "similar" they view
various comparison groups. For instance, we asked immersion students and
controls to consider various reference people (e.g., Americans, Italian-Canadians, English people from England, French people from France, monolingual or
bilingual ECs and FCs) and then to rate on 9-point similarity scales (running
from very similar to very different) each possible pair of reference people, with
pairs presented in a random order (e.g., Americans and French people from
France; Italian-Canadians and monolingual ECs). We also included in the list
"my teacher" and "me."

Multidimensional scaling (MDS) has proven valuable in several Canadian
studies of social perception (cf. Christian, 1976; Frasure-Smith et al., 1975;
Taylor, 1976). With MDS, the bases for making similarity-dissimilarity judge-
ments are left to the respondent. Using respondents' dissimilarity judgments as
data, MDS produces a configuration of the various reference people that summa-
rizes and graphically describes the perceived closeness or distance between and
among reference groups. It also uncovers some of the dimensions respondents
use in making their judgments.

In 1977, we used the MDS procedure with EC Grades 5 and 6 students in two
types of French immersion programs and compared them with EC controls. Our
aim was to obtain a clearer picture of the social attitudes of these students, in
particular, a better view of the affective consequences of French immersion
programs. The same Anglophone students had been tested for their stereotypes,
as already described; as of 1977, we found a strong immersion effect, due mainly
to the sour attitudes of the EC controls. The MDS configurations of the same
respondents indicated that the early immersion experience tended to reduce the
perceived dissimilarity of English Canadians and French Canadians to a significant degree. This rapprochement took place mainly because "bilingual FCs"
were brought closer to "bilingual ECs" in the thinking of the immersion students, relative to the EC controls, and because the "self" concept was placed
closer to a cluster formed by "bilingual ECs" and "bilingual FCs." There is
also a trend (which is not statistically significant) for the immersion students to
bring "monolingual FCs" closer to "bilingual FCs" and thus indirectly closer

to "self." In short, the early immersion experience seems to have reduced the feelings of social distance and separation between French- and English-speaking Canadians. The value of the MDS methodology is that it provides a means of interpreting data that one might miss with a commonsense approach. Thus, it is interesting to learn that the rapprochement of French and English groups took place mainly through the feeling on the part of early immersion pupils that they have become similar to "bilingual ECs" who in turn are seen as similar to "bilingual FCs" who in turn are similar to "monolingual FCs." Instructive as the method is, we need to test it further on new groups because here we used subjects who in the 1977 testing period had shown a clear immersion effect for stereotypes of FCs. The question remains: Would we get similar results with MDS for groups who had not shown an immersion effect at the level of stereotypes?

Mixed Procedures: Scaling and Questioning.   The feeling and reaction tendency features of attitudes can also be measured profitably through open-ended questions that produce responses that can later be rated and scaled by judges. This mixed-method procedure was the basis of an important recent study conducted in the spring of 1979 (Blake, Lambert, Sidoti, & Wolfe, 1981). In this case, Anglophone immersion students at both Grade 6 (end of elementary school) and Grade 11 (end of high school) levels were compared with EC controls who had FSL experiences only. In addition, FC students at the Grade 6 and 11 levels were introduced in the comparison, half of them being bilingual in English and half being essentially monolingual in French. Some 360 students were included in this survey, which was conducted in English and French.

Here are some examples of the questions asked and the scoring procedures employed. For the "*friends*" question, each student was asked: Do you have any close friends who are French Canadian (Canadien anglais)? If yes, how many? Then came the "*similarities*" question: What, in your opinion, are the main similarities between English-speaking young people and French-speaking young people? Please try to give three examples of similarities. Next was the "*differences*" question: What, in your opinion, are the main differences between English-speaking and French-speaking young people? Please try to give three examples of differences. Then the "*status of English-French relations*" question: In Canada today, opinions differ greatly about how well English-speaking and French-speaking people are getting along. Some people feel that relationships are bad and there is much tension between the two groups. Others feel that English-French relationships are just becoming comfortable now, and are even improving. What are your views on this issue? Then came the "*problems*" question: In your opinion, what are the two most important problems separating English-speaking and French-speaking Canadians? Finally, they were asked: If you feel that there are difficulties between English-speaking and French-speaking Canadians, then we would like your ideas about what could be done so that

English- and French-speaking Canadian young people would get along better. Two or three suggestions would be appreciated.

FC respondents were tested for skill in English and were categorized as monolingual or bilingual, providing two subgroups comparable to the immersion and EC controls for the EC respondents.

To score the open-ended questions, all responses were analyzed and scaled by two judges working independently. For instance, responses to the *similarities* question were coded and assigned a score from 1 to 6 on a scale ranging from *superficial similarities* to *profound, deep similarities.*'' Interjudge reliability of code assignments was found to be .95 for this scale. A similar scale was used for the *differences* question which also had a high interjudge reliability. For the *status of English-French relations* question, a 7-point scale was developed, with a continuum from *bad with much tension* to *good; atmosphere comfortable.* For the *problems facing English and French Canadians* and the *suggestions for improvement* questions, the essential ideas were preserved while accomplishing some summarization. Some 25 categories were developed for each question.

The results of this study are valuable and instructive because they provide several clear contrasts in attitudes and perspectives between English- and French-speaking Canadians on the one hand, and between those who had become bilingual (whether FC or EC) and those who had not. There were many examples of such contrasts. For instance when asked what they saw as the major problems separating ECs and FCs, the Anglophone pupils at Grade 6 (both immersion and controls) concentrated on ''language domination,'' ''group domination'' and ''separation'' as major divisive problems. In today's Quebec, these are clearly the concerns of Anglophones rather than Francophones, since French has become the only official language and the main language of work, and FCs hold nearly all political power positions. Not surprisingly the FC pupils had more trouble agreeing on what constitutes a problem. They mentioned ''language differences'' especially and general factors like ''stubbornness and resistance to getting along.''

The suggested solutions at the Grade 6 level showed similar contrasts. The Anglophones (both immersion and controls) emphasized ''greater political tolerance for Anglophones,'' reflecting their (and their parents') definition of the central problem. The Anglophones also suggested ''mixing pupils in bilingual schools'' and instituting ''student exchanges.'' In contrast, the Francophones suggested sending EC pupils to French schools as a possible solution.

Clearly ethnicity itself shapes quite different outlooks on Canada's current intergroup tensions, and this probing procedure effectively brought some of these differences to light. What is even more interesting for us is that, even at the Grade 6 level, being bilingual or not is more important than one's ethnicity in shaping certain perspectives. Thus, being bilingual (through immersion schooling for the EC students or through less formal means for the FC students) seems to provide the insight that the solution to Canada's troubles calls for the ''elimination of prejudice and discrimination." No such solution is seen in the responses of the EC controls or the FC monolinguals!

At the Grade 11 level, many more subgroup contrasts emerged. The subtle differences in the thinking styles of these late teenagers are fascinating. For instance the most popularly cited problem for all subgroups was "language differences," stressed particularly by the monolingual Francophones. Although there is a consensus that language differences cause trouble, there are quite different underlying themes associated with language differences. For both EC and FC bilinguals—who have already overcome the language barrier—the major problem shifts from language to "group domination," "group segregation" and "stubbornness" and "personal resistance to change." For EC monolinguals, Canada's malaise is traceable to "separatist" tendencies and "national disunity" coupled with language differences. For FC monolinguals, the major problems are "language differences," "domination by the English," and "differences in customs and culture."

The suggested solutions offered by the Grade 11 students display a wide range of sophistication. For instance, the bilinguals (both ECs and FCs) call for greater intergroup contact between English- and French-speaking Canadians much more frequently than do the monolinguals. Bilinguals, in other words, indicate that factors other than language differences are involved and argue that increased "contact" between the ethnic groups is required in order to improve the situation. The same theme is seen in the relative stress given to "travel throughout the country" as a solution. Both EC and FC bilinguals see more value in travel than monolinguals do.

A sharp contrast is seen between the EC controls and the immersion students at Grade 11. The controls were distinctive with the suggestion that greater political tolerance be given Anglophones, a solution that likely reflected their concerns about separation and disunity. Interestingly, the Grade 11 immersion students did not list this alternative at all. Their suggestions for the reduction of tensions reflect more sensitivity and better understanding of the meaning of the separatist movement in Quebec, e.g., the underlying feelings of inferiority among French Canadians and the unfairness of treatment they believe they have received in Canada. Because of their language skills, the bilingual Anglophones appear to be less worried than monolinguals about the current signs of political intolerance toward Anglophones because they are much better able to cope in modern Quebec. What is distinctive in the thinking of the immersion students is the need they see for people to learn about one another's culture. Presumably because they have been taught Canadian history from both English and French Canadian perspectives by teachers from the two backgrounds, they apparently see the value of dual-perspective teaching and the need for more of it. They were also distinctive in the emphasis placed on mixing Anglophones and Francophones in bilingual school systems. This theme was stressed substantially more often by the Grade 11 immersion students than by any other group. Incidentally, this same theme was noted in the thinking of other Grade 11 immersion students who participated in an earlier study (Cziko, Lambert, & Gutter, 1979).

The distinctive feature of the FC students' thinking at Grade 11 was the suggestion that student exchanges (where students from one ethnic group could visit in the other group's home) would help reduce tensions. They also emphasized the need to develop bilingual skills, in particular mutual bilingualism where ECs would learn French. However, they did not suggest, as the Anglophone students did, that bilingual schools are a solution, nor did they mention mixed FC-EC social and recreational activities. They supported instead exchanges— home-to-home or school-to-school—of a temporary, occasional nature.

The main conclusions we draw from this investigation is that early bilingual and bicultural experiences produce not only the obvious practical results (e.g., a profound impact on language skills), but also some other, and perhaps more important, changes in the realm of attitudes and ideas about intergroup coexistence. We found that our bilingual subjects were better able to make friends in the other ethnolinguistic group earlier in life. Furthermore, those with early immersion experience perceive French-speaking and English-speaking Canadians as being more similar in terms of human qualities than monolinguals do. This more receptive, less ethnocentric attitude was evident at Grade 6 and one could argue that it could be further developed by educators and parents by promoting occasions for intergroup social contacts at the elementary school level. By Grade 11, all groups shared a common view of the essential similarity of the two ethnic groups. Nonetheless, the older bilingual children stood out in their modes of assessing the problems facing Canadians and in the insights they had for reducing intergroup tensions. We assume that early bilingual-bicultural experiences promote such attitudes and help to open the minds of the bilingual youngsters. Our argument is that by becoming functionally bilingual in the other group's language and learning about their culture and values, the bilingual sees beyond the simple solution that learning the other group's language will make for intergroup harmony. Their perspective is more sophisticated, for they see a need to learn about, to go to school with, and to interact socially with members of the other group as the crucial factors in peaceful coexistence. Our guess is that the bilinguals may be more sophisticated in the solutions they suggest for reducing intergroup tensions because of their knowledge of, and sensitivity to, the other group's point of view.

OVERALL CONCLUSIONS

There are two interrelated issues dealt with in this paper, one concerned with the nature of attitudes and their measurement, the other with an educational intervention or "treatment" that should, theoretically, improve or change the attitudes of young people in a socially desirable direction. The treatment paradigm involved separate cohorts of Anglophone pupils at various grade levels in public schools who were in French "immersion" programs. "Immersion" pupils were compared with carefully matched Anglophone "control" pupils following a conventional English language program. At the start of the program the parents of the immersion and control pupils were in some cases tested and found to have basically similar patterns of social attitudes; in other cases, we had to presume that the two parental groups had equivalent attitudes. The working hypothesis was that learning thoroughly another ethnic group's language and learning about that group through a teacher who is a native informant would have a favorable impact on pupils' attitudes toward that group and the associated culture. Thus we expected to find immersion versus control differences in attitudes, what we called an "immersion effect."

In testing for the immersion effect, attention was given to theoretically different components of attitudes, a stereotype component, measured through semantic rating scales, versus a feeling or a reaction tendency component, measured through direct questioning and multidimensional scaling procedures.

Overall, the actual findings confirmed our expectations, but more than that, they provided several new insights into the ways attitudes function, in particular how certain clusters of attitudes can develop in such a way that one's perspective on society will become more mature and sophisticated. It appears that becoming bilingual and bicultural is an effective way of enriching young people's social perspectives.

With respect to pupils' stereotypes, the following findings are noteworthy.

1. Although not pronounced nor consistent, the immersion experience did have statistically significant effects on pupils' stereotypes of FCs: the stereotypes of immersion pupils were either slightly more favorable or less unfavorable than those of the control pupils, in general.

2. The ratings assigned to FCs, however, fell within the 4- to 5-point range on 7-point scales, indicating that Anglophone stereotypes of FCs were neutral to slightly favorable at best.

3. The immersion effect on stereotypes was not necessarily an amelioration of perceptions of the other ethnolinguistic group, for just as often the effect was an essentially neutral view of FCs, which nonetheless contrasted with the harsh, sometimes aggressive views expressed by the control pupils.

4. The stereotypes of immersion pupils reflected local administrative policies and idiosyncrasies, e.g., biases toward European French people in classes where the teachers were European; biases against FCs in classes where non-representative FC pupils were integrated into immersion programs. Stereotypes also reflected broader political tensions in the province.

5. The immersion experience had no negative or dampening effects on pupils' self-views or views of their own ethnic group.

6. The effects of immersion on stereotypes are more pronounced at the start of the programs (at Grades 1 and 2 for programs starting at kindergarten, and at Grades 7 and 8 for those starting at Grade 7). The effect appears to wear off with time.

7. It is also possible that the less marked differences between immersion and control groups in the later grades is due to a gradual improvement over time of the stereotypes of the control pupils. Since all control pupils had FSL training from Grade 1 on, that training could have beneficial effects which accumulate over time.

With respect to the feeling and reaction tendency components, the following findings are noteworthy.

1. The immersion effect is more evident in the feelings and reaction tendencies of pupils than was the case for stereotypes. Thus even in cases where there were no immersion-control differences in stereotypes (e.g., at Grades 4 and 5 in the 1970–71 testing), there were large, statistically reliable immersion effects with different questioning procedures. Thus, immersion pupils were much more likely than controls to say they had come to appreciate and like FCs, that they could easily imagine themselves being FC, that they liked the intensive study of French and wanted to continue, and so forth.

2. Also at the other grade levels, where the stereotype differences were less pronounced, there were important immersion-control differences in feelings and reaction tendencies towards FCs. For instance, at the time of leaving high school, the immersion students relative to controls not only showed high degrees of skill in French and a confidence to work, study and live in mainly French settings, but also showed a greater willingness and desire to meet and interact with FCs. They also showed more frustration because such interaction is difficult to achieve in the Canadian society.

3. We conclude, therefore, that the immersion experience broadened pupils' "social perspectives" more than conventional education did in the sense that immersion students asked more searching questions of society. For example: Why it is that various social barriers exist (religious, ethnic, linguistic) that discourage intergroup contacts in neighborhoods, schools, and in work and social settings?

4. The notion of "social perspectives" implies that there may be some higher-order aspect of attitudes that is often overlooked in the more conventional definitions of attitudes. The present research suggests to us that attitudes can cluster into higher-order, generalized orientations that encompass not only a tolerance for another group, but also a knowledge of,

appreciation for, and interest in people from that group. A person's "social perspective" would be enhanced by learning enough about the other group and its members to be sensitive to their values, expectations and wishes, and by coming to realize (a) that the other people are much like one's own people and oneself, and (b) that social systems often work against people getting to know and appreciate one another.

5. The data from the scaling procedures supported the notion of a maturation of social perspectives: e.g., immersion students reduced the perceived distance between their ethnic group and FCs more so than did the controls. Likewise, at the early grade levels, immersion pupils saw more similarities between FCs and ECs than did the controls.

6. Finally, the immersion students at the high school level showed broader social perspectives when asked to diagnose and suggest solutions for the problems that separate FCs and ECs in Canada today. The immersion experience appears to have provided them with mature and productive insights into society, e.g., that simplistic solutions, like getting to know one another's language, are not final answers. They seemed to realize that getting to know the other language and the other culture well is only a start, that behind the other language and culture are people who apparently are very much like their own people, and who are vulnerable to suspicions, threats and fears of other groups unless real opportunities are provided by the society for equitable group contact and interaction, starting at early school years. These insights were not apparent in the thinking of the monolingual control students, and we suspect this is so because they had not been given the opportunities to learn the other language thoroughly nor learn enough about the other group.

REFERENCES

Blake, L., Lambert, W. E., Sidoti, N., Wolfe, D. (1981). Students' views of intergroup tensions in Quebec. The effects of language immersion experience. *Canadian Journal of Behavioral Science, 13,* 144–160.

Christian, J. D. (1976). *Psychological differentiation and definition of the self: Multidimensional scaling approach.* Unpublished doctoral dissertation, McGill University.

Clément, R., Gardner, R. C., & Smythe, P. C. (1977). Motivational variables in second language acquisition: A study of Francophones learning English. *Canadian Journal of Behavioral Science, 9,* 123–133.

Cziko, G., Holobow, N., & Lambert, W. E. (1977, March). *A comparison of three elementary school alternatives for learning French: Children at grades four and five.* Unpublished manuscript, McGill University, Department of Psychology.

Cziko, G., Holobow, N., & Lambert, W. E. (1977, April). *Early and late French immersion: A comparison of children at grade seven.* Unpublished manuscript, Psychology Department, McGill University.

Cziko, G., Holobow, N., & Lambert, W. E., & Tucker, G. R. (1977, December). *A comparison of three elementary school alternatives for learning French: Children at grades five and six.* Unpublished manuscript, McGill University, Psychology Department.

Cziko, G., Lambert, W. E., & Gutter, R. (1979, November). The impact of programs-in-a-foreign-language on pupils' social attitudes. *Working Papers in Bilingualism* (pp. 13–28). O.I.S.E., Toronto.

Cziko, G., Lambert, W. E., Sidoti, N., & Tucker, G. R. (1980). Graduates of early immersion: Retrospective views of grade 11 students and their parents. In R. St. Clair & H. Giles (Eds), *The social and psychological contexts of language.* Hillsdale, NJ: Lawrence Erlbaum Associates.

Ervin, S. (1954). *Identification and bilingualism.* Unpublished manuscript, Harvard University.

Frasure-Smith, N., Lambert, W. E., & Taylor, D. M. (1975). Choosing the language of instruction for one's children: A Quebec study. *Journal of Cross-Cultural Psychology, 6,* 131–155.

Gardner, R. C. (1981). Second language learning. In R. C. Gardner & R. Kalin (Eds.), *A Canadian social psychology of ethnic relations.* Toronto: Methuen.

Gardner, R. C. (1982). Language attitudes and language learning. In E. B. Ryan & H. Giles (Eds.), *Attitudes towards language variation.* London: Edward Arnold.

Gardner, R. C., Glicksman, L., & Smythe, P. C. (1978). Attitudes and behavior in second language acquisition: A social psychological interpretation. *Canadian Psychological Review, 19,* 173–186.

Gardner, R. C., & Lambert, W. E. (1972). *Attitudes and motivation in second language learning.* Rowley, MA: Newbury House.

Gardner, R. C., & Lambert, W. E. (1959). Motivational variables in second language acquisition. *Canadian Journal of Psychology, 13,* 266–272.

Gardner, R. C., & Smythe, P. C. (1975). *Second language acquisition: A social psychological approach* (Research Bulletin No. 332). London: University of Western Ontario, Department of Psychology.

Genesee, F. (1978). Scholastic effects of French immersion: An overview after ten years. *Interchange, 9,* 20–29.

Genesee, F., & Hamayan, E. (1980). Individual differences in second language learning. *Applied Psycholinguistics, 1,* 95–110.

Genesee, F., Morin, S., & Allister, T. (1974a). *Evaluation of the 1973–74 grade 7 French immersion class: June 1974.* Instructional Services, Protestant School Board of Greater Montreal.

Genesee, F., Morin, S., & Allister, T. (1974b). *Evaluation of the 1973–74 Pilot grade 11 French immersion class.* A report submitted to the Protestant School Board of Greater Montreal.

Genesee, F., Rogers, R., & Holobow, N. (1982, July). *The social psychology of second language learning: Another point of view.* Unpublished manuscript, McGill University.

Guindon, H. (1971). Social unrest, social class, and Quebec's bureaucratic revolution. In B. Blishen et al. (Eds), *Canadian society: Sociological perspectives.* Toronto: Macmillan.

Lambert, W. E. (1967). The social psychology of bilingualism. *Journal of Social Issues, 23,* 91–109.

Lambert, W. E., Frankel, H., & Tucker, G. R. (1966). Judging personality through speech: A French Canadian example. *Journal of Communication, 16,* 305–321.

Lambert, W. E., Gardner, R. C., Barik, H. C., & Tunstall, K. (1963). Attitudinal and cognitive aspects of intensive study of a second language. *Journal of Abnormal and Social Psychology, 66,* 358–368.

Lambert, W. W., & Lambert, W. E. (1973). *Social psychology.* Englewood Cliffs, NJ: Prentice-Hall.

Lambert, W. E., & Tucker, G. R. (1972). *Bilingual education of children: The St. Lambert study.* Rowley, MA: Newbury House.

Lambert, W. E., Tucker, G. R., & d'Anglejan, A. (1973). Cognitive and attitudinal consequences of bilingual schooling: The St. Lambert project through grade five. *Journal of Educational Psychology, 65,* 141–159.

Mowrer, O. H. (1950). *Learning theory and personality dynamics.* New York: Ronald Press.

Swain, M. (1974). French immersion programs across Canada. *Canadian Modern Language Review. 31,* 117–128.

Taylor, D. M. (1976). Ethnic identity: Some cross-cultural comparisons. In J. W. Berry & W. J. Lonner (Eds.), *Applied cross-cultural psychology.* Amsterdam: Swets & Zeitlinger.

Taylor, D. M., Meynard, R., & Rheault, E. (1977). Threat to ethnic identity and second-language learning. In H. Giles (Ed.), *Language, ethnicity and intergroup relations.* London: Academic Press.

Wolfe, D., & Lambert, W. E. (1979). Graduates of early immersion: A follow-up study. Unpublished manuscript, McGill University.

A Social-Cognitive Perspective on Bilingualism: Comments on Lambert and Taylor[1]

E. Tory Higgins
New York University

It is a pleasure for me to be discussant on these two chapters because I was born in Montreal, was an undergraduate at McGill, and, most of all, because the first social psychology course I ever took was with W. E. Lambert. That course was a major influence on my interest in social psychology and, more generally, on my interest in the relation among language, thought and society. So it is fun for me to be involved in discussing these chapters. Also, it is fun because of the impact of the work of both Lambert and Don Taylor on second-language learning—after all, how many people have done such important research that they name whole regions after them, as in Wally's case with St. Lambert?

In my comments I talk about two issues—motivational factors in the acquisition of a second language and the consequences of bilingualism—and make some general comments about each of them, relating to what has been said so far and to some ideas of my own.

First, with respect to motivational factors in the acquisition of a second language, Lambert and Taylor have certainly done the pioneering work in this area, along with their colleagues. What interests me is the consideration of this issue in terms of a model that I have been developing that derives from many areas of social science—pragmatics, anthropology, sociolinguistics, speech and communication, and so on. It is a model of communication that I refer to as the "communication game," which is simply a steal from Wittgenstein's "language game," who was one of the first to talk in these terms. One important aspect of

---

[1]This paper is a transcript (with some minor modifications) of the author's discussion during the conference of the papers presented by Lambert and Taylor, with some of Lambert's remarks on the author's comments being included as well.

this model is its emphasis on the fact that communication has a variety of goals. That would seem obvious. But in many areas of psychology, and especially in experimental social psychology, the discussion of communication has centered around only one goal—information transmission. Certainly that is one important goal of communication, but there are a variety of goals in communication.

Another important set of goals in communication is social relationship goals, the idea that people communicate in order to form or maintain a relationship with someone or some group. But in addition to social relationship goals, there's what Goffman would call "face" goals or impression management goals, the idea that we communicate in order to make ourselves look good and to get others to make favorable judgments of us. In addition to face goals, there are "social reality" goals. We often communicate just to obtain consensus on what everyone thinks about something so we can know what "reality" is. One of the classic examples, of course, is Schachter's early work on the psychology of affiliation where he found that when people are anxious and they have a choice of who to wait with, they prefer to wait with other people than to wait alone but only if those other people have experienced the same event and only if they are allowed to talk. So people have a motivation to be in a communication situation where they can share some experience to get some understanding of what it means.

There is another communication goal that isn't talked about very much and hasn't been talked about much in this conference. That goal is entertainment. Another reason why people communicate is because it is fun—for the sheer pleasure of it. Partly because it is something else we can do, just like we can dance or sing or skip or whatever—we can talk. In fact, it is one of the things we most enjoy doing.

Distinguishing among these different kinds of goals has a long history. And yet the framework that Lambert and Taylor have been working with, I believe, enriches this notion of a "communication game." I also think this notion might enrich their framework. The task goal is very similar to what they call the "instrumental" goal. The social relationship goals are similar to their "integrative" goals. These two cases are fairly straightforward mappings between these two models. What is interesting is how the third variable, social or ethnic identity, fits in. I think it has features of both face goals and social reality goals, as well as social relationship goals. Perhaps it is because of its multifunctional nature that social identity is so important.

Now it may be that social or ethnic identity means something in addition to these goals, but I feel it would be interesting to think about ethnic identity in terms of how it relates to each of these goals, such as "face" goals. I think, in fact, that one aspect of the negative motivation from ethnic identity works in this way. That is, some people may be motivated not to acquire a second language because they don't want to be embarrassed by poorly speaking the language of that "other" group. Social reality goals may also contribute to negative motivation. Consider the case where a minority group is trying to learn a second language. They might feel that they're going to lose their sense of social reality by learning a second language. The threat to ethnic identity is in part the threat of loss of social reality—their social reality.

Entertainment goals haven't really been looked at in terms of this model. There is a component of "integrative goals" that seems to suggest entertainment—that you're sort of enjoying it. But there's an aspect of entertainment that appears to be left out of the model at this point—the idea that just as it is fun to speak your language it is fun to speak another language.

(Wally Lambert: That usually goes into the integrative part). Yes. But it might be interesting from that point of view to subdivide integrative into social relationship goals and entertainment goals to see what kind of impact that would have.

Let me switch gears now and talk about the second issue that came up in both talks, as well as in earlier talks today—the consequences of bilingualism. I especially enjoyed Wally's discussion of social-affective consequences of bilingualism because one of the points I wanted to make was that the literature on bilingualism seemed to emphasize cognitive rather than social consequences, including Wally's earlier pioneering work. I think that it was a problem when people said that learning a second language has positive consequences as we did not know what the social consequences were. And just as it was mistaken in the fifties to say that learning a second language was a bad thing, to say it is a good thing in the eighties without knowing what the social consequences are is jumping the gun. We need to know more about the social consequences, which was Wally's point and I second that strongly. I think it is important to collect data on social consequences in the sense of attitudes, but I am not sure that is sufficient. Other kinds of social consequences are social-cognitive consequences—consequences for making judgments of other people and consequences for one's memory about other people.

Let me give you a little background on the idea that I wish to discuss. When you consider social concepts, especially trait words like friendly, aggressive, independent, aloof, smart, and so on, one must distinguish between the meaning of the word and the referent. Now it may seem ridiculous for me to make that point when Ogden and Richards made it many years ago. But it is surprising how often we forget the implications of maintaining this distinction. What I am getting at is that there is a difference between the meaning of a word and the actual social event that will come to mind when you use the word. This difference is demonstrated in my recent research where the meaning of a word stays the same, but because the standard changes, the referent is different.

Let me give an example of what I mean by that. Take for instance the word *friendly*. The meaning of the word *friendly* is literally "more friendly than the standard." When you say "Tom is friendly," that is a comparative assertion and the meaning of the assertion is "Tom is more friendly than the average person," or "Tom is more friendly than some standard." Now the referential meaning is going to depend therefore on the standard that you have for friendliness. Let us say, for instance, that you are 2 years of age. You haven't much exposure to people. Ten years go by and the distribution of instances of friendliness changes. Now you have a different standard. The point is that the meaning of the word hasn't changed. The meaning is still "more friendly than the standard." But what has changed is the standard.

If you see Tom perform certain behaviors, you say: "Oh, Tom is friendly because he is more friendly than the standard." Now you don't see him for 10 years. You remember that he's friendly. "Oh yeah, Tom is friendly," Then you say to yourself, "Gee, why was he friendly?" What you do is reconstruct Tom's behavior to be consistent with that label. This is a classic Bartlett-type phenomenon, and what you get is distortion over time if the standard has changed between the time that the behavior was labeled and the time that the label is used to recall the behavior. This is the kind of research that I've been doing, where the meaning of the word stays the same but one manipulates the standard, which does cause major errors in memory.

The implications of this process, I believe, are quite interesting for bilingualism and especially for the kind of bilingualism that is involved in biculturalism. In fact, it may provide a way of distinguishing between the bicultural versus unicultural bilingual. The situation I am interested in is exactly the situation where you may find a bicultural bilingual, for example, an American-Spanish bilingual who has a trait term like *friendly* where the meaning of the word is the same in both English and Spanish, "more friendly than the average person," but the standard of "friendliness" is different.

(Lambert: I think there's where you can get some challenge. It is fascinating because friendship in French takes on a different form, you know. We use "friend" loosely in English, apparently, and the French restrict "friend" to a very select, small group. Thus, in Spanish you may have the same. So you have got to be careful about the identity of words between languages.)

Yes! But I'm going to restrict myself to comparative trait assertions because when you are talking about specific objects the meaning can be different since the optional features of what people have in mind may be different. The case of comparative assertions is better because there are many languages, especially Romance languages, where comparative trait assertions mean the same thing. Even if it is restricted to that, it would be important because all trait terms are comparative trait assertions and that's what we use when we talk about people. So, even if it only had to do with personality traits it would have significant implications for our impressions of people, our attitudes, and our social memory.

Now the situation I am thinking of is a case where the two words have the same linguistic meaning, "greater than the standard," but because it is bicultural, the standard might be very different in the two cultures. The average friendly person in Spanish culture may be very different from the average friendly person in English culture. My question is this—what happens when you get a child who is the kind of bicultural bilingual we have been talking about, who speaks one language at home and one language at school? What happens when this child goes to school, meets somebody for the first time and sees a set of behaviors. Think of the Spanish child who is going to an English school. These are children who speak Spanish at home but speak only English at school. Think of the boy who goes to school and becomes bilingual in the first two or three years, meets someone, Tom, has a relationship with him, and decides that Tom is friendly in English. Then he goes home. Now he is talking Spanish and his mother says:

"Did you have a nice day?"

— "Oh, I met this boy named Tom"—spoken in Spanish.

— "What is he like?"

— "Tom is friendly."

What I am suggesting is that in order to say "Tom is friendly" in Spanish he is actually distorting his memory of the behavior that he observed when he called him friendly in English, because the words have the same meaning but the standards are different. You actually have to distort your memory for it to fit. Then he goes back to school. Now he has a distorted memory of Tom. He meets Tom again, Tom behaves in the same friendly manner but appears to behave in a different manner because it is different from the stored memory. So here's a child who perceives an inconsistency in Tom's behavior.

I haven't collected any data on this yet. That's a real advantage at this point because I can create any scenario I want, and I want to point up the fact that we don't know, without data of this nature, whether the social-cognitive consequences of bilingualism are negative or positive. The negative scenario is the one I have just described, which is that the child perceives an inconsistency in Tom's behavior. What does inconsistency cause? Well, we know that inconsistency causes negative affect, uncertainty, a sense of unpredictability, a sense of lack of control.

Now let us consider the positive scenario. The positive scenario is that the child, by the fact that he has these different standards, develops an appreciation for variability. He starts noticing all kinds of variability among people. Well, what does variability cause? We know from the research on ingroup-outgroup perception by Tajfel and others, and I have done some work on this as well, that if you perceive variability, you become less stereotyped. In fact, that is what a stereotype is—it is a perception of *lack* of variability. So, if you perceive variability, you become less stereotyped. And I know from my own work that if you perceive variability you don't assume that others are doing things because they're black or because they are Spanish or because they are white or anything else. So what we have is a reduction in stereotyped judgments of others.

And, even more directly, if this child has more than one standard then there is a reduction in ethnocentricism because one of the definitions of ethnocentricism is that one makes judgments in terms of a single standard; namely, the standard of one's culture. As Roger Brown said years ago in "Words and Things," the worst thing about ethnocentricism is that you always make judgments in terms of one standard, your group's standard, and assume that is the only standard. That is the danger. If bicultural bilinguals use more than one standard, they may be less ethnocentric and that is the positive scenario. But the point is that only research will tell.

V

BIDIALECTISM

13

The Linguistic and Sociolinguistic Position of Black English and the Issue of Bidialectalism in Education

John D. Roy
Brooklyn College, City University of New York

The linguistic and sociolinguistic factors that surrounded the importation of Africans as slaves are not paralleled in the immigration of other groups. The importation of peoples with different native languages and the grouping of them together in a social stratum structurally removed from English resulted in the formation of an emergency language—a West African English Pidgin.

This emergency language developed out of the earliest contact of Africans with English speakers. Spencer (1971) cites evidence that establishes that this emergency Afro-English Pidgin was in use in West Africa barely 20 years after the establishment of the first British fort there and was the medium of communication in the English slave trade.

The great number of West African languages, and the practice of purposefully varying the loading points in order to mix the language groups and thus lessen the chance of shipboard insurrection, are two of the facts that favored the development and use of a West African-English emergency language functioning as a means of communication both between the English and the Africans, as well as between Africans of different language groups. Cruickshank (1916) cites William Smith, Surveyor to the Royal African Company who made a voyage to Guinea in 1726. He notes:

> The languages in the Gambia are so many and so different that the natives on one side [of the river] cannot understand those on the other, which is a great advantage to the Europeans, who trade there for Slaves. . . . The safest way is to trade with different nations on either side, and having some of every sort on board there will be less the danger of any plot. (p. 1)

This Afro-English emergency language was also the medium of communication on the plantations of America. Newly arrived Africans learned, primarily from fellow slaves, the medium of communication that was used in the new world between Africans who didn't share a common language, as well as between master and slave (Dillard, 1972).

The social and cultural context of ancestral African languages was replaced by the environment of the plantation and its system of communication. As a result, the children of the West Africans learned the emergency hybrid language system that combined English words with elements of West African language structure rather than the ancestral African languages of their parents or the socially distant English. The emergency language system then became the native language of these first-generation Afro-Americans. A native language which develops in this way is defined as a creole (Hall, 1966).

The Plantation English Creole that developed in America was the carrier of the ideas, actions and values of the slave society. It was a coherent natural language system not very different in structure from the English Creoles that can be heard today in rural West Indian villages and in parts of the Sea Islands of South Carolina and Georgia.

English Creole existed as the low status language in a 'diglossic' (Ferguson, 1959) pair with English. Contact with the high-status language variety, English, produced a process through which stigmatized, low-status linguistic features of English Creole began to give way to English forms as hypothesized by English Creole speakers. Various segments of slave society had different language needs and different access to English. House servants had more exposure to English than did field hands; town dwellers more exposure than did their rural counterparts. Over time, generations had more and more contact with English through location, employment and education and more of the stigmatized features were dropped and more of the forms hypothesized as English were added. Successive generations transmitted to their children a less marked, creole system except in those areas where there was only minimal contact with English. This process of language change, a process of differential linguistic acculturation termed decreolization, is responsible for the movement of Plantation English Creole toward English and for the range of social, regional and individual dialects that have been described as Black English (BE) and Black English Vernacular that can be heard in the urban and rural Black communities today (Roy, 1984).

The fabric of the sociolinguistic situation just described has not changed significantly for much of the Black population. Black English, like English Creole, remains the low status dialect used in Black communities that remain at a considerable social distance from English. Processes of linguistic change similar to those that once occurred in transformation of English Creole into Black English are now affecting Black English as it continues to converge on English. These processes involve the acquisition of Standard English (SE) features as well as the avoidance of certain stigmatized Black English features and the attempt by parents to transmit a "better" English to their children.

To those familiar only with clearly bilingual situations, the change from English Creole to Black English to English may seem an inordinately lengthy and painful process. Successive generations of non-English speaking immigrant groups gain competence in English relatively quickly either through the development of bilingualism or the adoption of English as their only language. The reasons for the slow pace of the linguistic acculturation of the descendants of African immigrants are both linguistic and sociolinguistic.

Immigrant groups that approach English from a clearly different first language with rare exceptions have not passed through the pidginization, creolization and decreolization processes that are responsible for the wide range of language forms that are present in communities using Black English. In the bilingual situation, there are clear differences between the vocabulary and the grammar of the native language and the target language, English. This is not the case in the relationship between English Creole and English, on the one hand, or between Black English and Standard English on the other. English Creole and Black English are both formed out of the lexical resources of English, but these lexical elements are embedded within historically different grammatical systems, many of the language subsystems of which are structurally different from English. Because of the similarity of the vocabulary and elements of the grammar, the systematic differences between the natively learned variety of Black English and the Standard English target are obscured (Roy, 1977).

The linguistic resources available to the child within a Black English speaking community during the period of language acquisition may contain a variety of language forms that range from deep Black English to Standard English. Because of the surface similarity and the opacity of the structural differences of the different language varieties in their environment, children in a Black English/Standard English environment cannot clearly identify the systematic differences between the low- and the high-status language varieties present around them. Brown and Bellugi (1964) noted that adults, in echoing their children's utterances, supply grammatical markers. This process of "imitation with expansion" provides children with models for the development of grammar from a base form of content words to include the relational concepts and categories of tense-aspect, number, possession, deixis, reference, location and so on. If in the period of language acquisition children are exposed to non-standard English grammatical models that, at the level of systematic identity are for the children, indistinguishable from the Standard English forms, they will acquire them and build a grammar that contains the features of the variety of Black English that is closest to them.

When speakers of non-standard Black English become aware of the low social value of Black English forms in certain public or formal situations, they seek to avoid these forms and to produce those of the high status language variety. The wide variety of expression that has emerged within Black English may be the result of the avoidance of stigmatized forms, as well as the structural interference (Weinreich, 1953) of Black English on the production of the forms of Standard English. Black English forms that speakers may want to avoid may be structurally important to their grammars, and the targeted Standard English forms that speakers may want to produce may interfere structurally with their grammatical systems, or may not be fully within their control. The result of attempts by individuals to alter their grammatical patterns, either temporarily (to respond to certain situations) or permanently, has been the production of considerable linguistic hypercorrection and innovation, some of which becomes a regular part of the language variety used by the individual and community. These innovations, neither Standard English nor the Black English forms they were developed to replace, form yet another layer obscuring the structural differences between the grammatical systems of the native and the target language varieties.

The high social distance between some Black English speakers and the community of Standard English speakers certainly affects both the availability of SE grammatical models and may affect the attitudes of the second dialect learner in such a way as to restrict the process of second dialect acquisition, as Schuman (1973) demonstrates it does in adult second language learning. The linguistic and sociolinguistic facts surrounding the immigration of Africans to the New World and the language experience of their descendants illustrate that the reasons for the apparent slowness of the change from English Creole to Black English to English are based in the complexities of the continuing processes of linguistic acculturation.

To examine the sociolinguistic and educational parameters that surround the issue of Black English/Standard English bidialectalism, some linguistic points must first be established. The first of these points is that each human language variety has an extremely complex rule-governed, interdependent 'system of systems' that enables humans to produce and interpret the meanings and the signals of their language. It can not be said that any one language variety is, in terms of its structure, any better than any other. This does not mean that a language that articulates the cultural experience of a band of hunters and gatherers deep in Amazonia has the vocabulary to deal with life in New York. But neither is the reverse true. Human languages meet the needs of the cultural experience of the social group that uses them.

The second point is that language varieties that coexist within the same environment may have different social values, particularly if one variety is used as a medium of wider communication. The language variety that has the higher social value is called a "Language" and the language variety with the lower social value is in popular parlance called a "dialect." It has been said with only slight flippancy that a Language is a dialect with an army.

The language varieties known as Black English are not dialects in the ordinary sense, in that unlike regional dialects, they have not diverged from a common language form, but rather are converging on English from the structurally different language system of English Creole. The differences between English and Black English are structurally important, involving the tense-aspect system of verbs, the systems of pluralization and possession and association, the systems of pronouns and comparatives, relative clause and question formation and negativization. These are important structural differences rather than the surface phonetic features of accent that mark the difference between one regional dialect and another (Roy, 1986, in press).

There is a wide range of dialectal differences between varieties of Black English, some of which are farther from the linguistic systems of Standard English than others. Speakers also have differing abilities in switching from Black English forms toward Standard English in contexts judged appropriate. The diversity within the communities is an important compounding factor in the processes of Black English/Standard English bidialectalism.

It is possible for children to be born into a community that includes Black English as an important part of its linguistic repertoire and for them to hear and perhaps acquire as part of their communicative competence such a variety of forms as "He here"; "He be here"; "He bes here"; "He does be here"; "He are here"; and "He is here." It is impossible for children to know during acquisition which of these forms are part of the language system assigned a high social value and which are not. It is impossible for children to recognize the limits of the converging grammatical systems flowing past them. The boundaries between the systems are opaque, as is even the fact that there are different language systems involved.

This inter– and intradialect variation is the result of language change in progress and it produces a situation that is at once both more difficult and less rewarding than that which faces the second language learner. It is less rewarding for the student, as Dennis Craig (1968) has pointed out, because the shared lexicon and the opacity of the systematic differences mean that the bidialectal student does not receive the rewards of learning something "new" as the bilingual student does. It is more difficult because learners and teachers seldom recognize or are prepared to deal with the systematic differences between the grammar of the student and the grammar of Standard English. Although there may be parental and educational pressure to speak Standard English, there is little effective help available from these sources; also there may be considerable peer pressure not to abandon the language of the group in favor of the language of an outside group seen by some as the oppressor (Roy, 1981).

It is on reaching school age that children learn that some of the language forms acquired from parents and peers, the language of first experience and discovery is, in some unexplained way, considered "bad" by an educational system that, in general, lacks the ability and, in some cases, the desire to provide them with the language variety that is "good."

Children who come from homes and communities where non-standard Black English is spoken can speak, hear, or read and interpret the sentence "They drive a red car" to mean that once in the past they drove a red car. This interpretation follows a grammatical rule present in most Black English varieties that unmarked action verbs signal a single past event. Teachers and books, however, interpret and produce sentences like "They drive a red car" to mean a habitual or usual occurrence. If the parent or teacher is asked about the time meaning, most may state that "They drive a red car" indicates the present. Similarly, the sentence "He does drive" is for the teacher an emphatic assertion of ability, whereas for the student "He does drive" may express merely a habitual occurrence.

These examples illustrate that the systematic differences between the dialects of Black English and Standard English can generate identical surface forms and that these surface forms have different meanings depending on the grammatical system that interprets them. William Stewart (in unpublished remarks) refers to this phenomenon as "pseudo-comprehension" because the speakers may not be aware that there has been a slip in the communication between them.

Teachers for the most part do not get around to explaining what "They drive a car" means nor do they get around to explaining the difference between "He drove a car" and "He has driven a car." They do not explain the tense-aspect system, or the passive or the use of quantifiers and negatives or relative clause formation because they do not themselves understand these things despite being expert speakers and writers of the Standard language. For like other speakers of Standard English, they can recognize that something is wrong in a sentence but have little idea of how what is right gets to be that way.

Limited by training and knowledge to teaching the techniques of analysis and elaboration and to the correction of error, the techniques of the traditional English class, teachers encounter a student population whose dialect is structurally different from English and are unable to teach what is needed. The technique of correction is heavily relied on, by some, in the hope that the correction of errors will enable students to learn the system of categories and marking of the English verb even if teachers themselves do not consciously understand them. There is perhaps the hope among some that if students make enough errors they will learn what is right. However, spot corrections are not adequate to illuminate or to teach target forms that are part of a highly systematic language structure that differs in complex ways from the highly systematic language structure that is the students non-standard dialect. The result of these efforts at correction, on both sides, is frustration and capitulation.

Contrast the anxious seriousness of the lower class Black students in the first and second grades who have come to school inspired by the hope for success of parents and family with the visible resentfulness, the result of adjustment to educational failure, of most of their brothers and sisters in junior high and high school and you will see the extent of the tragedy. The failure of the educational establishment to deal effectively with language differences results in the appalling levels of reading failure and incompetence in the writing of Standard English that characterize schools that serve students who are influenced by Black English.

At the level of national policy, the failure of the English teaching establishment takes a more bizarre form (see Stewart 1974b). The current policy of the college writing arm of the National Conference of the Teachers of English (NCTE) was set forth in a resolution in College Composition and Communication (CCCC, 1974). This resolution is entitled "Students' Right to Their Own Language" (SROL), and states that the teaching of Standard English to speakers of non-standard dialects is not only unnecessary but is actually "immoral" (CCCC, p. 3). To support this claim, the resolution asserts that "Language scholars long ago denied that the myth of a standard American dialect has any validity" (CCCC, p. 3).

This assertion ignores the fact that all advanced societies, at least from the time of the Greeks, have had standard languages. It runs counter not only to common sense but also to the opinions of linguists specializing in English. Halliday et al. (1964) state the generally held position regarding standard American English:

Halliday et al. (1964) present the generally held position that standard American English is a norm that refers to those forms of inflectional morphology and syntax which are used widely by educated American speakers and that differs only in minor details from the norm accepted elsewhere in the English-speaking world.

This "myth" of Standard English, the SROL resolution asserts, was created and is perpetuated in "an attempt of one social group to exert its dominance over another" (CCCC, p. 3). The teaching of Standard English is not a matter of cultural imperialism; rather, standard languages are a product of the needs of a complex society to communicate precisely over wide areas. It is important to remember that there is nothing inherently better about the standard dialect as language: it is merely the standard system.

To exemplify the claim (CCCC, p. 6) that SE is only trivially different from non-standard dialect, the resolution presents the following sentences:

1. Mary's daddy is at home.
2. Mary's daddy is to home.
3. Mary daddy home.

The resolution incorrectly asserts that "Preference for one form over another, then, is not based on meaning or even exactness of expression, but depends on social attitudes and cultural norms."

However, from the point of view of both the speaker as well as the hearer, the differences are not trivial. The range of possible meanings of sentence (3) within Black English includes:

> (a) Mary's daddy is home.
> (b) Mary's daddy's home.
> (c) Mary, daddy is home.
> (d) Mary, is daddy home?

The individual who produces sentence (3) may not control either the phonological or the syntactic processes involving word-final s, which is used in SE for the marking of the non-trivial systems of pluralization, tense, possession, and the contractions of "is, was, has." The Standard English speaker, hearing or reading sentence (3) would probably say that the sentence is ungrammatical English and that the meaning can not be arrived at with certainty using the grammatical processes known and accepted throughout the English speaking world.

The difference between sentences (1) and (2) centers on the meaning difference between "at" and "to." Are these trivial differences of meaning? Are Americans willing to lose the distinction between "Get that at the bank." and "Get that to the bank." merely because the SROL resolution asserts that the distinction between "at" and "to" is based on an attempt by one social group to dominate others? The claim that the distinctions between these grammatical markers does not effect "meaning," and exact communication is not only an absurd attempt to define away the problem but also a refusal to address the needs of many of the students in our schools and colleges.

The claim that judgments of grammaticality are the product only of "social attitudes and cultural norms" runs counter to the assertion of Chomsky and the Generative-Transformational school of linguistics that judgments of grammaticality are an inherent part of the basic human apparatus for acquiring and producing language.

Although the resolution's statement, "Unfortunately, many employers have narrowly conceived notions of the relationship between linguistic performance and job competence" (p. 14) recognizes the reality of the labor market, their argument goes on to suggest an improbable solution: "Since English teachers are in a large part responsible for the narrow attitudes of today's employers, changing attitudes toward dialect variation does not seem an unreasonable goal, for today's students are tomorrow's employers" (p. 14).

The NCTE thus assigns to English teachers more blame than they deserve and more power than they have ever had or ever could have to change the linguistic fabric of the society. Teachers are required to be crusaders against what is incorrectly seen as linguistic imperialism, rather than becoming more competent at teaching the standard language as a second dialect to those who need to learn it. This approach is an attempt to escape the problems of the teaching of English and has consigned a large group of students to third class positions in society.

Carol Reed (1981) considers this call to change language attitudes from the point of view of a student, who asks, "how are we to negotiate our way through the society during the hundred years or so it may take (him and his friends) to convince the American public and especially the American employer to appreciate the legitimacy of our dialect" (p. 141).

The SROL declaration asserts the students' right to their own language by advocating an incorrectly motivated and improbable process of attitude change. It assures the students of their right to resist what is claimed to be the linguistic and cultural oppression involved in the learning of Standard English, thus tragically ensuring their lack of success.

By equating the teaching of Standard English with oppression, the SROL has achieved a politically convenient, though patently dishonest and actually tragic solution to the problem of the inability to teach Standard English. Unfortunately, the SROL resolution has achieved a warm welcome among some sections of the academic community. David Shores (1977/1978), in writing about the SROL, cites several articles recommending the SROL to teachers. He states that the SROL statement has been well received.

By restricting the teaching and learning of what these students need to know in order to communicate effectively in this society, the radical myopia of the SROL resolution combines with the systemic incompetence in teaching Standard English to deny to even more students the chance they might have had of succeeding. Humans naturally possess the ability to be multi-dialectal. Denying the importance of teaching standard language to those who need to learn it condemns them unnecessarily to the position of being unable to communicate with the society at large.

The current situation surrounding Black English/Standard English bidialectualism is not the fault of the isolated teacher so much as it is the fault of the educational establishment as exemplified by the NCTE position.

The NCTE position can be seen as a response to the 'deficit' theory in American education. During the late 1950s and the early 1960s, the idea was prevalent that there was a deficiency in the language ability of Black children. There was even the claim that ghetto Black children were essentially without logical and orderly language. The work of linguists, William Labov among others, did much to establish the validity of Black English, to counter the assertion that BE is illogical, and to refute the assertion that Black children have a deficit of language ability. At the same time, Labov's work on variation theory examined BE and on incomplete data and examining only the sound system of BE concluded that BE was in deep structure similar to SE. He has since revised that position and acknowledges the Creole origin position presented above and advanced in the 1960s and early 1970s by Bailey (1965), Stewart (1964, 1969a, 1969b, 1974a) and Dillard (1967, 1972).

However, the educational establishment needed and wanted to hear that BE was only trivially different from SE because it was unable to deal with the problems posed by dialect differences. At all levels of educational policy, the similarities between the dialects are emphasized, the differences trivialized, and the assertion that children are competent in all the dialects of both BE and SE are all positions that are prevalent. In general, the problem has been defined away and the implementing of programs that would address the needs of the students influenced by Black English is avoided because that would result in classes that, in most areas, would contain mostly Black students leaving administrators open to charges of segregation.

Yet there has been and continues to be an intuitive recognition that the dialectal differences between BE and SE cause learning problems. Currently, the difficulties that Black students encounter in attempting to bridge the cultural and linguistic gaps between these language systems have been labeled as pathological. Thus, ghetto schools may claim that upwards of 50% or more of their students are afflicted with any number of a set of pseudo-scientific "learning disabilities." Thus, treating linguistic difference as pathology has become the most popular tactic for many school systems. It is a situation that is tragic for the self-image of the student and tragic in the long run for the society because the remedy does not address the nature of the educational problem.

To rectify this situation, the following points must be recognized:

- Students need to achieve productive competence in the grammar of Standard English in order to achieve educational, social and economic mobility in this society.
- The acquisition of Standard English as a second dialect can be an additive process and need not reject or excise the dialect form of family and peers.
- It is essential that teachers possess the knowledge necessary to do their job. The teachers of English who deal with speakers of non-standard Black English need to be trained so that they know enough about Standard English and Black English to teach systematically those forms of Standard English that are needed by their students.
- Teaching approaches, methods and techniques need to be developed and implemented that go beyond the techniques employed to teach those who already know the standard dialect and address the students who possess the structurally different forms of Black English.

English teachers must learn to recognize the systematic influence of Black English in the work of their students and to develop strategies for making their students aware of the fact that there are different language systems involved and aware of the systematic differences between them. Transformational exercises, contrastive exercises of the type used in English as a Second Language classes, role playing, rewriting/translating from one dialect to the other, and the development of editing skills are methods that might be included. The objective is for students to learn to recognize what is not standard in their language and writing and to be able to confidently produce the forms of the standard dialect in appropriate situations.

Teachers should be able to recognize errors in the use of Standard English as the product of historically different language systems that are in contact, rather than signals of an inability to learn, to reason, or to be organized. They also must be able to understand that language forms are themselves neutral tools of human communication that have a historic existence and a social and psychological utility. There is a need to recognize that these factors have little to do with the social value assigned by the society to language forms that are different from the standard norm of the educated elite. Students need not be deprived of the dialect of their family and friends; but they clearly need to learn Standard English for educational, social, and economic mobility. They have not done so to a large extent because their school systems and their teachers have not been prepared or able to teach them.

The situation outlined here is not facile. Strong and courageous efforts must be made in order to address the tragic imcompetence in the teaching of English and in the English teaching establishment. For those many students who enter school eager to learn but who do not succeed because their dialect forms are different in a complex way from the language of the school, there is a real need for a bidialectal approach to the teaching of students who are influenced by Black English.

REFERENCES

Bailey, B. L. (1965). Toward a New Perspective in Negro English Dialectology. *American Speech, 40,* 171–177.

(CCCC) (1974). *College Composition and Communication, 25,* (special issue).

Craig, D. R. (1971). Education and Creole English in the West Indies: Some sociolinguistic factors. in D. Hymes (Ed.), *Pidginization and Creolization of Languages* London: Cambridge University Press.

Brown, R. & Bellugi, U. (1964). Three Processes in the Child's Acquisition of Syntax. *Harvard Educational Review, 34,* 133–151.

Cruickshank, J. G. (1916). *Black Talk: Being notes on Negro dialect in British Guiana with (inevitably) a chapter on the vernacular of Barbados.* Demerara: The Argosy.

Dillard, J. L. (1967). Negro children's dialect in the inner city. *The Florida FL Reporter, 5*(3).

Dillard, J. L. (1972). *Black English: Its history and usage in the United States.* New York: Random House.

Ferguson, C. A. (1959). Diglossia. *Word, 15,* 325—340.

Hall, R. A. (1966). *Pidgin and creole languages.* Ithaca: Cornell University Press.

Halliday, M. A. K., Mcintosh, A., and Strevens, P. (1964). *The linguistic sciences and language teaching.* London: Longmans.

Labov, W. (1966). *The social stratification of English in New York City.* Washington, DC: Center for Applied Linguistics.

Labov, W. (1969). The logic of non-standard English. *The Florida FL Reporter 7* (1) 60–74.

Labov, W. (1972). *Sociolinguistic patterns*. Philadelphia: U. of Pennsylvania Press.

Reed, C. E. (1981). Teaching teachers about teaching writing to students from varied linguistic, social and cultural groups. In M. F. Whiteman (Ed.), *Writing: the nature, development and teaching of written communication. Volume 1: Variation in writing: Functional and linguistic-cultural differences*. Hillsdale, NJ: Lawrence Erlbaum Associates.

Roy, J. D. (1986 in press). The Structure of Tense and Aspect in Barbadian English Creole. In M. Gorlach and J. Holm, ed. *Focus on: the Caribbean*. Amsterdam and Philadelphia: John Benjamins.

Roy, J. D. (1984). *An Investigation of the Processes of Language Variation and Change in a Speech Community in Barbados*. Doctoral Dissertation, Columbia University. Ann Arbor: University Microfilms.

Roy, J. D. (1981). Remediation for the teaching of remedial English, in C. Schoen (Ed.), *The City University of New York Writing Supervisor's Conference Proceedings 1981*. New York: City University of New York.

Roy, J. D. (1977). *On the origin of English Creole: Evidence from the lexical structure*. Masters Thesis, Columbia University, New York.

Schuman, J. H. (1973). *Second language acquisition: The pidginization hypothesis*. Doctoral Dissertation, Harvard. Ann Arbor: University Microfilms.

Shores, D. (1977/78). Another look at students' right to their own language. *Illinois School Journal, 57* (No. 4) Winter.

Spencer, J. (Ed.). (1971). *The English language in West Africa* London: Longmans.

Stewart, W. A. (1964). Urban Negro speech: Sociolinguistic factors affecting English teaching. In R. Shuy, (Ed.), *Social Dialects and Language Learning*, NCTE, Bloomington.

Stewart, W. A. (1969a). Sociopolitical issues in the linguistic treatment of Negro dialect. In J. E. Alatis, (ed.), *Monograph Series on Language and Linguistics, no. 22*. Washington, DC: Georgetown University.

Stewart, W. A. (1969b). Historical and structural basis for the recognition of Negro dialect. In J. E. Alatis (Ed.), *Monograph Series on Language and Linguistics, no. 22*. Washington, DC: Georgetown University.

Stewart, W. A. (1974a). Acculturative processes and the language of the American Negro. In W. W. Gage (Ed.), *Language in its social setting*. Washington, DC: The Anthropological Society of Washington.

Stewart, W. A. (1974b). The laissez-faire movement in English teaching: Advance to the rear? *The Florida FL Reporter 12* (1&2):81–90, 98–99. Reprinted in M. A. Lourie and N. F. Conklin, (Eds.), (1978). *A pluralistic nation: The language issue in the United States* (pp. 333–356). Rowley, MA: Newbury House.

Weinreich, U. (1953). *Languages in Contact*. New York: Linguistic Circle of New York.

Continuities/Discontinuities in the Function and Use of Language as Related to Situation and Social Class

William S. Hall
University of Maryland

William E. Nagy
University of Illinois, Champaign-Urbana

There is a long tradition in cognitive social science linking language and thought. A more recent tradition in social science research links language functioning and use to schooling. Differences in patterns of language use may reflect or embody differences in how communicative or cognitive strategies are brought to bear on specific types of tasks in specific situations. The purpose of the present chapter is to describe socioeconomic status differences in one aspect of communication: the use of words of internal state. These are words that when used literally refer primarily to internal states, processes, or experiences. This includes words about cognition (*think, remember, know*), emotions (*happy, afraid, love*), perception (*see, smell, pain*), and intentions and desires (*intend, want, wish*) (See Hall & Nagy, 1986). Internal state words have both cognitive and educational significance; they play an important role in certain types of classroom discussion, and their use is linked to cognitive strategies and skills involved in metacognition (cf. Baker & Brown, 1980; Flavell, 1978).

SITUATIONAL VARIATION

Concurrent with increaseing interest in language differences between individuals of various social groups has come a growing focus on differences in the speech of the same individual in different situations. An early study by Labov (1964) illustrates very well some important aspects of the interaction between situational and social variation. Figure 14.1 represents differences in the pronunciation of *r* by speakers from different socioeconomic levels, at different levels of formality.

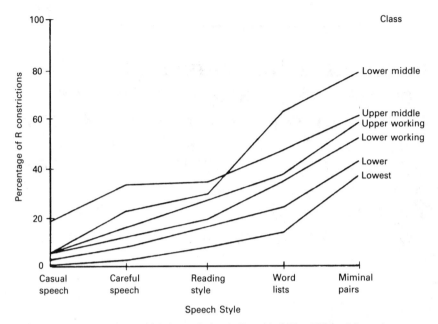

FIGURE 14.1.   Use of *R*-Constriction in New York City SES and Speech Style

This figure is originally from William Labov, "Phonological Correlates of Social Stratification" in John J. Gumperz and Dell Hymes (Eds.), *The ethnography of communication,* special issue of the *American Anthropologist,* Vol. 66, No. 6, p. 171. It is reproduced here from Robbins Burling, *Man's many voices,* New York: Holt, Rinehart & Winston, 1970, p. 93.

There are four particular aspects of this figure that we wish to draw attention to:

1. Both the situational and social differences are quantitative rather than qualitative; they manifest themselves in terms of the percentage of the time that a certain pronunciation is used. This does not mean that there cannot be some social or situational differences that are qualitative; however, much of such variation will consist in the relative frequency with which a certain form or pattern occurs.

2. Note that the most careful speech of the lowest group in Labov's study shows more *R*-constriction than the casual speech of even the upper middle-class group. Thus, there is in some sense a real "overlap" between the speech patterns of even the extreme ends of the social scale. This is of course not necessarily the case with all instances of social and situational vairation; but in many instances,

such variation will be one of degree, with much overlap between the patterns of different groups, rather than consisting of qualitative and absolute differences.

3. Note that in this case the situational differences are as large as the social differences. The magnitude of differences between the speech types of a single social group in different situations is the same as, or greater than, that of the difference between different social groups at any one given level of formality. Again, this is not necessarily the case; there may be instances where social variation in language patterns is far greater than any situational variation within the social group. However, situational variation is at least potentially as great as social variation—a point that we will return to shortly.

4. Note that there are differences in the way that different social groups respond to a given situation. In this case, all groups show a similar pattern, using a higher percentage of R-constriction in more formal circumstances—but the lower middle-class group shows a much more extreme difference in this regard than any of the other groups. It has been suggested that this is due to the uncertainty of being the second-highest group; the lower middle-class speakers, when in a formal situation, outdo the upper middle-class speakers in trying to sound upper middle class (cf. Labov, 1964).

The example just discussed involves variation in phonology. Not surprisingly, early work in language variation, e.g., Labov (1966), tended to focus on this area; phonology, being one of the more accessible aspects of language structure, has also been the first area of major focus in other fields such as historical linguistics and dialect geography. A title such as that of Sankoff (1973), "Above and beyond phonology in variable rules," gives an indication of the direction that progress in language variation study has taken, expanding "upwards" into syntax and semantics. However, the same social and situational factors that influence pronunciation (e.g., the age, sex, social class, mood, and personality of the speaker; the role and status of the addressee; the formality and the topic of the conversation) play a role in variation in syntax, vocabulary, and all other levels of linguistic patterning.

Cole, Dore, Hall, and Dowley (1978) document some of the more specific effects that situational variation can produce. Likewise, Matthew, Connelly, and McCleod (1978), investigating the speech of a five-year-old in three different situations (alone, with a friend, and with the mother) found substantial variation, both in syntactic complexity (the child used far more six-word or longer utterances with the mother than alone or playing with a friend) and in speech act types (the child used more commands alone than with the mother; presumably it used commands more often when taking on the adult role in the discourse).

The four points mentioned in regard to phonological variation in the example from Labov are also found to apply to nonphonological variation as well. Variation in other aspects of linguistic patterning may be quantitative rather than qualitative, and there may be substantial overlap between groups; situational variation may be of the same magnitudes as, or greater than, social-class-based variation; and different social groups manifest different patterns of situational variation.

This is crucial to the study of social variation in language patterns in a number of ways. First of all, there may be genuine social-class-based differences in language that appear in some situations and not in others. For example, Snow et al. (1976), studying the speech of Dutch mothers of three socioeconomic levels, found significant class differences in one situation (free play) but not in another (telling a story based on pictures in a book).

Second, what appears to be social-class-based variation in language may in fact be an artifact of the different responses different social groups may have to the "same" situation. Cazden (1970), in a review of research on social-class-based language differences, concludes that in most of the cases studied, the differences that were found were due to differences in the ways that children from different backgrounds react to a situation, rather than to any difference in linguistic ability supposedly correlating with social class. This calls into question any study of social-class-based language differences that does not carefully control for potential differences in the effects of the situation on the subjects involved. Cooper (1975), for example, in a critique of Bernstein's early work, points out that one of the settings used to collect data—a group discussion of capital punishment—may not have been as interesting, or as familiar, or as comfortable, to the working-class subjects as to middle-class subjects.

Then, the research presented in this chapter focuses on social class variation along with situational ones. Specifically, the chapter focuses on the way that differences between the home and school situations may influence children's use of internal state words at school. The issues here can be stated in terms of the "mismatch hypothesis." The mismatch hypothesis postulates that learning difficulties experienced by children from minority or "non-mainstream" backgrounds are caused by a discontinuity between the home and school environments—that is, a discrepancy between the expectations, strategies, and schemata that work at home, and the cognitive and motivational demands of the classroom. For children of the mainstream culture, on the other hand, there is a fair degree of continuity between home and school in terms of culture, patterns of language and behavior, and types of strategies for interacting with adults.

Two more specific, independent hypotheses about internal state word usage can be formulated within the mismatch model.

First of all, it might be argued that schools demand a high degree of "meta-behavioral awareness," and that different cultures or social groups do not provide children with the same amount of preparation in this area. By meta-behavioral awareness we mean the ability to analyze, and verbally describe, the emotions, thoughts, and intentions of a person or fictional character. Such analysis is typical of classroom discussion, especially relating to reading stories, even in early grades. The use of internal state words to talk about feelings, thoughts, and intentions is clearly an important aspect of the child's preparation for this type of school activity, and it is possible that children from some socioeconomic levels or ethnic groups receive more of such preparation at home than do others. Analysis of the internal state word usage of the adults in the children's environments at home and school will indicate whether or not this is the case.

The first hypothesis, then, is that there is a mismatch or discontinuity between the internal state word usage of adults at home versus at school experienced by children from non-mainstream families. A second hypothesis can be formulated concerning the internal state words produced by the children. If children from non-mainstream backgrounds experience a mismatch of some sort between the home and school environments, there is likely to be some indication of this in terms of their response to the school situation. The internal state word usage of the children is a measure of one aspect of their response that is of clear educational significance.

It should be noted that these two hypotheses are independent: there may be a mismatch in the internal state word usage of adults at home versus at school, but this may not be reflected in the internal state word usage of the children. Conversely, there may be a mismatch between the home and school environments that has nothing to do with internal state word usage of adults, which however influences the internal state word usage of the children.

The research discussed in this chapter tests these hypotheses in measuring differences in children's speech between home and school situations. It also contributes to a more general theory of register or situational variation (cf. Halliday, 1978). In the following pages we define internal state words, discuss the rationale for choosing internal state words for investigation, and present the results from the analyses of internal state word usage in natural conversation in the home and school environments of 4½-to-5-year-old children.

COGNITIVE IMPLICATIONS OF INTERNAL STATE WORD USE

Variation occurs in all aspects of language; in pronunciation, grammar, choice of lexical items, discourse-level phenomena, and so on. We are interested in language as a transmitter and reflector of culture and cognitive styles, and are, therefore, interested in language variation along dimensions that will be of direct cognitive and educational significance. This excludes from our consideration differences in pronunciation (e.g., *fas'* vs *fast*) or grammar (*I don't have any* vs. *I don't have none*). Such differences may correlate with important social distinctions, and relate in important ways to attitudes on the part of both speakers and hearers; but there is no distinction in conceptual content associated with differences in pronunciation or grammar alone. We therefore focused our investigation on aspects of language, or differences in patterns of language use that would be likely to influence the socialization of cognitive modes in children; these have to do with the content and functions of language, rather than with formal properties of phonology or syntax.

The use of internal state words is crucially linked to cognitive strategies in three related areas: the acquisition and organization of internal state concepts; the understanding of stories and discussion of stories; and metacognitive skills in general.

The scope of the present research is primarily to document what differences there are in the use of internal state words between different social groups, and then to interpret these differences, as far as this is possible, in terms of reasonable hypotheses about the effects these differences should have on the child's cognitive development.

PREVIOUS RESEARCH ON SOCIAL-CLASS-BASED DIFFERENCES IN INTERNAL STATE WORD USE

There is a substantial body of research on social-class-based language differences (cf. Bernstein, 1971, 1973) that has significant implications for, and makes some specific predictions about, class differences in patterns of internal state word use.

In an early study on class differences in language use, Schatzman and Strauss (1955, using as data transcriptions of interviews with people who had experienced a tornado, and taking the extreme cases on educational and income distribution) found that lower class subjects were less likely, when describing human behavior, to talk about motivation. They also found a class difference in the frequency of "you know"—this conversational device was more common along lower class speakers than middle-class speakers.

In the "positional" mode of control (cf. Bernstein, 1971, 1973) which is associated with restricted code, and asserted to be more typical of the working class, regulation of a child's behavior is in terms of external behavior and the positional status of the participants. In the "personal" mode of control, associated with elaborated code and supposedly more typical of middle-class families, more emphasis is given to motivation and intention in controlling the child's behavior. Also, in the positional mode of control, they are simply enforced rather than discussed. This would suggest that internal state words would be used with greater frequency by members of the middle class (although the difference might be manifested in different types of usage rather than in overall frequency).

In Bernstein (1973) are articles by several different authors exploring the implications of his theories in more detail. Some of the articles make more explicit claims about internal state word usage.

In data based on questionnaires in which mothers estimated their own usage patterns in response to a series of specific questions, Henderson (1973) found that middle-class mothers talked more about cognitive topics than about affective/interpersonal topics, and more about cognitive topics than did working-class mothers. On the other hand, working-class mothers talked more about affective/interpersonal topics than about cognitive topics, and more about affective/interpersonal topics than did middle-class mothers.

If one could assume that Henderson's methods accurately reflect the mothers' actual usage (this is somewhat questionable), that English social-class differences are similar to those in America, and that more talk about cognitive or affective/interpersonal topics will increase the frequency of the corresponding internal state word categories, then this research makes specific predictions about class differences we might expect to find in the internal state word usage in our data.

A slightly earlier study done in America had somewhat similar results. In a study of spontaneous story telling of fourth graders, von Raffler, Engel, and Sigelmen (1971) compare the speech of middle/upper-class whites and lower/middle-class blacks (thus confounding race and socioeconomic status). They found that a higher percentage of black children referred to internal states than did white children (71% vs. 46%), but that there were differences in the type of internal states referred to. Internal state references by the white children were mostly *think* and *know*; references to internal states by black children related to emotions and ambitions.

These results seem to confirm the class differences in choice of topic noted in Henderson (1973) but do not confirm the overall impression one gets from the descriptions of restricted and elaborate codes, that lower working-class persons do not use language to explore intentions and feelings.

Thus, internal state words do figure in claims that have been made about social-class-based language differences that might be of educational and cognitive significance. However, the research up to now has suffered from lack of a broad data base that takes situational variation into account and includes naturalistic conversation by children and their caregivers in the home.

INTERNAL STATE WORDS—WHAT THEY ARE

The current research centers on the analysis of data from the project outlined in Hall and Nagy (1979). Procedures were developed for coding internal state words, that is, for identifying instances of internal state words in naturalistic data and categorizing certain aspects of their use and function in the context of discourse; these procedures were then applied to the large corpus of conversation described earlier, and the resulting data subjected to analyses of various kinds.

Internal state words, or words of internal report, have meanings primarily concerned with internal processes, states, and experiences. This includes words about cognition (e.g., *think, know, believe, remember, figure out*), about emotions (e.g., *fear, angry, sad, happy*), about perceptions—both the five senses (*see, hear,* etc.) and the more "internal" perceptions (e.g., *dizzy, thirsty, ache*), about desires (*want, wish, desire*), and about intentions, choices, and decisions.

Internal state words are words that by virtue of their lexical meaning refer, when used literally, to internal states and processes. The word *jerk* (as in, *I could kill that jerk*) *expresses* the speaker's internal state or attitude, but does not *refer* to it, as would a word like *angry* or *upset.* To take a different kind of example, the words *did something* in a sentence like *I don't know what she said, but it sure did something to him,* may well refer to an internal state or experience, but not by virtue of the lexical meanings of these words.

Many words imply or presuppose information about internal states, but are not primarily about internal states themselves. For example, *complain* presupposes a certain type of attitude on the part of the speaker, but is primarily a verb of speaking. There are also words about capacities, such as *blind* or *intelligent,* which relate to internal states and processes, but which do not refer directly to internal states or processes as such.

Lexical ambiguity complicates the process of determining what should be considered an instance of an internal state word and what should not. *See,* for example, is a perceptual internal state word in *Did you see the firetrucks?* and a cognitive internal state word in *I don't see how you can do that.* However, it is presumably not an internal state word at all in a sentence like *He went to see his grandmother,* since it seems to be more or less synonymous with *visit* in this context.

In naturalistic data there will of course be several types of borderline cases where it is not clear whether some state, processes, or experience can be considered "internal" (that is, "mental" or "psychological"). (The theoretical issues involved in such cases have been discussed in detail in Hall and Nagy, 1986). However, the majority of words occurring in everyday conversation are rather prototypical examples of our basic internal state categories.

We have divided internal state words into four major categories:

1. *Cognitive.* Words in this category are about cognition, awareness, consciousness, knowledge, understanding, attention, thinking, belief, or certainty. Some of the commonly occurring cognitive words are:

think	know	remember	forget
understand	figure out	belief	believe
guess	assume	wonder	pretend

2. *Affective.* Words in this category relate to emotions. Some of the commonly occurring affective words are:

like	love	hate	afraid
sorry	angry	annoy	glad

happy	mad	mood	regret
prefer	sad	scared	upset

3. *Perceptual.* These words relate either to the five senses or to a person's awareness of his/her own body, e.g., pain or hunger. Some common perceptual words are:

see	look	hear	watch
listen	taste	hurt	pain
hungry	ache	tired	thirsty

4. *Intentions and Desires.* This category includes words for internal states that relate to goals—what a person intends, chooses, or wants. Some common words in this category are:

want	wish	intend	would like
plan	mean	decide	change one's mind
choose	hope		

In coding for usage, the most important distinction in our work is what we have labeled the "semantic/pragmatic" distinction, which can be expressed in the following question: Is a given instance of an internal state word being used to refer to and communicate about an internal state? More briefly, is it being used literally?

Semantic, or literal, usages, are those instances where the internal state word is used to refer to an internal state, as for example the *know* in *Maybe you know the answer.* Pragmatic, or nonliteral usages, are those instances where the lexical meaning of the internal state word contributes *indirectly,* if at all, to the propositional content of the sentence. A typical example of this would be the *know* in *Ya know, there ought to be a law.* (See Hall & Nagy, in press).

Semantic uses of internal state words can be further subdivided into reflections and non-reflections. *Reflections* are assertions by the speaker about his/her own current internal state, or questions about the addressee's current internal state.

One motivation for this distinction is the concept of *metacognitive experience.* For our purposes, we can adopt the following, somewhat modified definition of metacognitive experience: a metacognitive experience is awareness of one's own current internal state. (This overlaps substantially, but not perfectly, with the following definition by Flavell, 1978: "Metacognitive experiences are conscious cognitive or affective experiences which occur during the enterprise (that is, some cognitive enterprise) and concern any aspect of it" (p. 233).

Reflections as defined above have the following relationship to metacognitive experiences: When a speaker makes an assertion about his/her own current internal state, he or she must necessarily be aware of that state; the assertion is an expression of that awareness. When a speaker asks a question about the addressee's current internal state, this presumably elicits awareness on the part of the addressee on his/her own current internal state.

We have excluded from our definition of reflections assertions by the speaker about the addressee's internal state (*You know what shoes they are*) as well as imperatives relating to the addressee's internal state (*Guess where I'm hiding*). These may of course also elicit awareness on the part of the addressee of his/her own current internal state, but the connection is not as direct as in the case of questions, where the speaker is explicitly trying to elicit such awareness.

The definition of reflections given above can be broken down into two main criteria:

First, for a semantic usage to qualify as a reflection, it must be an assertion about the speaker's internal state or a question about the addressee's internal state. Thus, the internal state word must be in the part of the sentence asserted or questioned. This largely restricts reflections to internal state words in the main clause of the sentence; relative clauses and many subordinate clauses are presupposed rather than asserted or questioned. Thus, example (1) and (2) below constitute reflections, whereas (3) and (4) do not:

1. I'm thinking about it.
2. Do you know what the answer is?
3. Somebody I know told me about it.
4. They say that I know the answer.

To summarize, the most general coding category is Internal State Words. There are two basic types of classification according to which this general category is further subdivided. One type of division is according to lexical classes; internal state words can be divided into four groups—Cognitive, Affective, Perceptual, and Intentions and Desires—on the basis of their lexical meaning. The second division of internal state words, intersecting with the first, is according to function. Internal state words are categorized as Pragmatic or Semantic depending on their use in context. There is a further classification by use: Semantic Internal State Words can be further divided into Reflections and NonReflections.

These coding categories, discussed in more detail in Hall and Nagy (1986), are a refinement of the categories designed for the investigation of internal state word use in naturalistic data given in Gearhart and Hall (1982).

The categories Cognitive, Affective, and Intentions and Desires are very similar to the three subcategories of the Internal response category of the Stein and Glenn (1979) story grammar: *Thoughts or cognitions* (e.g., "Mary thought John was obnoxious"), *feelings or affective responses* (e.g., "Mary was very angry"), and *goals or desires* (e.g., "Mary wanted to hit John"). For the purposes of story grammar, it does seem best not to include Perceptual words in the category of internal responses. But in this research, internal state words are of interest because of their implications for metabehavioral awareness. We would consider perceptual awareness (e.g., the ability to analyze a perceptual array into a set of geometrical or mathematical relationships) as being related to metabehavioral awareness (e.g., the ability to analyze the emotions of a person or those of a fictional character).

Most words have a number of meanings, so the fact that a word occurs in a given category means only that it has at least one meaning that belongs in that group. Whether or not a specific instance of that word in the conversation belongs in that category must be determined on the basis of the context.

The overall goal in this research was to identify those factors that are associated with differences in internal state word use by the target children. We also want to answer questions such as the following, concerning predictions made by specific versions of the mismatch hypothesis that can be formulated regarding our data: Do children from nonmainstream backgrounds experience a discontinuity or mismatch between the internal state word use of adults at home and that which they encounter in the speech of adults at school? Does the speech of children from nonmainstream backgrounds reflect a discontinuity in the use of internal state words that might reflect a mismatch of culture between home and school experienced by these children?

SUBJECTS

To answer questions such as these, we searched a corpus generated by 39 target children and those with whom they spoke as well as those who spoke in the situations where they were present. Conversations occurring in two situations are discussed here. The unit from which the internal state words were coded was a turn to speak.

Categorization of the internal state word was carried out by two independent judges who worked from transcripts of the original tapes. The transcripts were distributed across race and SES to minimize confounding due to practice, and each judge coded approximately half the transcripts in each race/SES group.

The transcripts incorporated the following information:

1. a number identifying the target child and his/her family;
2. a code representing the race/SES group of that family;
3. a code identifying the speaker of each particular line of the transcript;
4. a code identifying the situation;
5. a sequential number identifying each line in the transcript;
6. an indication of incidences of simultaneous talk;

7. the actual text of the utterance;
8. a code indicating whether or not the utterance contained a question; and
9. the number of words and turns spoken by each speaker in the situation.

In addition, there was also, interspersed through the transcript, the contextual information provided by the experimenter during the taping. This information was useful in interpreting the discourse; for example, to whom a given remark was addressed, or the type of activities in which the participants were involved.

To assess agreement between the two judges, the transcript of a randomly selected subject was coded by both judges. The agreement among the judges as to what constituted an internal state word was 94%. The addressee of a particular internal state word was commonly identified 77.5%. The disagreements here usually involved uncertainty about the exact identity despite agreement about the age and sex of the addressee. Only 5% of the total judgments involved disagreement about whether the target child was the addressee. The assignment of each internal state word to a particular lexical category showed 92.0% agreement. The identification of the object of the internal state word (that is, to whose internal state the word referred) resulted in common judgments in 84.4% of the cases. Finally, the judgment as to whether the internal state word represented a Reflection or not was made in common for 84.7% of the internal state words. In general, the interrater agreement across all judgments is remarkably high for data of this sort.

RESULTS

Formation of Dependent Variables

Since no attempt was made during the taping phase of this study to control the target child's interactions, the amount of speech available for each target child and his/her principal interactants varies quite widely. Table 14.1 shows the means, standard deviations, and ranges of both the number of words and the number of turns for the target children and their principal caretakers. It is apparent from this table that the absolute frequency of occurrence of each of the coding categories will be, in part, dependent on the amount of speech sampled. In fact, frequencies for each speaker have an average correlation of .73 with the number of words spoken and .71 with the number of turns taken.

There are two typical ways to deal with methodological problems of this sort. One method is to treat the words and turns as covariates; in essence, to partial out their influence from the internal state word categories. The other method is to divide the variables of interest as a less direct (and frequently less precise) way of partialing out their influence. When the correlations among the internal state word categories were computed according to both methods and compared, the

TABLE 14.1
Means, Standard Deviations, and Ranges of Number of Words and
Turns by Principal Speakers

Person	Number of Words			Number of Turns		
	M	SD	Range	M	SD	Range
			Dinner			
Target children	1809.53	909.38	230-3810	314.43	153.30	54-770
Mothers	1998.06	1410.42	23-4955	272.61	174.11	5-714
			Directed activity			
Target children	505.46	235.38	17-969	110.81	51.97	8-209
Teachers	1702.81	733.15	436-2667	193.65	85.45	60-472

mean differences were negligible: .02 for per word versus words controlled and .09 for per turn versus turns controlled. Thus the use of proportions does not appear to be substantially less precise at reducing contamination than partialing. Based on this, as well as the fact that proportions are more conceptually meaningful and interpretable, we decided that dependent variables would be formed as proportions of the number of words.

Proportion variables typically have positively skewed distributions, and our variables are no exception. Thus for purposes of statistical analysis, the variables were arcsine-transformed to make their distributions more normal. All reported means and patterns of means, however, are based on the more meaningful untransformed variables.

Selection of Dependent Variables

Our coding procedures described in detail earlier, categorized the internal state word tokens occurring in the corpus in terms of the following categories:

Semantic Categories
    Reflections: Cognitive Reflections
                          Affective Reflections
                          Perceptual Reflections
                          Intentions and Desires Reflections
    Nonreflections: Cognitive Nonreflections
                          Affective Nonreflections
                          Perceptual Nonreflections
                          Intentions and Desires Nonreflections

Quotes and Songs
Pragmatic Categories: Conversational Devices
Indirect Requests
Rhetorical Questions
Exam Questions
Hedges
Opinion Questions
Attentional Devices

The following steps were taken to reduce this set of categories to a workable number of dependent variables: First of all, we chose to group together conceptually similar variables that individually were too low in frequency to be subject to reliable analysis. Second, we chose to focus on functional rather than lexical categories.

As a result, all pragmatic categories except attentional devices were grouped into a single category labeled nonliteral usages. Attentional devices were kept as a separate category. Nonreflections were similarly treated as a single category. Only in the case of reflections did we construct separate variables based on the lexical class of the internal state words. Songs and quotes were too infrequent to be analyzed.

We also included in the analysis some supercategories: First, reflections, including all four lexical classes of reflections; second, semantic usages, including both reflections and nonreflections; and finally, internal state words, which includes all kinds of internal state words (semantic, pragmatic, or quotes and songs) occurring in the transcript. The variables included in our analyses and the inclusion relationships among them are represented in Fig. 14.2.

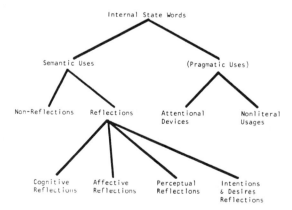

FIGURE 14.2. Class-Inclusion Relationships Among Internal State Word Variables

SELECTION OF SPEAKERS FOR ANALYSIS

The variables we chose can be defined for any speaker or group of speakers within a situation. Certain speakers and groups of speakers are of special relevance to our purposes.

The target children were of course the focal point of the data collection and are the focus of this analysis as well. They are the only individuals consistently present in both home and school situations, thus allowing for an analysis of situational variation in the speech of the same person.

The speech of target children is also of special interest to us because we are interested in the process of cultural transmission—that is, how a child learns patterns of language usage from the speech in his/her environment. Our target children, aged 4½ to 5 years, were still at an age when their understanding of internal state concepts is developing (cf. Wellman & Johnson, 1979).

The speech of other participants was of interest to us primarily insofar as it explained, or failed to explain, situational variation in the speech of the target children.

There are three sets of speakers who can be considered to comprise the linguistic environment of the target children. One of these contains only the primary caregiver (presumably the mother in the home environment and the teacher in the school environment). Another possible set contains all adults in the target children's environment. At home, this would include fathers, grandparents, and any other adults present (either coincidentally or on a regular basis) during the dinner situation. At school, this category consists almost entirely of teachers. The experimenter is present in the classroom, but speaks relatively little, and there are very few teachers' aides. A third definition of the target children's linguistic environment would include all speakers other than the target children themselves.

Although the third of these definitions has an obvious validity for some purposes, we have excluded it from our analyses for the following reasons: First of all, since the families in our sample differ in composition—some have only one child, others have several—comparison of internal state word usage across families would be difficult to interpret, since children and adults may differ substantially in their internal state word usage. Thus, a measure of the child's linguistic environment that included other children might reflect the age composition of the family more than consistent differences in internal state word use. Second, this measure of the environment of the child would incorporate a degree of redundancy. We are interested in measuring the influence of situational factors on the internal state word use of the target children. The speech of the other children, if included in the measure of the target child's linguistic environment, would incorporate factors influencing the target child's speech, but also the response of the other children to those same factors.

Because of this potential problem, in looking at the speech in the target child's environment, we concentrated on two measures: (a) the speech of the primary caregivers (the teachers and mothers) and (b) the speech of all adults in the target child's environment.

RESULTS OF DATA ANALYSIS

We begin by presenting our data in terms of the results of situations × race × SES and race × SES analyses of variance (ANOVAs) on the internal state word variables representing the speech of the target children, the speech of their primary caregivers (mothers and teachers), and of all the adults in their home and school environments. Then we try to account for variations in the target children's internal state word use.

Across-Situation Analyses

Several types of analyses were performed to investigate the effects of situation and social group membership on the target children's pattern of internal state word use. First of all, situation × race × SES analyses of variance were performed for all our dependent variables on the following groups of speakers:

1. Target children at home and at school. Since the setting is obviously a repeated factor in this case, the target children for whom data were not available at both school and dinner were excluded (N for analysis = 36).

2. Primary caregivers (teachers at school and mothers at home). For two target children, the mothers were not living at home and hence not present at the dinners. One mother spoke only five turns (23 words) in the course of the two dinners, using no internal state words at all; it was decided to exclude her from this analysis as well (N = 37 teachers, 35 mothers).

Tables 14.2–14.4 present all the significant effects found by these analyses. Because it is consistent with the organization of our subsequent discussion, the results are grouped according to the independent variables involved, rather than by groups of speakers. Table 14.2 contains all main effects of situation, Table 14.3 all significant interactions of situation with race and/or SES, Table 14.4 all effects of race and SES that do not involve situation.

Situation Main Effects.   For the target children, all significant main effects of situation involve a difference in means in the same direction; the target children use more Affective Reflections, Perceptual Reflections, Nonreflections, all Semantic Uses, and Nonliteral Usages at home than at school. It must be kept in mind that these variables represent proportions with the total number of words spoken as the denominator. Strictly speaking, one must say not that the children use more Semantic Internal State Words at home than at school, but that Seman-

TABLE 14.2
Main Effects of Situation on Internal State Word Variables

	Speakers		
Variable	Target Children (df = 1,32)	Teachers and Mothers (df = 1,64)	All Adults in Environment (df = 1,67)
Cognitive reflections	$F < 1$	$F < 1$	$F = 8.25**a$
Affective reflections	$F = 28.96**a$	$F = 12.91**a$	$F = 24.93**a$
Perceptual reflections	$F = 8.29**a$	$F < 1$	$F < 1$
CAP reflections	$F = 5.16*a$	$F < 1$	$F = 18.33**a$
Intentions and desires reflections	$F = 2.92$	$F = 16.42**a$	$F = 12.19**a$
All reflections	$F = 3.47$	$F = 13.45**a$	$F = 20.75**a$
Nonreflections	$F = 5.53*a$	$F < 1$	$F < 1$
Semantic usages	$F = 5.04*a$	$F = 8.11**a$	$F = 9.11**a$
Attentional devices	$F < 1$	$F = 11.07**b$	$F = 6.93*b$
Nonliteral usages	$F = 10.59**a$	$F < 1$	$F = 12.37**a$
All internal state words	$F = 4.12$	$F = 2.91$	$F = 6.40*a$

[a]Home mean is greater than school mean.
[b]School mean is greater than home mean.
*$p < .05$
**$p < .01$

tic Internal State Words constitute a larger proportion of the children's speech at home than at school.

Looking at the adult speech the children are exposed to—both in terms of primary caregivers (mothers and teachers) and all the adults in the environment—a similar pattern is seen. In the case of the speech of all adults (for which more of the main effects of situation are significant), there are proportionately more Cognitive, Affective, and Intentions and Desires Reflections used at home than at school; the same holds for Cognitive, Affective, and Perceptual Reflections taken as a group (CAP reflections), for all Reflections, all Semantic Uses, Nonliteral Usages, and all Internal State Words. The only exception is for Attentional Devices, which are used more by adults at school than by adults at home.

In comparing the relationship of the speech of the target children and adults, three different patterns emerge from an inspection of Table 14.2. First, for two variables—Affective Reflections and Semantic Uses—there is a significant home-school difference found among adults, and a corresponding significant difference among the target children. Second, for almost all the other variables,

TABLE 14.3

Interactions Involving Situation on Internal State Word Variables

| | Speaker | | | | | | | | |
| | Target Children (df = 1,32) | | | Mothers and Teachers (df = 1,64) | | | All Adults (df = 1,67) | | |
Variable	Race	SES	Race & SES	Race	SES	Race & SES	Race	SES	Race & SES
Cognitive reflections	1.83	1.73	1.03	<1	<1	3.53	<1	<1	2.77
Affective reflections	2.71	<1	<1	2.34	<1	6.71*	<1	<	7.82**
Perceptual reflections	<1	2.37	<1	1.69	2.55	<1	<1	2.15	1.43
CAP reflections	3.63	<1	1.92	1.42	<1	5.43*	<1	<1	3.84
Intentions and desires reflections	3.28	1.34	<1	<1	<1	<1	1.26	<1	<1
All reflections	5.94*	<1	3.16	3.64	<1	4.60*	1.55	<1	3.64
Nonreflections	2.73	4.63*	1.71	<1	3.72	<1	<1	2.92	<1
Semantic usages	9.22**	<1	1.65	2.85	<1	2.25	<1	<1	1.62
Attentional	1.92	1.68	3.41	<1	<1	<1	2.59	<1	<1
Nonliteral usages	<1	<1	1.51	4.08*	<1	<1	4.46*	<1	<1
All internal state words	13.11**	<1	<1	<1	2.28	2.60	<1	2.13	1.47

*p < .05
**p < .01

TABLE 14.4
Race and SES Main Effects and Interactions

| | Speaker | | | | | | | | |
| | Target Children (df = 1,32) | | | Teachers and Mothers (df = 1,64) | | | All Adults (df = 1,67) | | |
Variable	Race	SES	Race & SES	Race	SES	Race & SES	Race	SES	Race & SES
Cognitive reflections	<1	<1	3.99	<1	1.15	<1	<1	<1	1.68
Affective reflections	<1	<1	<1	<1	<1	<1	<1	<1	<1
Perceptual reflections	2.04	1.09	<1	1.08	2.35	<1	<1	6.50*[b]	<1
CAP reflections	<1	1.32	3.74	<1	<1	<1	<1	<1	<1
Intentions and desires reflections	2.34	<1	<1	2.80	<1	<1	5.86*[a]	<1	<1
All reflections	<1	1.20	2.45	<1	<1	<1	<1	<1	1.30
Nonreflections	2.02	<1	<1	<1	<1	<1	1.27	<1	<1
Semantic usages	1.80	1.33	1.78	<1	<1	<1	<1	<1	1.51
Attentional devices	13.94**[a]	1.29	4.93*	4.77*[a]	<1	<1	1.78	<1	<1
Nonliteral usages	<1	<1	1.69	<1	<1	<1	2.77	3.04	<1
All internal state words	4.34*[a]	<1	<1	<1	<1	<1	<1	<1	<1

[a]White mean is greater than black mean.
[b]Working-class mean is greater than middle-class mean.
*p < .05
**p < .01

there is a significant home-school difference among adults, but no significant difference among the children. (Among the variables under discussion here, the pattern of means among target children, though nonsignificant, was always in the same direction as the significant differences among the adults.) The third pattern, perhaps the most interesting of the three, involves the two variables Perceptual Reflections and Nonreflections, for which the target children show a significant situational difference, whereas neither the primary caregivers nor the adults in general show such a difference. Moreover, in the case of Nonreflections there is almost no difference at all in the means for the adults in the home versus school environments. In the case of Perceptual Reflections, where children have a significantly higher mean at home than at school, the adults (both primary caregivers and adults in general) show a nonsignificant difference in the opposite direction.

This illustrates a point that will become even clearer in further results. Specifically, the use of internal state words by the target children reflects the internal state word use of the adults in their environment to a certain extent and in certain respects, but there are also important aspects of the target children's internal state word use that cannot be accounted for in terms of the internal state word use of the adults around them.

Interactions of Situation With Race and/or SES.   The significant interactions in the speech of the target children reported in Table 14.3 were each followed up by post hoc testing. The Tukey test was used for all pairwise comparisons, and the Scheffe method was used for the non-pairwise comparisons. A significance level of .05 was used for all post hoc testing.

The significant situation × race interactions suggested that black children had lower means at school than at home for Reflections, Semantic Uses, and Internal State Words. At school, white children had higher means than black children for Semantic Uses and Internal State Words; white children at home also had a higher mean than black children at school for Semantic Uses and Internal State Words. Furthermore, it was found that the mean for the black target children at school was significantly lower than the means for the other three cells (black children at home and white children at home and at school), taken as a group for Reflections and Internal State Words. Also, the combined black home and white school means were higher than the combined white home and black school means; this was significant for Semantic Uses and Internal State Words. The significant situation × SES interaction for Nonreflections indicates that the mean for middle-class target children at home is higher than the mean for middle-class target children at school.

The situation × race interaction—the fact that the black target children's mean at school for Reflections, Semantic Uses, and Internal State Words is lower than their mean at home, and lower than white target children's means at both home and school—bears crucially on the theoretical issues and hypotheses central to the present research. There is apparently something about the school situation, or the black target children's response to it, that causes them to use proportionately fewer internal state words than the white target children use at school. One of the chief goals of further analyses is therefore to identify as far as possible the situational factors influencing the children's internal state word use, and to see to what extent these factors contribute to the situation × race interaction.

The interaction takes on a different character for the analyses involving teachers and mothers, however. The significant situation × race × SES interaction for Reflections has the following pattern: at home, the white middle-class mothers have the highest mean, and the black middle-class mothers have the lowest mean; at school, the teachers of black middle-class target children have the highest mean, and the teachers of white middle-class target children have the lowest mean. The same pattern holds for CAP Reflections, and almost the same pattern for Affective Reflections as well.

The situation × race interaction for Nonliteral Usages, on the other hand, indicates that the mean for black mothers is higher than the mean for white mothers. This order is reversed among teachers. The same pattern obtains for the interaction in the adult environment at home and at school.

In the case of overall situational variation, there was similarity, at least for some variables, between the children and the adults in their environment. In both cases, there was a general tendency to use more internal state words in most categories at home than in school, both on the part of the target children and the adults. In the case of the interactions of situation with race and SES, however, there is no apparent similarity between the target children and the adults in their environment. More specifically, no trace of the situation × race interaction in the target children's use of Reflections, Semantic Uses, and Internal State Words can be found in the speech of their primary caregivers or of the adults in their environments. Therefore, it appears that an explanation for this interaction in the speech of the target children will have to be sought elsewhere than in the internal state word use of the adults in their environment.

Main Effects and Interaction of Race and SES.   Finally, we want to take note of any overall race or SES differences independent of the effect of situation (see Table 14.4). Among the target children, race main effects indicate that white target children use more Attentional Devices, and more Internal State Words in general, than do black target children. This pattern holds for the use of Attentional Devices among primary caregivers, and for the use of Intentions and Desires Reflections in the adult environments. The significant main effect of SES on the use of Perceptual Reflections by adults in the environment indicates a greater use of this category of internal state words in the environments of working-class target children.

It should be noted that the main effects of race and SES in our data are both rather few and also rather specific. White target children do use more internal state words in general than do the black target children, but, as it is seen in the following analyses, this difference holds only at school, not at home. The white target children also use more Attentional Devices (that is, they say "Look!" more often), but there are no other main effects of race found among the target children.

Among primary caregivers, the only significant effect of race or SES is again in the use of Attentional Devices. And among adults in the environment, there is only one significant main effect each for race and SES; in both cases, a specific subcategory of reflections is involved.

Within-Situation Analyses

Race × SES ANOVAs were also performed on all dependent variables *within* each situation for each group of speakers analyzed in the previous ANOVAs (that is, target children, mothers and teachers, and all adults). The results of these analyses are summarized in Tables 14.5 and 14.6.

There are significant effects of race in the speech of the target children at school. As was indicated by the situation × race interaction in the across-situation analyses above, the black target children show fewer Semantic Uses and Internal State Words than the white target children at school, even though there is no such racial difference in the home situation.

The Influence of Adult Internal State Word Use on Target Children

Having now presented data on variation in the target children's use of internal state words, we want to see to what extent this variation can be accounted for in terms of other measurable aspects of the target children's communicative environment. An obvious place to start is with the internal state word use of the adults whose speech the target children hear at home and in school. There are two basic reasons why we might expect the internal state word use of the target children to resemble that of the adults in their environment. First, since the children are learning the language largely from the adults in their environment—especially the home environment—one would expect similarities between adults and children in at least some aspects of their speech. Second, both the adults and children in a given situation may be similarly affected by some aspect of the situation that influences internal state word use (for example, the general topic of conversation).

One measure of similarity between the internal state word use of children and adults is to compare the patterns of means. In Table 14.4, for example, it can be seen that the racial differences in the target children's use of attentional devices (white children use more of them than do black children) is found in the speech of their primary caregivers as well. On the other hand, the Situation × Race interaction on semantic usages and internal state words found in the speech of

TABLE 14.5
Within-Situation Effects of Race and SES at Home

	Speaker								
	Target Children (df = 1,34)			Mothers (df = 1,31)			All Adults (df = 1,34)		
Variable	Race	SES	Race & SES	Race	SES	Race & SES	Race	SES	Race & SES
Cognitive reflections	1.97	1.13	1.66	<1	<1	<1	1.05	<1	<1
Affective reflections	2.41	<1	<1	2.48	<1	2.62	<1	<1	4.32*
Perceptual reflections	2.56	3.82	<1	3.34	<1	<1	1.67	1.60	1.47
CAP reflections	6.14*[a]	<1	<1	<1	<1	2.06	<1	<1	<1
Intentions and desires reflections	<1	1.93	<1	3.99	<1	<1	12.4**[b]	<1	<1
All reflections	2.62	2.27	<1	3.87	<1	1.15	2.60	<1	<1
Nonreflections	<1	2.74	1.50	<1	3.69	<1	1.76	8.92**[c]	<1
Semantic usages	2.59	<1	<1	2.89	1.11	<1	<1	2.85	<1
Attentional devices	9.10**[b]	<1	<1	1.30	<1	1.37	<1	<1	1.31
Nonliteral usages	<1	<1	<1	<1	<1	<1	<1	2.16	<1
All internal state words	1.94	<1	<1	1.01	2.08	1.26	<1	3.85	<1

[a]Black mean is greater than white mean.
[b]White mean is greater than black mean.
[c]Middle-class mean is greater than working-class mean.
*p .05
**p .01

TABLE 14.6
Within-Situation Effects of Race and SES at School

| | Speakers | | | | | | | | |
| | Target Children (df = 1,33) | | | Teachers (df = 1,33) | | | All Adults (df = 1,33) | | |
Variable	Race	SES	Race & SES	Race	SES	Race & SES	Race	SES	Race & SES
Cognitive reflections	<1	<1	2.81	<1	<1	4.17*	<1	<1	4.01
Affective reflections	<1	1.43	1.23	<1	<1	4.21*	<1	<1	3.53
Perceptual reflections	<1	<1	1.31	<1	4.24*b	<1	<1	4.86*b	<1
CAP reflections	<1	<1	4.20*	1.01	<1	3.80	<1	<1	3.24
Intentions and desires reflections	3.63	<1	<1	<1	<1	<1	<1	<1	<1
All reflections	3.68	<1	3.96	<1	<1	3.87	<1	<1	3.41
Nonreflections	3.02	2.19	<1	<1	<1	<1	<1	<1	<1
Semantic usages	5.88*a	<1	2.45	<1	<1	1.79	<1	<1	1.81
Attentional devices	5.56*a	<1	3.22	3.74	<1	<1	3.31	<1	<1
Nonliteral usages	<1	<1	2.03	5.25*a	<1	<1	5.64*a	1.13	<1
All internal state words	9.03**a	<1	1.04	<1	<1	1.46	<1	<1	1.42

[a] White mean is greater than black mean.
[b] Working-class mean is greater than middle-class mean.
*p .05
**p .01

target children (see Table 14.3) is not present at all in the speech of their primary caregivers or of the adults in their environment in general. As might be expected, certain aspects of the children's internal state word use mirror that of the adults in their environment more closely than others.

Correlational Analyses

The relationship between the speech of target children and the speech in their environments was investigated in more detail in terms of correlational analyses. For each variable indicating an aspect of internal state word use, correlations were performed to determine to what extent the speech of the target children resembled the speech in their environments, as represented by (a) the primary caregivers (teacher and mother), (b) all adults in the environment, and (c) all speakers in the environment. These correlations are shown in Table 14.7.

It is interesting to note that all the significant correlations are positive, and, with the exception of the significant positive correlation between the target child and total environment at home for semantic usages, all the significant relationships involve reflections, or some subcategory of reflections. Specifically, at school there is a significant correlation between the target child and his or her adult environment for affective reflections, perceptual reflections, CAP reflections, intentions and desires reflections, and all reflections. At home, there is a significant correlation for every category of reflections; that is, for all those significant for the school environment as well as cognitive reflections. Because reflections, by definition, are intimately related to the speaker and/or hearer in the current situation, it appears reasonable to hypothesize that the "immediacy" of reflections—that is, the fact that they refer to the speaker's or addressee's own current internal state—leads them to show a high degree of correlation between the target child and its environment. Because they are especially related to the "here and now," they may be more strongly influenced by situational factors such as the general subject matter that affects all participants in the conversation in a similar fashion.

As can be seen in Table 14.7, the speech of the target children generally correlates more strongly with the speech of all adults than with the speech of the primary caregiver alone, and more strongly still with the speech of all speakers in the environment.

Table 14.8 presents these same correlations, computed across situation. These correlations reflect the degree to which the speech of the target child at school is influenced by the speech in the home environment, and the degree to which the speech of the target child at home is influenced by the speech in the school environment.

A comparison of Tables 14.7 and 14.8 reveals that, in general, any similarity between adults' and childrens' internal state word use is within situations, rather than between situations. The internal state word use at home does not have a

TABLE 14.7
Within-Situation Correlations Between the Target Child and Different Measures of the Linguistic Environment

| | Situation | | | | | |
| | School | | | Home | | |
Internal State Word Use Variable	Teacher Only (N = 37)	Adults (N = 37)	All Speakers (N = 37)	Mother Only (N = 35)	Adults (N = 38)	All Speakers (N = 38)
Cognitive reflections	.280	.271	.300	.217	.605**	.611**
Affective reflections	.491**	.496**	.501**	.311	.519**	.555**
Perceptual reflections	.162	.170	.361*	.035	.239	.434**
CAP reflections	.398**	.424**	.433**	.177	.441**	.547**
Intentions and desires reflections	.348*	.304	.493**	-.033	.211	.376**
All reflections	.343*	.329*	.414**	-.065	.177	.387**
Nonreflections	-.244	-.243	-.245	-.193	.108	.063
Semantic usages	-.004	-.002	.000	-.100	.219	.355**
Attentional devices	-.037	-.052	.183	-.131	.056	.043
Nonliteral usages	.184	.176	.182	.331	.250	.318
All internal state words	.048	.049	.048	-.196	.078	.237

*p < .05, two-tailed
**p < .01, two-tailed

TABLE 14.8
Across-Situation Correlations Between the Target Child and Different Measures of the Linguistic Environment

	Situation					
	Target Child at Home			Target Child at School		
Internal State Word Use Variable	Teacher Only (N = 33)	Adults at School (N = 36)	All Speakers at School (N = 36)	Mother Only (N = 36)	Adults at Home (N = 36)	Speakers at Home (N = 36)
Cognitive reflections	.366*	.378*	.349*	-.031	.212	.193
Affective reflections	.296	.292	.297	-.174	-.006	.072
Perceptual reflections	.078	.095	.010	.000	-.057	-.171
CAP reflections	.099	.114	.209	-.055	.214	.132
Intentions and desires reflections	-.073	-.063	.059	.074	.092	.088
All reflections	.046	.026	.099	.040	.116	.048
Nonreflections	-.154	-.104	-.177	-.232	-.287	-.267
Semantic usages	.181	.177	.247	.002	.037	-.066
Attentional devices	.262	.223	.114	.024	-.115	-.109
Nonliteral usages	.157	.123	.000	.183	.303	.380*
All internal state words	.326	.330*	.300	-.067	.076	.026

*$p < .05$, two-tailed
**$p < .01$, two-tailed

measurable influence on the child's speech at school; similarly, the internal state word use in the school environment does not have much influence on the target child's speech at home. One exception to this is that the target child's use of cognitive reflections at home correlates positively with the use of cognitive reflections in the school environment, regardless of the particular definition of the environment (teachers, adults, or all speakers). The target children's overall use of internal state words at home also correlates with the use of internal state words by adults in the school environment. The only significant influence of the home environment upon the target children's speech at school is represented by a positive correlation between the target children's nonliteral usages at school and the nonliteral usages of the total environment at home.

The sharp contrast in magnitude of correlations between Tables 14.7 and 14.8 suggests that target children's use of internal state words, to the extent that it is influenced by the speech of adults in the target children's environment, is largely accounted for by the internal state word use of adults *within* the situation. Very little of the target children's use of internal state words in school can be predicted from the speech that the children are exposed to in the home, nor can their use of internal state words at home be predicted from the internal state word use they encounter at school.

One specific hypothesis we are interested in evaluating in terms of our data is that children from nonmainstream backgrounds experience discontinuity or mismatch between the internal state word use of adults at home and that which they encounter in the speech of adults at school. This might be the case, for example, if there were great differences by race or SES in the use of internal state word usage encountered by children from the different groups at school. In this case, some children (presumably the "mainstream" or middle-class children) would experience a fair degree of continuity between the internal state word usage encountered at home and at school. Other children, nonmainstream or minority poor children, would find that the internal state word use of adults at school was quite different from what they had experienced at home. Our data give no support for this hypothesis. As was seen in Table 14.4, there are only a few, very specific effects of race or SES in the internal state word use of adults either at home or at school. Any home-school discontinuity would show up as a Situation × Race, Situation × SES, or Situation × Race × SES interaction in the speech of adults. There are a few such significant interactions (see Table 14.3), but except for those involving nonliteral usages, the pattern of means involved is not consistent with the mismatch hypothesis (e.g., the home-school difference is greater for the white middle-class mothers and teachers than for the other race/SES group). Therefore, except for the case of nonliteral usages, there is no evidence of a home-school mismatch in the internal state word use of adults for the mainstream children in our sample.

Indirect evidence for a mismatch could be found by comparing the speech of the target children at home and at school to assess the degree of continuity between home and school in terms of *their* internal state word use. Table 14.9 presents the correlations between the target children's home and school internal state word use, calculated separately for the two racial groups.

Table 14.9 does in fact show a pronounced difference between the two racial groups. For four variables-intentions and desires reflections, reflections, semantic usages, and internal state words—the white target children show a significant similarity in their speech between home and school. It can be noted that the last three of these four are superordinate categories representing an increasingly general picture of internal state word use. However, there are no significant correlations between home and school for the black target children, and the differences in the magnitude of correlations between home and school for blacks and whites are significant for these same four variables. For these variables, then, the white target children show a high degree of similarity between their internal state word use at home and at school. This suggests that for those factors controlling internal state word use they are also experiencing a definite continuity between the home and school environments. For the black target children, on the other hand, there is no measurable similarity between their internal state word use at home and at school. This seems to suggest that, with respect to those aspects of the environment that influence internal state word use, they are experiencing some discontinuity or mismatch between the home and school situation.

TABLE 14.9
Correlations by Racial Group Between Target Children's
Internal State Word Use at Home and at School

Variable	Whites (N = 17)	Blacks (N = 19)	Z
Cognitive reflections	.108	.005	.28
Affective reflections	.021	.434	1.21
Perceptual reflections	.045	−.261	.85
Intentions and desires reflections	.705**	−.202	2.96*
All reflections	.613**	−.422	3.18**
Nonreflections	−.273	.228	1.40
Semantic usages	.699**	−.081	2.59**
Attentional devices	.338	−.145	.56
Nonliteral usages	.342	.284	.18
Internal state words	.714**	.013	2.44**

*$p < .05$, two-tailed
**$p < .01$, two-tailed

SES DIFFERENCES IN CORRELATIONS

In light of the above results (Table 14.9), parallel analyses were performed comparing correlations calculated separately for the two SES groups. Tables 14.10 and 14.11 show the correlations between internal state word use patterns of target children and the adults in their environment, at home and at school, respectively. As can be seen in these tables, none of the differences in correlations between the middle and working classes are significant either at home or at school. Thus, SES does not seem to play a role in determining the way in which the target children relate to the internal state word use of the adults in their environment, either at home or at school. It must be noted, of course, that in two cases there are correlations that reach significance for the middle class but not the working class. At home, there is a significant positive relationship between the use of reflections by the middle-class target children and the adults in their classrooms. However, in neither case is the difference between the correlations for the middle class and the working class significant.

Also of interest is the degree of similarity between the target children's internal state word use at home and at school. Table 14.12 presents the correlations for the different internal state word variables between the children's home and school internal state word use patterns. In this case, none of the differences

TABLE 14.10
Correlations by SES Group Between Internal State Word
Use of Target Children at Home and Adults in the Home

Variable	Middle Class (N = 17)	Working Class (N = 19)	Z
Cognitive reflections	.590**	.647**	.25
Affective reflections	.629**	.590**	.17
Perceptual reflections	.272	.145	.36
Intentions and desires reflections	.298	.234	.19
All reflections	.296	.162	.39
Nonreflections	−.203	−.013	.53
Semantic usages	.575*	.165	1.33
Attentional devices	−.356	.075	1.22
Nonliteral usages	.154	.326	.50
Internal state words	.368	.072	.86

$*p < .05$, two-tailed
$**p < .01$, two-tailed

TABLE 14.11

Correlations by SES Group Between Internal State Word
Use of Target Children at School and Adults in School Environment

Variable	Middle Class (N = 17)	Working Class (N = 19)	Z
Cognitive reflections	.257	.306	.15
Affective reflections	.624**	.434**	.27
Perceptual reflections	.398	−.285	1.95
Intentions and desires reflections	.392	.262	.40
All reflections	.521*	.240	.91
Nonreflections	−.220	−.352	.39
Semantic usages	.095	−.084	.49
Attentional devices	−.058	−.154	.27
Nonliteral usages	.193	.146	.13
Internal state words	−.041	.101	.39

*$p < .05$, two-tailed
**$p < .01$, two-tailed

TABLE 14.12

Correlations by SES Group Between the Home and
School Internal State Word Use of the Target Children

Variable	Middle Class (N = 17)	Working Class (N = 19)	Z
Cognitive reflections	.301	−.097	1.11
Affective reflections	.503*	.059	1.35
Perceptual reflections	−.075	−.206	.78
Intentions and desires reflections	−.030	.575**	1.87
All reflections	−.073	.051	.34
Nonreflections	.242	.086	.44
Semantic usages	.227	.007	.64
Attentional devices	.546*	−.101	1.95
Nonliteral usages	.112	.565**	1.44
Internal state words	.299	−.002	.85

*$p < .05$, two-tailed
**$p < .01$, two-tailed

between correlations for the two SES groups are significant. However, the patterns of correlations differ in an interesting way: the middle-class children show a similarity between home and school in their use of affective reflections and attentional devices, and the working-class children have a similarity between home and school in their use of intentions and desires reflections and nonliteral usages.

In general, these results, taken together with those in Tables 14.9–14.11, suggest that race is a more important factor than SES in determining the target children's adjustment to the classroom situation.

Effects of Home and School Environments on Children's Speech in School

The findings just discussed describe the effects of certain aspects of communication patterns in a situation on the speech of the target children in that situation.

TABLE 14.13
Comparing Correlations Between Target Children's Internal State Word
Use at School with Indices of Conversational Structure at Home and at School

Target Child Internal State Word Use	Indices of Conversational Structure					
	Percent of Primary Caregiver's Internal State Words Addressed to				Percent of Internal State Words by all Speakers Addressed to Target Child	
	Target Child		Children			
	Home	School	Home	School	Home	School
Cognitive reflections	.181	.198	.221	.003	.127	.289
Affective reflections	−.173	−.040	−.179	−.141	−.287	−.103
Perceptual reflections	.073	.078	.040	.154	−.020	.147
Intentions and desires reflections	.053	.009	.042	.191	−.135	−.125
All reflections	.014	.092	.091	.122	−.107	.036
Nonreflections	.531**	.258	.400*	.023	.294	.161
Semantic usages	.185	.185	.217	.122	−.008	.098
Attentional devices	.244	.396*	.433**	.064	.326*	.324
Nonliteral usages	.218	.396*	.165	−.228	.174	.378*
All internal state words	.291	.350*	.373*	.079	.124	−.240

*$p < .05$, two-tailed
**$p < .01$, two-tailed

TABLE 14.14
Comparing Correlations Between Target Children's Internal State
Word Use at School with Indices of Conversational Structure at
Home and at School

Target Child Internal State Word Use	Indices of Conversational Structure					
	Number of Turns by Child		Percent of Turns by Child		Percent of Turns by Primary Caregiver	
	Home	School	Home	School	Home	School
Cognitive reflections	.031	.376*	.231	.296	.072	.118
Affective reflections	.149	.147	.016	.181	−.233	−.365*
Perceptual reflections	.176	−.105	.113	.171	.086	.192
Intentions and desires reflections	.126	.106	.014	.012	−.035	−.470*
All reflections	.147	.192	.114	.154	−.060	−.237
Nonreflections	.063	.473**	.413**	.465*	.213	−.380*
Semantic usages	.162	.332*	.243	.293	.011	−.340*
Attentional devices	−.042	.104	.290	.378*	.047	−.253
Nonliteral usages	.179	.295	.222	.364*	.201	.052
All internal state words	.172	.351*	.356*	.432*	.062	−.357*

*p < .05, two-tailed
**p < .01, two-tailed

However, the mismatch model presumes that there are also cross-situational effects. Specifically, we want to look for ways in which patterns of communication at home may influence the child's response to the school situation. Tables 14.13, 14.14, and 14.15 present correlations between indices of the patterns of communication at home and school and the target children's internal state word use at school.

For some variables, of course, there are only within-situation effects. For example, the target child's internal state word use at school correlates with the number of turns spoken by the target child at school, but not with the number of turns the target child speaks at home. Similarly, the target child's school internal state word use correlates with the percentage of turns taken by the teacher, but not with the percentage of turns at dinner spoken by the mother. Nor do the number of adults present at dinner, the percentage of turns at dinner spoken by adults, or the percentage of turns at dinner spoken by the experimenter have any influence on the target children's internal state word use at school.

The remaining four variables, however, do evidence cross-situational correlations. The higher the percentage of the mother's internal state words addressed to

TABLE 14.5
Correlations Between Target Children's Internal State
Word Use at School with Indices of Conversational
Structure at Home

Target Child Internal State Word Use	Indices of Conversational Structure		
	Number of Adults Present at Dinner	Percent of Turns at Dinner Spoken by	
		Experimenter	Adults
Cognitive reflections	.298	−.059	−.007
Affective reflections	.072	.068	.152
Perceptual reflections	−.108	.085	.105
Intentions and desires reflections	.107	−.184	−.155
All reflections	.182	−.160	−.105
Nonreflections	−.037	−.253	.214
Semantic usages	.164	−.236	.032
Attentional devices	.014	−.124	.106
Nonliteral usages	−.007	−.091	.170
All internal state words	.149	−.286	.029

*$p < .05$, two-tailed
**$p < .01$, two-tailed

the target child at home, the more nonreflections the target child uses in school. The higher the percentage of mothers' internal state words addressed to children in general, the more nonreflections, attentional devices, and internal state words the target child uses at school. And the greater proportion of the turns at home that the target child has, the more nonreflections and internal state words the child uses at school.

The influence of the home environment on the child's use of nonreflections in school is noteworthy. The more attention the target child receives (in terms of internal state words), and the larger the target child's share of the conversation at home, the more nonreflections he or she uses at school. This is interesting, first of all because these same factors do not correlate significantly with the target child's use of nonreflections at home, and second because of the possible developmental implications of use of nonreflections. Nonreflections involve more displacement or abstraction than reflections, and hence may indicate a more advanced type of usage.

An important implication of the pattern of correlations in these tables is the specific nature of the influences of home and school environments on children's speech. First of all, most of the influences are situation specific; for example, the percentage of the mother's internal state words addressed to the target child influences the target child's use of attentional devices at home, but nonreflections at school. Second, as this same example also illustrates, specific aspects of the communication patterns in a situation can affect very specific aspects of the child's speech. Any model of the influence of home and school environments on children's speech must therefore allow this degree of specificity and detail. Overall measurements like Mean Length of Utterance (MLU) will be far too crude to assess the effects of situational factors on patterns of language use (cf. Cole et al., 1978).

IMPLICATIONS FOR THE MISMATCH HYPOTHESIS

No evidence was found for any mismatch between home and school environments for minority or poor children, as far as the internal state word use of adults was concerned. However, the speech of white target children at school is related strongly both to their speech at home and to the speech of the adults in the school environment. The speech of the black target children at school, however, shows no relationship either to their own speech at home or to the speech of the adults in the classroom. This suggests very strongly that (a) the black target children's relationship to the school situation is significantly different from that of the white target children; and (b) the relationship between the home and school environments is different in the experience of the black and white target children. This could be the result either of a home-school mismatch experienced by the black target children that is not reflected in the variables we have investigated, or of differential treatment of the two racial groups in school in terms of teaching styles or patterns of interaction. Our findings suggest strongly that such a mismatch or difference does exist, but not in the internal state word use of the adults as such. Rather, it appears that patterns of interaction both at home and in the classroom have significant effects on the use of internal state words by the children at school.

Likewise, our data failed to support one particular version of the mismatch hypothesis, namely, the hypothesis that the home environments of some non-mainstream children would provide them with less experience in metabehavioral analysis than did the home environments of white middle-class children. However, the results of our analyses do suggest that the black children in our sample experienced some sort of mismatch between home and school, although this mismatch did not directly involve the internal state word use of adults. Three types of evidence point to the existence of some sort of mismatch:

First, there is the reduced use of internal state words by the black target children in the school situation. Although this finding permits more than one interpretation, it is certainly consistent with the hypothesis that the black children found the school situation different from the home situation in important ways.

Second are the racial differences in the adult child correlations at home and at school. At home, there are some racial differences, and it is in the black families that there are the highest correlations between children's and adults' internal state word use. At school, on the other hand, racial differences are found for a larger number of variables and it is the white children who show the highest correlation with their teachers. Lack of correlation in internal state word use patterns does not mean lack of communication. However, differences in the degree of correlation between adult and child internal state word use does suggest differences in the nature of the communication. A high correlation between adult and child internal state word use suggests that both adults and children are being affected by situational factors—e.g., the topic of conversation and the activities the speakers are engaged in—in parallel ways. A lack of correlation indicates that the situational factors affect adults and children differently. Thus a higher correlation could be interpreted as indicating a greater similarity or reciprocity between the roles of adults and children in the situation. A lack of correlation could indicate some breakdown in communication, or simply a greater degree of distinction between the roles of adults and children in the conversation.

A third type of evidence for some sort of home-school mismatch is found in the correlations between children's speech at home and children's speech at school. For four internal state variables, the white children show a significant home-school correlation while the black children show none. The white children's speech at school, then, is largely predictable from their speech at home; as far as internal state words are concerned, they seem to be using similar speech patterns in the two situations. The lack of correlation on the part of the black children indicates that not only do these children tend to use fewer internal state words in school, but also that their school internal state word use is not at all predictable from their speech at home. This indicates that for the black children, the school situation demands a substantially different set of verbal strategies and skills.

Analyses of those indices of the patterns of communication for which we had information indicated no clear explanation for the specific cause of the black children's reduced use of internal state words at school. However, our data show that the different functional categories of internal state words are sensitive to very specific kinds of situational factors. The racial difference in the children's speech at school should ultimately be traceable to particular teaching strategies or styles, or to some differences between home and school communication patterns. To identify these, though, would require detailed categories for coding mothers' and teachers' speech and behavior beyond the score of the present work.

ACKNOWLEDGMENT

The research on which this chapter is based was supported by a grant from The Carnegie Corporation of New York to William S. Hall. The preparation of this manuscript was supported by the National Institute of Education under Contract No. US-NIE-C-400-76-0116, The Department of Psychology, and the Computer Science Center of The University Of Maryland, College Park.

REFERENCES

Baker, L., & Brown, A. L. (1980). *Metacognitive skills and reading* (Tech, Rep. No. 188) Urbana: University of Illinois, Center for the Study of Reading. (ERIC Document Reproduction Service No. ED 195 932).

Bernstein, B. (1971). *Class, codes and control: Vol. 1. Theoretical studies towards a sociology of language.* London: Routledge & Kegan Paul.

Bernstein, B. (Ed.) (1973). *Class, codes, and control: Vol. 2: Applied studies toward a sociology of language.* London: Routledge & Kegan Paul.

Cazden, C. (1970). The situation: A neglected source of social class differences in language use. *Journal of Social Issues, 26*(2), 35–60.

Cole, M., Dore, J., Hall, W., & Dowley, G. (1978). Situational variability in the speech of preschool children. In M. Ebihar & R. Gianutsos (Eds.), *Papers in anthropology and linguistics* (pp. 65–105). New York: New York Academy of Sciences.

Cooper, B. (1975). Language differences and educational failure (Occasional Paper 3). University of Sussex, Education Area. (ERIC Document Reproduction Service No. ED 121 067).

Flavell, J. H. (1978). Metacognitive development. In J. M. Scandura & C. J. Brainerd (Eds.), *Structural/process theories of complex human behavior* (pp. 213–245). Alphen a. d. Rijn, The Netherlands: Sijthoff & Noordhoff.

Gearhart, M., & Hall, W. S. (1982). Internal state words: Cultural and situational variation in vocabulary usage. In K. Borman (Ed.), Children in a changing society. Hillsdale, NJ: Lawrence Erlbaum Associates.

Halliday, M. A. K. (1978). *Language as social semiotics.* Baltimore: University Park Press.

Hall, W. S., & Nagy, W. E. (1979). Theoretical issues in the investigation of words of internal report (Tech. Rep. No. 146). Urbana: University of Illinois Center for The Study of Reading. (ERIC Document Reproduction Service No. ED 177 526).

Hall, W. S., & Nagy, W. E. (1986, pp. 26–65). Theoretical issues in the investigation of internal state words. In Irwin & Myrna Gopnik (Eds.), *From models to modules: Studies in cognitive sciences from the McGill workshops.* Norwood, NJ: Ablex.

Hall, W. S., & Nagy, W. E. (in press, 1987). The semantic-pragmatic distinction in internal state words. *Discourse Processes.*

Henderson, D. (1973). Contextual specificity, discretion and cognitive socialization: With special reference to language. In B. Bernstein (Ed.), *Class, codes, and control (Vol. 2,* pp. 48–80). London: Routledge & Kegan Paul.

Labov, W. (1964). Phonological correlates of social stratification. In J. Gumperz & D. Hymes (Eds.), The ethnography of communication [Special issue]. *American Anthropologist, 66*(6), 164–176.

Labov, W. (1966). *The social stratification of english in New York City.* Washington, DC: Center for Applied Linguistics.

Matthew, M., Connolly, K., & McCleod, C. (1978). Language use, role, and context in a five-year-old. *Journal of Child Language, 5,* 81, 99.

Sankoff, G. (1973). pp. 44–59. Above and beyond phonology in variable rules. In C. Bailey & R. Shuy (Eds.), *New ways of analyzing variation in english.* Washington, DC: Georgetown University Press.

Schatzman, L., & Strauss, A. (1955). Social class and modes of communication. *American Journal of Sociology, 60,* 329–338.

Snow, C. E., Arlman Rupp, A., Hassing, Y., Jobse, J., Joosten, J., & Vorster, J. (1976). Mother's speech in three social classes. *Journal of Psycholinguistic Research, 5,* 1–20.

Stein, N. L., & Glenn, C. G. (1979). An analysis of story comprehension in elementary school children. In R. Freedle (Ed.), *New directions in discourse processing* (Vol. 2). Hillsdale, NJ: Lawrence Erlbaum Associates.

von Raffler Engel, W., & Sigelman, C. (1971). Rhythm, narration, description in the speech of black and white school children, *Language Sciences, 18,* 9–14.

Wellman, J., & Johnson, C. (1979). Understanding of mental processes: A developmental study of "remember" and "forget." *Child Development, 50,* 79–88.

15

Coping or Groping? Psycholinguistic Problems in the Acquisition of Receptive and Productive Competence Across Dialects

William A. Stewart
The Graduate School and University Center of the City University of New York

Despite a certain amount of good-natured complaining about the differences between British and American English, perhaps best illustrated by the variously phrased and attributed witticism that England and America are divided by a common language, it is nevertheless possible for Americans and Britons to follow even fairly rapid discourse in each other's dialects with relative ease and apparent accuracy.[1] This is undoubtedly most true just so long as *standard* varieties of British or American English are involved, but with that qualification the same international ease of comprehension would extend to standard Irish, Canadian, Australian, New Zealand, and South African English as well, and to only a slightly lesser extent to the standard English of India, Hong Kong, Singapore, and those African and Caribbean states having English as their official language.[2]

An obvious reason for this high degree of comprehensibility between widely dispersed varieties of standard English is that standardization and literacy have minimized structural differences between them. Once *non*standard dialects of various kinds are included in the picture, however, structural uniformity begins to break down over geographical and social distance, and the intercomprehensibility of dialects becomes increasingly limited as the structural differences between them grow greater. In some cases, two dialects may be structurally

---

[1]The term *dialect* is used here in the linguist's sense of a structurally identifiable sub-variety of a language. In this use, there is no connotation of low prestige or structural deviation from a literary or official norm.

[2]A *standard* dialect (see footnote 1) or language variety is one in conformity with codified norms defining "correct" usage, and is the form most often spoken by educated people and used in official documents, literary works, and formal situations. Popular dialects that deviate from the standard dialect(s) are called *nonstandard* dialects.

different enough so that either is virtually impossible for speakers of the other to understand. Where this is so, the relationship between the two dialects of the same language approaches that between two different but related languages.

At this point, two more complications must be added to the notion of structural differences between dialects—and between languages, for that matter. The first is that, instead of being distributed more or less evenly throughout the various structural domains of dialecfs or languages, the differences between any two may be concentrated in one structural domain or level. Thus two dialects (or languages) may differ primarily in aspects of pronunciation, or of vocabulary, or of sentence structure or other features of their respective grammars. Moreover, these different kinds of structural differences (phonological, lexical, syntactic, morphological, semantic—to use the more precise linguistic terms for them) can each have a differential effect on cross-dialectal comprehension. Indeed, as is demonstrated later, they seem almost to scale in this respect, with phonological differences most easily resolved, semantic differences posing great difficulties, and the others in between.

The second complication in the notion of structural differences between dialects or related languages is an occasional (perhaps not so rare after all) comprehension asymmetry. That is, given dialects or related languages A and B, speakers of A find it intrinsically easier to understand B than the other way around. (What "intrinsically' means here is that the asymmetry is not due to different degrees of cross-dialectal exposure for the two populations, or to such extra-linguistic factors as a difference in the social status of A and B.) A well-known case of such an asymmetry involving related languages is the markedly greater ease with which speakers of Portuguese understand Spanish than vice-versa. The comprehension asymmetry in this case seems to arise from the greater complexity of Portuguese phonology and morphology. A simple illustration of how this works is furnished by a morphological example involving the Spanish (1) and Portuguese (2) forms of "general" (adjective) and the derivationally associated "generality" (noun):

(1)   *general : generalidade*
(2)   *geral   : generalidade*

It will be noted that the Portuguese derivational paradigm contains all the morphological information for the Spanish forms, but not vice-versa, so that (ignoring differences in pronunciation) the Portuguese speaker will recognize Spanish *general* in his own *generalidade* and thus be able to equate it with Portuguese *geral* (or so equate it through some underlying shape from which both *geral* and *generalidade* are derived), but the Spanish speaker's derivational paradigm gives him no information that will relate Portuguese *geral* either directly or indirectly to his own adjective *general*. Such structural differences between Spanish and Portuguese, existing in the domains of phonology and syntax as well as morphology, and compounded many times over in number and complexity, could account in large part for the overall comprehension asymmetry that exists across the two languages.

Following through on the implications of the foregoing example, it is not at all evident that the Portuguese speaker's greater ability to understand Spanish, if indeed it derives from these kinds of cross-language structural relationships, will be matched by a greater ability to produce accurate Spanish as well. For, while that fragment of the Portuguese grammar specifying *geral:generalidade* contains (for historical reasons) information allowing the correct identification of Spanish *general,* no Spanish-specific information as such is included. This means that there is nothing to constrain the production for Spanish of a Portuguese-like adjectival form *geral,* which is in fact non-existent in Spanish.[3] And so for the rest of Spanish, insofar as the possibility goes of simulating it from the content of Portuguese grammar.

What one is seeing here is an indication of still another kind of asymmetry— this time not between the abilities of different speakers of different languages or dialects, but rather between different abilities for one and the same speaker with respect to a single language or dialect. In general, it involves the ability of an individual to comprehend a much greater range of dialectal variation than that individual uses, or probably even can use. One established way of referring to this phenomenon is as the asymmetry between *receptive* and *productive* competence, where *competence* is one's ability to use language—any language, or a particular language.

Such an asymmetry was posited in the case of the Portuguese speaker's receptive and productive competence in Spanish (assuming, of course, a Portuguese speaker who had not actually learned to speak Spanish); and while the Spanish speaker's receptive competence in Portuguese (again assuming no specific learning of it) would be less than the Portuguese speaker's receptive competence in Spanish, it would be considerably greater than the Spanish speaker's production competence in Portuguese. Nor need separate (if related) languages be involved; returning to the illustration which opened this paper, the highly mutually intelligible standard dialects of English used throughout the world, an American not specifically instructed in British English would certainly not be able to speak it with even the remotest approximation to the ease and accuracy with which, as a speaker of American English, he could understand it.[4]

---

[3]The writer, who has spoken both languages since childhood, has actually heard *geral* (though with a successfully Spanish pronunciation of the *g*) in Brazilian attempts to speak Spanish in Uruguay and Argentina.

[4]This does not mean that it is impossible to be productively bidialectal, and competently so. Individuals who are fluent in the production of two or even more dialects of the same language abound, just as bilinguals and multilinguals do. The point is that apparent receptive competence is not necessarily evidence of productive competence in the same dialect or language, which leaves it an open question whether apparent cross-dialectal receptive competence in itself amounts to bidialectalism in any real sense—especially in cases, such as between standard varieties of British and American English, where the dialects are structurally quite similar throughout.

An important point needs to be made at this juncture concerning the receptive/productive competence asymmetry as it applies over dialects (or related languages) which are increasingly structurally different from the variety in which a monodialectal/monolingual speaker has both productive and receptive competence. If a monodialectal speaker of a standard variety of American English were to be tested for receptive competence (as determined by ease and accuracy of comprehension) for the following dialects, in order: standard British English, standard Irish English, standard Indian English, Yorkshire dialect, Southern Counties Scottish, Orkney and Shetland Islands Scottish, one could assume with confidence that his receptive competence score would start quite high, decline with something of an abrupt drop from standard Indian English to Yorkshire dialect (corresponding to an increase in structural differences), and end quite low for Shetland Islands Scottish, which can sound for all the world like a foreign language to an uninitiated American. Then, if the same American were tested on productive competence in the same series of dialects (using, say, a native speaker's judgment of the structural accuracy of the attempt), the subject could be expected to score abysmally on the more deviant dialects, but might receive a surprisingly high score on the ones structurally close to his own. Such a result could give the impression that such an individual's productive competence across unacquired dialects is scalar, and in fact far from low for dialects structurally similar to his own. And yet the subject has by definition low productive competence in all the dialects tested for. What is happening in such a case is that either real or apparent structural similarities between the subjects own dialect and that of the task can mask low productive competence when the subject compensates for it by producing the forms he knows.

Although the illustration just given of this problem was hypothetical, being contrived with a wider structural range of dialects than is to be found in the experimental literature, a somewhat more subtle version of it is to be found in the psycholinguistic literature on language development in lower class black American children (e.g., Ervin-Tripp, 1972), when the researcher is attempting to assess a Black English speaker's acquisition of the rules of Standard English grammar. In a discussion of the acquisition of the Standard English rules for tense marking and person agreement in the copula, something like the following data might be given for a typical subject:[5]

(3)   a. She my sister.
       b. He be mean.
       c. You is a nice lady.
       d. They bees in my school.

---

[5]The data display is somewhat reconstructed for brevity, though the range of copula variants remains typical.

e. This is my doll.

f. I'm hungry.

Concerning such a display, the researcher points out that, while (3a—d) are clearly nonstandard in the form of the copula employed, (3e, f) are actually in conformity with Standard English rules in this respect. This is then offered as evidence that the subjects have incorporated Standard English grammatical rules into their linguistic repertory, i.e., are acquiring productive competence in Standard English and are therefore becoming (or have already become) bidialectal. Variation between Nonstandard and Standard English copula, as in (3a—f), is not necessarily inconsistent with this conclusion, since it could conceivably represent code switching.

In fact, the data in (3a—f) is analytically far more ambiguous than it might appear at first glance, and could actually be giving a false impression of bidialectal productive competence that the speaker of (3a—f) in reality does not have. An interpretation of the data as consistent with at least incipient bidialectal productive competence depends upon (3e—f) truly being produced by internalized Standard English rules for copula use, which means that they should not only satisfy Standard English grammar but be unaccountable for by the nonstandard grammar which produced (3a—d). Yet it is not at all certain that either of these conditions really obtains. For one thing, there is the possibility—one might even say the probability—that (3e) has been generated by the same rule(s) of nonstandard Black English grammar that produced (3c), the apparent Standard English agreement in person and form in (3e) being entirely fortuitous. Indeed, if the nonstandard rule(s) involved here were of the variable kind proposed by Labov (1969; also as chapter 1 in Labov, 1972), with variability in this case between *is* and $\emptyset$ (no overt copula), then at least (3a, c, e) could have been produced by the same nonstandard grammatical rule(s). And if *I'm* can in some varieties of Black English be, not a combination of pronoun plus contracted *am,* but rather a morphemic variant of *I* borrowed whole from Standard English (as proposed in Stewart, 1966), then (3f) could actually be another instance of the "zero copula" construction of (3a).[6]

The remaining sentences (3b, d) are unlikely to be mistaken for Standard English, since they contain an "invariant" *be* which is used in many varieties of Black English to mark an aspectual distinction between (by its presence) [+ ITERATIVE], indicating repeated action or extended state, and (by its absence)

---

[6]Although a Black English structurally unitary (monomorphemic) treatment of *I'm* (diagnostic: *I'm here: Here I am* = polymorphemic or contractional *I'm; I'm here: Here I'm is/am* = monomorphemic *I'm*) might appear to be concentrated in children's speech, the widespread occurrence of monomorphemic *it's* and *that's* (diagnostic: *It's OK: It's can't happen; That's all right: That's don't matter*) in the speech of even elderly adults should caution against assuming a purely developmental cause.

[–ITERATIVE], indicating a unitary action or restricted state (Fasold, 1969, 1972; Labov, 1969, 1972; Stewart, 1966, 1967).[7] If this applies to sentence (3f), it would be unambiguously [−ITERATIVE], rather than ambiguously [±ITERATIVE] as its Standard English equivalent would be.

Finally, the form written *bees* in (3d) represents invariant *be* with an added *-s* which certainly does not follow Standard English rules of grammatical accord, since it occurs with a plural subject. But a verbal suffix *-s* does exist in some varieties of Black English, where it can function as a marker of [+HABITU-ATIVE] (Stewart, 1969a) or as a phonetically salient marker of [−PAST].[8]

From the foregoing analysis it should be clear that data of the type (3a—f) offers virtually no clear evidence of the acquisition of Standard English gram-matical rules by a Black English speaker who might produce them. Even the most apparent cases of Standard English grammar being used, sentences (3e) and (3f), turn out to be questionable in this regard. If Black English is a decreolizing creole language, as has been argued (Dillard, 1972; Stewart, 1967, 1968, 1969b, 1974a), and copular structures of the kind evident in (3a—f) were compared with earlier creole equivalents, evidence of a shift toward Standard English gram-matical forms and rules would be readily apparent. But this change has been long in process, and such Standard English-like features as *I'm* (especially mono-morphemic *I'm*) and full-form copula *is* (especially without third person singular agreement) could well have been incorporated into Black English usage genera-tions ahead of present-day speakers of the type represented by the hypothetical producer of sentences (3a—f).

Some present-day speakers of Black English do display a knowledge of some or all of the forms and rules associated with the Standard English copula. Others do not seem to have done so, but may well have acquired Standard English forms and rules pertaining to other areas of grammar; to these, they may perhaps later add Standard English copula forms and rules. No claim is being made that speakers of Black English cannot acquire productive competence in Standard English; but it is being suggested that the structural relationship between Black English and Standard English is such that, at any given point, the apparent productive competence in Standard English displayed by Black English speakers may not always be real. What is more, these same cross-dialectal structural

---

[7]This Black English [+ ITERATIVE] marker is often referred to in the linguistic literature as "invariant *be*" because, unlike Standard English *be*, it is never internally inflected to *is, was,* etc. Although *is* and *was* certainly exist as copular forms in most varieties of Black English, they do not behave syntactically like inflected forms of *be*. At the same time, so-called invariant *be* can take external inflections, especially *-s*.

[8]The [+HABITUATIVE] sense of *-s* is more likely with active verbs (e.g., *I walks to school*), while its [−PAST] function is particularly useful with stative verbs (*I knows what I knows*). In some cases, the [+HABITUATIVE] use of *-s* can be clearly distinguished from its [-PAST] use by occurrence in [+PAST] grammatical contexts, as when it combines with the *-ed* ending (*I staysed up in Florida for one year* "I remained down in Florida for a year").

relationships must make the acquisition of productive competence in Standard English by a Black English speaker (or vice-versa) an extremely difficult enterprise. For, given the linguistic ambiguity of grammatical function words and inflections whose forms are shared across the dialects but whose meanings differ, how is the speaker of the one dialect to make correct inferences about the rather different grammar behind the sometimes quite familiar verbal output in the other dialect? After all, if a Standard English speaking research psychologist or psycholinguist can mistake some Black English uses of *is* as evidence of Standard English grammar, then why might not a Black English speaker take a Standard English use of *is* as in conformity with his own grammar—hence evidence that the two dialects are alike in this regard so that he, the Black English speaker, already knows Standard English to that extent? In such a case the second-dialect learning process, slow and difficult at best, can be short-circuited entirely.

In kind, the structural relationships just considered between American Black English and Standard English, posing such difficulties for cross-dialectal learning, do not appear to be typical of structural relationships between dialects around the world—or even in the United States, for that matter. In the case of the relationship between local dialects and Standard English in England, which may be taken as an example of the more traditional one, cross-dialectal differences are for the most part phonological and lexical. That is, the dialects are differentiated from each other by the use of different words for some things, but primarily by the way in which shared words—and this includes the vast majority of words—are pronounced. Apart from the effect of differences in pronunciation, grammatical differences between traditionally related dialects are few indeed.[9] With respect to the grammatical function words in particular, the same-form-different-meaning relationship which held in the American Black English case is almost nonexistent. In short, one could say that traditional dialect relationships involve superficial differences on top of an underlying unity, whereas the Black English case shows evidence of superficial similarities masking underlying differences.

There are indeed instances of the American Black English kind of dialect relationship in other parts of the world, or cases that show traces of such a relationship, but these almost always involve a history of the language having been learned as a foreign language by a part of the speaker population. Irish dialects of English are a mild instance of this—mild in part because of the dynamics of the spread of English in Ireland over the last three and a half centuries, and mild in part because Irish and English were historically related languages to begin with. More well-defined cases exist where the original lan-

---

[9]Wright (1905) devoted five-sixths of a discussion of the structural differences between British dialects of English to phonology and the remaining sixth to what he called *accidence,* mostly morphology with only a bit of syntax. While some of this difference is undoubtedly due to the underdeveloped state of syntactic theory and knowledge in his day, it also must in part reflect the actual nature of the structural relationships between British dialects.

guage or languages of the foreign population bore no relationship to the language they set out to acquire. In some of these cases, particularly where the second language learning was entirely informal, enough inadvertent restructuring of the second language could take place to create new varieties of it which had something of the character of related foreign languages rather than dialects. These are the so-called *pidgin* and *creole* varieties of English and other languages of mercantile, military, and colonial expansion (Hall, 1966; Todd, 1974, 1984).[10] Where a pidgin or creole has continued to coexist with the related standard language, as in the case of creole and Standard English in Jamaica, the creole (because of its low social status) may undergo a certain amount of structural change, called *decreolization*, in the direction of the standard language, while the latter (because it is usually learned as a second language by creole speakers) may undergo creole influence. Intermediate varieties are created through this reciprocal influence, and these in turn blend with each other to give rise to a *creole-to-standard continuum* (Bickerton, 1975).

Movement across such a continuum characteristically consists of word-form changes, which may proceed fairly rapidly and in the process merely mask some fairly substantive grammatical differences between the two ends. Because of this masking effect, changes in the underlying grammatical structure become increasingly difficult for the naive speaker and educator alike to monitor. In other words, except for the degree of structural differentiation covered by the span from the variety most unlike the standard dialect to the standard dialect itself, structural relationships within the creole continuum are very much like those that hold between American Black English and Standard English. Nor should this be particularly surprising if, as already suggested, Black English is a late decreolizing creole. As such, it would represent the remnant of a North American colonial or plantation creole continuum from which the more creole end had either disappeared completely or become restricted to the South Carolina and Georgia coast as an otherwise mysterious dialect of undocumented origin known locally as Gullah or Geechee.

By the early 1950s it had become a matter of public knowledge and professional concern that the academic performance of black children as a group was significantly below that of white children in most American public schools. Psychologists and linguists soon began to focus on one particular area of academic achievement in which black children (again, as a group) seemed to perform especially poorly: language use. For some of the linguists who had already had experience with educational problems in the Caribbean, the details of American

---

[10]There has been much discussion concerning the processes that might have given rise to pidgin and creole languages, as well as typological issues relating to their classification. Although these questions are not pertinent to the present paper, it is worth mentioning that an interesting debate has developed concerning the role of an alleged innate universal grammar in the formation of creole languages (Bickerton, 1981).

black children's problems with school language looked strikingly familiar. Ethnically correlated dialect differences were therefore suspected, looked for, and some found rather quickly. Since the notion of a creole predecessor to American Black English had not previously been a part of the history of black speech as assumed by American dialect geographers and historians of the English language in North America, a debate arose as to whether the nonstandard speech of black Americans had vestigial creole features, or was merely a variant of the nonstandard speech of southern whites. Most linguists did agree, however, that there was some degree of language conflict in the classroom. Those who did not accept a creole origin for the nonstandard speech of black Americans, and who therefore did not expect structural differences between it and Standard English to be cognitively problematic, simply urged teachers to be more tolerant and understanding. Those linguists who were convinced that Black English was a post-creole, and as such could give rise to creole continuum-like coping problems in the classroom, proposed the development of special pedagogical materials to help Black English speakers learn Standard English with a minimum of linguistic uncertainty.

Although some educators expressed tentative interest in the proposal for special Standard English curriculum materials for Black English speakers, most black educators and community leaders strongly opposed the idea. In large part, their opposition arose from a fear that special curriculum materials for black dhileren, no matter how linguistically justifiable, would be likely to result in the resegregation of those children. By the late 1960s, black opposition to cross-dialectal curriculum materials had been fanned into considerable heat by a misunderstanding (perhaps created or reinforced by early discussions on bilingual education for Hispanics) that the purpose of such materials was actually to teach black children to speak, read, and write Black English.

At this point, the educational establishment was ready to back off completely from the issue. But back off to where? It was, after all, the late 1960s, by which time it had become even clearer that black children tended to have special difficulties with the Standard English component of the curriculum. Moreover, linguists had by then demonstrated that there really was a linguistic entity that they called *Black English* (sometimes *the Black English Vernacular*) and that its structural features might make standard English difficult for its speakers to learn. Clearly, with regard to the school language achievement problems of black children, the educational establishment was caught between the Scylla of an ineffectual traditional curriculum and the Charybdis of controversial curriculum innovation. But if one linguistic notion had gotten the educators into potential trouble, another was to rescue them from it. For they soon found recourse in the receptive/productive competence asymmetry.

Irony in the turn of events is one of the little things that make life interesting, so it is interesting that, if the perception of a need for special curriculum materials for American Black English speakers had its inspiration in the study of education across a creole continuum in the Caribbean, so too did the countering notion of receptive competence between Black English and Standard English have a precursor in a claim made by a student of Caribbean creoles. Touching on the question of intelligibility across the Jamaican creole continuum, David De-Camp (1971) notes: "The varieties of Jamaican [creole-to-standard] English themselves differ to the point of unintelligibility; but some Jamaican English is mutually intelligible with standard English," (p. 350).

And of course he notes the even more obvious fact that no Jamaicans seem able to speak all the varieties across the continuum, and some appear quite limited in the range they can produce. But, operating within a generative theoretical notion of a homogeneous speech community and an "ideal speaker-listener" whose productive and receptive competence are identical, DeCamp (1971) attempts to argue that participants in the Jamaican creole continuum have not only receptive but also productive competence across the entire continuum range. The earlier reported comprehension failure between varieties is left unexplained, but production failure is ascribed to sociolinguistic factors:

> One could well argue that the individual speaker's limitation to a span of the continuum, the fact that no one speaker can command the entire range of varieties, is a matter of performance rather than of competence, analogous to his inability to speak sentences beyond a certain level of complexity. The theoretical competence of the 'ideal speaker-listener' could be defined as spanning the entire continuum, including full command of all the switching rules between any one point and another. We could then look for socioeconomic explanations of the manner in which the actual performance of real speakers falls short of this ideal competence. (p. 368)

Describing the Guyanese creole continuum a half-decade later, Derek Bickerton (1975) differs with DeCamp concerning intelligibility between the varieties: "Indeed, one may often observe speakers in the same conversation producing at widely different levels and yet continuing to understand one another perfectly" (p. 196).

Yet the examples of this that he cites on the same page are far from convincing. In any event, Bickerton notes individual limited productive range, as De-Camp did in Jamaica. And, like DeCamp, he wants to claim that the limitation is a matter of performance, rather than competence. But he wants to do so for a different reason: to explain claimed cross-continuum intelligibility.

> It would seem more plausible to argue that a speaker in a creole system both produces and understands by virtue of the same set of internalised rules, and that the striking asymmetry which often exists between receptive and productive capacity arises through performance factors: in particular, limitations on opportunities for actual use of (and hence, full familiarisation with) particular varieties, imposed by particular life-styles, and overt social restrictions on what occupants of given roles may or may not say. (pp. 197–198)

In other words, the continuum participant can understand all varieties for the simple reason that he can speak all varieties. If he is never observed to speak anything remotely approaching all varieties, well, it is just that he has no wish to speak some, and no one will let him speak others. An implicit claim in all this is that one can know a language variety without ever using it. Yet, right in the middle of the last passage quoted from Bickerton, there is that seemingly contrary statement about limitations on use of a language variety giving rise to a lack of "full familiarisation" with it.

The particular theory of linguistic competence to which both DeCamp and Bickerton are beholden is indeed unfriendly to the possibility of a productive/receptive competence asymmetry, because the theory holds these abilities as equivalent. It is not the case that, given apparent evidence of greater individual receptive competence than productive competence across the creole continuum, DeCamp and Bickerton needed to resolve the asymmetry by expanding their claims for individual productive competence to match the observed receptive range—much less by expanding both to cover the entire continuum. They could have remained just as faithful to a theory of competence that is neutral on productive and receptive abilities by reacting skeptically to apparent evidence of receptive competence where this seemed to range far beyond the individual's apparent productive competence. Why, then, did DeCamp and Bickerton opt for expanding observed productive competence to a theoretically much wider ranging ability? The answer would seem to be that, for them, productive competence was equated with the performance aspect of the theoretical competence-performance distinction (see Valian, 1979, for a historical overview) in terms of which they are attempting to describe individual competence within a creole continuum. Receptive competence, manifested in terms of comprehension ability, would then most accurately represent true competence in such a competence-performance distinction, and as such it would be a more reliable measure of real (even if unattested) productive ability as well. DeCamp and Bickerton thus allowed an assumed range of individual receptive competence for which there was only equivocal evidence to define an individual productive range for which there was no direct evidence at all.

Moving directly to the question of comprehensibility between American Black English and Standard English, William Labov, in his study of the language of Harlem teenagers, came to a similar conclusion. In a now famous experiment, he asked his Black English speaking subjects to repeat Standard English sentences containing embedded yes-no questions, such as

(4) I asked Alvin if he knows how to play basketball.

in which yes-no question embedding is carried out with a complementizer, *if*, and re-reversal of question word order. Approximately half of the subjects gave responses of the equivalent form

(5) I ask Alvin do he know how to play basketball.

which has the more direct Black English embedded construction. Describing the experiment in some detail, Labov (1972) comments on these results:

> In the most obvious view, we can observe that the subject failed to perform the task required. But we cannot overlook the fact that [5] is the correct equivalent of [4]; it has the same meaning and is produced by the nonstandard rule which is the nearest equivalent to the standard rule. (p. 62)

Accordingly, he concludes:

> Since the [subject] does perform the translation, it is clear that he does understand the standard sentence. He then rapidly produces the correct nonstandard equivalent [5]. Understanding here must mean perception, analysis, and storage of the sentence in some relatively abstract form . . .
>
> From these considerations, it is clear that the [subject] is perfectly competent in (at least this) aspect of the standard grammar. (p. 63)

Finally, he goes on to generalize from this conclusion to the theme, now already familiar from DeCamp and Bickerton in other contexts, that "the gears and axles of English grammatical machinery are available to speakers of all dialects, whether or not they use all of them in everyday speech" (p. 64).

But if "English grammatical machinery" is there for all to use, Labov's experiment can hardly be said to have demonstrated the fact. For there remains the crucial question of whether sentences like (4) might not be quite transparent as to meaning because of high structural redundancy and low semantic ambiguity. Indeed, it is difficult to see why a listener would need a knowledge of the Standard English rules for embedding questions in order to determine that there is a question inside (4), since it starts out with *ask*. One probably would need minimal grammatical cues, such as Subject-Verb-Object word order, but little else. It would be interesting to see a comprehension test of sentences like (4) stripped of all their dialect-specific morphology and syntax, e.g., to

(6)   I-ASK-ALVIN-HE-KNOW-HOW-PLAY-BASKETBALL.

Once a probable meaning is inferred for such a string, the appropriate grammatical structure from any dialect can be used in the "repetition." In a sense, this is translation; but it is a kind of translation that does not depend on a knowledge of more than one grammar.[11]

---

[11]Those who have learned or taught a foreign language in classroom settings, especially where written translation exercises were involved, will recognize this strategy as responsible for some fairly accurate translations by rank beginners.

It was undoubtedly this current of expressed scientific opinion on cross-dialectal competence, emanating from respected linguists who had done research on black subjects, that eventually reached American educators and became the authority for advocacy of a laissez-faire policy on the teaching of Standard English to Black English speakers. This policy was articulated in the form of a position paper, *Students' Right to Their Own Language,* which was drafted in the course of 1971–1974 by a special committee of the Conference on College Composition and Communication, finally published by them in 1974 (Committee on CCCC Language Statement, 1974) and co-supported by the National Council of Teachers of English.[12]

The position taken on cross-dialectal competence by the Committee on CCCC Language Statement is essentially that of DeCamp (1971), Bickerton (1975), and Labov (1972), except that it is less competently articulated, dogmatic in tone, and seeks to trivialize the observable grammatical differences beteen Black English (never actually mentioned directly) and Standard English:

> Although they vary in phonology, in vocabulary, and in surface grammatical patterns, the differences between neighboring dialects are not sufficiently wide to prevent full mutual comprehension among speakers of those dialects. (Committee on CCCC Language Statement, 1974, p. 4)

If "neighboring dialects" is taken as meaning closely related dialects of the traditional kind (i.e., that have evolved out of a common ancestor and exist in adjacent territories) then the statement is essentially correct. But it is precisely for this reason that the issue of the historical origin of Black English is important; a decreolized creole and its related standard are certainly not "neighboring dialects" in this historical sense and therefore should not be expected to have the characteristics of such a relationship.

Following up on this alleged close relationship between the various dialects that come together in American public schools, but for some reason treating a restatement of the claim just made as if it were new information, the position paper goes on to say:

> Another insight from linguistic study is that differences among dialects in a given language are always confined to a limited range of *surface* features which have no effect on what linguists call *deep structure,* a term that might roughly be translated as "meaning". (Committee on CCCC Language Statement, 1974, p. 6)

Certainly Black English and Standard English have surface structural differences between them—phonological differences and morphological differences. But that is certainly not all; the Black English invariant *be* has been

---

[12]The history of the position paper is discussed in an in-depth review of it by Stewart (1974b).

shown to mark an aspectual difference for which Standard English has no equivalent. Nor does it appear to be readily comprehended accurately by persons who do not actually know Black English grammar. The public schools are full of middle-class, monodialectal, Standard English speaking teachers who daily hear black children making the be/non-be ([+ITERATIVE]/[−ITERATIVE]) distinction consistently and repeatedly, and yet have no idea of its meaning. Would the CCCC Language Statement Committee consider Black English invariant be a mere surface-structural feature? Then why is its grammatical meaning not understood by speakers of other dialects? Was the Committee perhaps unaware of its existence? Long discussions of it had already been in the linguistic and English-teaching literature for half a decade. So, if the Committee was aware of the existence of Black English invariant be and its grammatical function, why was it not mentioned? Or, at least, why did the Committee continue to claim that differences between dialects were *always* confined to surface structure? Whatever the answer to these questions may be, the general effect of the position paper was to put the teaching of Standard English on the defensive, and to considerably discourage further research on the pedagogical effect of dialect differences. Total receptive competence across dialects became educational dogma. When the CCCC/NCTE laissez-faire policy on English teaching was finally abandoned by the profession at large (and, it would seem, somewhat by the organizations that originally sponsored it), it was not because the notion of total cross-dialectal receptive competence began to be questioned; it was simply because a shift in the values of the larger society had brought about the reimposition in the English class of what the CCCC Language Statement Committee would have referred to as "surface-structure" norms.

Earlier in this paper, it was suggested individual productive competence across dialects may sometimes appear to be more so (more competent, that is to say) than it proves actually to be. Now that certain claims for cross-dialectal receptive competence—particularly over the variants in a creole continuum—have been examined and found not totally convincing, it is perhaps worth wondering whether receptive competence across dialects might not sometimes also appear more competent than it really is. One must remember that in most real world, cross-dialectal interactions, impressionistic evidence of comprehension consists for the most part of an absence of any indication—particularly by the listener—of its failure. And this means that the listener must be aware that he failed to comprehend at some point. One likely cause of this awareness would be the use by the speaker of some unfamiliar word (or unfamiliar pronunciation of a familiar word, thereby causing it not to be recognized) or expression. The use of an unfamiliar grammatical construction might have the same effect, though in such a case the listener would have recourse to the kind of comprehension by lexical scanning mentioned in the discussion of Labov's experiment. There is, however, a kind of cross-dialectal unfamiliarity that would be quite likely to cause comprehension failure, yet highly unlikely to be noticed—or at least recognized as a linguistic problem—by the listener: interdialectal ambiguity. A word or grammatical inflection or syntactic construction can be said to be interdialectally ambiguous if its surface form is shared by the two dialects but its meaning is not, or, more precisely, if it has at least one meaning in one dialect that it does not have in the other. A lexical example of interdialectal ambiguity involving Standard English and Gullah (or Geechee), a decreolizing form of creole English spoken in coastal South Carolina and Georgia. Sentence (7a) is Standard English; sentence (7b) is Gullah in Standard English orthography:

(7) a. The girl chased the boy and kissed him back.
    b. The girl chase the boy, kiss him back.

The linguistically sophisticated reader will perhaps guess that tense of the verbs in (7b) is probably ambiguous, i.e., [±PAST], but since this is true within Gullah itself the ambiguity is not interdialectal. The interdialectally ambiguous item is the word *back,* interpreted in either direction. In Standard English, its semantic specification is roughly [+REPEATED, +RECIPROCAL], whereas in Gullah it is [+REPEATED, ±RECIPROCAL]. This means that, ignoring the verb tense problem, (7b) has both a Standard English interpretation (7a) and another, (8):

(8) The girl chased the boy and kissed him again.

Now, the interesting thing about (8) is that it is not an interpretation of (7b) that a Standard English speaker (that is, one who does not also know Gullah or some other related variety of creole English) would be likely to come up with, even if the context suggested that there was something wrong with interpretation (7a). After all, the Standard English speaker knows what adverbial *back* means, if he knows nothing else![13]

Because of decreolization, syntactic interdialectal ambiguity between a decreolizing creole and its related standard language is more likely than between any other kind of dialect relationship. And syntactic interdialectal ambiguity must, if anything, be even more problematic for cross-dialectal receptive competence than lexical interdialectal ambiguity, because so much more can go on at the syntactic level. The following example actually occurred, and involved a

---

[13]Even if the linguistic context makes the use of a particular word seem bizarre to one who does not speak that dialect, there is no guarantee that either the linguistic or nonlinguistic context will suggest the correct interpretation. The Irish English construction *be after* + Verb + *-ing* is, by the present writer's experience, consistently misinterpreted as "be in pursuit of + Noun," hence "be about the business of + Verb + -ing" by American English speakers (provided, of course, that they have not had a great deal of exposure to Irish English), no matter how clear the context makes it that such an interpretation is problematic. The construction usually means "have (just) + Verb + -en" (Bliss, 1979; pp. 299–300).

question (9a) posed in Standard English to a Gullah speaker, who answered with (9b). Emphatic stress is indicated by italics:

(9)   a. Had Joe left when *you* left?
       b. No, Joe leave *before* I leave.

Since (9b) translates as (10a), the Gullah-speaking listener had obviously mis-comprehended (9a) as meaning (10b):

(10)   a. No, Joe left *before* I did.
        b. Did Joe leave when *you* left?

This miscomprehension (which could also have occurred with speakers of other varieties of Black English outside Gullah territory) is an inevitable consequence of the fact that, at the particular stage of decreolization of the listener, *had +* Verb is not unambiguously equivalent to Standard English *had* + Verb + *-en,* but rather can also be equivalent to Standard English Verb + *-ed.*

Interdialectal ambiguity between Black English and standard English was noted almost half a century ago by the anthropologist Melville Herskovits, who, seeing it in the context of a general theory of New World Negro acculturation, termed it *masking* (Herskovits, 1941; see also Dillard, 1972, for a continuation of the term). Subsequently, the term *camouflaging* has been used for the same phenomenon (Spears, 1982; Stewart, 1968). In any case, whether in reference to culture or language, the phenomenon probably originated as inadvertent rein-terpretation in the acculturative or second language learning process, and never was the result of an intentional effort to conceal or deceive, despite the romantic appeal of such a notion.

Because this kind of interdialectal ambiguity involves shared surface patterns whose meanings are falsely equated, the resultant communication breakdown is not likely to be perceived as linguistic in nature. Rather, it may be attributed to faulty information or an erroneous conclusion, as was evidently assumed for (9a) by the speaker of (9b). Even when there is an awareness that the problem is linguistic, it is not likely to be clear which shared structures are interdialectally ambiguous and which are not. In either case, the resultant comprehension prob-lems will not be easily resolvable, and may continue to make themselves felt either as semantic bizarreness or structural indeterminacy generalized throughout the discourse.[14]

In summary, there seem to be good reasons to question the uncritical assump-tion of general receptive competence across dialects, particularly if the inter-

---

[14]Elsewhere (Stewart, 1984) I have referred to this kind of unperceived interdialectical mis-comprehension as pseudocomprehension.

dialectal relationship exists across a creole continuum, or in the aftermath of one. Since American Black English is in all likelihood a decreolized creole, and since at least one controlled study has turned up statistically demonstrated evidence of comprehension problems with Standard English on the part of Black English speaking children (Berdan, 1977)—and, most important of all, since the success of public education with those who need it most hangs in the balance, the empirical study of the linguistic and psycholinguistic mechanism involved in productive and receptive competence across dialects ought to be an important research agenda.

ACKNOWLEDGMENT

The material in this paper is in part derived from research supported by a grant (GS-39814X) from the National Science Foundation.

REFERENCES

Berdan, R. (1977). Polylectal comprehension and the polylectal grammar. In R. Fasold & R. W. Shuy (Eds.), *Studies in language variation*. Washington, DC: Georgetown University Press.

Bickerton, D. (1975). *Dynamics of a creole system*. Cambridge: University Press.

Bickerton, D. (1981). *Roots of language*. Ann Arbor: Karoma Press.

Bliss, A. (1979). *Spoken English in Ireland: 1600–1740*. Dublin: Dolmen Press.

Committee on CCCC Language Statement. (1974). *Students' right to their own language*. Urbana: National Council of Teachers of English. [*College Composition and Communication:* 25 (No. 3) Special issue]

DeCamp, D. (1971). Toward a generative analysis of a post-creole speech continuum. In D. Hymes (Ed.), *Pidginization and creolization of languages*. Cambridge: University Press.

Dillard, J. L. (1972). *Black English in the United States*. New York: Random House.

Ervin-Tripp, S. (1972). Children's sociolinguistic competence and dialect diversity. *Early childhood education: Seventy-first Yearbook of the National Society for the Study of Education*, Part 2. Chicago: National Society for the Study of Education.

Fasold, R. (1969). Tense and the form *be* in Black English. *Langauge 45*,

Fasold, R. (1972). *Tense marking in Black English*. Washington, DC: Center for Applied Linguistics.

Hall, R. A., Jr. (1966). *Pidgin and creole languages*. Ithaca: Cornell University Press.

Herskovits, M. J. (1941). *The myth of the negro past*. New York: Harper Brothers.

Labov, W. (1969). Contraction, deletion, and inherent variability in the English copula. *Language, 45*,

Labov, W. (1972). *Language in the inner city: Studies in the Black English vernacular*. Philadelphia: University of Pennsylvania Press.

Spears, A. K. (1982). The Black English semi-auxiliary *come. Language* 58:850–872.

Stewart, W. A. (1966). Social dialect. In *Research and planning conference on language development in disadvantaged children*. New York: Yeshiva University.

Stewart, W. A. (1967). Sociolinguistic factors in the history of American Negro dialect. *Florida FL Reporter, 5*. [Reprinted in H. B. Allen & G. N. Underwood (Eds.), *Readings in American dialectology*. New York: Appleton-Century-Crofts, 1971]

Stewart, W. A. (1968). Continuity and change in American Negro dialects. *Florida FL Reporter, 6*. [Reprinted in Allen & Underwood 1971 (see at Stewart 1967)]

Stewart, W. A. (1969a). On the use of Negro dialect in the teaching of reading. In J. C. Baratz & R. W. Shuy (Eds.), *Teaching black children to read* (pp. 156–219). Washington, DC: Center for Applied Linguistics.

Stewart, W. A. (1969b). Historical and structural bases for the recognition of Negro dialect. In *Monograph Series for Languages and Linguistics, 22*. Washington, DC: Georgetown University.

Stewart, W. A. (1974a). Acculturative processes and the language of the American Negro. In W. W. Gage (Ed.), *Language in its social setting,* (pp. 1–46). Washington, DC: Anthropological Society of Washington.

Stewart, W. A. (1974b). The laissez-faire movement in English teaching: Advance to the rear? In A. C. Aarons (Ed.), *Issues in the teaching of standard English. [Florida FL Reporter:* 12. Reprinted in M. A. Lourie & N. F. Conklin (Eds.), *A pluralistic nation: The language issue in the United States.* Rowley, MA: Newbury House.]

Stewart, W. A. (1984, January). From xenolect to mimolect to Pseudocomprehension: Structural mimicry and its functional consequences in decreolization. Paper presented at the meeting of the Section of Linguistics, New York Academy of Sciences. (To appear in the *Annals* of the Academy.)

Todd, L. (1974). *Pidgins and creoles.* London: Rutledge & Kegan Paul.

Todd, L. (1984). *Modern Englishes: Pidgins and creoles.* Oxford: Basil Blackwell.

Valian, V. (1979). The wherefores and therefores of the competence-performance distinction. In W. E. Cooper & E. C. T. Walker, (Eds.), *Sentence processing: Psycholinguistic studies presented to Merrill Garrett.* Hillsdale, NJ: Lawrence Erlbaum Associates.

Wright, J. (1905). *English dialect grammar.* Oxford: Henry Frowde.

Author Index

299

Subject Index